THE

SANSKRIT BUDDHIST LITERATURE

OF

NEPAL

THE

SANSKRIT BUDDHIST LITERATURE

OF

NEPAL.

BY

RAJENDRALALA MITRA

GYAN

Published by

Gyan Publishing House
5, Ansari Road
Daryaganj, New Delhi-110002
Phone: 011-47034999, 9811692060
E-mail: books@gyanbooks.com

Distribution Network
gyanbooks.com
India, USA, Canada, UK, Australia

ISBN: 978-93-6280-226-2 (PB)
First Published, 1882

2nd Impression 2024

Printed at: Gyan Press, Delhi.

THE SANSKRIT BUDDHIST LITERATURE OF NEPAL
Author: RAJENDRALALA MITRA

THE

SANSKRIT BUDDHIST LITERATURE

OF

NEPAL.

BY

RÁJENDRALÁLA MITRA, LL. D., C. I. E.

CALCUTTA:

PRINTED BY J. W. THOMAS, BAPTIST MISSION PRESS.

AND PUBLISHED BY

THE ASIATIC SOCIETY OF BENGAL, 57, PARK STREET.

1882.

PREFACE.

About sixty years ago a young Englishman, placed by the exigencies of public service amidst strangers in an inhospitable and till then little-known clime, occupied himself in collecting materials, which have since afforded the key to the religion of one-fifth of the human race. That Englishman was Brian Houghton Hodgson, and a brief notice of his career in India may not be out of place here.

Born at the close of the last century, he entered the Bengal Civil Service as a writer on April 30, 1818. According to the rules of the Service at the time, he had, on his arrival at Calcutta, on August following, to attend for a year the College of Fort William, and pass through the usual course of training there. His career at the College was a highly satisfactory one, and he distinguished himself greatly by his zeal, assiduity and successful study of the Persian language. On August 20, 1819, he was appointed Assistant to the Commissioner of Kumaon, which office he exchanged, on the following year, for that of Assistant to the Resident of Kathmandu. His services in these two offices were well-spoken of, and in two years (November 23, 1822) he was promoted to the Foreign Office, as Officiating Deputy Secretary in the Persian Department. At the beginning of 1824 he returned to Kathmandu to assume charge of the Post Office there; but he did not hold it long. In March 1825, he reverted to his former office of Assistant to the Resident, which he held till he was himself appointed Resident in January 1833. His career as a Resident extended from that time to the close of 1843, when he retired from the Service. His sojourn in Nepal thus extended over a period of twenty-one years. In 1848, he returned to India, and lived for nine years at Darjiling as a private resident, engaged in literary and scientific pursuits.

Gifted with intellectual powers of the highest order, thoroughly well educated, and possessing indomitable energy, Mr. Hodgson was always most laudably employed, and the result of his labours placed him in the foremost rank as an accomplished man of letters and a highly successful cultivator of science in India.

Of his services to Government no notice need be taken here. Suffice it to say that he repeatedly received cordial thanks for them, and all along enjoyed the fullest confidence of his employers. To him is especially due the credit of frustrating, at a very critical period, the intrigues which were being carried on for the overthrow of English supremacy in India by the Sikhs, the Sindhians, and the Marhattas during the first Afghan war when the country was denuded of British troops. During the years 1838 to 1842 he was instrumental in intercepting twenty-three missions from Kathmandu to the plains, and in holding back the Nepal Durbar from avenging the defeat it had sustained in 1816. His wisdom, tact, influence, and judicious management also contributed largely to secure for the British Government the coöperation of Nepalese soldiers during the Mutiny of 1857-58.

His literary labours may be noticed under two heads: first, what were undertaken for Government; second, what were rendered to the republic of letters. Under the first head come the various memoirs and reports which he submitted to Government in his official capacity. The ordinary round of duties devolving on an Assistant in an Indian embassy is limited enough; but an officer in a foreign Court has many opportunities of collecting and digesting valuable information, and

Mr. Hodgson utilised them to the utmost. While working as Assistant to the Resident, his attention was first directed to the military organisation of Nepal, and his studies resulted in two memoirs giving details regarding the then existing force of the Nepal Durbar, the military tribes and races from which it was drawn, their tribal names and classification, their physical and moral qualities as soldiers, their pay and discipline, as also the manufacture of their arms and ammunitions. He closed his memoirs with the suggestion that the British Government should obtain through the Durbar the services of a large body of the Gurkha soldiery, so as, on the one hand, to reduce the chances of collision with Nepal, and, on the other, to remove the homogeniety of the Bengal army. The memoirs were very favourably received, and elicited the hearty thanks of Government; but the suggestion was not acted upon until many years after.

Mr. Hodgson next turned his attention to the commerce of Nepal with the people of the plains on this side, and with those of Central Asia and China on the other. For some time before the first Nepal war this commerce was extensive, and Mr. Hodgson's object, in the papers he wrote on the subject, was to furnish practical directions, routes and details about travelling, and custom house charges, with a view to revive that commerce, and divert the people from their warlike propensities. The topographical and statistical information compiled in those papers was of high importance, comprising as they did translations of some old itineraries from Kathmandu to Darjiling, and of all principal military routes in the valley of Nepal.

The legal administration of the country also found in him an able and most faithful historiographer. The administration was purely Hindu, absolutely untouched by foreign influence for several centuries, and in it he very justly recognised the outcome of ancient Indian Brahmanic laws developed by Indian administrators. His essay on this subject appeared in the *Researches* of the Asiatic Society of Bengal, and for the first time gave to Europeans a faithful and complete picture of the social condition of the people of Nepal. The opinion of the Bengal Government on this report was thus expressed—"This subject is one which possesses much interest, whether for the legislator, the historian, or the philosopher. In Hindustan we look in vain for any traces of Hindu legislation or government. The Moslem conquerors have everywhere swept them away. And if we wish to enquire what are the features of the Hindu system of Jurisprudence and Judicature it is in Nepal we must seek for the answer. Mr. Hodgson is the first who has enabled us to obtain a precise and definative view of the subject. His information was transmitted to the Governor-General, and the Governor-General deemed it of sufficient importance to authorise its publication."

During his sojourn in Nepal Mr. Hodgson was greatly impressed by the evils which resulted from the borders of the Nepal territory, serving as an Alsatia to the criminal classes of India. The weakly governed dominion of the king of Oudh was a rich field of adventure for men of this class, and when hard-pressed they always found a secure asylum in those borders. Nor were their operations confined to Oudh. Well-organised parties sallied forth from the Terai every year, and committed depredations over the whole of India, as far as Dakkhan, returning from their expeditions, heavily laden with booty, during the rains when Thuggi and highway robbery were the least productive. Before devising means for the suppression of the evil, Mr. Hodgson deemed it expedient to collect information from the robbers themselves and others familiar with the subject, and compiled a large mass of authentic depositions and facts for which he received the most cordial acknowledgments of Government. They ultimately, but after some delay, led to the establishment of the Thuggi Department, which has completely broken up the organized bands of robbers which had been for a long time the opprobrium of every civilized Government in India.

The next subject to which reference should be made is Indian Education. The battle fought between the Anglicists and the Orientalists during the administration of Lord William Bentinck, was of too stirring a character to escape the notice of Mr. Hodgson. Remarkable alike for the force and massiveness of his intellect and for his disinterestedness and devotion to the well-being of the people of this country, he plunged into it with characteristic intrepidity. But he joined neither the Anglicists led by Lord William Bentinck, Mr. Macaulay, Mr. Trevelyan and Dr. Duff, nor the Orientalists who were represented by Dr. Wilson, Dr. Tytler, Mr. Thoby Prinsep and Mr. John Colvin. He could not for a moment believe that the English language could under any circumstance be made the vernacular of the two hundred and forty millions of India, and he cherished equal doubts about the fitness of the Sanskrit and the Arabic languages for the every-day use of the various nationalities and races who inhabit this vast country. He adopted, therefore, a middle course. Without detracting from the merits of the English language and of the ancient classics as instruments of intellectual culture for the select few, he held that education to be effectual for the masses must be imparted through the medium of the current vernaculars. In Europe vernacular languages had achieved wonderful success. They had dispelled the impervious gloom of the Middle Ages, and inaugurated an era of widespread intellectual enlightenment, the like of which the world had never before seen; and he urged that, under similar circumstances, the vernaculars of India were well able to accomplish the same object. This *via media*, however, did not commend itself to men's minds at the time. People in power then were so wedded to their extreme opinions that they could not listen to what appeared to them to be a mere compromise, and the admirable letters in which Mr. Hodgson put forth his views in the columns of the local newspapers and afterwards published in book-form were to a great extent neglected by them. But the letters did not fail to attract the attention of persons who had not fallen in with the theories of the two contending parties, and the testimony borne by these regarding the soundness of his arguments, must have been a source of great satisfaction to the learned author. In a letter to the Political Agent at Bhopal, in 1838, the late Dr. John Wilson, of Bombay, than whom few could speak with greater emphasis on questions relating to Indian education, remarked—"Mr. Hodgson's advocacy of the vernaculars is most powerful and convincing. They must be the medium of the regeneration of India, as they have been such of every country on the face of the globe." In the same year the official Report on Education in Bengal (p. 200) contained the following: "No one has more earnestly urged the duty of communicating European knowledge to the natives than Mr. Hodgson; no one has more powerfully shown the importance of employing the vernacular languages for accomplishing that object; no one has more eloquently illustrated the necessity of conciliating the learned and making them our coadjutors in the great work of a nation's regeneration." Five years after, in his address to the Medical College of Calcutta, Professor Sir William O'Shaughnessy said—"The progress of the principles of Normal and Vernacular Education cannot now be checked. These facts (see his address to the Medical College students) have deprived the anti-vernacular party of even a pretext for advocating the exclusive use either of English or of the learned native tongues. Let those who wish well to India, and desire to see its inhabitants flourish in knowledge, visit the secondary schools of the new Medical College, and they will see the first fruits of the Normal system. I have felt it an imperative duty to publish these important facts. It is the only contribution I can offer to the measures of the eminent and wise philanthropist under whose auspices normal instruction is now claiming public support." Truth once put forth can never be lost, and it is gratifying to notice that for the last thirty years Mr. Hodgson's opinion has been very widely accepted, and much has already been done in India to accord to the vernaculars their right place in the curriculum of education.

The next question of local value to which Mr. Hodgson addressed himself was the fitness of the Himalaya mountains for the settlement of Europeans. He had watched with lively interest the introduction of tea-planting at Darjiling, and knowing how intimately that industry was connected with that of European colonization in this country, he came to the conclusion that, though the plains would not, and could not, be inhabited permanently by Englishmen, no objection would apply to the hills, and if adequate and remunerative occupations could be found for them there, the problem would at once be solved. The then Lieutenant-Governor of Bengal was struck by this opinion, and desired Mr. Hodgson to furnish him with a memorandum thereon. The report furnished pleased him much, and "he ordered its publication along with some of the author's previous Essays to make up an entire number of the 'Selections from the Records.' No. XXVII was the result, whereby most of the aforementioned papers, though in themselves hardly official, became so by adoption."

The papers above noticed form but a small fraction of the writings of Mr. Hodgson. A keen observer, master of a facile pen, and enthusiastically devoted to study, he neglected no opportunity of taking notes of all that appeared before him, 'whether performed by man or produced by nature;' and his writings are as varied as they are voluminous, bearing the most satisfactory evidence of his ardent zeal, unremitting industry, and profound learning. Man formed the central figure of his study, and he devoted a great part of his time to researches into the elucidation of the ethnic relations, the languages, the ancient history, the literatures, and the handicrafts of the different tribes of men who fell under his observation. His ethnologicial papers* include

* The following is a list of the papers:—

1. On the Languages, Literature, and Religion of the Bauddhas of Nepal and Bhot. As. Res. vol. XVI.
2. On the Aborigines of the Sub-Himalayas. Jour. A. S. B. vols. XVI.
3. Ethnography and Geography of the Sub-Himalayas, *ib.*, vol. XVII, p. I.
4. On the Chepáng and Kúsunda Tribes of Nepal, *ib.*, vol. XVII.
5. Comparative Vocabulary of the Languages of the broken tribes of Nepal, *ib.*, vols. XXVI and XXVII.
6. On the several Dialects of the Kiranti language, *ib.*, vol. XXVI.
7. Vayu Vocabulary, *ib.*, vol. XXVI.
8. Vayu Grammar, *ib.*, vol. XXVI.
9. Bahing Vocabulary, *ib.*, vol. XXVI.
10. Grammar of the Bahing dialect, *ib.*, vol. XXVII.
11. Origin and Classification of the Military Tribes of Nepal, *ib.*, vol. II.
12. Classification of the Newárs; or People of Nepal Proper, *ib.* vol. III.
13. Sifan and Horsok Vocabularies. On the Trans-himalayan Tribes of Hor-Yeul, Sog-Yeul, and Sifan, *ib.*, vol. XXII.
14. On the Tibetan Type of Mankind, *ib*, vol. XVII, p. II.
15. Caucasian and Mongolian Affinities, *ib.*, vol. XXII.
16. Comparative Vocabulary of the several Languages and Dialects of the Eastern Sub-Himalayas from the Kali or Ghogra to Dhansri, *ib.* vol. XVI.

17, 18. On the Aborigines of the North East Frontier (Assam and south of it), *ib.*, vols. XVIII and XIX.

19. Indo-Chinese borderers and their connection with the Himalayan and Tibetan tribes, *ib.*, vol. XXII.
20. On the Aborigines of the South of India; cultivated and uncultivated, *ib.*, vols. XVIII, XIX.

all the different and till then almost unknown tribes of the Eastern Himalayas to the Indo-Chinese borders, and several of Central and Southern India as far as Ceylon, and the information collected have been pronounced by competent judges to be of high scientific value. Speaking of one of them—the litttle volume on the Kooch, Bodo and Dhimal tribes,—Dr. Latham writes: "The Kooch, Bodo and Dhimal, is the title of one of Mr. Hodgson's works, and it is a model of an ethnological monograph." Speaking more generally, he says, "Next come in brilliant succession the labours of Botta, Layard, and Rawlinson, to which may be added the bold yet cautious criticism and varied observations of Hodgson, illustrating the obscure Ethnology of the Himalayan Indians." Chevalier Bunsen, in his 'Philosophy of Universal History,' is equally emphatic in his estimate of Mr. Hodgson's works. According to him, "our highest living authority and best informant on the Ethnology of the native races of India is Mr. B. H. Hodgson, who uses Tamilian as the general name of the Non-Aryan races."

Dr. Hooker dedicated his "Rhododendrons of Himalaya" to Mr. Hodgson, "whose researches into the physical geography and especially the ethnology of the people of the Eastern Himalaya," he said, "are beyond all praise." Professor Owen, in his report to the British Association, May 1863, bore the following testimony on the subject: "Mr. Hodgson, my accomplished and scientific friend, has contributed an important element to the Ancient History of India, by his Buddhist researches, and he has now established an additional claim to the gratitude of the Ethnologist, by the collection he has made of the skulls of various tribes." Dr.

21, 22. On the Aborigines of the Nilgiris, two papers, *ib.*, vol. XXV.

23. On the Aborigines of the Eastern Ghâts.

24. On the Aborigines of Ceylon.

25. On the Aborigines of Central India, J A. S. B., vol. XVII.

26. On the Kooch, Bodo and Dhimal Tribes, *ib.*, vol. XVIII.

Barnard Davis, on the same occasion, said: "Mr. Hodgson early and constantly felt that the most interesting object of natural history is man himself, and he devoted his unremitting attention to the study of the many curious tribes with whom his long residence in India brought him in contact. He studied the physical and philological aspects of the subject, and was at infinite pains to gain a knowledge of the ideas as well as languages of these races. One of the most complete Ethnological Essays ever written, is Mr. Hodgson's book on Kooch, Bodo, and Dhimal Tribes." Other authorities, equally distinguished, have spoken in similar terms of Mr. Hodgson's ethnological works, but I shall forbear to quote them.

Mr. Hodgson's researches into religion are limited to that form of it which prevails in Nepal—the Buddhism of S'ákya Siñha as it manifested itself in that Alpine region on its expulsion from Hindustan,—but he has done more on that subject than any other European writer.* Before his

* The following are the titles of his essays on this subject:

1. Sketch of Buddhism, derived from the Bauddha Scriptures of Nepal. Trans. R. A. S., vol. ii.

2. Quotations in proof of the above. Jour. R. A. S., vol. V.

3. On Buddhist Symbols, *ib.*, vol XVIII.

4, 5. On the Resemblance of the Symbols of Buddhism and Sinaism. Quart. Ori. Mag., vol. VII, two papers.

6. On the Bauddha Literature and Religion of Nepal. As. Res., vol. XVI.

7. Sketch of Buddhism. Jour. As. Soc., vol. V.

8. On Bauddha Inscriptions, *ib.*, vol. III.

9. On Ancient Inscriptions, *ib.*, vol. III.

10. On Sarnath Inscriptions, *ib.*, vol. IV.

11. On the Ruins of Samaran (Simroun), *ib.*, vol. IV.

12. Remarks on an Inscription in the Runga and Tibetan characters from Nepal, *ib.*, vol. IV.

13. On the Relics of the Catholic Mission in Tibet and Nepal, *ib.* vol XVII, p. II.

14. A Bauddha Disputation on Caste, Trans. R. A. S., vol. III.

time all that was known of Buddhism was crude, vague and shadowy, derived from secondary and by no means reliable sources. He it was who established the subject on a sound philosophic basis. To quote the language of M. Csoma de Körös, than whom no European had studied the literature of Tibetan Buddhism with greater success, "Mr. Hodgson's illustrations of the literature and religion of the Buddhists form a wonderful combination of knowledge on a new subject with the deepest philosophical speculations." The opinion of the illustrious savant, Eugène Burnouf, in regard to one of Mr. Hodgson's papers is equally emphatic. In his Introduction to the History of Buddhism, he says, "In the *Asiatic Researches* for the year 1828 was contained a dissertation by Mr. Hodgson, full of ideas entirely new regarding the languages, literature, and religion of Nepal and of Tibet; and this first essay contained also an account of the different philosophical schools of Buddhism, which has never since been surpassed or equalled. This first memoir yet further teemed with value as bringing to light, among other important discoveries, the grand and theretofore wholly unknown fact that in Nepal there existed numerous Buddhist works composed in Sanskrit, the original language of Buddhism." Altogether he has written 18 papers on the subject, and they are replete with most varied and instructive information. Much has been done since, but no one can even now write on Buddhism with any accuracy who has not thoroughly studied Mr. Hodgson's essays.

Reference has already been made to Mr. Hodgson's Memoirs on Law, Legal Practice, Police and Administration of Justice in Nepal. On economic subjects there are extant

15. On the Primary Language of the Buddhist Writings. Jour. As. Soc., vol. VI.

16. European Speculations on Buddhism, *ib.*, vol. III.

17. Remarks on M. Remusat's Review of Buddhism, *ib.*, vol. III.

18. Translation of the Napalia Devata Kalyana, *ib.*, vol. XII.

papers by him on the Wool of Tibet, on the Cultivation of Hemp in Nepal, on the Paper of Nepal, and on the Silk-worms of India.*

No one can live on the Himalayas without being deeply impressed by the sublime scenery around him, and to students of science it affords the richest field for enquiry and research. The lofty snow-capped peaks, the wonderful glaciers, the intricate river systems, the high tablelands, the fertile valleys, the flora and the fauna, so peculiar, so characteristic, so distinct from everything of the kind seen in other parts of the globe, are all fraught with instruction of the deepest interest to science, and Mr. Hodgson devoted himself to their study with the greatest ardour. Few were at the time better qualified by previous training, habit of research, and scientific acumen to do them adequate justice, and the various essays and notes he has published on the Physical Geography, Topography† and Fauna prove the suc-

* The titles of the papers are:

1. On the Law and Legal Practice of Nepal, Jour .R. A S., vol. 1.
2. Some Account of the Systems of Law and Police in Nepal, *ib.*
3. On the Administration of Justice in Nepal, As. Res., vol. XX.
4. On the Wool of Tibet, Trans. Agri. Soc. of India, vol. VIII.
5. On the Cultivation of Hemp in Nepal, *ib.* vol. V.
6. On the Paper of Nepal. Jour. A S. B. vol. I.
7. On the Silk-worms of India, Jour. Agri. Soc. of India, vol. II.

† The following are the titles of the papers on Physical Geography and Topography:

1. On the Physical Geography of the Himalayas, *ib.*, vol. XVIII, p. II.
2. On the snow line in the Himalayas, *ib.*, vol. XVIII.
3. Memorandum on the seven Kasis of Nepal, *ib.*, vol. XVII, p. II.
4. Route from Kathmandu to Tazedo on the Chinese frontier, As. Res., vol. XVII.
5. Route of two Nepalese embassies to Pekin, with remarks on the watersheds and plateaus of Tibet, J. A. S. B., vol. XXV.
6. Route from Kathmandu to Darjiling, *ib.* vol. XVII, p. II.
7. Measurement (official) of the great Military Road throughout Nepal, from Kumaon to Sikim, *ib.* 18 (?)
8. A cursory Notice of Nayakote, *ib.*, vol. IX.

cess with which he prosecuted his researches. Adverting to the essay on the Physical Geography of the Himalaya Mountains and Tibet, Baron Humboldt remarked, "La chaine de l'Himalaya 'a eu dans ces derniers temps des savants observateurs, M. Hodgson et le Capt. Strachey, que réunit une grande variété connaissances solides." Studying Mr. Hodgson's statements and map, proving the identity of the Sampu and the Brahmaputra rivers, the great Indian geographer, Pemberton, remarked, "I consider this so satisfactory that nothing but ocular demonstration to the contrary could now shake off my conviction."

The fruits of his zoological researches are contained in a series of one hundred and twenty-three papers,* alike remark-

* Their titles are :

1. On the Mammalia of Nepal, Jour. As. Soc., vol. I.
2. On the same continued up to 1841, *ib.* vol. X.
3. On the Mammalia of Tibet, *ib.* vol. V.
4. On the same up to 1842, *ib.* vol. XI.
5. Catalogue of the Mammals of Nepal and of Tibet brought down to 1843, M'Clelland's Journal, 1843.
6. On the Rats, Mice, and Shrews of Nepal (to complete the Mammal Catalogue up to 1843) Ann. and Mag. of Nat. History, 1845.
7. On the Geographical Distribution of the Mammals of Nepal, Proc. Zool. Soc. 1847.

[See XXVII of Selections, Art. Phy. Geog. of Nepal, J. A. S.]

8. Characters and Descriptions of the New Mammals from Nepal, *ib.* vol. I.
9. Description of the Chiru Antelope, *ib.* vol. I.
10. Further account of ditto *ib.* vol III.
11. Description and Characters of the Wild Dog of Nepal, *ib.* 1833.
12. On various Zoological subjects, *ib.* vol. III.
13. Synopsis of the Ghoral and the Thar, *ib.* vol. IV.

14 to 17. Wild Goat and Wild Sheep of the Himalaya with remarks on the Genera Capra and Ovis, *ib.* vols. IV, V, XII and XVI.

15. On the Lachrymal Sinus in Antelope, Thâr and Cervus Aristotelis, *ib.* vol. III.
16. On a new form of the Hog kind or Porcula Salvania, *ib.* XVI, p. I.

able for great originality, minute observation, keen acumen, high critical skill, and thorough knowledge of the requirements of scientific classification. Most of the species of mammals and birds were, when described by him, new to science and typical, and the light thrown by them on the fauna of the Himalayan and trans-Himalayan regions is immense. To show this I cannot do better than quote, as I have so often done above, the opinions of those who are best able to speak authoritatively on the subject. "Mr. Hodgson's labours," says Dr. Hooker in his

17. On a new species of Badger from Tibet, J. A. S., vol. XVI, p. II.
18. On the Wild Goat and Wild Sheep of Nepal, As Res., vol. XVIII.
19. On the Ratwa Deer, *ib.* vol. XVIII, p. II.
20. On Cúon Primœvus, J. A. S. B., vol. I.
21. On Ursitaxus Inauritus, *ib.* vol. V.
22. On three new species of Paradoxurus, with remarks on the structure, and habits of the genera, *ib.* vol. III.
23 On Antelope Hodgsoni, *ib.*, vol. I.
24. On the Black Antelope, Gleanings in Science, vol. II.
25. On a new species of Felis, *ib.* vol. III.
26. On the Musk Deer, *ib.* vol. III.
27. On the Cervus Jarai, *ib.* vol. III.
28. On the Jharal Goat, *ib.* vol. III.
29. On the Chiru Antelope, *ib.* vol. III.
30. On Nepal Zoology, J. A. S. B., vol. I.
31. On a new Lagomys and a new Mustela, inhabiting the northern region of Sikim and the proximate parts of Tibet, *ib.* vol. XXVI.
32. Specific description of a new species of Cervus, *ib.* vol. IV.
33. On the Wild Goat of Nepal, *ib.* vol. V.
34. On Zool. Nomenclature, *ib.* vol. V.
35. On the new genus Ursitaxus, As. Res. vol. XIX.
36. On the Gauri Gau, *ib.* vol. VI.
37. On a new genus of the Plantigrades, *ib.* vol. VI.
38. On Bibos, a new Bovine genera typed by the Gauri Gau, *ib.* vol. VI.
39. On the Hare of the Gangetic Provinces, the Himalaya and Tibet, *ib.* vol. IX.
40. On the genera Semno-pithecus et Macacus with description of three new species, *ib.* vol. IX.

Himalayan Journal, "have extended over twenty-five years during all which time he has seldom had a staff of less than

41. On Cervus Elaphus of the Saul Forest of Nepal, As. Res. vol. X.
42. On the Marmots of Himalaya and Tibet, *ib.* vol. X.
43. Illustrations of the genera of the Bovinæ, part 1. Skeletons of Bos, Bibos and Bison, the individuals examined being the common Bull of Nepal, the Gowri Gao of Nepal, and the Yak, *ib.* vol. X.
44. Of a new species of Lagomys, inhabiting Nepal, *ib.* vol. X.
45. On a new organ in the genus Moschus, *ib.* vol. X.
46. Classical Terminology of Natural History, *ib.* vol. X.
47. Second Paper on the Marmots of Himalaya and Tibet, and on a new species of Rhinolophus, *ib.* vol. XII.
48. On a new species of Cervus Dimorphe, *ib.* vol. XII.
49. On the structure and habits of Prionodon Pardicolor.
50. On the Hispid Hare of the Saul Forest, J. A. S. B. vol. XVI.
51. On the Genera of the Ruminants, *ib.* vol. XVI.
52. Summary of the Vespertilionidæ of Nepal, *ib.* vol. IV.
53. Summary description of two new species and Flying Squirrel *ib.* vol. XIII.
54. On three new species of Musk inhabiting the Himalayan districts, *ib.* vol. VIII.
55. Summary description of four new species of otter, *ib* vol. VIII.
56. On the Anatomy of Ailurus, Porcula, and Stylocerus, with corrections of the paper on Ruminants, *ib.* vol. XVII.
57. Addendum to the Anatomy of Ailurus, *ib.* vol. XVII p. II.
58. On the Cat-toed Plantigrades of the Himalaya, *ib.* vol. XVII.
59. On the Polecat of Tibet, *ib.* vol. XVIII.
60. On a new species of Himalayan Mole, *ib.* 1849.
61. On the domesticated Goats and Sheep of the sub-Himalayas and Tibet, *ib.* v. XVI, p. II.
62. On Budoreas Taxicolor, a new genus of Bovine Antelopes, *ib.* vol. XIX.
63. Description of a new species of Himalayan Mole, *ib.* XXVII.
64. On a second new species of Himalayan Lagomys, *ib.* XXVI.
65. On the Shou or Tibetan Stag, *ib.* vol. XIX.
66. Further Account of the Shou, *ib.* vol. XX.
67. On the Ponies of Tibet and Himalaya, Ben. Sport, Mag., 1840 (?)
68. The Jharal Hunter's Song, *ib.* 1840.
69. On two species of Wild Sheep inhabiting the Himalaya, with remarks on the craniological characters of the Ovis and its allies, Jour. As. Soc. vol. X.

two to twenty persons of various tongues and races employed as translators, collectors, artists, shooters, and stuffers. By

70. On the Wild Ass and Wolf of Tibet, McClelland's Jour. Nat. History, 1847.
71. On the Pigmy Hog of the Saul Forest, J. A. S. B., vol. XVI.
72. Postscript to ditto, *ib.* vol. XVI.
73. On a new species of Porcupine, *ib.* vol. XVI.
74. Definitions and descriptions of new genera and species of Nepal Birds, not heretofore published in India, Proc. Zool. Soc., 1845.
75. Catalogue of Nepal Birds collected between 1824 and 1844, Zool. Misc. 1844.
76. Reprint of the above Catalogue in India for reasons assigned, Jour. As. Soc., vol. XXIV.
77. Additions to the Bird Catalogue of 1844, bringing it down to 1854, Curà Moore, Proc. Zool. Soc., 1854.
78. On Ninox, a new piscatory genus of the Strigine family, *ib.* vol. V.
79. On the structure and habits of Elanus Melanopterus, *ib.* vol. VI, 75, 18 (?)
80. On sundry new species of Nepalese Cinnyris, Ind. Rev., 1, 272. 18 (?)
81. On new Nepalese species of Edolian and Ceblepyrine Shrikes, *ib.* 324, 18 (?)
82. On new species of the more typical Laniïdæ, *ib.* 445, 18 (?)
83. On the new genus Niltava, *ib.* 18 (?)
84. On the new forms of the Parianæ and Leiotrichanæ, *ib.* 18 (?)
85. On a new species of Partridge, Proc. Zool. Soc., 1833.
86. On the Scolopacidae of Nepal, *ib.* 1834.
87. On Nepalese Birds, *ib.* 1845.
88. Description the Aquila Nepalensis, As. Res. vol. XVIII.
89. On the Migration of the Grallatores and Natatores. Gleanings in Science, vol. II.
90. On the Homrai Buceras, *ib.* vol. II.
91. Notes on the Ornithology of Nepal, A. R. vol. XIX.
92. On a new species of Bucerine Bird (Aceros Nepalensis), G. in S. vol. I, 1829.
93. On the Scolopacidae, *ib.* vol. II.
94. On the new species of Buceros, J. A. S. B., vol. II.
95. On Aquila Nepalensis, *ib.* vol. II.
96. On Circoectus Nepalensis, *ib.* 1833.
97. On Nepal Zoology, *ib.* vol. II.

unceasing exertions and princely liberality he has unveiled the mysteries of Buddhism, chronicled the affinities, lan-

98. On the Bearded Vulture of the Himalaya, J. A. S. B., vol. IV.
99. On the Red-billed Erolia, *ib.* vol IV.
100. Summary description of some new species of Falconidæ. *ib.* vol. V.
101. Addition to the Ornithology of Nepal, *ib* vol. V.
102. Notes on Zoological Nomenclature, *ib.* vol. V.
103. On new species of Columba, *ib.* vol. V.
104. On new Incessores, *ib.* vol. V.
105. On Charadriadæ, *ib.* vol. V.
106. On Falconidæ, *ib.* vol. V.
107. On Yunxinæ, *ib.* vol. V.
108. On Certhiadæ, *ib.* vol. V.
109. New species of Hirundinidæ, *ib.* vol. V.
110. On Indian Thrushes, *ib.* vol. VI.
111. Indication of a new genus of Incessorial Bird, *ib.* vol. VI.
112. Description of three new species of Wood-peckers, *ib.* vol. VI.
113. On a new genus of the Sylviadæ, *ib.* vol. VI.
114. On some new genera of the Raptores, *ib.* vol. VI.
115. New species of Scolopacidæ, *ib.* vol. VI.
116. On a new genus of the Pheasant group (*Crossopticon Tibetanum*), *ib.* vol. VII.
117. On Cuculus, *ib.* vol. VIII.
118. Notice of a new form of the Glaucopinæ or rasorial crows, inhabiting the northern region of Nepal, *ib.* vol. X.
119. On Conostoma Æmodium, *ib.* 1841.
120. Description of a new genus of the Falconidæ, *ib.* vol. XII.
121. Catalogue of Nepalese Birds presented to the Asiatic Society, *ib.* vol. XII.
122. Additions to the above Catalogue. *ib.* vol. XII.
123. On a new species of Partridge from Tibet. (*P. Hodgsonæ*), *ib.* vol. XXV
124. On the new genus Merva, *ib.* vol. XII.
125. On the Charj or Otis Bengalensis, *ib.* vol. XVI.
126. On a New Genus of the Meropidæ, J. A. S. B, vol. V.
127. A new Genus of the Picadæ, also two new species of the Genus Sitta, *ib.* vol. V.
128. Two new species of Meruline Birds from Catamandu, *ib.* vol. VIII.
129. On a a new species of Plecotus, *ib.* vol. XVI.
130. On a new genus of the Fissirostrial Tribe at Catimandu, *ib.* vol. VIII.

guages, customs and faiths of the Himalayan Tribes, and completed a natural history of the quadrupeds and birds of these regions. Throughout the Bird and Quadruped departments of our national Museum, Mr. Hodgson's name stands prominent." Dr. Jerdon says, "Mr. Hodgson, for many years our accomplished Minister at the Court of Nepal, has added largely to our knowledge of the birds of the Himalaya, few of which escaped his notice. His papers are distinguished by deep research and great acumen, and are very full of details of structure."

The following extract from the Natural History Review for April 1865, p. 156, is also worthy of notice:

"About the year 1832, Mr. B. H. Hodgson, for many years British resident at the Court of Nepal, began his labours. This gentleman, it may be fairly said, has distinguished himself far beyond all his fellow-workers, by the great extent of his collections, and the numerous observations he has given to the public on almost every branch of Natural Science. Before Mr. Hodgson commenced his residence in Nepal, the Zoology of that country and of the high ranges of the great adjacent mountain-chain was almost unknown in Europe, and the novelties, which it fell to his lot to discover and describe, were consequently both striking and numerous. With the utmost liberality Mr. Hodgson has from time to time presented the whole of his enormous collections to the British Museum, and to other scientific institutions in this country, and though it is much to be regretted that he has never collected the whole of his scattered writings into one connected series, this deficiency has been to some extent supplied by two catalogues of Mr. Hodgson's collections, published by the Trustees of the British Museum in 1846 and 1863 Referring to the list of Birds in the second edition of this catalogue (prepared, we believe, by Mr. G. R. Gray,) it will be seen that the species of this class of Vertebrates obtained by Mr. Hodgson, in Nepal, Sikim, and Tibet number no less than 168. Nearly the whole of these are represented in our National Collection, through Mr. Hodgson's munificence, by several specimens in skins as well as by drawings made from life, and in many instances by skeletons or portions of skeletons."

The time, trouble, and expense incurred in collecting materials for the above contributions were immense. Hunters, taxidermists, collectors, draftsmen, copyists, and translators had to be organised and trained, their works constantly watched and directed, and their charges all defrayed from a private purse; and, amidst his onerous official duties and private literary occupation, Mr. Hodgson cheerfully did all that was necessary or desirable. Of the work done by his staff of hunters and taxidermists, some idea may be formed from the fact that no less than a total of 10,499 specimens, including 9,512 birds, 903 mammals, and 84 reptiles &c., all their handiwork, were presented to the British Museum, besides several thousands more to the Asiatic Society of Bengal and other scientific bodies. Duplicates from these collections have been distributed to the chief European and American Societies.

The draftsmen were employed in drawing natural history specimens and ethnological, architectural and antiquarian subjects, as also maps, plans, routes &c. The drawings were made of one uniform size, folio, each containing one or more subjects. There is no record to show the total number of drawings prepared under the superintendance and at the expense of Mr. Hodgson; but he presented 1,241 sheets containing drawings of birds and 567 sheets of mammals to the Zoological Society of London; 55 sheets of reptiles &c. to the British Museum; 46 sheets of ethnological illustrations to the Christie Collection; 61 sheets of ditto to the Anthropological Society of London; 66 sheets of architectural drawings to the India Office Library; and 24 sheets of architectural and 258 sheets of archælogical drawings to the Institute of France. The last were accompanied by a large mass of MSS., mostly in Sanskrit, explanatory of the Buddhist drawings. It is to these that M. Burnouf repeatedly refers in his great work on the History of Indian Buddhism.

Mr. Hodgson's collection comprised a great number of ethnographical specimens, mostly crania, which have been given to the British Museum. It included, moreover, three trunks full of MSS. of various kinds, in Sanskrit, Newárí, Persian, and English (mostly unpublished essays, papers and notes by Mr. Hodgson, and translations from old Indian records), which had been amassed for the full exposition of the history, institutions, races and tongues, revenue and commerce of Nepal and other Indian places. The whole of this collection was presented to the India Office, in August 1864, along with a detailed catalogue of its contents. The catalogue is too long to be copied here, but the following extract from the report of the Librarian of the India Office will give an idea of the value attached to the collection by a competent judge.

"Mr. Hodgson's present to our Library is indeed one of eminent importance, if only embracing materials from which, for the first time, the history, political, religious and linguistic, of Nepal might be digested by a competent scholar. That a person duly qualified to undertake such a compilation be found is highly desirable; though no one in any wise so ably as the learned donor himself could execute an account of a people, among whom, in the advantageous and responsible position of British Resident at the Court of Kathmandu, Mr. Hodgson passed nearly a quarter of a century. At least it is earnestly to be hoped that Mr Hodgson's health will still render it practicable for him to contribute a single chapter, and that a most valuable one, to the history of Nepal, in a narrative of the measures by which he succeeded, on more than one critical occasion, in restraining the Nepalese from disastrous irruption into the plains of India. The influence that effectuated this check, was wholly personal to Mr Hodgson, and yet the service here referred to, though of momentous import, has never, it occurs to me, been recognised.

"The Sanskrit and other oriental MSS. sent by Mr. Hodgson are a priceless addition to our collection. Of most of these there are no other copies in Europe."

Among the papers contained in this collection was a number of vocabularies of the non-Aryan vernaculars of India and its frontiers, and these have been most satisfactorily utilised in Dr. W. W. Hunter's Non-Aryan Dictionary.

There are yet two other contributions made by Mr. Hodgson to the cause of knowledge which require to be noticed here. The first is a collection of zylographs, comprising two complete sets of the great cyclopedias of Tibet, the Kahgyur and the Stangyur. Each set is made up of 334 bulky volumes, printed with wooden blocks on Tibetan paper, in the Indian puthi form, and comprises the whole circle of the sacred literature of the Tibetans. Analyses of these grand compilations have been published by M. Csoma de Körös in the last volume of the *Asiatic Researches* and in the Journal of the Asiatic Socity of Bengal, and they show the high value of the works for a correct understanding of the religion of Buddha as current beyond the Himalayan range. The number of copies extant of these grand compilations is exceedingly limited. The *Kahgyur* alias *Kangyur* includes no less than a hundred volumes, arranged under the three grand divisions of *Dulva, Do,* and *Sherchin,* whence their common name *De-not-sum,* Sanskrit, *Tripithaka,* "The three Repositories." This is obviously of the same character as the Buddhist Tripithaka as now known in China and Japan, of which Rev. S. Beal has lately published a useful catalogue, though the order of arrangement and the contents are not the same. The whole of the works in either case is strictly sacred or religious. The name Kahgyur means "translations of commandments," and the works are avowed to be translations of texts existing between the 7th and the 13th centuries, mostly in the 9th, in the language of Magadha.

"The Stangyur is a compilation in Tibetan of all sorts of literary works, written, mostly by ancient Indian Pandits, and some learned Tibetans, in the first centuries after the introduction of Buddhism into Tibet, commencing with the seventh century of our era. The whole makes two hundred and twenty-five volumes. It is divided into two classes – the རྒྱུད and མདོ *Rgyud* and *Mdo,* (Tantra and Sútra classes in Sanskrit). The 'Rgyud,' mostly on Tántrika rituals and ceremonies, makes eighty-seven volumes. The 'Mdo,' on science and literature, occupies one hundred and thirty-six volumes. One separate volume contains hymns or praises of several deities or saints. And one volume is the Index of the whole." (*Asiatic Researches,* XXI, 553.) Only a few of the richer monasteries of Tibet possess these zylographs: beyond Tibet they were unknown. The works were first printed in 1731, from blocks which are still in use in a monastery near Testrilhua-po. Mr. Hodgson obtained two sets, the second set, now in the India Office, from the Grand Lama of Thibet. The first set is now preserved in the Library of the Asiatic Society of Bengal.

The second contribution refers to Sanskrit-Buddhist works, of which Mr. Hodgson discovered a great number in Nepal. The existence of these was before his time perfectly unknown, and his discovery has entirely revolutionized the history of Buddhism as it was known to Europeans in the early part of this century. The total number of works discovered is not known, but it is believed that the works when carefully arranged and indexed will amount to about two hundred. Copies of these works to the total number of 381 bundles have been distributed so as to render them accessible to European scholars. Of these eighty-five bundles comprising 144 separate works were presented to the Asiatic Society of Bengal; 85 to the Royal Asiatic Society of London; 30 to the India Office Library; 7 to the Bodleian Library, Oxford; 174 to the Societe Asiatique, and M. Burnouf. The last two collections have since been deposited in the Bibliotheque Nationale of France.

The character of these works was first noticed by Mr. Hodgson in his Essays. He was thus not only the discoverer of these most ancient and authentic records, but also the first intelligent exponent of their nature and value, both in their ritualistic and in their philosophical aspect, and very appropriately did Burnouf address him, in the dedication of his *Saddharma-puṇḍarika,* "comme fondateur de la veritable etude de Buddhisme." Elsewhere he added, "Quand aux dogmas generaux de Buddhisme il n'y a rien dans le *Saddharma-puṇḍarika* que ne se trouve dans vos excellents memoires. Vous avez tracé d'une maniere compléte et hardie le plan de l'edifice de Buddhisme." It should be added, however, that the plan adopted by Mr. Hodgson was to give the result of his researches, and not to describe at length the contents of the works found by him, and his notices, therefore, served more to excite than to allay curiosity in regard to those texts.

M. Burnouf, working on the codices that were sent to France, produced, in 1844, his 'Introduction a l'Histoire du Buddhisme indien.' None can speak too highly of the industry, the ability, and the critical acumen displayed in this learned essay; but in it the nature of the materials was subordinated to the historical facts deducible from them, and the MSS. therefore remained comparatively unknown. His next venture was a translation of one of the works, the *Saddharma-puṇḍarika*—"le Lotus de la bonne Loi,"—and it affords an excellent specimen of the nature, character, style, and subject of the Nepalese collection.

The MSS. presented to the Royal Asiatic Society of Great Britain have the benefit of a nominal catalogue prepared by Professors Cowell and Eggling, but no analysis of any of them has yet been published. Mr. Bendall has, I hear, in hand an edition of the *Vinaya-Sútra,* and M. E. Senart promises a recension of the *Mahávastu Avadána,* taken probably from the Paris collection.

Of the Calcutta collection one work, the Lalita-Vistara, was published by me several years ago, and brief notices were added of seven others in its Introduction; but the rest, until lately, had never been touched. Even the list preserved of it was corrupt, sometimes describing the same work under two or three names as different works, at others giving one name for four or five or more works. These mistakes arose chiefly from the fact of two or more different works having been written continuously in a single volume without any break in the pagination, and in cursory examination, only the first and the last page of each codex having been read to make out the name of the volume.

In order to bring to a focus all the information available regarding the MSS. brought away from Nepal by Mr. Hodgson, Dr. W. W. Hunter published, last year, a catalogue, giving the names of all the works comprised in the several collections; but the list given in it of the Calcutta collection, compiled by me from the records of the Asiatic Society's office, is, I am sorry to observe, for the reasons aforesaid, not correct. Whether similar errors, owing to similar causes, exist in the European lists or not, I cannot make out; but on the whole the Catalogue is a useful compilation, and the thanks of oriental scholars are due to its learned author for the service he has done them by its publication.

When the MSS. were discovered, opinion was divided as to their age and authenticity. While men like Burnouf, Prinsep, Wilson and others accepted them to represent the oldest records of Buddhism, those who had directed their attention to the Páli texts of Southern Buddhism thought otherwise; and the discovery and decipherment of the As'oka edicts strengthened their position a great deal. It was urged that since the Páli of the edicts was the oldest type of that language, and it was unquestionably the vernacular of India within 250 years of Buddha's ministry, and since it was equally unquestionable that Buddha sought proselytes among the unlettered classes of society, he must have addressed them in the vernacular dialect of the time, and the most authentic and ancient record of his religion necessarily must be found in the Páli language. This, however, is a *non sequitor*. Admitting, for the sake of argument and not as facts, that the premises are correct, it does not follow that the religion of S'ákya Siñha must exist in the Páli language. The language used in preaching to the masses is not the language that is ordinarily used, nor is it fit, for the development of abstruse philosophical ideas; and the southern Páli texts do not pretend that they are *verbatim* reports of S'ákya's preachings. It would be absurd to suppose that in the 6th century before Christ there was any organisation for *verbatim* reports, and that such organisation was brought into operation to take down the sermons and lectures of an itinerant hermit addressed to the lower orders of the people. It must follow that the teachings of the saint were recorded by his followers, long after date, when the effect of those teachings had been thoroughly established, and there was a desire created to know what he had taught; and that the records contained the substance of the teachings as remembered by those who reduced them to writing. In such a case it is by no means necessary that even the language should be the same which was used at the time of preaching. To quote the opinion of Mr. Hodgson (*Essays*, p. 121)—" The preaching and the spreading of the religion is a very different thing from the elaboration of those speculative principles from which the religion was deduced. In the one case, the appeal would be to the many; in the other to the few. And whilst I am satisfied that the Buddhists as practical reformers addressed themselves to the people, and as propagandists used the vulgar tongue, I think those philosophical dogmata which formed the basis of the popular creed, were enounced, defended, and systematised in Sanskrit. I never alleged that the Buddhists had eschewed the Prákrits, I only denied the allegation that they had eschewed the Sanskrit; and I endeavoured at the same time, to reconcile their use of *both,* by drawing a distinction between the means employed by their philosophers to establish the principles of their religion, and the means employed by their missionaries to propagate the religion itself." History fully supports the validity of this position; but not to travel out of India I may appeal to a parallel case of recent date and unquestionable authenticity—that of Chaitanya of the 15th century—to prove the fact. The lectures of that saint were delivered in three languages: Bengali in Bengal, Uriah in Orissa, and Hindi in the North Western Provinces, but they have been all reduced to Bengali in the *Chaitanya-charitámṛita,* while his philosophical doctrines occur in Sanskrit. So strong was the influence of Sanskrit in this case that the followers of the saint have thought fit even to annex to the Bengali text a Sanskrit commentary. In the 6th century before Christ, this influence of the Bráhmanic language must have been infinitely more powerful, and it is difficult to suppose that its use was then avoided even in philosophical disquisitions. Were it otherwise, still the fact is patent that the Buddhists themselves, both Northern and Southern, admit in the most unqualified terms that their scriptures, including the teachings of the founder, were compiled, not during the lifetime of the teacher, but at three convocations held from time to time during 250 years after his death. This admission is a settler. To contradict it would be to attach to *à priori* arguments an importance which logically they cannot claim.

Nor are the premises on which the theory is based at all tenable. The Páli of the Edicts was, doubtless, the language of record and the Court language of As'oka; it was probably also, with more or less local variations, the vernacular of the Indo-Aryan races; but it is far from being a proved fact, that it was the common vernacular of all the different races, Aryan and non-Aryan, who peopled India in former times. Nay, the presumption is strong that the case was quite the contrary. Unity of language implies or presupposes not only unity of race, unity of religion, and unity of political condition, but also unity of climatic influences. Sounds are the outcome of the vocal organs; but those organs, though formed on the same model and structurally are identically the same, are not in the same state of development and tension under all circumstances. The gutturals of northern climes, which we have to "hiss, spit and sputter all," cannot be naturalised in the tropics. The guttural K of the Persians is entirely lost by their descendants in India, even in the second generation. The early Indo-Aryans had the same K, as we find in the Prátis'ákhyas, but it has long since been lost. The Bengali organs of speech in the Gangetic delta cannot control the sounds which are natural to the people of Central and North West India. Hence it is that among the descendants of the Aryan immigrants one single language, the original Sanskrit, got converted into the different vernaculars that are now current. The process of change was even more powerfully in operation at the time of As'oka, when social intercourse among the different tribes was more limited than it is now. Then, at that time, the non-Aryan races were more powerful and better organized than now, and they spoke in very different dialects. And under the circumstances it was impossible for the Páli to have been the common vernacular of all at the time of As'oka. It might have been the *lingua franca,* but certainly not the vernacular or the household language of all classes.

Three hundred years before the time of As'oka the case was even stronger. Society was much more divided, the different tribes were more isolated, and the influences which regulate the decay and regeneration of languages much more actively in operation; and it was impossible for

S'ákya Buddha to make himself intelligible to his mixed Aryan and non-Aryan audiences in one common language. He must have adapted his language to the capacity of his hearers, and if we had *verbatim* reports of his lectures, they would have shown that he did not speak in the same dialect at Magadha and at Srávastí. There is then the evidence of the Gáthá, which has been so largely quoted in Buddhist works to prove the authenticity of the Sanskrit narratives, to show that the popular language of the Aryans at the time of As'oka's death and for some time before it, was the Gáthá and not the Páli. (*Cf.* Introduction to my edition of the Lalita-Vistara.) And this suggests the question—was it the Gáthá, or some now unknown archaic form of Páli, or the Gáthá in varying forms to suit local circumstances, that S'ákya used in his preachings? There is nothing reliable to answer this question; but whatever it was, it was not pure Sanskrit, nor was it the same everywhere. A preacher anxious to win the heart of his hearers and secure proselytes could not adopt any language but that which would appeal directly and tellingly upon the hearers. The Sanskrit could not do so in the time of S'ákya Siñha, *ergo* the language of S'ákya was not Sanskrit, but one or more vernaculars, and the same must have been the case with his successors. Anyhow with the unquestionable and living proof of the Gáthá, we cannot unhesitatingly accept the Páli.

Professor Lassen, following Turnour and the Ceylonese accounts, is of opinion that Mahendra arrived in Ceylon in 245 B. C., and he or his successors taught the religion of S'ákya orally, without any text, for one hundred and fifty years, until between 102 and 75 B. C. the Pitakataya was committed to writing in Páli and its commentaries in Cingalese (*Mahavanso*, Ch. 33), and five hundred years after that Buddha Ghosa translated the latter into Páli. (Idem, Ch. 37.) Dr. John Muir does not subscribe to this opinion. He says, "It is also difficult to concur in Lassen's opinion as to the period at which the Páli or Mágadhi was introduced into Ceylon. Mahendra and his followers, who were no doubt numerous, must necessarily have carried with them the language of their native country; and not only so, but they may have been the bearers of numerous works written in that language. For it is not easy to receive literally the account given by the Ceylonese writers of the time, at which their religious works were first committed to writing, or to suppose that the foreign propagators of Buddhism, who would at first be ignorant of Cingalese, should, at the period of their arrival, have had no records in their own language of the new religion which they were introducing, or that these records should not have been safely handed down to their successors." While fully subscribing to Dr. Muir's argument, I cannot help thinking that the expressions, "the language of their native country" and "records in their own language," are calculated to mislead. The language of the records must have been that in which they were *preserved* in their native country, and not necessarily their native vernacular. In case of the Jesuit Missionaries in Southern India, the language of the Bible they introduced was not the vernacular of their native country; and what was true of the Missionaries was equally so of the Buddhist propagandists. At the time of Mahendra (245 B. C.) two, if not three, convocations of the Buddhist clergy had already been held and their scriptures finally settled, and the books carried must have been what were so settled at the convocations, and these were certainly not written in Páli or Mágadhi; for the Páli of the Pitakataya is not the Páli of As'oka's edicts, and the Mágadhi, as we know it, could not have been in existence when the Páli was current, for it is unquestionably a later evolution of the Sanskrit than the Páli. To say the Mágadhi of the original texts must have been different from the dramatic Mágadhi, is to give up the contention altogther, for we then come to something unknown and non-existent. It follows consequently, that the premises with which the advocates of the Páli theory start must fall to the ground, and with them the conclusion about the claim of the Páli to be the language of the original texts.

The discovery of the Chinese translations of original Buddhist records has placed in the hands of scholars a new mass of evidence which goes a great way to solve this vexed question. These records are avowed to be translations, not from Tibetan or Páli texts, but from the *Fan*, the language of the Bráhmans, *i. e.*, the Sanskrit. Some of these translations date from the 1st century of the Christian era, and most of them were prepared between the 3rd and the 9th centuries. These facts incontestably prove the existence of some Sanskrit originals at a time long anterior to the date of the Páli translations of Ceylon.

The question then arises, are the MSS. discovered by Mr. Hodgson the representatives of those originals? That some of them are not so, and of comparatively recent date, is fully admitted; but there are others whose claims to authenticity and antiquity cannot be questioned. Their names are given in the Chinese versions, and that circumstance alone is sufficient to vindicate the justice of their claim. It is to be regretted that the public has not before it translations of all these Chinese versions to compare with Mr. Hodgson's Sanskrit texts, but from what little it has, ample evidence is found in favour of the Nepalese texts. The Ceylonese, the Burmese and the Siamese versions of the life of S'ákya as preserved in Páli are deeply tinctured with local colouring. They give us pictures of the places where they were produced, and not of India, and the languages in which they are preserved are of a much later date than even the monumental Páli of As'oka,* whereas the Chinese version, as seen in Mr. Beal's 'Romantic Legend of Sákya Buddha,' is purely Indian, perfectly devoid of local colouring, and it is impossible to believe that it had been taken from any Páli original.

Mr. Beal's work is a mutilated version of the original Chinese, many descriptive portions being omitted; but such as it is, it "is a translation of the Chinese version of the '*Abhinishkramana Sútra*' done into that language by Djnanakuta, a Buddhist priest from North India, who resided in China during the Tsui dynasty, *i. e.*, about the end of the sixth century A. D. It would seem from a consideration of the title of the seventeenth chapter, 'Leaving the palace for religious life,' that originally the story of the 'Abhinishkramana' was simply that of Buddha's flight from his palace to become an ascetic. Afterwards, the same title was applied to the complete legend (as in the present work), which includes his previous and subsequent history. A very valuable date, later than which we cannot place the origin of the story, may be derived from the colophon at the end of the last chapter of the book. It is there stated that the 'Abhinishkramana Sútra' is called by the school of Dharmaguptas *Fo-pen-hing-king;* by the Sarvástivádas it is called *Ta-chwang-yen* (great magnificence, *i. e.*, 'Lalita-Vistara'); by the Mahásanghikas it is called *Ta-sse, i. e.*, Mahâvastu." (Beal's Introduction, p. v.) This description shows that it is made up of three distinct Sanskrit works, the *Abhiniskramana Sútra*, the *Lalita-Vistara*, and the *Mahávastu*,—all relating to the life of Buddha, and it is hopeless to expect that it should closely represent any one of

* Westergaard and Kuhn take the Ceylonese Páli to be the language of Ujjaíni, a local Prákrit, and Oldenberg places its original home in Southern India (Andhara and Kalinga); neither place connected with the original nidus of Buddhism.

the three originals. It is observable, too, that Asiatic translators have never observed the rigid scrupulousness of the modern European rules about faithful translation, where the *ipsissima verba* of the original is carefully preserved, and even the turn of the style, language and idiom is attempted to be reproduced. Ordinarily a general concordance in feature is all that Asiatics think necessary, and much latitude is allowed in ornamentation. It is, nevertheless, not difficult to show which parts of the Chinese version have been taken from which work, for the correspondence in language even in the purely descriptive portions, which refer not to the speeches of the principal actors, is as close as can reasonably be expected, if we bear in mind the peculiarities of the Sanskrit and the Chinese idioms. To give an instance: chapter VII of the Chinese version (page 35), giving an account of the descent of the Bodhisattva, opens with the following:

"At this time Prabhápála Bodhisattva, the Winter being now passed, and the opening month of Spring arrived, when all the flowers and the trees put out their scents, the vernal air, soft and serene, neither too cold nor hot, the young grass and other verdure freshly come forth, brightly shining on every side, at the time of the junction of the constellation Kwei (with the sun)" &c.

This subject is treated of in the 6th chapter of the Lalita-Vistara, and in my translation (p. 94) it commences with the words:

"Thus, Bhikshus, the Winter having passed away, in the fullness of the Spring season, in the month of Vaiśákha, when the sun was in the constellation Viśákhá, the trees were covered with leaves, and loaded with exquisite flowers and blossoms. The earth was covered with a carpet of green. The evils of great heat or cold were then absent, and everywhere there was calm and quietness. At such a time the Bodhisattva &c. &c."

It is obvious that the translators have arranged their words and sentences with a keen eye to the English idiom, and the Chinese translation has judiciously omitted the name of the Hindu month, which would have been useless and puzzling to Chinese readers, the name of the constellation being quite sufficient for them. These divergences apart, it is undeniable that this portion of the Chinese version is a counterpart of the Sanskrit Lalita-Vistara as we have in Mr. Hodgson's collection. Other instances of such close correspondence in language may be multiplied *ad libitum*, and the portions taken from the *Mahávastu* also affords similar correspondence; but we look in vain for such coincidences in the Southern versions. There even the speeches of the saint and his divine mother, which from their sanctity should have been most faithfully preserved, appear to be quite distorted. The details, too, of the narrative have been very materially altered, so as to show that we have in them an imperfect outline of the story and its substance. To give an instance. The Lalita-Vistara gives the dream of Máyá in these words:

"A noble elephant, white as silver or snow, having six tusks, well-proportioned trunk and feet, blood-red veins, adamantine firmness of joints, and easy pace, has entered my belly." (p. 94).

The Tibetan version has:—

"Un éléphant blanc comme la neige et l'argent, à six défenses, aux pieds, à la trompe superbes, à la tête rouge, à la démarche agréable, aux membres forts comme le diamant, le plus beau des éléphants entrait en elle, et jamais elle n'avait vu, ni entendu (dire) qu'on éprouvât un pareil bien-être." (Foucaux, p. 61).

The Chinese text has—

"Bôdhisatwa having then descended into the womb of Mâya the Queen, she in the midst of her sleep had a dream to this effect, 'she thought she saw a six-tusked white elephant, his head coloured like a ruby (or red pearl) &c. descend thro' space and enter her right side.'" (Beal, p. 37.)

All these three Northern versions it will be seen, are closely similar, and unquestionably produced from one source. But we fail to perceive anything like this similitude in the Southern narratives. The Burmese version of Bishop Bigandet (p. 29,) says:

"Opposite this mount and facing the cave where Maia sat surrounded by her attendants, rose another mount, where Phralaong, under the shape of a young white elephant, was roaming over its sides in various directions. He was soon seen coming down that hill, and ascending the one where the princess lay on her bed, directed his course towards the cave. On the extremity of his trunk, lifted up like a beautiful string of flowers, he carried a white lily. His voice, occasionally resounding through the air, could be heard distinctly by the inmates of the grotto, and indicated his approach. He soon entered the cave, turned three times round the couch whereupon sat the princess, then, standing for a while, he came nearer, opened her right side, and appeared to conceal himself in her womb."

The Siamese version follows this account pretty closely, but not quite faithfully. It says—

"Then they led her to a golden palace, standing on a silver mountain, and prayed her to rest on a couch with her face turned to the west. Then she saw a golden mountain, whereon the Royal Being that should be Buddha marched in the form of a white elephant. The most admirable of white elephants, leaving the mountain of gold, came to the foot of the mountain of silver, and passed round to its northern side. In his beautiful trunk he held a newly expanded white lotus flower. He ascended the mountain, and having trumpeted loudly, entered the golden palace. Thrice he marched around the couch, and at the end of the third circuit, he appeared to enter her right side, and pass into her womb." (Alabaster's Wheel of the Law, p. 98).

None, I venture to think, will be disposed to accept these Páli versions to be the archetypes of the Chinese text, or to doubt for a moment that the Sanskrit original as we have it in Mr. Hodgson's collection supplied the model for it. If so, the fact being admitted that the first Chinese version of the Lalita-Vistara was prepared in the first century of the Christian era, the inference is unavoidable that the Sanskrit original had existed for at least two to three centuries before that time to have acquired the necessary antiquity and religious authority to be fit for acceptance as the scriptures of the Buddhists, and worthy of translation by the people of China. This brings us to the Convocation held under the auspices of As'oka; but for the reasons assigned in the Introduction to my edition of the Lalita-Vistara, it is impossible to believe that that work was produced on that occasion (*cf.* pp. 56-7), and we must go back to the synod of Kálás'oka. Now, the Lalita-Vistara as we have it at present is a compound of two different works—a prose version in pure Sanskrit, which substantiates its statements by quotations from a metrical and simpler version in the Gáthá dialect. I pointed out this fact twenty-seven years ago (Journal, As. Soc. for 1856), and it has since been generally accepted. At the last Oriental Congress, held at St. Petersburg, it was announced as a new fact, but in no way controverted. The interval between the synod of Kálás'oka and the Nirváṇa cannot be extended to much more than a hundred to a hundred and forty years. If we admit the originality of the Páli we have to believe that within that period, the original life of the saint in Páli was first rendered into Gáthá and then into Sanskrit, and that the most ancient and authentic Páli having been lost, the author of the Sanskrit text was obliged to quote the Gáthá for his authority. This would be absurd, and the Páli theory must, therefore, be abandoned.

It is to be regretted that evidence is wanting to prove in the above way the authenticity of the other works of the collection under notice; but the evidence available in favour of the assumption that the more revered portions of the scriptures were compiled at the same, or about the same, time at which the Lalita-Vistara was got up is by no means stinted. It would be unreasonable and opposed to every law of inference to suppose that the Lalita-Vistara was the only work got up at the time; and if any faith is to be placed in the accounts of the convocations, held avowedly to preserve the scriptures from corruption and interpolation, and to settle disputed points of doctrine and of discipline, the conclusion is forced on us that several works, besides the Lalita-Vistara, were compiled on those occasions. And as a number of Mr.

Hodgson's texts are written in the same style as that of the Lalita-Vistara, and quote the Gáthás in support of their statements, it would be perfectly reasonable to accept them to be of the same age. Moreover, as the Gáthá was not adequate for the precision necessary for abstruse philosophical discussions, and no language existed in India in former times which was so well fitted for the definition of various shades of philosophical thought as the Sanskrit, it would be by no means unreasonable to suppose that Sanskrit alone, without the Gáthá, was used for philosophical works, and as the philosophy of Buddhism form the corner-stone of the doctrine of Buddha, some works on the subject must have existed from the earliest date. At any rate, the Páli originals of the present Sanskrit works must first be found before the argument above set forth can be fairly traversed. This argument is the same which Páli scholars used before the discovery of the Sanskrit texts, and it is perfectly legitimate.

There was a time when it was urged that the rational character of the Páli narrative was of itself proof sufficient for their antiquity and originality, and James Prinsep went the length of admitting that "if the rationality of a story be a fair test of its genuineness, which few will deny, the Páli record will here bear away the palm." The publication of some of the original Páli texts has since completely set this argument at rest. The quotations given above leave us little room for choice on the score of rationality. They are alike legendary, and full of romantic fables. Were they otherwise, still the question at issue would not be influenced one way or other by it. Plausibility is no proof in law, nor can it be in history. If we admit the reverse of the position, we have to accept all the society novels and stories of the day as history. The argument is that the Chinese texts were taken from Sanskrit originals, and that those originals are now before us in the MSS. discovered by Mr. Hodgson;

and this is borne out by their close correspondence in name, language and matter. If this be admitted, as it must be, the high value of the discovery cannot be gainsaid.

This question, however, of the antiquity of the MSS. apart, the services rendered by Mr. Hodgson to the cause of literature and science generally have called forth the warmest acknowledgments from all who are able to appreciate them. The quotations given above, express the opinion of some of the ablest critics on the subject, and associated bodies have not been slow in bearing their testimony to their value. The Asiatic Society of Bengal, whose transactions have been so greatly enriched by the contributions of Mr. Hodgson, presented him, on the occasion of his retirement from India, an address, elected him an Honorary member, and voted a marble bust which now adorns its meeting-room. The Royal Society of London, the highest scientific association on the face of the earth, elected him a Fellow; and another body no less distinguished and more exclusive, the French Academy, elected him a Foreign Member. The dignity of the Knighthood of the Legion of Honor, was bestowed on him by the French Government. He has now retired from the field of active labour, carrying with him the respect and esteem of all cultivators of science, and the warmest wishes of his friends and admirers for his long life and prosperity in his happy home in Gloucestershire.

To turn now to the immediate object of this Preface. The total number of MSS. presented by Mr. Hodgson to the Asiatic Society of Bengal was 86 bundles, including 170 separate works on various subjects. They vary in extent from a few s'lokas to a hundred and twenty thousand stanzas. The great bulk of the works refers to the history, philosophy, morality, and rituals of the religion of Buddha; a few are devoted to miscellaneous subjects. To classify them according to the scheme of the Nepalese Buddhists as described by Mr. Hodgson in his essays, (pp. 11 f.), I find, is impracticable. The codices do not in their colophons always give the names of the classes to which they belong, and the definitions of the classes as supplied to Mr. Hodgson by his informants are obviously arbitrary, and do not suffice to help me. An old classified catalogue would have been of much use; but such a record does not exist. Taking no note of a primer on grammar,* another on versification,† a collection of moral maxims,‡ obviously Hindu, a commentary an a Jain astronomical work,§ a treatise on precious stones,|| and a few rituals, the whole of the works are narrative, in each case the author relating what he had heard himself or from some one of what Buddha said on particular occasions about particular subjects, and in so far the form of the works supply no clue to their classification. The subjects, too, are not unoften so varied in each work that they afford no help. The threefold division of the Southern Buddhists—the Sútra, the Vinaya, and the Abhidharma—is nowhere prominently marked in the Nepalese texts. Judging by the nature of the works, the Sútras may be said to be represented by the "nine dharmas" of the Nepalese. Some of them are called Maháyána, others Mahávaipulya, but none Sútra only. M. Burnouf takes the simple Sútras to be the most ancient, but on insufficient grounds, for he had only one work of the kind before him, and it was by no means a satisfactory one. I have none to refer to.

The Vinaya by name is represented by a single commentary on a work which is not included in the collection before me, and, to judge from the character of the commen-

* Prayoga-mukha.

† Chhandomṛita-latá.

‡ Chánakya-śárasaṅgraha.

§ Súrya-prajṉapti-ṭíká.

|| Maṇi-parikshá.

tary, I have in it a treatise on philosophy, and not on moral discipline as the class is said to include. M. Burnouf noticed this absence in the collection which he examined. He says, (p. 33,) "la collection de M. Hodgson n'offre pas d'ouvrages qui se placent dans la classe du Vinaya, comme elle en possède qui appartiennent à celle des Sútras. Dans les deux listes que j'ai citées plus haut, le nom de *Vinaya* ne se présente qu'une seule fois, et encore n'est-il pas employé avec ce caractère de généralité qu'il a dans l'expression de *Vinaya piṭaka* 'le Recueil de la discipline.' Il figure seulement sur le titre d'un traité philosophique, le *Vinaya sútra,* dont j'ai indiqué l'existence tout à l'heure, et duquel il me suffit de dire en ce moment qu'il n'est pas attribué à Çàkyamuni." It is obvious, however, that the moral stories which figure so prominently in the collection under the name of Avadána, are the representatives of Vinaya works. The stories are intended to illustrate the deserts of virtue and vice, and *pro tanto* they are lessons on morality. In Ceylon there is a large class of works under the name of Játakas. These narrate the prominent incidents in the former lives of S'ákya Buddha. Many stories in the Nepalese collection also bear the same common name, but they occur in compilations which have the generic title of Avadánas. In fact, the Avadána of the Nepalese is the class of which the Játaka is an order. The former treats of the anterior lives of S'ákya Buddha as well as of other persons, whereas the latter is confined to S'ákya only.

The Abhidharma of the Ceylonese includes philosophical works; and the Prajnápáramitás and their commentaries take its place in the Nepalese collection.

Apart from the above, there is a large number of works in the Nepalese collection which bear the name of Dháraṇí. They begin in the usual style of Sútra works, with the set form, "thus has it been heard by me, that when Bhagaván sojourned in such a place," &c., &c., and, like the Sútras, bear no author's name, and in this respect they may be called simple Sútras, but they supply, each one or more, charms to be worn as amulets, and must be of a much later date than that of S'ákya Buddha and his earlier disciples. The atheistic and the later theistic Bauddhas could not have invoked the name, as the Dháraṇís do, of Tárá, or Vajrasattva, or Avalokites'vara to preserve them from snake-bites, malarial fevers, and demons. They are obviously imitations of the Hindu Kavachas from the Tantras, of which a great many were translated into Tibetan between the 7th and 13th centuries of the Christian era.

Believing in the authenticity and great historical value of the MSS. presented to the Asiatic Society by Mr. Hodgson, Mr. Arthur Grote, when President of the Asiatic Society of Bengal, often urged me to examine them and prepare an analysis of their contents; but the magnitude of the task deterred me. The total number of MSS. was 86 bundles representing, according to the Indian mode of reckoning, nearly a million and a half of verses, written in the, to me, very unfamilar Newári character, bristling with errors, full of uncouth and unknown technical terms, and abounding in quotations in a dialect which was but imperfectly intelligible to me. To master them thoroughly was the task of a life-time, and, having regard to my official and other pressing works, I could not take it up. Mr. Grote, however, did not like to see his project dropped altogether, and, after his retirement from India, suggested the plan of dividing the task among two or more persons, and the Council of the Asiatic Society having accepted it, and agreed to defray the cost of preparing and printing an analysis, Paṇḍit Harináth Vidyáratna was employed to read the texts and prepare, under my direction and supervision, abstracts of their contents in Sanskrit. The Paṇḍit read about two-thirds of the total number of the texts. Paṇḍit Ráma-náth Tarkaratna read the large *Prajnápáramitá*, and Paṇḍit Kámákhyánáth Tarkavágís'a three of the smaller works. The rest fell to my lot. I had also frequently to compare the Paṇḍits' abstracts with the originals, and this involved the necessity of a great deal of very hard and tedious reading. It was originally intended that I should translate all the abstracts into English, but during a protracted attack of illness, I felt the want of help, and a friend of mine, Bábu Haraprasád S'ástrí, M. A., offered me his co-operation, and translated the abstracts of 16 of the larger works. His initials have been attached to the names of those works in the table of contents. I feel deeply obliged to him for the timely aid he rendered me, and tender him my cordial acknowledgments for it. His thorough mastery of the Sanskrit language and knowledge of European literature fully qualified him for the task; and he did his work to my entire satisfaction. I must add, however, that I did not deem it necessary, nor had I the opportunity, to compare all his renderings with the originals. In preparing the abstracts it was found that my Paṇḍits could not always master the true import of the philosophical terminology of the Buddhists, nor could they condense with sufficient clearness the diffuse disquisitions about obscure dogmas to make them fit for presentation to the public. The attempt, therefore, to review the dogmas was abandoned, and attention was directed mainly to the narratives and the stories about the previous births of Buddha, which have been so largely illustrated in the ancient sculptures of India. Even in this respect, however, some limit had to be put to the length of the stories. Some of the stories are very long, extending over a hundred to two hundred pages, and all are decked out with a good deal of descriptive ornaments and tedious details. To reproduce them in their entirety would require not one, but many, volumes, and I had, therefore, to satisfy myself with their bare outlines—their skeletons—omitting all flesh and blood which give them their vividness and interest for the faithful. But reduced and attenuated as they are in the following pages, they will, I believe, prove useful in elucidating Buddhist traditions and sculpture, and in conveying a fair idea of the nature and contents of the newly discovered literature.

8 Maniktollah,
July 27, 1882.

CONTENTS.

N. B.—The MSS. as now arranged in the Asiatic Society's Library bear the Nos. shown here.

THE

SANSKRIT BUDDHIST LITERATURE OF NEPAL.

No. B. 26.

ABHIDHA'NOTTARA ALIAS AVADA'NA-STOTRA TANTRA.

अभिधानेात्तरं ।

Substance, yellow Nepalese paper, 12 × 3. Folia 205. Lines on a page, 6. Extent in s'lokas, 3100. Character, Newári. Date, Newári Samvat 805 = A. C. 1685. Appearance, old. Prose and verse. Very incorrect.

A treatise of the Tantra class, containing mystic mantras and directions for the worship of demigods and good and evil spirits of various kinds. Anonymous. The scene is laid in the abode of a Guhyaka of the name of Vajrakrodha Ḍákiní, ("the imp of lightning passion,") where the great Tathágata Vajrasattva once sojourned. There certain other Tathágatas solicit him to impart to them a knowledge of the secret science of destroying the net of the imp of lightning passion (*Vajrakrodha-ḍákiní-jála-samvarábhinottarottara-hridaya*,—the full name of the woık); and the knowledge is imparted in a series of sixty-five lectures. After defining the time, the place, and the persons fit for the worship of various kinds of imps, the spirit of Vajrasattva is directed to be meditated upon in the essence of certain letters of the alphabet, which constitute the víjamantras. In his heart the worshipper should reflect upon a central point, and over it the syllable *yam* forming a blue atmosphere, thereupon a brilliant red triangular halo formed by the syllable *ram*, thereupon a frost-like watery glow formed by the syllable *vam*, and thereupon a four-cornered yellow-coloured terrene globe formed by the syllable *lam*. He must then meditate on the wheel diagram, which he should imagine to consist of eight red-coloured spokes placed on the globe aforesaid. The form of the demi-goddess is fierce, four-mouthed, twelve-armed, &c., and the víjamantra for her is *Om hum áh mahásukham.* In this way the rituals for the performance of the rites and the worship of certain other divinities named are given at length. The divinities, imps, and rites are: Samvaravajra, Píṭhaparva, Vajrasattva, Píṭhadevatá, Bheruka, Yogavíra, Piṭhamálá, Mátrikábheda, Ádikarmika-yoga, Vajravira, Sadyoga-samvara, Amrita-sanjivaní, (raising the dead), Yogini, Kulaḍáka, Yoginí-yoga-hridaya, Buddha-kápálika Yoga, Vajrasattva, Manjuvajra, Naváksharáliḍáka, Vajraḍáka, Varsháyana, Kavachadvaya Chomaka, Ḍákíní Chomaka, consecration of pictures, daily service for Yoginís, meditation on the seven-syllabic mantra, Vajra-yoga-sádhana, Gardhavákára-yoga, the five cries, the fourfold goddess, Vajrabhaírava-krodhádhipati yoga, meditation on Vajrakrodha, Janmapas'ubhávaná, and Átmabháva. The Yoginis, whose worship is particularly enjoined, are described as women fair as the pith of the lotus stalk, with lotus-like pink eyes, fond of white garments, odorous as fresh sandal paste, and devoted to the adoration of Sugata and his successors. There are several kinds of these; some are called Kulajás, others Bráhmís, others Rudrás. The Ḍákinís are women of a bright red complexion, having the aroma of the lotus, benign countenances, red eyes and nails, and fondness for decorating their rooms with pictures of lotus flowers. They belonging to the race of Padmanetra. In course of the work several charms and amulets are given to protect persons from the attacks of evil spirits, diseases and other evils.

Beginning. ओँ नमः श्रीचक्रसम्बराय ।
सज्यते यत्र पर्य्यन्तं सर्व्वबुद्धविकुर्व्वितैः ।
क्रियते वज्रसत्त्वेन तद्गीतधर्म्मधातुकं ॥
श्रीमते वज्रडाकाय डाकिनीचक्रवर्त्तिने ।
पञ्चज्ञानत्रिकायाय त्राणाय जगतो नमः ॥
यावत्यो वज्रडाकिन्यश्छिन्नसङ्कल्पबन्धनाः ।
लोकहत्यापवर्त्तिन्यस्तावतीभ्यो नमो नमः ॥
एवं मया श्रुतमेकस्मिन् समये भगवान् सर्व्वतथागतः वज्रक्रोधडाकिनीगुह्यकोद्येषु विजहार । तत्र सर्व्वतथागता भगवन्तमनादिनिधनं श्रीवज्रसत्त्वमध्येषयन्ति स्म, देशयतु भगवन् ! सर्व्वतथागत ! वज्रक्रोधडाकिनीजालसम्बरणाभिधानोत्तरोत्तरं हृदयं ।

End. स्वाध्यात्माश्रययोगेन स्वधर्म्मात्तरभावना ।
यथा तथा विकल्पेन चान्यथारूपभाव्य च ॥

चित्तसम्मोहमासाद्य मन्युमुत्पाद्य इन्द्रियं ।
यथा तथा विमोचेण अन्यथारूपदर्शयेत् ॥

Colophon. इत्यभिधानोत्तरे स्वात्मभावपूजापटलः पञ्चषष्टितमः ॥

No. A. 13.

ABHIDHARMAKOS'A-VYA'KHYA'.

अभिधर्म्मकोशव्याख्या, मूलसहिता ।

Subtance, Nepalese paper of a yellow colour, 18 × 6. Folia, 338. Lines on a page, 12 to 13. Extent in s'lokas, 19,266. Character, Newári. Date, ? Prose. Generally correct.

A series of Aphorisms on the principles of Buddhist philosophy. By Vasubandhu. With an elaborate commentary, by Yasomitra A'chárya. The aphorisms are brief and terse, and so constructed as to express their meaning by their case-marks, without the aid of verbs, as is the case with the Sútras of Bráhmanical writers, and totally unlike the Sútras of the Buddhists, which are generally loose, verbose and prolix. The commentary also follows the style of the Hindu philosophers, and discusses the questions raised, with reference to their philosophical bearings, but supplies no *vṛitti* or literal meaning. The logical precision of the Hindu writers is, however, to some extent wanting, both in the text and the commentary: the categories are also different. The work is divided into eight chapters, each called a *Kos'asthána* or 'receptacle.' The first chapter opens with a discussion about *dharma* or religious duty, which is said to be of two kinds,—one *Sás'rava* leading to transmigration, and the other *Anás'rava*, or that which effects emancipation from the bond of mundane existence. Then follow descriptions of the twelve sentient organs which constitute corporeality; these include the five sensory organs, eyes, ears, &c., and seven desires, collectively called the *adhyátmika dhátus*. The second treats of organic and mental functions (*indriya*), which are reckoned at twenty-two. They comprise vision, audition, smelling, taste, touch, living, thinking (manas), feminity, masculinity, sensation of pleasure, ditto of pain, ditto of ease, ditto of uneasiness, ditto of indifference, ditto of earnestness, ditto of vigour, the sense of memory, ditto of meditation, ditto of knowledge, the desire of command over unknown persons (*anájñátamájñásyámíndriya*) that of command (*ájñendriya*), the sense of being commanded, (*ájñátendriya*). The third treats of the different order of beings (*kámadhátu*) resulting from our carnal desires, *káma*. The subject of the fourth chapter is the relation which our actions bear to our future life, or the manifestation of the soul in different forms of animal life in accordance with actions performed in previous lives. The fifth describes the pain and suffering resulting from transmigration. The sixth refers to meditation on the attributes of the Deity (*I's'vara*). The seventh treats of knowledge, which is of two kinds, carnal (*Laukika*) and transcendental or that which results from Yoga meditation. The eighth explains *Samádhi* or concentration of the mind on the Divinity—the only means of salvation open to man.

The work is of great importance as a repository of the various metaphysical theories of the early Buddhists. It takes up, one after another, all the various topics which engaged their attention; points out their character; notices their authors; decides upon their merits with great tact and learning; and forms altogether a valuable work of reference on the subject. M. Burnouf, in his *Introduction a l'Histoire du Buddhisme Indien* (p. 563), has the following appreciative remarks on this work : Les observations les plus générales entre celles que m'a suggérées l'examen de ce volumineux traité, embrassent trois points principaux. Le premier concerne la rédaction et le système du commentateur; le second, les indications qu'il donne sur d'autre ouvrages, indépendamment du sujet qu'il traite; le troisième porte sur le sujet lui-mème. En ce qui touche la rédaction et le systéme du commentateur, il faut reconnaitre qu'il appartiant à la bonne école des glossateurs indiens. Yaçômitra possédait certainement toutes les ressources de la langue sanskrite, et il en a fait une excellent usage pour explication du texte primitif. Sa glose est á la fois grammaticale et philosophique. Il suit, pour la grammaire, l'êcole de Pāṇini ; et quant au systême philosophique, il développe les opinions exposées ou seulment indiquées, dans ceux des livres cannoniques qu'on nomme *Sútras*. De lá vient la qualité de *Sautrántika* ou philosophe de l'êcole des Sûtras, qu'il prend dans un grand nombre de passages. Sous ce rapport, les indications que renferme ce commentaire sont aussi nombreuses que variées, et on y rencontre presquè 'à chaque page des fragments plus ou moins étendus de ces traités, dont plusieurs se retrouvent dans les volumes que nous possédons à Paris. L'examen d'un tell livre met à mes yeux l'authenticité des Sútras à l'abri de toute contestation; et il rend à la littérature sacrée des Buddhistes un service du mème genre que celui que les commentaires philosophiques des Bráhmanes rendent aux Védas, qu'ils citent á tout instant."

Beginning. यः सर्वथा सर्वहतान्धकारः संसारपङ्कादजगदुज्जहार । (?)

महाबलो ज्ञानसमाधिदृष्टो यः पञ्जरं जन्ममयं विदार्य्य ।
विवेश निर्वृत्यटवीं प्रशान्तां तं शास्तृनागं शिरसा नमामि ॥
परमार्थशास्त्रकृत्या कुर्व्वाणं शास्त्रकृत्यमिव लोके ।
यं बुद्धिमतामग्र्यं द्वितीयमिव बुद्धमित्याहु ॥
तेन वसुबन्धुनाम्ना भविष्यत्परबन्धुना जगतः ।
अभिधर्म्मप्रत्यासः कृतोऽयमभिधर्म्मकोशाख्यः ॥
अभिधर्म्मभाष्यसागरसमुद्धृतस्यास्य शास्त्ररत्नस्य व्याख्या मया कृतेयं यथार्थनाम्ना स्फुटार्थेति ॥ १ पत्रं ॥

उक्तानीन्द्रियानीति। प्रथमस्य द्वितीयस्य च कोशस्थानस्य सम्बन्धोपनिपाततां(?) दर्शयन्नाह। उक्तानीन्द्रियाणीति ॥ ४७ प० ॥

इदमिदानीं वक्तव्यमिति द्वितीयस्य तृतीयस्य च कोशस्थानस्य सम्बन्धप्रदर्शनार्थमिदमुक्तं कामरूपारूप्यधातुवैचित्र्येन चित्तादीनां कृतो निर्देश इति ॥ ॥ १२२ प० ॥

तीर्थकरविप्रतिपत्त्या समुत्पादितसन्देहः पृच्छत्यथ यद्येतदिति विस्तरः ॥ १७७प०

कर्म्मजं लोकवैचित्र्यमित्युक्तमिति चतुर्थस्यादावुक्तं। अतोऽनेन सम्बन्धेन अनुशयोपन्यास इति सम्बन्धं दर्शयति ॥ २१९ प० ॥

पञ्चमस्य षष्ठस्य च कोशस्थानस्य सम्बन्धमुपदर्शयन्निदमुपन्यस्यति। उक्तं यथा प्रहाणमित्यादि ॥ २४९ प० ॥

षष्ठात् कोशस्थानात् अनन्तरं सप्तमस्योपन्यासे सम्बन्धं दर्शयन्नाह ॥ चान्तयश्चोच्यन्ते ॥ ज्ञानानि चेति विस्तरः ॥ २९६ प० ॥

सप्तमादनन्तरमष्टमस्य कोशस्थानस्योपन्यासे सम्बन्धं दर्शयन्नाह ॥ ज्ञानाधिकारेणेति विस्तरः ॥ ३१६ प० ॥

End. अवधारणात् पञ्च धातवो रूपादयस्तदन्यधर्म्मधातुप्रदेशेनेन्द्रियमिति सिद्धं ॥ ॥ ४७ प० ॥

विचिकित्सया सम्यग् दृष्ट्या च कुशलमूलप्रतिसन्धानादितिवचनात्। चित्तलाभः चित्तप्रतिलम्भः अतद्वतः पुद्गलस्य नैरसमन्वागतस्येतिवचनादिति ॥ ॥ १२२ प० ॥

इयता हि कालेन तेषामायुषः परिसमाप्तिरिति ॥ १७७ प० ॥

कुशलत्वाच्चासंस्कृताभ्यामाकाशप्रतिसङ्ख्यानिरोधाभ्यामुत्कृष्टतर इति ॥ २१९प०॥

यदि परिहाणिरभविष्यत्। स एव युगपत् पञ्च परिज्ञा अलप्स्यतेति ॥ २४९प०॥

तदन्य आनन्तर्य्यमार्गाख्यैः क्लेशान् प्रजहातीति सिद्धं ॥ २९५ प० ॥

देवादीनां कर्म्मजा यथा तेषां बोधिसत्त्वानामिति ॥ ३१६ प० ॥

योऽधीत्य सर्व्वशास्त्राण्यभिमतविद्यो यशोमित्रः ।
स इमां कृतवान् व्याख्यां व्याख्यास्यन्यास्त्वसन्तुष्टः ॥

Colophon. आचार्य्ययशोमित्रकृतायामभिधर्म्मकोशव्याख्यायामष्टमं कोशस्थानं समाप्तं ॥ ॥ ३२८ प० ॥

No. B. 3.
AS'OKA AVADÁNA.

अशोकावदानं ।

Substance, Nepalese paper of a yellow colour, 16 × 5". Folia, 276. Lines on a page, 8. Extent in s'lokas, 9,660. Character, Newári. Appearance, old. Verse. Incorrect.

An account of the early life of As'oka, and of his conversion to Buddhism, and tales and anecdotes related to him by a Yati named Upa Gupta, with a view to illustrate the morality of the Bauddha religion. The name of the author is not given, but the work professes to be a record of the history of As'oka which a sage, named Jayas'rí, related to his audience at the Kukkuṭa Víhára, situated in a garden called Upakaṇṭhikáráma, on the bank of the Ganges at Páṭaliputra. There is a Kukkuṭa Vihára in Behar, but that is not on the bank of the Ganges; this must therefore be different.

Mr. Hodgson says the class of works called *Avadána* includes treatises on "the fruits of actions or moral law of mundane existence."* According to Burnouf: "Ils s'occupent, en effet, comme le dit la liste nepalaise, du fruit des œuvres; qui signifie *légende, récit légendaire*, ainsi que l'entend Csoma de Cörös, d'áprés les interprètes tibetains du Kahgyur. Ces légendes roulent d'ordinaire sur ces deux sujets, l'explication des actions présentes par les actions passées, et l'annonce des récompenses ou des peines réservées pour l'avenir aux actions présentes. Ce double objet est, on le voit, nettement résumé dans la definition de la listes népálaise, à laquelle il ne manque que la traduction littérale du mot sanskrite."†

The conclusions arrived at by Burnouf are—1st, that the Avadánas of the Nepalese represent the second division of the Buddhist scriptures, or that which includes the Vinaya or discipline. 2nd, That this discipline is not taught dogmatically as in the Sútras, but illustrated by examples, anecdotes and stories. 3rd, That they refer to all matters relating to Buddhist rules of conduct, both for householders and for the clergy, and monks, as well as to forms of rituals, and mode of life under all

* Illustrations of the Literature and Religion of the Buddhists, p. 23.

† Introduction a l'histoire du Buddhisme, p. 64.

circumstances. 4th, That we have in them the history of Buddhism both of the time of S'ákya, and of his successors for a long period.* These facts will be illustrated at length in the analyses which will follow of the several Avadánas which occur in the collection now under notice.

The genealogy of As'oka begins with Bimbisára, king of Rájagriha, who was a contemporary of S'ákya. His lineal descendants successively were—

2. Mahípála.	7. Turakuri.
3. Udayís'a.	8. Mahámaṇḍala.
4. Muṇḍa.	9. Prasenajit.
5. Kákavarṇí.	10. Nanda.
6. Sahali.	11. Vindusára.

These names occur in the life of As'oka given in the Divya Avadána, except the 2nd, 3rd, 4th and 7th which have been differently given, Ajátasatru appearing for Mahipála, Udayin for Udayís'a, Muyin or Udayibhava, for Muṇḍa and Tulakuchi for Turakuri or Turakuvi. In the absence of necessary MSS. it is impossible to ascertain how far these differences are due to copyist's errors. Apparently they are. The lists given in the Páli annals and in the Vishṇu Puráṇa are more seriously discrepant. They stand thus :—

Vishṇu Puráṇa, Vol. IV, pp. 180—186.	*Maháwanso*, pp. 15—20.
1. S'is'unága.	1. Ajátasattu.
2. Kákavarṇa.	2. Udáyibhaddhako.
3. Kshemadharman.	3. Anuruddhako.
4. Kshattraujas.	4. Mundo.
5. Vidmisára, or Bimbisára.	5. Nágadasako.
6. Ajátas'atru.	6. Susunágo.
7. Darbhaka.	7. Kálás'oko.
8. Udayás'va.	8. Ten sons of the last, no name given.
9. Nandivardhana.	
10. Mahánandi.	9. Chandagutto.
11. Sumálya &c., the nine Nandas.	10. Bindusáro.
12. Chandragupta.	
13. Vindusára.	

The other Puráṇas give many different versions of the names above noted, (see Mr. Hall's Notes in *loco cit.*). The Páli names are

* Ibid, p. 47.

obviously not so authentic as the Buddhist ones from Nepal. The latter were very early translated into the Chinese and have therefore better claim to confidence. At the same time it should be observed that the omission of the name of Chandragupta from the latter is significant. Coupled with the fact mentioned by the Nepalese writer that Vindusára came to Magadha from Rájagriha, it suggests the idea that Chandragupta was the sole king of his race, and that the Mauriya line commenced and ended with him. The Páli annals make Vindusára the son of Chandragupta. If so he could not have come from Rájagriha to take possession of his ancestral kingdom of Magadha. This is, however, not the place to enter into a discussion on the subject.

According to the work under notice Vindusára of Rájagriha became the king of Páṭaliputra, and his eldest son was Susima. When Vindusára was reigning at Páṭaliputra, a Bráhman of Chámpápuri presented to him a daughter named Subhadráṅgí. The damsel was extraordinarily beautiful, and a soothsayer having foretold that she would be the wife of a great king and mother of a universal monarch, the father made the present with a view to help the prophecy. The immediate fruit of this presentation did not, however, prove satisfactory to Subhadráṅgí. Immured in the palace she was, through the jealousy of the princesses of the zenana, doomed to menial service. Among other low occupations she was ordered to acquire the art of a barber, whereby, she was told, she would gain the goodwill of the king. When well proficient in the art she was ordered by the princesses to go and shave the king. She did so, and acquitted herself so well that the king offered to grant her any boon she wished. She prayed for his society; but the king denounced her on account of her being of the low caste of a barber. She explained that she was only acting the part of a barber by order of the princesses of the palace, but that she was a Bráhmaṇí by birth, and had been presented to the king expressly with a view to his marrying her. The king, thus reminded of her history, granted her wish, and made her the chief queen of the palace. As'oka was the first fruit of this union. He was so named because the mother emancipated herself from her sufferings by his birth, the word meaning "griefless." The lady had a second son named Vigatas'oka, which word has a similar meaning. As'oka was very unruly and troublesome, and his father made him over for training to an astrologer, named Piṅgalavatsa, who foretold that the boy would succeed his father on the throne of Páṭaliputra.

When the prince had attained his majority, his character did not mend; he was found so troublesome, that it was deemed advisable to get rid of him by deputing him to quell a mutiny which had broken out at Takshas'ilá, at a great distance from the seat of the empire. His efforts proved successful, and he was well received by the people of that place. In the meantime his elder brother Susima created disturbances at Páṭaliputra, and offended the chief minister, through whose intrigue he too was sent to Takshas'ilá, and As'oka was recalled therefrom.

Soon after, the king fell ill, appointed As'oka his successor through the instigation of the minister, but, much against his own will, and died. Susima, disappointed of his patrimony, rose against his younger brother, and attacked Páṭaliputra; but As'oka, through his able minister Rádha Gupta, soon overpowered him, and, to prevent future disturbances, ordered his ministers "to lop off the heads of all the trees in the royal garden with their flowers and fruits," in the same sense in which Tarquin the Proud lopped off the heads of the "tallest poppies" in his garden to instruct his son as to what he should do. The ministers demurred, and so he himself struck off their heads, and, retiring to a garden with the ladies of the palace, enjoyed the pleasures of life to the utmost.

Noticing one day that some of the ladies had broken the branches of an As'oka tree, he was very much annoyed, and directed a wicked man named Chaṇḍagirika, "the fierce mountaineer", to burn them to ashes on a large fire, and this was immediately done. The mountaineer, however, soon after met his deserts. Sárthaváha, a rich merchant, had proceeded to sea in the company of a hundred other merchants, and there had a son born unto him, who was named Samudra. On his way home, after twelve years, falling into the hands of pirates, he was deprived of all his effects, and murdered along with all his companions. His son Samudra alone escaped, and led the life of a beggar. Once he came to the house of the mountaineer to beg alms, and was set upon, but could not by any means be murdered. Surprised at it, the mountaineer reported the circumstance to As'oka. The king came to see the strange beggar, heard everything from him, and then cut off the head of the mountaineer.

The miracle wrought by the beggar worked on the mind of the king; and he became attached to the religion of Buddha. He caused a chaitya to be erected at the Kukkuṭa garden, and deposited in it some relics of Buddha. He then caused a chaitya and other religious edifices to be erected at Rámagráma. Coming thence to the river Ganges, he was requested by the Nágas to go to their country, and there he caused religious edifices to be erected. At the request of the people of Takshas'ilá, he caused 3,510,000,000 stupas to be erected for the deposit of relics. By his order the Yakshas erected, on the shores of the sea, ten million stupas for the same purpose.

After this a son was born unto him named Kunála, who soon distinguished himself in all that was taught him.

Subsequently, on one occasion As'oka went to a Yati, at the Kukkuṭa garden, to study the true religion, and, at the suggestion of that recluse, sent for, from the Urumuṇḍa Hill, a Yati named Upa Gupta, to whom he assigned the monastery of Venuvana, or the "Bamboo Grove." This saint was the son of Gupta, a rich man of Mathurá, who had been converted by one Soṇavásí, a mendicant who resided on the Urumuṇḍa Hill, and presented his three sons As'va Gupta, Dhana Gupta and Upa Gupta to his tutor. A prophecy of Buddha is quoted, according to which the birth of Upa Gupta was to take place a hundred years after his demise (*mama nirvritimárabhya s'atavarshagate upaguptanáma bhikshurutpatsyati.*) (Fol. 23-2-1.) This chronology, however, does not accord with the statement that As'oka was the thirteenth from Bimbisára, a contemporary of the great teacher. A contemporary of As'oka could scarcely be born within a hundred years of the reformer's death. Such a prophecy, however, was needed to exalt the rank of the great teacher who became the spiritual guide of so mighty a sovereign as As'oka. Having studied Buddhism under this tutor, As'oka caused, at every Buddhist resort, a Maṭha to be established for the adoration of the "Three Jewels."

When the teacher retired to his own hermitage, As'oka caused a proclamation to be issued declaring Buddhism to be the religion of his country. His chief queen Pavishyarakshitá was, however, annoyed at his forsaking the old family religion, and, through a secret agent, got the sacred tree where adoration was paid, to be cut down. As'oka was much grieved at this ; but, through the miraculous power of his religion, he restored it to life. He deputed Supiṇḍola Bharadvája, a Yati, from the Mandár Hill, to preach the true religion everywhere over his empire, and celebrated with great pomp the quinquennial humiliation and conference, giving a great profusion of wealth, raiment and food to the clergy.

About this time he also celebrated the marriage of his son Kunála with a maiden named Kánchanamálá, and soon after deputed the son to quell an insurrection in Takshas'ilá, a distant province, which seems to have been ill at ease under the house of Bimbisára. Kunjarakarṇa, the chief of the rebels, succumbed to the powerful army which followed the prince, and peace was soon restored. The insurrection, however, would appear to be a feint, and the real reason, as in the case of Susima and As'oka himself, was the removal of a troublesome prince from near the throne; for it is stated, apparently by way of euphemism, that soon after the deputation, the king saw in a dream the prince's face all pale, haggard, and dried up, and, being informed by astrologers that that portended one of three things, *viz.* loss of life, retirement from the world as a hermit, or loss of sight, wrote a letter to Kunjarakarṇa to deprive the prince of his eyesight, as the least of the three evils. The mandate was duly carried out through the instrumentality of a Chaṇḍála—the task having been held as too cruel to be executed by any person of a higher caste. It is not a noteworthy fact that after this Vítas'oka, the younger brother of the king, should retire to the hermitage of Upa Gupta, and afterwards accept from Guṇákara, a disciple of that teacher, consecration as a houseless hermit. This renunciation of the world did not, however, enable him to escape with his life. It so happened that at this time a professor of the Nirgrantha school, who reviled the religion of Buddha, had got a picture painted, representing himself with the likeness of Buddha lying at his feet, and this he had circulated widely in the province of Puṇḍravardhana, and As'oka, hearing of it, had proclaimed a price (some dinars) on his head. A cow-herd (A'bhira) had heard of this, and one night taking Vítas'oka, with his long beard, matted unkempt hair, and uncut nails, to be the Nirgrantha, cut off his head, and presented it to the king with a view to obtain the promised reward. The sight of the head deeply grieved the king; and he sought from Upa Gupta, his spiritual guide, religious consolation for his many acts of cruelty.

A hundred folia of the text are devoted to the life of As'oka as given above. The incidents narrated are the same as those given in the Divya Avadána, translated by Burnouf;* but the language is different, the one being a prose work, and the other a poetical version. The rest of the work is made up of lectures delivered by the teacher for the consolation of his royal pupil.

The first lecture is devoted to the celebration of a fast in honor of a chaitya (*chaitya-vrata*), and the religious merit derivable therefrom.

* Introduction á l'Histoire du Buddhisme indien, pp. 358, 435.

The second expatiates on the merits of devotion to Buddha, and on the propriety of confessing to him one's sins, praying for redemption. The third is on desire to be useful to mankind. The next five lectures have for their themes, contentment *(samprasáda)*; the suppression of the passions and indifference to carnal suffering *(kshánti-páramitá)*; relinquishment of works tending to birth, death and hell, and devotion to Buddha *(vírya páramitá)*; the abstraction of the mind from worldly affairs, to be centred in meditation *(Dhyána-páramitá)*; and the conviction that all things are illusory, and Buddha alone is true *(Pajñá páramitá)*. These are followed by a story in which seven maidens obtained preeminence by devotion to Buddha. It forms the subject of a distinct work, *(Sapta-kumáriká Avadáná)*, and will be noticed under that head. The means of salvation and the evils of mundane existence are then descanted upon, and they are followed by a long string of stories in illustration of various duties incumbent on householders and hermits, and of proper and improper conduct.

Prasenajit and Ajátas'atru were rival kings who long fought with each other for supremacy. Thrice had the former been defeated, but, a rich banker helping him with a thousand pieces of gold, on the fourth occasion he became successful. To evince his gratitude he placed the banker on the throne for seven days, during which the latter did a great deal to promote the spread of Baudha religion.

A householder was a great reviler of the Baudha religion, but was converted by the sight of some miracles performed by Maudgalyáyana. He then worshipped S'ákya with great devotion, and beheld the miracle of lights of various colours issuing from the mouth of the great Saint.

The person of a Brahman's wife, when *enciente*, smelt most offensively. Astrologers declared the cause to be the presence of a Preta (an evil spirit) in her womb. She brought forth an ugly brat whose body smelt like a putrid substance, and who was fond of feasting on aquatic weeds unfit for human food, whence his name Durgandha Jambála. After roaming about in many places, Jambála sought the shelter of Bhagaván when he sojourned at Kuṭágára near the Karkaṭa tank, in the suburbs of Vais'ali. The Lord converted him, and, when asked by his followers the cause of the fœtid odour, said, that it was due to his having, in a former life, abused a Yati.

Once when Presanajit, king of S'rávasti, was retiring from Jetavana, after adoring Bhagaván, five hundred geese came to him, and announced that the king of Pánchála had been greatly pleased to notice Prasenajit's devotion, and was coming to congratulate him on his conversion to the true faith. Prasenajit let loose the geese in the tank near the monastery, and retired. The geese, hearing the discourses of Bhagaván, were released from their anserine form, whereupon they repaired to the highest heaven. Bhagaván explains that the geese were Bráhman Buddhists who, hearing the evil teaching of some Tirthikas, had wavered in their belief, and were therefore punished by being doomed to be born as geese. From the genealogical table above given it will be seen that Prasenajit was the 9th from Bimbisára, a contemporary of S'ákya, and could not have been a contemporary of the great teacher; but such anachronisms are frequent in the Avadánas. The Tirthikás appear to have been Jains; some say they are Bráhmanas.

A youth of the name of Viditajasá of the S'ákya race, solicited Bhagaván, when he was at Kapila A's'rama, to make him a monk. The lord declined, because he was a youth, and had not obtained his father's sanction. Sanction was, after some difficulty, obtained and he was ordained. His claim to the distinction was, that he had, in a former life, replaced a flag which had been knocked down by some wrestlers whom he overcame in fight.

King Prasenajit had a very ugly daughter, by name Kutsitá, whom he gave away to one Gañga. The husband, ashamed of his bargain, and apprehensive of ridicule from his relations, kept her confined in a room. The relatives wished much to see her, and once proposed that at a festive assembly whoever would come without his wife would be fined five hundred pieces of coin. Every one came to the assembly with his wife, except Gañga, who paid the fine. Kutsitá heard of this, and, to relieve her husband of the trouble she caused him, repaired to a jungle to commit suicide. Just after applying the noose round her neck she prayed to Buddha. Rays of light from the person of the Lord came to her rescue, and by their touch converted her into a handsome woman. Thus metamorphosed she returned home. In the mean time the relatives had plied Gañga with so much wine that he became insensible, and lay on the ground. Seizing this opportunity they went to the house of Gañga, and were surprised to behold the most handsome woman they had ever cast their eyes on. Returning to the place of feasting they congratulated Gañga on the possession of such a beauty. He took the remarks of his relatives to be mere banter, but, on return home, was himself surprised to behold the change. The lady soon after obtained her husband's permission to become a mendicant, and was duly ordained by the Lord. The cause of her ugliness is related to be her fault, committed during a former life, in having expelled from her home a Pratyeka Buddha named Virúpa, after insulting him for his ugliness.

A king of the Kaurava race, while reigning at Káshṭhanagara, wished to be a hermit. The Lord refused to ordain him until he had obtained the permission of his wife and relatives. He did so, and was ordained. His good fortune was due to various acts of piety performed in former lives, which are detailed at length.

When sojourning at Jetavana near S'rávasti, S'ákya Siñha once dwelt on the importance of giving presents to worthy persons, and, in illustration of this subject, said, that when, after many successful ventures and loaded with valuable commodities including sandal-wood of the kind called Gos'irsha, a number of merchants were returning home from Rákshasa-dvipa (island of genii), a violent hurricane arose, and every moment threatened them with destruction. Beholding this, some offered their prayers to Tirthikas, some to Chandra, some to S'akra, some to Agni, some to Varuṇa, and so on, but to no avail. One of them, named Punyasena, prayed Hetúttama, a Bodhisattva who dwelt near his abode. Immediately the vessel was cast on shore, and the merchants returned home. Just at the time Hetúttama happened to be laid up with a burning fever, and his medical advisers recommended an unguent of Gos'irsha to be smeared on his person. Knowing that the drug was to be had only from Punyasena, king Chandráloka offered four lacs of coins for a supply of it. Punyasena declined the offer, but, carried the drug to the hermit, and cured his suffering with it. The result of this act of beneficence was, that the person of the merchant became most beautiful and redolent with exquisite aroma, and all the wealth he had lost at sea was found in the bottom of the well behind his house.

Bhava S'armá, a Bráhman of S'rávasti, was one night about to go to his lady love, when his old mother stood in the way, and prevented him. He felt vexed and killed her; but when he came to his mistress and told her of what he had done for her love, she was annoyed, and sent him away from her house, as she would not associate with a matricide. Deeply mortified, he consulted certain Bráhmaṇas, and through their advice, performed all the expiatory ceremonies enjoined in the Vedas, but they failed to afford him consolation. At last he retired to the wilderness, and, by the advice of a Bhikshu, performed the rite called *ashṭáṅga upasadha*, (the cleansing of the eight members of the body,) and, then going to the Lord at Jetavana, got himself ordained a hermit, and obtained peace of mind.

Madhurasvara, a householder, had left some wealth with misers. The wealth, so deposited, was all destroyed by fire. The householder taught the misers the true religion, and they got their wealth back. Some robbers next attempted to rob them, and he saved them. He then became a prisoner in lieu of some mendicants, and remained tied hand and foot in a field. Some robbers came to kill him; but Bhairaví Deví, with a retinue of five hundred imps, came to his rescue; his bonds fell off, and he rose high up in the sky like a flamingo, whereupon the robbers fled, and he became a devoted hermit.

One Padmaka, beholding, in his youth, a dead body, felt disgusted with the world, and, obtaining the permission of his parents, became a hermit. When at Mathurá, he entered the house of a prostitute for alms. The frail one was charmed with the beauty of his person, and sought his love. He was disgusted, and immediately left her house. To overcome him she employed a Chaṇḍálí, who lighted a fire and by the force of her enchantments brought him thither; but, rather than yield to the wishes of the two wicked women, he offered to jump into the blazing fire, and kill himself. His enticers were terrified, and at last took his advice, and became mendicants.

The Lord Jina was once in the Nandana garden of Indra, and there, amidst the gods, performed many miracles for their edification. He performed the meditation (samádhi) called *Durgati-sodhana*, and instantly millions of rays of diverse colours issued from his body, and blessed the gods. He then performed the *Rajádhishthána* meditation, and similar rays issued from his turban, purified all classes of beings, and returned back to their place. Then issued from his person the *Hrit* mantra, and the sound of it at once translated the dwellers of hell to heaven. Then from his turban issued the sound of *Guhya* mantra, and it excited in all created beings a desire to adore the three Ratnas. Similarly the *Munindrahrit* mantra issued therefrom and excited in all creation a desire to adopt the Bodhi religion. Then the *Sarvajinopahrit* mantra issued forth in great effulgence, and wrought salvation for all the greatest sinners; thereupon bright lights issued from the head of all the saints, and the Lord closed his instruction by explaining the secret knowledge of the great Dháraṇí.

In Mr. Beal's Tripíṭhaka three works are mentioned as bearing on the life of As'oka; the first is *A-yu-wang-pi-u-king*, which is the same with the As'oka Avadána. The name of its translator is lost. The second is *A-yu-wang-chun* or a history of As'oka rájá; it was "translated by Ngan-fa-kin of the Western Tsin dynasty (circ. 265-313), belonging to the Ngan-sih (Assíka Parthian country). The third is named *A-yu-wang-wan-muh-yun-in*, and refers to the circumstances which induced As'oka to put out the eyes of his son.

Beginning. ওঁ নমঃ সর্ব্ববুদ্ধায় বোধিসত্ত্বেভ্যঃ।

यः श्रीमाल्लोकनाथस्त्रिभुवननिलये मारसैन्यान् विजित्य
लोकानां पुण्यहेतोः सततशुभकरीं बोधिचर्य्यां दिदेश।
तं बुद्धं शाक्यसिंहं सकलगुणनिधिं श्रीघनं बोधिराजं
नत्वाऽशोकावदानं सकलहितकरं बोधिहेतोः प्रवक्ष्ये॥
येनैव त्रिजगल्लोकं पालितं पुत्रवत् सदा।
जयन्तु शासनान्यस्य मुनीन्द्रस्य जगद्गुरोः॥
नत्वा तं श्रीघनं नाथं महाबुद्धं मुनीश्वरं।
तत्प्रसादादहं वक्ष्ये रत्नदानावमालिकां
एवं मया श्रुतं पूर्व्वं यथा मे गुरुभाषितं।
तथाहं सम्प्रवक्ष्यामि तच्छृणुध्वं सुभाषितं॥
तद्यथासीन्महीखण्डे आर्य्यावर्त्ते रसोत्तमे।
मगधभूप्रदेशेऽत्र गङ्गातीरे पवित्रिते॥
नगरं पाटलीपुत्रं भूकान्तातिलकोत्तमं।
सुभिक्षं कमलावासं सर्व्वसम्पत्समृद्धितं॥
साधुजनसमाकीर्णं विद्वज्जननिषेवितं।
सर्व्वदा मङ्गलोत्साहप्रवर्त्तनाभिनन्दितं॥
ईतिभिरनभिक्रान्तं स्फीतं क्षेमं शुभाश्रयं।
सत्यधर्म्मालयारामसुरम्यं स्वर्गसन्निभं॥
तस्योपकण्ठकारामे दिव्यालङ्कारमण्डिते।
जयश्रीर्नाम सर्व्वज्ञो बोधिसत्वो महासुधीः॥
भिक्षुभिः श्रावकैः सार्द्धं विजहार जिनात्मजः।
तदा सोऽर्हन्महाभिक्षुः सर्व्वसत्वानुकम्पया॥
बोधिसंवरमारभ्य सद्धर्म्मं समुपादिशत्।
तच्च धर्म्मामृतं पीत्वा सर्व्वे लोकाः प्रमोदिताः॥
सत्कृत्य श्रद्धया नित्यमुपस्थाय विशेभिरे।
तदा ते भिक्षवः सर्व्वे स्थविरं तं जयश्रियं॥
कृताञ्जलिपुटा नत्वा प्रार्थयन्नेवमादरात्।
भदन्त श्रोतुमिच्छामो भगवज्जातकावलीः॥
कस्मिन् वंशे समुत्पन्नो बोधिं प्राप्य जिनोऽभवत्।
कथं तेन मुनीन्द्रेण बोधिराससाधितोऽभवत्॥
तत् सर्व्वं समुपादिश्य सर्व्वान्नः परिबोधय।
इति तैः प्रार्थ्यमानः स जयश्रीः स्थविरो यतिः॥
तान् सर्व्वान् श्रावकान् भिक्षून् समामन्त्र्यैवमब्रवीत्।

शृणुध्वं भिक्षवः सर्व्वं यदशोकेन भूभुजा ॥
पृष्टार्हतोपगुप्तेन भाषितं तत् सुभाषितं ।
गुरुणा मे यथोद्दिष्टं तथा वो वक्ष्यते मया ॥

End. एवं जयश्रीर्मुनिराजकल्पः सम्बोधिचर्य्याप्रविकाशहेतोः ।
सर्व्वान् स्वशिष्यान् प्रतिबोधयन् स प्रज्ञां दिदेश स्वयदानमालां ॥
श्रुत्वाऽपि ते सर्व्वे उदारचित्ताः शिष्याः सलोका अनुमोदमानाः ।
सद्धर्म्ममाश्रित्य सदा चिरत्नं भक्त्या भजन्ति स्म सदा प्रमोदैः ॥

Colophon. इति श्रीअशोकावदानमालायां दुर्गतिपरिशोधनधारणीमण्डलपरिवर्त्तो नाम षट्त्रिंशोऽध्यायः ।

No B. 6.

AVADA'NA S'ATAKA.

अवदानशतकं ।

Substance, yellow Nepalese paper, 15 × 4½ inches. Folia, 176. Lines on each page, 9. Extent in s'lokas, 6248. Character, Nágara. Date, ? Appearance, old. Verse and prose. Incorrect.

A collection of stories in illustration of miracles performed by Buddha. Compiled by Nandis'vara Achárya. According to the name of the work, there should be a hundred tales; but the codex under notice contains only ninety. The stories are puerile and of little interest. They open and conclude in very much the same way in every case, and repetitions are frequent. The language is simple, and of the peculiar verbose style common in Nepalese Sanskrit works. Nothing is known of the author; but the work is of considerable antiquity. It appears to be the same with the *Pih-u-king* of the Chinese, which was translated from the Sanskrit by one Guṇabhadra. The Sanskrit name of the Chinese work as given by Mr. Beal is *S'atávadána Sútra*, (Catalogue of the *Buddhist Tripíṭhaka*, p. 88). The following are brief abstracts of the stories.

STORY I.—Once upon a time, the great Buddha lodged in the Bamboo grove (*Venu-vana*) on the side of the Kalandaka tank at Rájagriha. There, he initiated Rájá Bimbisára into his doctrines, and, by preaching, converted thousands to his faith. There lived, at this time, in a retired village named Dakshiṇagiri, one Sampúrṇa, a Bráhman as rich as Kuvera. Some of his relatives embraced the Buddhist religion, and spoke highly of it before him. One day he fell on his knees and adored Buddha. The Lord appeared before his votary attended by Ánanda. Sampúrṇa received him with every manifestation of reverence due to a god, and waited the pleasure of the Lord. Of him the Lord sought food and drink, both for self and his retinue of Bhikshus. When a thousand begging vessels were filled with all the dainties of the time, a voice from heaven declared " the vessels of a thousand Bhikshus are full."

At the manifestation of this miraculous voice, Sampúrṇa fell, like a felled tree, at the feet of the Lord, and importuned him for instruction in Bodhi knowledge. The Lord lent a willing ear to his importunities, and, calling to mind the doings and sufferings of his votaries in his former existences, smiled. Rays, blue, red, yellow and white, shot forth from his smiling lips. Some of these proceeded upwards and some downwards; the latter cooled the fiery regions of hell and warmed the chill blush of Stygian wind, liberating multitudes of suffering sinners, who repaired to the regions of the gods and of men, and there took new births. Those rays which preceded upwards, reached the regions of Brahmá and others, and there recited the two following Gáthás :—

" Commence the good work, give up the world, and be obedient to the command of Buddha."

These rays afterwards turned thrice round Buddha, and disappeared in his head-dress. When Buddha had a mind to reveal the past, these rays, issuing from his teeth, disappeared in his back ; when he wished to speak of the future they vanished in his front ; when he thought to speak of hell they fell at his feet ; and when of perfect knowledge they lost themselves in his head-dress.

After the disappearance of these rays the Lord addressed Ánanda, saying, " this Bráhman is sure to become a great Buddha, endowed with mercy, memory, the three qualities, and the ten powers, observant of the six articles of our faith and adorned by universal benevolence." The Lord then taught Sampúrṇa the perfect knowledge.

II.—When dwelling in a lofty tower on the lake Markala, in the vicinity of Vaishali, the Lord, while on a begging excursion, entered the house of one Siñha, a general of the royal army, who offered him welcome. The brilliancy of the Lord's person attracted tke notice of Yasomatí, daughter-in-law of Siñha. She enquired of her father-in-law how she could be as brilliant. He replied, by becoming a votary of the Lord.

Thereupon she invited Buddha and his companions, satisfied them with various dainty dishes, and adored the Lord by throwing flowers at his feet. These flowers forthwith went to the lofty tower and formed a gemmed parasol of such exquisite beauty as even the most skilled artist would fail to imitate. She fell at the feet of the Lord, and prayed for admission to the ranks of his followers. The Lord addressed A'nanda, saying, "This Yasomatí is destined to become a great Buddha, Ratnamatí by name."

III.—When the Lord sojourned in the garden of Anáthapiṇḍada in the Jeta grove at S'rávasti, there lived at S'rásvasti a rich usurer who had obtained a son by worshipping Indra and other gods. The son, named A'nanda, grew up under the care of his parents. But he was weak in the loins, and even at the age of six years could not walk, though by his sharpness and intelligence he readily, at the time, mastered all the sciences of his day. The usurer was very sorry at the ailment of his son, and wept bitterly for his sad lot.

The omniscient Lord, knowing all this, presented himself one day at the usurer's house. The boy, seeing him marked with all the 32 signs of greatness, suddenly rose up from his seat, received him with great reverence, and enquired about his health. The parents of the child wondered at this miraculous cure.

The Lord smiled and said, "This boy will become a great Buddha."

IV.—A merchant at S'rávasti carried his mercantile transactions beyond the sea. In two successive voyages his vessels were wrecked. He escaped with his life with great difficulty, his splendid fortune being drowned in the sea.

He started on a third expedition with the firm conviction that the Lord Buddha was the greatest and most merciful of gods. This time fortune smiled on him; after a prosperous voyage he returned laden with riches from the Jewel Island. After his return he bought two Kárshápaṇa worth of incense, and at the Jeta grove burnt it before the Lord. The smoke rose up in clouds and covered the sun. The astonished merchant invited Buddha and all his Bhikshus, feasted them to their fill, and showered precious stones with a lavish hand among them. These stones rose up in the air, and there formed a splendid tower and a brilliant gemmed umbrella over the Lord's head. The merchant fell on his knees and asked instruction in supreme knowledge.

The Lord said to Ánanda, "This man will become a perfect Buddha, Ratnottama by name."

V.—In S'rávasṭi there was a patriarch as rich as Kuvera. When Devaputra fell from heaven he, under the name of Chaṇḍika, became the son of that patriarch. Chaṇḍika for a long time suffered from a burning sensation throughout his body. Obtaining no relief from medicines, he meditated on Buddha. The Lord kindly presented himself before Chaṇḍika, and granted him a medicine obtained from Indra. It effected an instant cure. Chaṇḍika feasted Buddha to his entire satisfaction and asked instruction in supreme knowledge.

The Lord said to Ananda &c.

VI.—Before the advent of Buddha Rájá Prasenajit used to worship the Tírthikas, but, after the appearance of that great preacher, he bowed to none but the great Lord. When the Lord was dwelling in the Jeta grove, a gardener of S'rávasti brought a big lotus flower as a present for the king.

A worshipper of the Tírthikas asked its price. At this time Anáthapiṇḍada came and doubled its value. They bade against each other with emulous pride till the price rose to a hundred-fold. Thereupon the gardener enquired about the whereabouts of Buddha, and, hearing of his great power from Anáthapiṇḍada, presented the flower to the Lord. Instantly the lotus swelled out to the size of a carriage wheel, and stood over Buddha's head. The gardener, astonished at this, asked instruction in supreme knowledge. The Lord said to A'nanda, "This man is to become a great Buddha, Padmodbhava by name."

VII.—When the Lord was dwelling in the Jeta grove, the kings of North and Śouth Kos'hala made war upon each other. Rájá Prasenajit came with a sorrowful countenance to the Lord, and begged him to bring about a peace. Whereupon the Lord proceeded to Benares where the king of North Kos'hala paid him a visit. Buddha preached before him the blessings of peace. His lecture had the desired effect. The king repented, and went to a monastery where he rose to the rank of an Arhat.

At the request of the Southern king Buddha lived for three months in his capital. The king bestowed on him the gift of a thousand pieces of cloth, and asked instruction in perfect knowledge.

The Lord said to A'nanda, "The king will become a perfect Buddha under the name Vijais for this good work."

VIII.—When the Lord resided in the Jeta grove, two bankers of S'rávasti quarrelled with each other. One was a Buddhist, the other a follower of a Tírthika named Púraṇa. Each held his object of worship to be the most powerful. The king Prasenajit convened a large assembly to settle their quarrel, and requested the disputants to worship each his own god. The flowers offered to Púraṇa fell to the ground, while those offered to Buddha flew like so many flamingoes (haṇsa) towards the Jeta grove. The worshipper of Púraṇa, astonished at his great mistake, deserted the altar of his god and falling on his knees, asked &c.

IX.—The ninth miracle is wanting.

X.—Once upon a time Ajátas'atru defeated Rájá Prasenajit in a great battle. The vanquished monarch, overwhelmed with grief at this sad reverse of his fortune, shut himself up in one of the innermost apartments of his seraglio. On this, a rich banker of S'rávasti incited the king to go again to war by offering him a large heap of gold. In this second battle Ajátas'atru was made a captive. Prasenajit went in triumph to the Jeta grove where the Lord was residing, carrying the captive in his train. There, before the Lord, he generously set the vanquished king at liberty.

Prasenajit did not forget the banker. He offered the man his throne for a week. During this week the banker-king had no other occupation but honoring the Lord and feasting his Bhikshus. At the expiration of his short reign, he fell at the feet of the Lord, and asked for supreme felicity.

The Lord addressed to A'nanda, saying, "This man will obtain his desired object. He will become a Buddha, Avayaprada by name."

XI.—The Lord was residing in a hamlet down the stream Ajeravatí, in S'rávasti. The inhabitants of that place were all boatmen. They cheerfully entertained the Lord with a share of their frugal fare, and sat round him in a retired spot, listening to him with great attention. From him the boatmen obtained each his desire.

The Lord revealed the secret of his great miraculous power to those Bhikshus who were desirous of knowing it in the following words:—

"Once on a time a Buddha, Bhagiratha by name, reached the banks of the Ganges with two thousand Bhikshus, on a travel round the country. A merchant, who was ferrying his goods over the stream with a number of his dependents, approached the Lord respectfully, helped him in crossing over the stream, and feasted him to his entire satisfaction. I am that merchant. I enjoy the supreme felicity by the virtue of my good works in my former existences."

XII.—Perambulating in the Kaurava country, the Lord one day reached its capital. There he summoned Indra and bestowed on him a quantity of sandal-wood from Gos'irsha. A few days later Indra, expecting favours from the Lord, anointed him with the sandal, and feasted him with rich viands. Wondering at the submission of the gods, thousands of the Kaurava race flocked round him to receive his blessing. By his precepts every one obtained what he desired.

The Lord addressed the Bikshus who desired to know the secret of his power, saying :—

"A great Buddha, Brahma by name, entered once the capital of a Kshatríya king, who prayed the Lord for staying there for a period of three months. During this short time, the king honored the Lord in every possible way. He offered him flowers, aromatics, incense, rich food, splendid robes and the sandal from Gos'írsha.

"O Bhikshus! I am that king; by virtue of my former good works I obtain this pújá from the gods."

XIII.—While the Lord was living in the Jeta grove a caravan of five hundred merchants missed their way in a sandy desert, and suffered greatly from the scorching heat of the meridian sun. Every moment their sufferings grew more and more intense. They prayed Varuṇa and others, but from none did they receive the least help. They then sought protection from Buddha. The Lord Buddha left the Jeta grove, and appeared before them. They welcomed him with ardent manifestations of respect. By the command of Buddha, Indra sent refreshing showers down, and fresh and delightful breezes blew from the south. The merchants, relieved of their sufferings, went to S'rávasti. There they obtained all they desired through the blessing of the Lord.

The Lord addressed the Bhikshus, saying; "In ancient days Chandana, a great Buddha, went to the capital of a king. The king prevailed upon the Lord by his entreaty to honor his capital with a temporary residence for three months. There was no rain for several years in the kingdom; the ministers advised the king to bathe the Lord with perfumed water. The Lord was delighted, and forthwith heavy showers of rain fell from the clouds. I made one of those that poured the perfumed water over the Lord's head."

XIV.—Once on a time the city of Náthakaṇṭha was desolated by a destructive epidemic. The suffering multitude prayed Indra and other gods for help, but to no effect. They then sought protection from Buddha. He appeared among them from his then residence in the Bamboo grove *(Venu-vana)* in Rájagriha, and granted them relief. The Bráhmaṇas of the place, grateful for the kindness of the Lord, listened to his preaching with great attention. They obtained all their desires through his lectures.

The Lord revealed to the Bhikshus the real cause of his great power. He said, "Chandana, a great Buddha, entered of yore the capital of a Kshatríya king. The king honored him greatly. I was that king; my great power resulted from that great man's blessing."

XV.—The Lord lodged in the Bamboo grove on the side of the tank Kalandaka. Ajátas'atru, the king of that place, was a great hater of the Buddhists. He made preparations for an extensive sacrifice. Bráhmans came to the sacrifice by thousands, but none to the Bamboo grove.

When the priests offered the oblation to Indra, the Lord, disguised in the form of that god, accepted it from them. People wondered at the visible appearance of the god, and came flocking to the sacred spot. To the great astonishment of the assembled multitude the Lord assumed his own form. Many turned Buddhist at this miracle and obtained whatever they desired from the great Lord.

The Lord revealed to the Bhikhus the following ancient story. "A Kshatríya king founded a splendid Vihára at the desire of Indradyumna, a great Buddha. I was that Kshatríya king who was blessed by Indradyumna."

XVI.—Ajátas'atru and Devadatta, two great enemies of the Buddhist faith, published a hostile criticism on the sacred books of that religion. Thereupon Indra visited the Lord, and himself superintended the decoration of the Bamboo grove, which rivalled Vaijayanta. At this the people went in crowds to receive blessings from the Lord, in spite of royal prohibition. The king was at last obliged to revoke his decree against the Lord's worship.

XVII.—There were five hundred musicians at S'rávasti. The king had a great taste for music. Supriya, a master musician, applied one day for permission to play on the Vína before him. The king took Supriya to Jetavana. Supriya's performance was quite charming.

But the Lord had, before this, from prescience of Supriya's design, invited Panchas'ikha, the prince of heavenly choristers. Panchas'ikha now played on a Vína the staff of which was set with gems and rubies. Every one was ravished. Supriya and his tuneful band, knowing the evanescent character of all worldly excellence, invited the Lord to a sumptuous feast, and solicited Bodhi knowledge. The Lord smiled, and said to Ananda; " These musicians will become Buddhas Varṇas'varas by name." Then he addressed the Bhikshus, saying, " This my great power is owing to my merit in feasting and delighting Prabodha, a great Buddha."

XVIII.—When the Lord was at S'rávasti an adulterer was led to the place of execution by an order from the king. Having fortunately met the Lord on the way, the convict prayed him for his own life. The Lord sent Ánanda to procure a reprieve from the king on the score of the convict's betaking himself to a monastery. As a monk the adulterer soon became celebrated for his piety and devotion.

The Lord said to the Bhikshus :—" In one of my former existences I was a Bráhmaṇa, Padas'ata by name. I gave Lord Indradhvaja an excellent dinner at that time. From him I got this my present power."

XIX.—When the Lord sojourned in the Bamboo grove, Bimbisára, the king of Magadha, approached him reverentially with drums beating and cymbals sounding, led him in a pompous procession to the capital, and feasted him magnificently.

The Lord said to the Bhikshus that in one of his former existences he, as a king, had honored Buddha Kshemankara in a similar way.

XX.—A rich banker in S'ravasti was converted to Buddhism by Maudgalyáyana. He gratified the Lord by inviting him to a dinner of a hundred dishes of delicious viands, and prayed for Bodhi knowledge. The Lord smiled, variously coloured rays of light issued from his teeth as described in miracle I. The Lord said to Ánanda, " This banker will become a great Buddda, Divyananda by name."

XXI.—Travelling in Magadha the Lord stood one day on the banks of the Ganges. The Bhikshus beheld a large stupa at a little distance, and enquired to whose honor it had been raised. The Lord replied ; "Brahmadatta was the king of Benares in ancient times. Being childless he worshipped many gods. Once he found in his garden tank a boy marked with all the 32 signs of greatness, born in a lotus, and seated on its seed vessel. He picked the boy up, and had him educated as his own son. At every step the boy took, lotus flowers issued from his feet and instantly withered and decayed. Kás'yapa instructed him in divine knowledge. He left the world, and, becoming a hermit, obtained supreme felicity.

XXII.—As the Lord was passing one day through a street of S'rávastí, a boy fetched a full-blown lotus from a gardener in the bazar, and threw it upon the Lord's head. The Lord smiled and said, "For this deed of merit this boy will become a great Buddha, Padmottara by name."

XXIII.—The wife of a sea-faring merchant vowed that she would, on the safe and speedy return of her husband, present to the shrine of Vishṇu, a golden wheel. On his arrival, true to her vow, she proceeded straight to the temple, but met the Lord Buddha in the midway. Observing him marked with all the 32 signs of greatness, she offered the wheel to him. The Lord smiled and said, On her attainment to the Bodhi knowledge, she will become a great Buddha, named Chakrántara.

XXIV.—On arriving before a large stupa, the Bhikshus in his retinue enquired of the Lord, to whom was the old stúpa dedicated? The Lord replied, to Das'as'iras. The gardener of a king named Brahmadatta found a little urchin one day on a lotus flower, and presented it to the king. The king named him Das'as'iras. On arriving to majority, he left the king, and became a hermit. As fire expires when fuel is consumed, so he obtained utter annihilation.

The Bhikshus enquired about the merits of Das'as'iras. The Lord replied that in one of his former existences Das'as'iras threw a lotus flower on Buddha Vipas'chit. From that Lord he obtained a boon, dissevering the bond of transmigration.

XXV.—A rich merchant of S'rávastí, considering the evanescent character of all worldly happiness, determined to buy the goodwill of the Lord at the sacrifice of everything else. The Lord prophesied that the merchant would become a great Buddha, Súkshmatvak by name.

XXVI.—The next merchant who obtained the Lord's favor was prophesied to obtain the name of Sítaprabha on his attaining nirváṇa.

XXVII.—The boatman who ferried the Lord across the Ganges in one of his numerous travels in Magadha was blessed to have the name Samsárottaraṇa when he should attain supreme felicity by the teaching of the Lord.

XXVIII.—A girl one day decked the Lord's feet with red sandalwood paste. When he went on his begging tour, the whole city of

S'rávastí was reddened with the paste. At this marvellous display of the Lord's power, the girl, on her knees, prayed for Bodhi knowledge, which the Lord granted her. She became a great lord, named Dharmádána.

XXIX.—A gardener presented the Lord at S'rávastí with a pilgrim's staff. The Lord took it, and planted it in the earth. Forthwith it swelled to the size of a big banian tree, covered all over with beautiful green foliage. At this miraculous power of the Lord, the gardener, &c. &c. His name was to be Nirmala.

XXX.—A band of intoxicated revellers was dancing and singing in a street of S'rávastí. The Lord presented himself among them. Their riotous indecent songs changed at once into hymns in praise of the Lord. They threw blue lotuses on his head. These flowers rose up in the air and there formed a rich parasol. At this marvellous display &c. They were each to be named Balgusvána on attaining Bodhi knowledge.

XXXI.—At one time the Bhikshus suffered greatly from an epidemic of jaundice. They enquired of the Lord the cause of such suffering. The Lord said:—"The people of Benares laboured under this very same disease in the reign of Padmaka. The physicians, unable to relieve the jaundiced by the medicines they had, advised them to bring a Rohita fish of a particularly large size. But this fish was nowhere to be found. The king, who loved his subjects greatly, unable to behold their sufferings, vowed to give up his life. He abdicated the throne in favour of his son, leaped from the terrace of his palace, and died. On his death he became a big Rohita fish. By the use of its flesh, every one obtained a thorough cure. After this the Rohita fish addressed his subjects in the following way: 'Come, O my people, I will teach you the excellent Bodhi knowledge, by which you will obtain nirváṇa.' They said 'You took for us so much pains, therefore when you become a Buddha we will become your disciples.'",

XXXII.—The Lord taught the doctrine that merit results from giving alms, and that a meritorious man can work miracles. He gave the following as an instance:

Once upon a time, the kingdom of one Brahmadatta being stricken by a severe famine, he numbered his people, weighed the grains in the country, and made it a rule that every one should get only one mouthful of food a day, only the king getting two. A Bráhmaṇ, who was not included in the census, demanded his portion. The king gave up half his share. Then Indra in the disguise of a Bráhman came to demand his share. The king, even at the risk of his life, gladly offered it to him. Indra greatly delighted, sent down a heavy shower of rain.

XXXIII.—Devadatta sent assassins to the Jetavana grove to kill the Lord. The Lord received the murderers very hospitably. The Bhikshus wondering at this, the Lord said :—"Bramhadatta, king of Benares, had by his queen Durmatí an only son Dharmpála by name. Durmatí, full of anger, envy and malice vowed one day, 'If I take anything in the king's household I shall drink my son's blood by cutting his throat.' At the nonfulfilment of the vow, the king in wrath commanded her to keep her word. The child cried pitiously in the agony of death. But the cruel mother would not relent. I am that Dharmapála, and this Devadatta is that Durmatí."

XXXIV.—A Bhikshu, who wanted to mend his nether garment, wept bitterly, not being able to thread the needle. He cried: "Who is there desirous of merit?" The Lord said he wanted merit. The Bhikshu, wondering, said, "O wonderful! wonderful! the Lord, who is a great Buddha himself, still thirsts after merit." The Lord replied, there was a king, Sibi by name, who gave different parts of his body for the benefit of small animals. To Indra he gave his eyes. At this, Indra granted him the Bodhi knowledge.

XXXV.—A king of Benares had a Yaksha for his spiritual guide. The Yaksha demanded for his food the flesh of the king's son. After much lamentation the king submitted to his demand. The cruel Yaksha then wanted to devour the queen. She too was sacrificed for the gratification of the spiritual guide. Then the king had to offer his ownself a victim to the unappeasable appetite of the Yaksha. When the king had already promised his own body, the Yaksha taught him the following verse—"Grief is always caused by our dear ones; we fear for their mishap. He who has none to love has none to fear or to grieve for." The king, in meek submission, said, "Do, Oh lord, as you like with my body." But he was agreeably surprised to find the Yaksha transformed into Indra, who held the prince in one, and the queen in the other, hand, and restored them to the king.

O Bhikshus! I am that king, Ánanda is the son, and Yas'odhará is the queen.

XXXVI.—Buddha, when preaching the doctrine of filial love and obedience, narrated the following story by way of illustration :

"When Maitrakaṇyaka was a mere child, his father, a rich merchant of S'rávastí, went to sea and died by shipwreck. On arriving at majority Maitrakaṇyaka enquired of his mother about the profession of his father in order that he may betake to it. His mother, unwilling to tell the truth, lest she should lose her son too in the sea, deceived him by saying his father was a menial servant.

"Maitrakaṇyaka took to that profession, and earned four kárshápaṇas. Next he turned a dealer in spices, and gained eight kárshápaṇas. On the first day of his career as a gold merchant he obtained 16 kárshápaṇas, on the second 32. All these earnings he made over to his mother. But on being apprised of the true profession of his father, he determined to start on a nautical expedition, and when his mother, with tears in her eyes, came to dissuade him from his purpose, he kicked her, and bid her be gone. At sea, a sea-monster (Makara) broke his vessel to pieces. He saved himself on a plank, and wandered in a state of utter destitution in the city of Ramanaka. He was, however, taken up and hospitably entertained by four Apsarasas, with whom he remained for several years. Then travelling southward he was met by a company of eight Apsarasas. By them he was whirled in a giddy round of pleasures for years together. Travelling again in the same direction he fell in with a band of sixteen Apsarasas, who also tried their best to make him happy. On the fourth time he was welcomed by a troop of thirty-two Apsarasas, who too spared no pains to make him joyous. These enjoyments he derived as a reward for having made over his earnings to his mother. But on the fifth time he happened to find himself in a city of iron. On entering it, a big burning iron wheel began to revolve over his head, from that time blood and pus became his only food. In this manner he remained there for sixty-nine thousand years. These pains were owing to his kicking and disobeying his mother. Then he determined to hold that iron wheel on his head for ever, that others may not suffer the same pains. Just at this charitable thought the wheel went up seven times the distance of the nether region and left him free.

"I am, O Bhikshus! that Maitrakaṇyaka."

XXXVII.—The Lord persuaded by his lectures the son of a rich banker to go to a hermitage, and lead a solitary life, unknown to the public. The Bhikshus enquired of the Lord the reason for this. The Lord said :—

In days of yore, there lived in a mountain-cave a sage with no other companion than a hare. The hare, coming to know, one day, that the sage was about to leave the place on account of a draught, requested him to postpone his departure till the next morning. The sage consented. The hare kindled a fire and was on the point of jumping into it, when he, out of love to the poor creature, promised to stay there even at the risk of his life. The hare, well pleased, turned his eyes towards heaven, and prayed Indra for rain. Forthwith there was a heavy shower of rain. The sage asked the favor of becoming the hare's disciple, when it should attain the rank of a Buddha.

The Lord said, "I am that hare, and the banker's son is that sage."

XXXVIII.—The Lord made no distinction as to proper and improper times in preaching the truths of religion. One day he preached while cleansing the Jetavana with a broom in hand. The Bhikshus admired his unwearied labour in the cause of truth. The Lord said:—

"Subháshitagaveshí, the son of Brahmadatta, ascended the throne of Benares, and ordered his ministers to search for good news [subháshita or gospel]. Indra, in the disguise of a Yaksha, brought him one. On the king's asking for a second, the false Yaksha made the king's falling or jumping into a fiery ditch heated by burning fire for seven days and nights, a condition of telling it. The king abdicated his throne in favour of his son, and, coming to the brink of the fiery lake, jumped into it. Forthwith it was filled with cold limpid water. Indra throwing off his disguise, taught him the following Gáthá:

"'Walk in the path of duty; do good to your brethren; and work no evil unto them. He, who confers a benefit upon a man, is lodged comfortably both here and in the next world.'

"O Bhikshus, I am that Subháshitagaveshí."

XXXIX.—One day the Lord entered the city of S'rávastí with his alms-dish in hand. A Bráhmaṇ, approaching him, drew a circle round where he stood, and cried, "Gautama, you should not cross this line until you have counted down five hundred kárshápaṇas to me." The Lord, seizing this opportunity to point out that good and evil deeds never go unrequited, obeyed the Bráhmaṇ. The news of this event went round the city. Many, even gods, offered their purses to the Lord's service; but he accepted none. At last when Anáthapíṇḍada paid his ransom, he made no objection. The Bhikshus asked, if Anáthapíṇḍada owed the Bráhmaṇ the money just paid. The Lord said, "The eldest son of

Brahmadatta went to his villa in the spring. There the minister's son played at dice with another, betting five hundred kárshápaṇas. He lost the wager; but did not pay the man as he ought to have done. I am the king's son, Anáthapíṇḍada, the minister's son, and this Bráhmaṇ is the winner at the play."

XL.—The Lord, while residing in the Gymnasium of Kús'í, ordered A'nanda to raise a platform commencing from the north, saying, that was the day for his nirváṇa. Subhadra, a traveller of Kús'í, had obtained supreme felicity from the Lord's teaching. From Subhadra the athletes of the place obtained the religion of Buddha. While lying on that platform the Lord revealed to the Bhikshus the following story, showing his relation with Subhadra and the athletes of the place.

"A certain king tracked a herd of deer in a cave, and aimed at them. The lord of the herd jumped into an impetuous stream and ferried over on his back one by one the deer. He did not rest until all were on the other side, although in so doing he was scratched all over by the hoofs of his burden, and blood flowed copiously from his back. I am that lord of the herd, Subhadra one of the herd, and the athletes are the other members of the flock."

The Bhikshus then enquired about the merits of Subhadra which raised him to such an eminence. While Lord Kás'yapa was on his way to nirváṇa, his nephew As'oka was living at a great distance. Unable to see his dear uncle in his last moments, As'oka gave vent to loud lamentation. A silvan deity, taking compassion on the boy, carried him to Kás'yapa by his power as a god. There both of them obtained valuable lectures from the Lord. The sylvan deity became an Arhat. Now he personates Subhadra.

XLI.—When the Lord was in the bamboo grove, Maudgalyáyana and S'áriputra, moved by the sight of the dreadful sufferings of a ghost, enquired its cause from the Lord. The Lord said: "A consumptive Buddha was advised by his physicians to use sugarcane juice. He entered the house of a rich banker of S'rávastí, and begged of him for some of the juice. The banker ordered his servant to see the Lord supplied. The wicked servant half filled a vessel with urine, then poured a quantity of sugarcane juice into it, and presented it to the Lord. For that one misdeed, the servant suffers this torture."

XLII.—Maudgalyáyana enquired the cause of the terrible torture of a ghost, whom he saw convulsed with pain at the cremation ghat. The

Lord said: "When the Lord Kás'yapa was at Benares, the wife of a house-holder was very ill-natured. A beggar one day asked alms of her. She bound him hand and foot to a prop, and gave him a good thrashing. She now suffers for her sins."

XLIII.—On another occasion the Lord gave the following aooount of the sufferings of a ghost.

When the Lord Kás'yapa was at Benares, a Bhikshu asked a palmful of water from a girl who was carrying a pitoher of water. She replied "Even if you die, Bhikshu, I won't grant you a drop." It is she who now suffers.

XLIV.—The history of another ghost who was at Gridhrakúṭa as given by the Lord is this—

Advised by physicians to take sweetmeats, a Buddha entered the house of a rich Bráhmaṇ. The Bráhmaṇ charged his wife with the entertainment of the lord. She gave him a dish of night-soil covered over with rice. She now feels the consequences of her wicked act.

XLV.—While the Lord was residing at Rájagriha, there were five hundred who hovered over the city in whirls. They fell in with Maudgalyáyana on his way to the city, and addressed him thus:—

"Know, holy man, we were five hundred bankers of Rájagriha. We gave no alms, we threw impediments in the ways of other's charity, and we accused innocent persons of holding communion with evil spirits. The result is, that we suffer infernal torture. We have our relatives in the city. Will you, holy man, request them to feed the lord Buddha for our sake. Thereby alone can we escape these torments." The relatives complied with their request. The Lord preached the transcendental doctrines of his faith, and the ghosts were ghosts no more.

XLVI.—The mother of Uttara, a shopkeeper of S'rávastí, was very miserly and ill-natured. After her death Uttara turned a hermit. The spectre of his mother appeared before him, and revealed to him her terrible sufferings. Uttara wept bitterly, for he loved his mother tenderly, feasted the Lord with rich viands and rescued his suffering mother.

XLVII.—Ánanda enquired one day the reason why a goblin, which he had seen, suffered so tremendously. The Lord said, "Lord Kás'yapa preached at Benares. Induced by his lecture a banker's daughter forsook the pleasures of the world. But her education was defective. She became conceited, she contemned the learned, and shut her eyes from the wise. For these three reasons, she became a hobgoblin ; bad smell issued from her body, and she lost the use of her eyes."

XLVIII.—A banker of S'rávastí, though a follower of the Lord, died very conceited owing to the defect of his training. When the Bhikshus disposed of his dead body, they found him transformed into a goblin. They requested the Lord to preach for the benefit of the conceited ghost. The banker ghost, by training his mind, rose to the chiefship of the spirits. In this form he still used to come to listen to the Lord's edifying speeches. He obtained great power; the odour of his body rose superior to that of all flowers.

XLIX.—Here is the reason of another ghost's terrible suffering as given by the Lord.

A banker had two wives. They were jealous of each other. One of them was in the family-way, the other contrived to mix a quantity of noxious drugs with the food of her rival. The miscarriage, as designed, took place. The guilty wife then swore before her relatives, "If I have had any hand in this foul deed, let god turn me to a ghost that eats her own son." She has now been turned to a suffering spirit.

L.—The miracle of Jambála, vide p. 12.

LI.—A rich banker of S'rávasti was very miserly. He heaped his gold in his garden where he lived. After his death, a black serpent, at whose very sight men lost their lives, took possession of the heap. Bimbisára, the king, knowing this, solicited the Lord for the discipline of the serpent. The Lord preached before the serpent and converted him. He became a Devaputra.

LII.—A Bráhmaṇ's son, Chandra by name, lived close to the premises of Anáthpiṇḍada, with whom he often went to hear the Lord preach. Dying a premature death, he became a Devaputra. One day the Devaputra found a Bráhmaṇ in the cremation ghat bewailing the loss of an only child who still lay lifeless in his lap. In the disguise of a Rishi the Devaputra consoled the mourning father, and induced him to receive the lessons of fortitude from Buddha. By him he was initiated to the true faith. This Bráhmaṇ was the adulterer of Benares (p. 14). Chandra was his son. The adulterer's son saved his father's life when he was sentenced to death as a thief by sacrificing his own life.

LIII.—A banker's daughter covered the Lord, when entering the city to receive alms, with three sál flowers. Then she climbed up a tree for more of them. She fell down dead, and was instantly transformed into a Devaputrí. She listened to the Lord's preachings and, "tearing the mountain of this existing body with the adamantine weapon of knowledge, obtained the fruit of being furnished with ears."

LIV.—Rájá Bimbisára, receiving the knowledge of truth from the Lord, had built a big stúpa over the Lord's nails and hairs in his zenana, and his maids cleansed the place every day. When Ajátas'atru obtained the throne by parricide, he prohibited the females to sweep the stúpa on pain of death. S'rímatí, a female slave, caring not at all for her life, washed it neatly and lighted it with a row of lamps. The king, in great rage, ordered her to the place of execution. After her death, she, as a Devaputrí, appeared before the Lord in the Bamboo Grove, and, "cleaving the mountain of human misery by the thunderbolt of knowledge," obtained all that is desirable.

LV.—Anáthapiṇḍada obtained permission from the king to solicit alms for the Lord, for the benefit of the whole population of the city. On an elephant rode the patriarch, receiving metallic vessels, bracelets and other ornaments as alms from his neighbours. A poor woman, who had an only cloth, threw it over the elephant from behind a hedge. The beggar knew instantly what the matter was, and bestowed on her rich presents. She went to the Lord and received the knowledge of truth from him.

LVI.—When Buddha was putting up at S'rávastí, Rájá Bimbisára of Rájagriha grew impatient at his absence. The omniscient Lord, perceiving this, started for Rájagriha at once. But he was detained for one night by the entreaties of a parrot in a forest. Apprized of the Lord's residence in the wood by the intelligence furnished by the parrot, Bimbisára, followed by the whole court, came out to receive him. Every one was highly delighted by the Lord's lectures. The parrot, fixing his mind on the Lord, died and turned a Devaputra. From heaven he regularly attended the Lord's teaching, and thus "cleaving the bond of human misery by the sharp knife of knowledge," obtained the highest bliss.

LVII.—While the Lord was at Rájagriha, Anáthapiṇḍada requested the king Bimbisára to send an ambassador to the Lord, inviting him to S'rávastí. He preached at that city. The messenger fixing his mind &c.

LVIII.—Journeying through different countries, the Lord entered a piece of forest where dwelt five hundred herds of buffaloes. A wicked animal ran at the Lord. To avoid the danger he created five lions. The buffalo fell submissively at the Lord's feet. The Lord took pity on the poor creature, taught him the sublime truths of the Buddhist faith. All impressions, he said, are transient, the soul has no attributes, the peace is nirváṇa. The buffalo became a Devaputra, &c.

LIX.—Devaputra Upañshada obtained the fruit of being furnished with ears by constantly attending the Lord in the Jetavana grove with five hundred of his men.

The Lord gave the following story to his Bhikshus, pointing out the merits of the fortunate god. In this very Kalpa Kás'yapa Buddha lived at Benares. Rájá Krika, in a splendid procession, proceeded to pay a visit to the Lord. The Bráhmaṇs, burning with the ambition of becoming as great as Krika, asked the Lord to point out to them a way by which they could obtain all they desired. The Lord said, "By the holy fast called Ashṭáñga." They kept the fast. One was successful, he was born the son of Krika. Another, failing, became a serpent. Hot sand fell incessantly on his body and tortured him greatly. He again kept the fast, and was this time more happy in the result. His next existence was as the son of a god. This Upañshada was the serpent.

LX.—Hañsajátaka miracle, given in the Bodhisattva Avadána.

LXI.—Suvarṇábha, or the golden-coloured, the son of a rich S'ákya, frequented the pipul-tree grove. In pursuance of the Lord's teaching he betook himself to a hermitage and attained the rank of an Arhat. The Lord said, in the ninety-first mundane period a Buddha, Vihas'yí by name, lodged in the capital of Bandhumat. After he attained nirváṇa the Rájá raised a stúpa to his honor. A householder, finding a golden coloured image in the stúpa, ornamented it with earrings, and prayed for having a Buddha for his preceptor, and becoming as beautiful as the golden image itself has that householder been born as Suvarṇábha.

LXII to LXXI.—All relate to men who attained Arhatships for their merit in ornamenting, clearing, and repairing the stúpa dedicated to the sage Vipasyi at the city of Bandhumatí.

LXXII.—A citizen of S'rávastí had a daughter, Supriyá by name; she was Jatismará, or one who remembered the history of her past existences. She chanted gáthás as soon as she was born. In her time the country was stricken by a famine, but she feasted the Lord and the legion of his Bhikshus with food procured by the power of working miracles. By the persuasion of the Lord she turned a hermit, and became an Arhat.

The Lord said, "In this very Bhadráku Kalpa she was the maid-servant of a rich banker. Lord Kás'yapa was then at Benares. The banker, her master, went with a full supply of provision to his country-seat; from his store she bestowed a large quantity on the Lord and was approved by the banker. Her fortune in this existence she owes to her good deeds in her past."

LXXIII.—S'uklá was the only daughter of a rich S'ákya at Kapilavastu. Many a prince sought the hand of the rich and beautiful heiress. Unwilling to marry she obtained her father's permission to betake herself to a hermit's life. She gradually rose to be an Arhat.

The Lord said, S'uklá in her former existence in this very Kalpa, entered Pravrajyá at the instance of Kás'yapa.

LXXIV.—Somá, the daughter of a rich Bráhmaṇ at S'rávastí could remember all she heard. Having become a hermit, she rose to be an Arhat. Her history was that in her former existence she forsook the world at the command of Kás'yapa.

LXXV.—On the day of Girivalgu-Saṅgama, a festival held at S'rávastí, people crowded from all quarters to the city. Among others came Kubalayá, a nátch girl, from the Dakshiṇápatha. She asked if there was any in the city that could surpass her in beauty. Being replied "Gautama, a S'ramaṇa," she instantly repaired to the Jetavana, and there displayed her charms before the Lord. But by a miracle the Lord destroyed all her beauty, and turned her into a hideous old hag. She fell at the Lord's feet, and he gave her true knowledge.

The Lord said, Kas'ísundara, the son of a Benares king, practised austerities in a secluded grove on the Himalaya. A Kumar girl fell in love with him, and endeavoured to seduce him by her charms. Finding him proof against her fascination, and mortified at the neglect of one she loved, she became a disciple of the great Kás'yapa. That Kumar girl is this Kubalayá.

LXXVI.—The daughter of Brahmadatta, king of Benares, refused to give her hand to any in the crowd of princes that paid their court to her. At last when Lord Kás'yapa came to live in the Rishipaṭṭana, she sought and obtained instruction in the Bodhi knowledge from him.

Some of her lovers wanted to carry her off by force. But she rose to the sky, and there displayed such miraculous power, that they all despaired of her hand, and went away.

The Lord said, Kás'ísundarí obtained her powers by an intimate attachment with Kaṇaka who flourished in this very Kalpa.

LXXVII.—Muktámálá of S'rávastí was so named from the row of pearls with which she was born. She attained Arhatship by attending the Lord in company with a daughter-in-law of Anáthapiṇḍada.

The Lord said, a banker presented his wife with a pearl necklace. The wife gave it to Kás'yapa, who was sojourning in Mrigadáva at Rishipaṭṭana in Benares. For that merit she was born with a row of pearls on her neck.

LXXVIII.—The Lord was at Kachangalá. An old woman, hearing from Ánanda that the Lord was thirsty, approached him with a pitcher full of water. At the sight of the Lord her breast heaved and gushed and she felt the affections of a mother. The Lord said, "This kind woman was his mother in five hundred of his former existences. In one of her former existences she mastered all the mysteries of dhyána, acquired the knowledge of proper and improper application thereof, and rose to the rank of a female Arhat."

LXXIX.—While the Lord was at S'rávastí, Prasenajit and Brahmadatta quarrelled with each other. During the progress of the war, Prasenajit begat a daughter, and Brahmadatta a son. They adjusted their differences on condition of their children's marriage with each other. Arriving at age Kshemá, the girl, expressed her desire of remaining a virgin and devoted to the Lord. Her father, alarmed, wrote to Brahmadatta to hasten the marriage. But Kshemá fled to the Lord for protection. He examined her carefully, and, instilling into her the knowledge of truth, raised her above the influence of vile passions. When the priest was just going to unite the young couple, Kshemá rose up to the sky where she displayed miracles. She came down thence, and with the permission of her father betook to hermitage. The Lord said, Kshemá in this very Bhadraka Kalpa delighted Lord Kás'yapa and obtained the boon of becoming the first among female disciples.

LXXX.—Virúpávadánam. Given in the Bodhisattva Avadána.

LXXXI.—Samudrávadánam. Ditto.

LXXXII.—A householder of S'rávastí had the mortification of finding all his children die as soon as they were born. He feasted the

Lord one day, and promised if his next child lived to devote him to the Lord's service. His next born was a long-lived one. The householder kept his word. Sumana, the boy, soon attained Arhatship under the edifying lectures of the benign Buddha.

The Lord said, the high position of Sumana is due to his merit in feasting the Lord Vipas'yí, and in decorating the stúpa raised over his tooth and nails.

LXXXIII.—For granting two dínars at the stúpa of Vipas'yí the donor, Hiraṇypáṇi a gambler, was born at S'rávastí, with two dínars always in hand; when the coins were removed they were instantly replaced by others. He frequented the Lord's dwelling, and easily attained the high position of an Arhat.

LXXXIV.—When the Lord was at S'rávastí the queen of Prasenajit gave birth to a son clad in the ochre vestment of an Arhat. No sooner was he born than he enquired whether the Lord was in that city. At the tender age of seven he was raised to the dignity of an Arhat.

The Lord said, When the son of Kṛika (*vide supra* LIX) wanted the permission of his parents to enter a hermitage, they made him promise his return after he had finished the study of the 'three receptacles.' He came back and taught his parents. He obtained Arhatship which he so richly merited.

LXXXV.—A pair of Yas'omitra's teeth oozed out continuous streams of water. By frequenting the Jetavana he obtained Arhatship.

The Lord said, in one of his former existences Yas'omitra, after entering the hermitage, supplied an old Bhikshu and his followers with water for a thousand years. The boon which he secured made him what he was now.

LXXXVI.—Just as the Lord landed at S'ankás'ya, Upapádika, a Bhikshu, received him with great honor. The Bhikshu was admitted into the rank of Arhats.

The Lord gave the following account of his merits—Five Bhikshus obtained true knowledge from Vipas'yí. One of them is this Upapádika.

LXXXVII.—Sobhita, the son of a rich S'ákya at Kapilavastu, betaking himself to the hermitage, obtained Arhatship.

The Lord said, "In Bhadraka Kalpa, Rájá Sobhita erected a stúpa over the hair and nails of Krakachchhanda in his own capital, Sobhavatí. On a festive occasion a brotherhood of friends proceeded to strew flowers on the stúpa. Sobhita, refusing to take part with them, was expelled from the company. Deeply mortified, he afterwards made sufficient amends for his misconduct. In another existence he obtained the favor of Kás'yapa, and, entering a mountain cave, cleansed the courtyard of a Buddhist stúpa.

LXXXVIII.—Kapphina, the young king of Dakshiṇápatha, had 18,000 young courtiers. Proud of this strong body of supporters, he insolently commanded the lords of six cities, S'rávastí, &c., to appear before him. They, in alarm, took refuge with the Lord. The Lord, in the following terms, challenged Kapphina to come and fight: "If you are standing do not sit, come with as much speed as you can." By wafting his magic wand aloft, he suddenly brought into existence an innumerable array of veterans of which he took the lead in royal robes. But when Kapphina was about to engage, a voice from heaven declared "Obey the command of Buddha," and he changed his mind. The Lord instructed him in the Bodhi knowledge, and raised him to the rank of an Arhat when he departed this world.

The Lord said, "A merchant of Bandhumatí feasted Lord Vipas'yí and founded a Vihára for him in the 71st mundane period. This very man in his other existence as Brahmadatta, king of Benares, gave wholesome diet to a Pratyaka Buddha who was ill, and raised a stúpa to his honor. For these merits he obtained Arhatship when living as Kapphina, king of Dakshiṇápatha.

LXXXIX.—A warder of a fort at Benares once snatched a quantity of food from a girl, and subsequently, putting himself to much suffering from want of food, gave it all to a Pratyeka Buddha. The Buddha showed him miracles. The man on his knees begged instruction in true knowledge, which was granted him. Born at S'rávastí, this man was named Bhadrika. He obtained Arhatship from S'ákyamuṇi.

XC.—When the Lord sojourned in a grove in the country of Sthula Koshṭaka, that country was under the rule of a king named Koravya. His brother's son, Ráshṭrapála, was a handsome youth, endowed with perfection in every limb and feature. While roaming about in the grove one morning he beheld the Lord proceeding with his followers to the city to collect alms. The signs of greatness on the person of the Lord made a strong impression on the susceptible mind of the youth, who fell at his feet, and solicited conversion. The Lord, however, declined to comply with the request until the youth should obtain the permission of his parents. This was, however, not easy of attainment, as his parents and their relatives and friends did not approve of the plan of the youth. The youth, however, was resolute, and his importunity prevailed. He got the permission, was duly ordained, and raised to the rank of an Arhat. The congregation was surprised at this, and begged of the Lord to explain how it was that Ráshṭrapála, a youth born in a royal family and possessing no preliminary training, should at once become an Arhat. The Lord replied that this was due to the accumulated deserts of good works done by him in former lives. Once on a time the king of Videha, defeated by his enemy, repaired to the wilderness, and, roaming about in great distress from thirst, met a Buddha, and sought his protection. This protection was duly accorded, and the king regained his metropolis and worshipped the Lord for three months, after which he begged that he may be able to acquire true knowledge. That king is now Ráshṭrapála and earns the fruit of his good work. This explanation, however, did not suffice to satisfy the audience. The feeling seemed to be that the work was not enough for so high a reward as Arhatship. The Lord, therefore, continued. Again in the kalpa when human life extended to twenty-thousand years the Lord Kás'yapa sojourned in the Deer Park near Benares. At that time Benares was under the rule of Kṛika, a pious king, under whose just administration the country prospered in every way, abounding in men, animals, good crops and flourishing commerce. The youngest son of this king paid a visit to the Deer Park at Ṛishipatana, and beheld the Lord impressed with 32 great signs and 80 minor indications of greatness, and resplendent with glory more brilliant than a thousand suns put together. Deeply impressed by the sight, he fell at the feet of the Lord, and, sitting aside, listened respectfully to the religious discourse which the Lord delivered. He then sought conversion, and Lord Kás'yapa was satisfied, and when the prince and his relatives sought his protection he had them duly converted. The prince planted an umbrella in honour of the Lord. That prince has now been born as Ráshṭrapála.

"Again, Bhikshus, there lived in former times in the city of Benares a poor Bráhmaṇ, who lived on tubers *(Mulika Bráhmaṇa)*. In order to collect tubers he used to repair to the top of a hill. On one occasion he there met a Pratyeka Buddha in distress, and did everything he could to relieve the distress by offering him all such refreshments as he could command. The Pratyeka Buddha benefitted greatly by his attention, and offered him a boon for his good deeds. The Bráhmaṇ begged that he may be devoid of all human passions, and his prayer was immediately granted. And the person who then was a poor Bráhmaṇ living on roots is now born as prince Ráshṭrapála. In his former existences he had undergone many trials and sufferings in the cause of true religion, to which he was always attached, and in return for it he is now born in a royal family and is endowed with so much personal beauty. And the ultimate reward of his devotion is that he is now come face to face with Arhatship, and acquired perfection in it. This shows that you should always avoid black acts, and betake to white ones which are sure at one time or other to bestow on you their much prized reward." The Bhikshus were greatly delighted by this narration.

This is substantially the same with the story of the king of the Kaurava race which occurs in the As'oka Avadána (*ante* page 14).

Beginning. जनपदचर्य्यायां पूर्णभद्र इति बुद्धो भगवान् सत्कृतो मानितः पूजितो राजभि राजमात्रैर्धनिभिः पौरैः श्रेष्ठिभिः सार्थवाहैर्देवैर्नागैर्यक्षैरसुरैः किन्नरैः महोरगैरित्यादि।

End. भगवानात्तमनसस्ते भिक्षवो भगवता भाषितमभ्यनन्दन्।

Colophon. इत्यवदानशतके नवमी उद्दानगाथा समाप्ता। समाप्तं चावदानशतकं। छन्न यं सुगतभाषितं। नन्दीश्वराचार्य्यपूर्व्वमिदानीं प्रकाशितं।
पूर्णभद्रो यशोमती कुसीदवणिजस्तथा।
सोमोवभिश्च पद्माकपञ्चालौ सूम एव च।
राजानं पश्चिमं कृत्वा वर्गो ह्येष समुद्दितः।

No. B. 38.

APARIMITÁYUR-DHÁRAṆÍ.

अपरिमितायुर्धारणी ।

Substance, Nepalese paper of a yellow colour, 7 × 3 inches. Folia, 22. Lines on each page, 5. Extent in s'lokas, 190. Character, Newari. Appearance, old. Prose. Generally correct.

A mystic mantra and the praise thereof as a means of promoting longevity. The work professes to have been related by Buddha himself, when sojourning at the Jeta Grove near S'rávastí, to Manjúsrí. The mantra consists of the following words :

ॐ नमो भगवते अपरिमितायुर्ज्ञानसुविनिश्चिततेजोराजाय तथागतायार्हते सम्यक्सम्बुद्धाय। तद्यथा । ॐ पुण्यपुण्य महापुण्य अपरिमितपुण्य अपरिमितपुण्यज्ञानसम्भारोपचित ॐ सर्व्वसंस्कारपरिशुद्धधर्म्मते गगणसमुद्गते स्वभावविशुद्धमहानयपरिवारे स्वाहा ।

"Om, salutation to the Bhagavat ; to the sovereign of endless life, wisdom and unfailing glory ; to the Tathágata ; to the Arhat ; to the perfect Buddha ; thus, Om, to the soul of the virtue of virtues, the great virtue, the measureless virtue, the knowledge of measureless load of virtue ; and Om, to the possessor of all purified and pure duty ; to him who can rise to the sky ; to the scion of the naturally pure and righteous race, may this be propitious."

This sentence is repeated a hundred times, and he who recites it, or writes it, or causes it to be written, or keeps it written in his house, or hears it recited, or promulgates it, or worships it with offerings of flowers, incense, aromatics, garlands, unguents, clothes, parasols, flags, bells, standards ; or wears it on his person, is said to receive the full measure of human life. The work is reckoned among the simple Sútras ; but it is obviously a charm intended to be worn as an amulet, and must be of a comparatively recent date,—an imitation of the Hindu charms of Tántric origin.

Beginning. ॐ नमः श्रीबुद्धाय । एवम्मया श्रुतमेकस्मिन् समये भगवान् श्रावस्त्यां विहरति स्म जेतवनेऽनाथपिण्डदस्यारामे महता भिक्षुसङ्घेन सार्द्धमर्द्धत्रयोदशभिर्भिक्षुशतैः सम्बहुलैश्च बोधिसत्त्वैर्महासत्त्वैः । तत्र खलु भगवान् मञ्जुश्रियं कुमारभूतं आमन्त्रयते स्म । अस्ति मञ्जुश्रीः उपरिष्ठायां अपरिमितगुणसञ्चयो नाम लोकधातुस्तत्रापरिमितायुर्ज्ञानसुविनिश्चिततेजो नाम तथागतोऽर्हन् सम्यक्सम्बुद्ध एतर्हि तिष्ठति ध्रियते यापयति सत्त्वानां धर्म्मं देशयति । शृणु मञ्जुश्रीः कुमारभूत

इमे जाम्बुद्वीपका मनुष्यका अल्पायुष्का वर्षशतायुषः तेषां बहून्यकालमरणानि निर्द्दिष्टानि। ये खलु मञ्जुश्रीः सत्त्वा अस्यापरिमितायुषस्तथागतस्य गुणवर्णकीर्त्तनं नाम धर्म्मपर्य्यायं लिखिष्यन्ति लिखापयिष्यन्ति नामधेयमात्रमपि श्रोष्यन्ति यावत् पुस्तकगतमपि कृत्वा गृहे धारयिष्यति वाचयिष्यति पर्य्यवाप्स्यति परेभ्यश्च विस्तरेण प्रकाशयन्ति पुष्पधूपगन्धमाल्यविलेपनचूर्णचीवरच्छत्रध्वजघण्टा-पताकाभिश्च समन्तात् पूजयिष्यन्ति। ये परिक्षीणायुषः पुनरेव वर्षशतायुषः सन्ति ये खलु मञ्जुश्रीः सत्त्वास्तस्यास्त्वपरिमितायुर्ज्ञानसुविनिश्चिततेजोराजस्य तथागतस्य नामाष्टोत्तरशतं श्रोष्यन्ति धारयिष्यन्ति वाचयिष्यन्ति तेषामायुर्वि-वर्द्धयिष्यन्ति।

End. इदमवोचद् भगवानात्तमनास्ते भिक्षवस्ते बोधिसत्त्वा महासत्त्वाः सा च सर्व्वावती पर्षत् सदेवमानुषासुरलोको गन्धर्व्वाश्च भाषितमभ्यनन्दन्निति।

Colophon. आर्य्यापरिमितायुर्नामधारणी समाप्ता।

No. B. 40.

BHADRAKALPA AVADÁNA.

भद्रकल्पावदानं।

Substance, Nepalese paper, $15\frac{3}{4} \times 5$ inches. Folia, 23. Lines on a page, 8. Extent in s'lokas, 7,110. Character, Newári. Appearance, old. Verse. Incorrect.

Thirty-four legends on moral subjects, related by Jayas'rí in reply to a query of Jinas'rí who wished to know some of the anecdotes related by Upa Gupta, to his royal pupil As'oka. The scene of the second narrative was the Bodhimaṇḍa of Buddha Gayá, and that of the first the Kukkuṭa Garden referred to in the As'oka Avadána.

Upagupta opens his narrative thus :—"When the Lord, after having obtained what he desired, thought of returning home, all the gods began to sing hymns in his praise. He taught them the sublime truths of his religion."

I. The first story is that of Yas'odhará, the forsaken wife of Buddha. Suddhodana's nephew, Devadatta, having been repulsed in his advances for her love, became her deadly enemy, and plotted several times to take her life. He accused her before his uncle, alleging that, unless she lives in guilt, how is it that when others become mothers in ten months from their first conception, she should remain big for eighteen. The king did not give credit to these allegations. Then he induced the king to abdicate in his favour for twenty-one days, promising at the end of that period to fetch his son Buddha back to him. During these twenty-one days he tried every means in his power to put an end to Yasodhará's life. He threw her into a tank; but she was protected and sent to her father by the king of serpents who happened to be there at the time. This tank was long celebrated as Gopátírtha from another name of Yasodhará. Thrown into a blazing fire she was miraculously protected by the coldness which the fire suddenly assumed. Precipitated from a high hill, she was saved by the kindness of a big monkey. At the expiration of the appointed time Devadatta, unable to fulfil his promise, was imprisoned by the king; but he was soon after released on the intercession of Yasodhará.

At the end of six years Yasodhará gave birth to a child as ugly as ugly could be. He was named Virúpa. Envious Devadatta taunted Virúpa, by saying, "O Virúpa, do you know your father's name? Buddha is gone these twelve years and you are at the age of six." Yasodhará consoled her son by saying, "Your father is gone in the search of a desire-fulfilling elixir. He will soon return, and change your ugliness into beauty. Do not believe in what envious Devadatta says to you."

II. After a stay of six years at Dharmadvípa, Lord Buddha presented himself at Benares with five of his followers. His residence was at Mrigadáva in Rishipaṭaṇa. There was at this time a band of thirty "sons of Belial" who revelled in all manner of licentiousness. One of them lost his mother Bhadráñgí who, in company with gods, came one day from the regions of bliss to hear the Lord's lecture. Bhadráñgí found these wicked people following two women of bad character; she found one of them, Kás'iká going away, and took this opportunity of correcting the gay lotharios. She presented herself before them in the guise of Kás'iká, and gradually and artfully led them to the Mrigadáva. There she prayed the Lord to bring these wicked young men to the right path. Immediately after she rose to the sky, and thence said: "If you are to come to me worship Tattágata, and renounce the path of evil." Following Bhadráñgí's advice, they proceeded to the Lord, who instructed them in his faith, and touched them with his right hand. Forthwith, their heads were miraculously shaved, and their garments miraculously changed into yellow rags. They were then sent by the Lord as apostles of his faith. They travelled from place to place in the guise of students (Brahmacháris), preaching the Buddhist gospel.

III. A company of professional sacrificers of Benares, who were absent on a sacrifice at Vrinda, returned and found thirty old vagabonds reclaimed. They immediately placed themselves under the Lord's tuition. The chief of the company was Luchira.

IV. There lived at Kus'álagram, inhabited by the Droṇas, one Púrṇa, a Bráhmaṇ, who, induced by a celestial voice, proceeded to the Himálaya, and there practised austerities to obtain favours from the Lord. He made thirty-four disciples. With these he proceeded to the Mrigadáva. The Lord touched them with his right hand. Forthwith they were transformed into so many Bhikshus.

V. Uttara and Nalaka were the two sons of one Jayí, the family priest of a king of Tvarkaṭa in the vicinity of Avanti. Uttara was versed in all the Vedas. Nalaka was a kind-hearted man; he wandered here and there as a hermit, unmindful of his study. They were both sent for their education to their uncle Drití, whose hermitage lay on the Vindhya Range. Drití advised them to proceed to the Lord at Mrigadáva, where they were initiated in the duties of silent hermits.

VI. Sabhika was a great controversialist. His mother was a perfect mistress of the art of disputation. She was educated by a Bhikshuṇí. She obtained the name of Mahádhí or great intelligence. By the merit of her good works she was cured of her bodily deformities for which she was exposed on her birth. She married one Vidyákara, only because she was defeated in a controversy with him. The fruit of this marriage was the great controversialist Sabhika. Sabhika, after having silenced all his antagonists, proceeded to Mrigadáva to measure his powers of ratiocination with the Lord. But on the first sight of that great man Sabhika fell on his knees, and begged him for instruction. By the Lord's command Uttara gave him the definitions of Sambuddha, Arhaṭ, S'ramaṇa, Bráhmaṇa, Snátaka, Dvija, Vaidika, Vipra, S'rotriya Brahmachárí, Ṛishi, Parivrájaka, Muni, Tapasví, Yati and Yogí. Within a short time Sabhika entered the hermitage.

VII. The story of Jas'odeví.

VIII. The story of Grihapati Svastika.

IX. After causing, on his way to Gana, a thousand boatmen to renounce the world, the Lord presented himself one day at the hermitage of the Kás'yapas. There he converted Fulvavilva Kás'yapa, Buddha Kás'yapa, Sarit Kás'yapa* and their nephew Upasena with

* The names are differently given in other works, Urnvilva occurs for the first, Nadí for the second, and Gaya for the third.

their numerous followers to his own faith. He gave the following story of their former lives:

"Three royal brothers, Indrarája, Siñharája and Bhadraràja, proceeded once upon a time from Kaluga to Hastina, where a Tathágata made his appearance, in order to worship him and receive his blessing. They invited him to their own kingdom, and on his death raised a Stupa to his honour. They begged of him the boon of ever remaining the servants of Sugata. They are now born as the Kás'yapas."

X. Once on a time, on the Lord's entrance into the Dharmáraṇya, seven hundred Ṛishis explained to him as many different modes of worship. The Lord pronounced them all, without exception, to be false. He explained to them the sublime truths of his own religion. They all obtained Nirváṇa by accepting his creed.

XI. Rájá Bimbisára heard one day his family priest teach the Dvátriñsat lakshaṇas, or the 32 signs of Buddhahood. From that time he became disgusted with the world, and panted for the knowledge of the true faith. Just at this time, the rumour of the Lord's appearance in the Jatavana grove reached his ears. He resolved on an interview with him. Great was his surprise when he found the great Ṛishi Kás'yapa sitting before the Lord, a convert to the Buddhist faith. By the Lord's instructions the Rájá regained the ease of his mind, and entered on a course of virtuous administration of his kingdom.

XII. Sáriputra and Maudgalyáyana were two foremost teachers among the early Buddhists. They were friends from their early boyhood. They were both proficient in all the sciences of their day. The real name of Sáriputra was Upatishya. He was the last of the seven sons of a Bráhman, Dharmapati of Náradagráma, near Rájagriha, by his only wife Sárí. Maudgaláyana was the son of Dhányáyana of Kelika, a village not far from Náradagráma. He was called Maudgaláyana because he was born in the Gotra or clan of the Maudgaláyanas. They both were converted by the Lord himself, and both soon rose to high rank among his followers. Dírghanakha, the maternal uncle of Sáriputra, envying the Lord's great fame, came boastfully forward to silence the Lord by arguments; but remained one of his most zealous partizans to the end of his life. Jeta, a Rishi, and A'nanda his friend were at this time made converts. Jeta presented the Lord a Vihára which still goes by his name.

XIII to XXXII. Short stories relating to the conversion of

various persons to the Buddhist faith by Buddha himself during his sojourn in the Jetavana grove. The converts were Kás'yapa, a rich Bráhmaṇa, Naradatta the nephew of Asita a Ṛishi, S'aktí a Brahmaní, Padmá her friend, seven hundred disciples of Rudraka, Rebata a Muni, Anáthapiṇḍada, Púrṇa and other inhabitants of S'rávastí. When going to his hermitage in the Veṇuvana at Rájagriha, he appointed Púrna at the head of the Sangha or Chárch of S'rávastí. While journeying through a forest, Buddha found a gang of robbers dividing their booty. The Lord, giving them an equivalent in gold, restored the stolen property to its owners. The robbers became his followers, and honoured him greatly when he lived at Rájagriha.

XXXII. The Bhikshus enquired of the Lord how was it that his mother (aunt) Gautamí, though blind, was called Sulochaná or perfect-eyed? The Lord gave the following explanation: A big white elephant was very fond of his mother. He migrated with his old mother from the Himálaya to the Vindhyan forest where provender was easily procurable. Finding one day a travelling merchant in great distress, the kind animal took compassion upon him, and extricated him from his difficulties. That ungrateful wretch informed the king of Benares, who was in search of a white elephant, of such an animal being available in the Vindhyan forest, a circumstance which led to the poor elephant's being tracked and caught. He was conducted to the Royal Menagerie at Benares. For weeks together the elephant did not take any food, but shed profusion of tears. On being asked the cause he gave vent to his filial apprehensions. The king granted him release. He hastened to find his old mother, with his heart beating with apprehensions. He found her in the forest, blind with tears. On his arrival her eyes cleared up, and she got back her sight. I am that elephant, and Gautamí is the old mother.

XXXIII. The story of Nalini; told in the Avadána-kalpalatá.

XXXIV. Invited by his father, Lord Buddha proceeded from Veṇuvana to his capital. The king paid a return visit to his son at Veṇuvana where he heard many edifying lectures. One of them contained the following story: Rájá Sudása of Benares had by a lioness a son named Sutasoma. When that son came to the throne he was in the habit of eating privately raw human flesh in the prison house. He was expelled by the nobles from the throne on account of this habit. Wandering in the forests, unattended and alone, he was met by his mother, the lioness, who carried him to celebrate a sacrifice of a hundred royal youths. After ninety-nine princes had been secured already, the ex-king went in search of Sutasoma whose adventures form the subject of another book, viz., Sutasomajátaka. The Lord said, I am that Sutasoma.

Beginning. ॐ नमो रत्नत्रयाय ।

नत्वा श्रीमत्त्रिरत्नं त्रिभवहितकरं सर्व्वलोकैकबन्धुं
जित्वा क्लेशान् समारान् अमलपददं मोक्षसौख्यैकमार्गं ।
वक्ष्ये श्रीशाक्यराजस्वपुरगतकथां सुन्दरीं मोक्षहेतुं
चातुर्वर्गाभिकाङ्क्षाः शृणुत बुधजनाः भद्रकल्पावदानं ॥
जयश्रीः पुनरुत्थाय समाधेर्बोधिमण्डपे ।
व्याख्यातुं श्रेघनीं धर्म्मां विजहार ससाङ्घिकः ॥

End. योऽसौ सर्व्वाधिपः श्रीमान् सुतसोमाभिधो नृपः ।
अहं हि भगवांस्त्वात्मा शाक्यमुनिरभूत्तदा ॥
श्रुत्वेति वाक्यं कथितं जिनेन प्रत्याययुक्ते सकला नृपाद्याः ।
प्रदक्षिणीकृत्य पद्मौ प्रणत्य सम्बोधिचर्य्यास्वभिलाषिणश्च ॥

Colophon. इति श्रीभद्रकल्पावदानेऽशोकोपगुप्तभाषणे सौदासोद्धरणे सुतसोमजातकं नाम चतुरधिकत्रिंशत्तमः परिसमाप्तः ॥

Old No. 815.—New No. B. 42.

BODHI-CHARYÁVATÁRA.

बोधिचर्य्यावतारः ।

Substance, palm-leaves, 11 × 2½. Folia 48. Lines on a page, 6. Extent in s'lokas, 1,100. Character, Newárí. Date ? Appearauce, old and smudgy. Verse. Generally correct.

A philosophical disquisition on the duties appropriate to Buddhist monks. The work is in ten chapters. Its author's name is not given. It opens with a dissertation on Buddhist disposition (*Bodhi-chitta*). This disposition is of two kinds, one called *Bodhi-praṇidhi-chitta*, or desire to acquire the true knowledge, and the other *Bodhi-prasthána-chitta*, or that disposition of the mind which obtains when that knowledge has been acquired. The second chapter treats of *Ishṭopadeshaṇá* or devotion to good work. This devotion is described to manifest itself in a desire to devote every thing good in this world to the worship of Tathágata and his sons. The third dwells on three topics, respectively called *Punyánumoda*, *Adhyesaná* and *Yáchaná*. The *first* is the disposition to virtue, wishing all creation to be free from pain and the troubles incident to existence ; the *second*, supplication to all the Buddhas of every quarter for the enlightenment of the minds of those who are immersed in pain ; the *third*, prayer to Jinas for the suppression of all sensuous desires—to wrest the soul from the bondage of the flesh. These lead to active benevolence, to the administration of medicines to the sick, food to the starving, relief to the poor, and the like,—all which promote the disposition to acquire the true knowledge. The fourth chapter enjoins the devotion of the mind to the mandates of the Buddhas and their sons, whereby alone can liberation from the bonds of transmigration be acquired. The fifth is devoted to the means of overcoming all sensuous desires. The sixth to perturbations of the mind and the propriety of suppressing them, as also the cultivation of forbearance (*kshánti-páramitá*) ; and the seventh to active penance (*Virya-páramitá*) or the subjugation of the passions by active exertion. The longings of the organs of sense and desires having thus been overcome, the eighth chapter, enters upon the subject of cogitation (*Dhyána-páramitá*) as to what is good and what is evil. Virtuous actions resulting from a desire to benefit one's own self, are described to be vicious, as they are prompted by a longing for rewards; this should be suppressed, and good should be done for the sake alone of doing it. Never should one proclaim his own merits, nor the demerits of others. Such cogitations settle the mind to meditation of that which alone is true. The ninth chapter is called *Prajñá-páramitá*. It describes the nature of the true knowledge, and in doing so, two doctrines are discussed : 1st, *Máyáváda*, or that which ascribes every thing mundane to Máyá or illusion ; and the 2nd, *Sunyatáváda*, or pure nihilism. The last chapter expresses a desire that whatever fruits may arise from the discussion and practice of the rules set forth in the work, may be to the glory of Buddhist devotion.

Beginning ॐ नम आर्य्यघोषाय ।
सुगतान् ससुतान् सधर्म्मकायान् प्रणिपत्यादरतोऽखिलान् स्ववन्द्यान् ।
सुगतात्मजसम्बरावतारं कथयिष्यामि यथागमं समासात् ॥
न हि किञ्चिदपूर्व्वमत्र वाच्यं न च सङ्ग्रन्थनकौशलं ममास्ति ।
अत एव न मेऽपराधचिन्ता स्वमनो भावयितुं कृतम्मयेदं ॥
मम तावदनेन याति वृद्धिं कुशलम्भावयितुं प्रसादवेगः ।
अथ मत्समधातुरेव पश्येदपरोऽप्येनमतोऽपि सार्थकोऽयं ॥
क्षणसम्पदियं सुदुर्लभा प्रतिलब्धा पुरुषार्थसाधनी ।
यदि नात्र विचिन्त्यते हितं पुनरप्येष समागमः कुतः ॥
रात्रौ यथा × × घनान्धकारे विद्युत्क्षणं दर्शयति प्रकाशं ।
बुद्धानुभावेन तथा कदाचिल्लोकस्य पुण्येषु मतिः क्षणं स्यात् ॥
तस्माच्छुभन्दुर्बलमेव नित्यं बलन्तु पापस्य महत् सुघोरं ।

तज्जायतेऽन्येन शुभेन केन सम्बोधि चित्तं यदि नाम न स्यात् ॥
कल्पाननल्पान् प्रविचिन्तयद्भिर्दृष्टम्मुनीन्द्रैर्हितमेतदेव ।
यतः सुखेनैव सुखस्य वृद्ध मुत्प्लावयत्य प्रमिताञ्जनौघान् ॥
भवदुःखशतानि तर्त्तुं कामैरपि सत्वव्य सनानि हर्त्तुकामैः ।
बहुसौख्यशतानि भोक्तुकामैर्नं विमोच्यं हि सदैव बोधिचित्तं ॥

End. मञ्जुघोषं न सम्पाति यदा क्षान्तिः शुभ ।
कल्यामित्र स्वन्देहं यम्प्रासादात् सर्व्वज्ञत ॥

Colophon. इति चर्य्यावतारे परि मन परिच्छेदो दशमः समाप्तः ।

No. B. 15.

BODHISATTVA AVADA'NA.

Substance, paper, 15 × 4¼. Folia 205. Lines on a page, 9. Extent in ślokas, 4,784. Character Newári. Date, unknown. Appearance, old. Prose and verse. Very incorrect.

A collection of legends regarding the former lives of the Bodhisattva. They were related at S'rávastí by the side of the tank Anavatapta, by the Lord Buddha himself, in a series of lectures to his disciples who composed the audience, the subject of the lectures being stories illustrating the means of obtaining *moksha*. After an eulogy on the extraordinary powers of Sáriputra (Mudgaláyana), the Lord gave an account of his ten sufferings, (See Bodhisattvávadána-kalpalatá,) and then recounted a series of stories each of which is called a Játaka. The stories relate chiefly to meritorious acts performed by Buddha in his previous existences.

Subhása Játaka. In one of his former existences the Lord was a king, Suprabhása by name. He was very irascible, and, in an angry moment, severely scolded an elephant driver, who in return spoke to him at length on the merits of charity, mercy, forgiveness, &c. This reacted on the mind of the king, who gradually began to long for Bodhi knowledge.

Vyághrí Játaka. In one of his numerous existences the Lord resided on the mount Kuláchala as a hermit. There he found a hungry tigress looking with a wistful eye at her newborn cubs. To relieve the poor creatures from being devoured by their hungry parent, the

Lord determined to offer his own body to her. He let himself fall from a high precipice, to the valley where the tigress was, and expired, thereby saving the cubs.

Sivi Játaka. As king of the Sivis the Lord, after bestowing the whole of his wealth on the poor, bestowed even his eyes to Indra, who begged them of him. Indra, pleased with his munificence, granted him heavenly eyes.

Kulmásapinḍí Játaka. Kulmáspindí, king of Kos'ala, was none else than the Lord himself. His maxim was that well-timed and well-placed charity is always laudable. A gift is never too small.

S'reshṭhi Játaka. The Lord was a ḅanker. A Pratyeka Buddha came to his door to beg. The wicked Mára prepared a hell at the door, but the virtuous banker fearlessly passed through the hell, and gave his alms.

Avisahyá s'reshṭhi Játaka. In the course of an infinite number of transmigrations the Lord was once born a rich and munificent banker. Indra stole all his property except a scythe for cutting grass and a bit of string for tying bundles of grass. The kind man used to gather grass, and sell it to relieve his poor neighbours.

S'as'a Játaka. Once on a time the Lord transmigrated into the brute world, and became a hare. He used to lecture on moral subjects to two of his friends, one a jackal, the other an ape. Indra demanded food of him. Having nothing else to give he jumped into a blazing fire, and requested Indra to eat his roasted flesh.

Agastya Játaka. The Lord was once born a rich Bráhmaṇ of the name of Agastya. He practised austerities in an island in the Southern sea, where Indra used to come and beg the Rishi's food and thereby deprive him of the means of sustenance. After four days the Ṛishi died of hunger.

Maitribala Játaka. The Lord was once born, a most charitable king of the name of Maitribala. He gave away whatever was asked of him; once he gave five portions of his flesh to five Yakshas who longed for human flesh, and asked it of him.

Visvambhara Játaka. Visambhara was the prince of the Sivis. He gave away an elephant much esteemed by the Sivis to a Bráhman. The Sivis complained of this before their king, the Prince's father, who banished Vísambhara from his kingdom. Visambhara went to the forest with his wife and children. A Bráhman begged as gift the boys. He was instantly complied with. Indra then demanded Visambhára's wife. Her too Visambhara gave away. Afterwards he was known as S'ákyamuni.

Yajña Játaka. King Yajña, or Buddha in a former birth, finding his kingdom afflicted by a drought, consulted the Bráhmaṇs as to the remedies for the evil. They advised him to perform a sacrifice. The king did not relish the idea, because it involved the slaughter of a large number of animals. He established alms-houses in every city, in every village, and in every street.

S'akra Játaka. In one of his previous existences the Lord was born as Indra, and when the Devas had to fight with the Asuras his prowess alone was sufficient to overpower the enemy.

Bráhmaṇa Játaka. The Lord was born in the family of a Bráhmaṇ. He went to a Guru who taught him many S'ástras. The Guru ordered all his disciples to procure the Dakshiṇá—the fees due to a guru—by theft. All consented, except that boy.

Unmádayantí Játaka. The Lord was the king of the Sivis. The maddening fairy-like beauty of Unmádayantí, wife of one of his ministers, captivated his heart. Some of his counsellors advised him to possess her by force. But the wicked advice was spurned by the king.

Supáraga Játaka. The Lord was named Supáraga. He was a clever merchant, and expert man of business. In his old age he, along with a number of other merchants, undertook a voyage to trade with the inhabitants of a coast named Bharu Kachchha. He, with his whole fleet, was one night overtaken by a terrible storm. Supáraga fell on his knees and prayed and worshipped Sugata. Instantly the storm blew over, the wind was hushed, the sea was calm. The fleet reached safe its place of destination, and the merchants enriched themselves by very profitable trade.

Matsya Játaka. Buddha was in the course of his transmigrations born a fish. He was the lord of all the fishes. He lived in a large ancient pond. He instructed his fellow-creatures by his edifying lectures on charity, righteousness, &c. Suddenly one summer the water of the tank was on the point of drying out. The fish-king looked toward the sky, and made a vow, saying, " I will never see the destruction of so many of my friends." On this Indra sent a heavy shower of rain, and filled the tank with water.

Vartakapota Játaka. Once upon a time a forest was on fire. The animals of the forest fled towards every quarter. One crippled, weak, wingless bird, unable to fly, solicited Agni to desist from burning. Instantly the fire was quenched. The wingless bird was the Lord himself.

Kumbha Játaka. In one of his existences the Lord was, under the name of Kumbha, king over the Devas. Finding his allies and his subjects much addicted to drinking, he rose up to heaven, and thence harangued them with the voice of thunder. The subject of course was Temperance.

Aputraka Játaka. In another existence, the Lord renouncing the world delivered a grand lecture on the transitory character of everything worldly, in order to rebuke those who re-entered the world after adopting the ascetic state. He said—the trouble of maintaining a family is a positive hindrance to Mukti.

Visa Játaka. The Lord was born in the family of a Bráhmaṇ. He had six brothers and a sister. All of them practised austerities. They were attended by only one servant girl. She gathered fruits, and divided them for the brothers and sister. Indra, for five successive days, stole the eldest brother's share, in order to examine the imperturbability of his temper. He was a little moved on the first day; on the second he suppressed his hunger; from the third he had no desire for eating.

S'reshṭhi játaka. Born in the family of a Bráhmaṇ, the Lord was named S'reshṭhi. He went to a hermitage. He baffled all the endeavours of his friends to bring him back to his home, by showing them by the clearest arguments that the highest pleasures are to be had only in a hermit's life.

Buddhabodhi Játaka. The Lord was born in the family of a Bráhmaṇ. He and his wife renounced the world together. They lived in the same forest. One day as the Lord, at the end of his austerities, was gathering dust at a beautiful spot, and his wife was repeating the meditative formula, in came a young king, who, captivated by the beauty of her person, at once ordered his servants to take her into his carriage. She cried loudly for help. Then coming to the hermit the king found him not the least agitated by the loss of his wife. He admired his firmness, begged his pardon, and restored him his wife.

Hañsa Játaka. In the series of existences from the lowest form of animalculæ to man, the soul of the Lord once entered the external cover of a king of the flamingoes who lived at Mánsarovar. He had a general as generous as himself. Brahmadatta, King of Benares, longing to have a sight of this virtuous pair, caused a splendid tank to be dug in the suburbs of his metropolis, which he had beautified at an immense cost. He issued a proclamation to the purpose that any bird coming to the tank would be perfectly safe. Some of the flamingoes who went to Mánsarovar were loud in the praise of the tank at Benares. The King of the flamingoes, with his faithful general, resolved to pay a visit to the famous tank. But when floating on its waters the king bird was caught by men who were kept on purpose by Brahmadatta. All his followers fled away at the time of his danger; but his general followed him wherever they led him. Brahmadatta seated them on a splendid throne, welcomed them, feasted them, and granted them liberty. The flamingo discoursed long on the advantages of virtue, and then took his departure.

Mahábodhi Játaka. Again in another existence the Lord, under the name of Mahábodhi, delighted his large audience with religious discourses flowing smoothly from his lips. He travelled from country to country, visiting many kings, and captivated men's hearts by his eloquence, at once soothing and persuasive. He was a hermit of the rank of an Ácharya. Men flocked to him by thousands. Some of the ministers of a King whom he visited warned him to keep a watchful eye upon the man. "He is a spy," they said, "come to deceive us by the power of his speech."

The King, thus advised, doubted the honesty of the sage. One day when the hermit came to his presence, the King did not salute him. The hermit, perceiving this change in the King's conduct, attempted to go away. The King said "Where do you go from us, Sir?" "You are unfit for religious discourse," was the reply, "I shall go to the forest." The King found it was no time then for detecting his knavery. He therefore allowed him to go, but requested him to come back after a while. The sage assented to this request. After practising in a forest four dhyánas and soon obtaining "five experiences," he returned to the King's court.

Many of the ministers came forward to refute the arguments of the pious hermit. One of them said: "Who can be the author of the color and fragrance of the lotus and the like? This earth is the result of nature (*svabháva*)." Another said—"It is impossible that this earth should be the result of an accident, and therefore have the wise concluded that it must have proceeded from one who is absolute mind and felicity." A third remarked, that the assumption of a single cause for objects of various nature resulting from diverse causes, is inconsistent. They must proceed from acts performed in previous lives, or attempts to do good would never be followed by pain. Another was of opinion that "woods of various shapes, colors and qualities could not result from the fruits of works performed in former existences; were it so, still woods destroyed do not again become woods, so the dead do not come to life again. Therefore we should seek happiness while we live." The hermit, perceiving that the King was fond of illustrations, retired to his hermitage. There, by a miracle, he created a large monkey, took out its skin, and made of it a covering for his own body, and repaired to the royal presence. Every one accused him of killing a monkey, and laughed at his conduct. "Why," asked the hermit, "if all this be either natural or brought about by previous work, I have done no wrong in killing a monkey."

After this argument, the King cared very little for the sophisms of the philosophers, but placed himself entirely under the guidance of the pious hermit.

Mahákapi Játaka. The Lord was once born a monkey, dwelling in a woody spot by the side of the Himálaya. A man, who had lost his way in the forest, while gathering fruits, fell from a lofty tree into a deep lake. The monkey, who was close by, rescued him by carrying him on its back over the steep precipice. At last weary with toil the poor creature fell fast asleep, appointing the man to watch him. The man wanted to kill the animal for its meat, and threw a stone at it, in order to effect his purpose. The sound of the stone broke the monkey's sleep. It found from what quarter it had come. It rebuked the man gently, and showed him his way out of the forest. In a short time the man died of a loathsome disease.

Sarabha Játaka. A Sarabha was chased by a king on horseback. While crossing a deep ravine the king fell into it. The Sarabha, seeing the horse without its rider, immediately perceived what had happened, and proceeded directly to rescue the king. This Sarabha was Buddha in one of his transmigrations.

Ruru Játaka. A man was carried down by an impetuous stream. He cried piteously for help. A golden-colored stag (*Ruru*) rescued him from danger. He made the man promise on no account to discover the place of the stag's residence and let him go.

Meanwhile the queen of the place had dreamt of receiving lectures from a stag as brilliant as gold. On receiving the promise of a large reward, that very man now betrayed his trust, and showed the king where the stag dwelt.

The king aimed his shaft at the stag. But the animal neared the king of his own accord, and asked him who had shewed him the place. On finding the man to be no other than he whom he had once rescued, the stag told the king of the man's faithlessness. The king wanted to kill him, but the stag interposed. The king was highly pleased with him, took him home, honored him, feasted him, and received lectures from him. He taught the royal family lessons of high importance in the true faith.

The stag was none else than the Lord himself.

Kapí Játaka. While bathing in a river a certain king found a very delicious fig (*Ficus religiosa*) floating down the stream. The king took it up and wanted to have more. He went high up the stream and found a big fig-tree inhabited by monkeys who lived solely on its fruits. One of them was seen sending the monkeys off from the sight of the royal army. The king, thinking him to be the chief, cut with an arrow the branch on which he stood. He declared himself to be the king of the monkeys, and discoursed long with the king on man's destiny and on virtue, charity, patience, penitence and so on.

This monkey chief was Buddha himself.

Kshánti Játaka. A hermit practised austerities in a wilderness. A king came into that forest with the ladies of his house. One day while he slept, the ladies, in the course of their walk, came to the hermit's grove. The hermit welcomed them, and extolled the powers of righteousness before them. The king, seeing a hermit amidst the royal dames, flew at him in a rage, and cut two of his fingers. Instantly he felt a burning fever. The hermit was the Lord Buddha.

Brahma Játaka. Once on a time the Lord, born in the regions of Brahmá, came down to earth and brought the king of Videha, who was ruining himself by associating with low companions, to the path of justice and virtue.

Hastí Játaka. An elephant supplied with his own flesh, the food to a hundred men who were banished from their houses, and were almost dying of hunger. This elephant was the Lord in one of his former existences.

Sutasoma Játaka. Subháshita, a Bráhman, was soliciting alms from Sutasoma, when suddenly there was a great uproar in the female apartment. Sutasoma, asking Subháshita to wait a little, went into the seraglio. King Saudása (*vide* Avadána-s'ataka, story 89) got hold of him, and carried him away. Sutasoma remembered the promise he had made to Subháshita, solicited Saudása to grant him a moment's leave that he may grant some money to the Bráhman. After long entreaty Saudása permitted him to go. Sutasoma, after redeeming his promise, returned as he had engaged. Saudása, highly pleased to find the prince a man of his word, permitted him to ask four boons. The boons Sutasoma asked were the following:—

That Saudása should always speak the truth, leave the slaughter of animals, liberate all captive princes, and give up eating raw flesh.

Though reluctant, Saudása nevertheless granted these boons.

This prince Sutasoma of the Kaurava dynasty was none else than lord Buddha in one of his previous existences.

Ayo Játaka. A royal youth once obtained permission from his parents to proceed to an hermitage. This prince was the Lord.

Mahisa Játaka. A buffalo, though constantly harassed by a wicked monkey, did not try to injure him. This buffalo was the Lord.

S'atapatra Játaka. A lion, that had a bone stuck into his throat, went to a S'atapatra, who, pitying the sufferings of the lion, took the bone out of his throat. The same lion, while devouring a large quantity of venison, was asked for a bit by the S'atapatra, who was at that time very hungry. But the lion gave him nothing. The S'atapatra was not the least moved by it. This S'atapatra was the Lord himself.

After this story follows a few verses enumerating the different merits of offering various things to Buddha, as also of reading and of hearing read works on the Buddhist religion.

Beginning. ओं नमः श्रीसर्व्वबुद्धबोधिसत्त्वेभ्यः ।
श्रीमन्तिसद्गुणपरिग्रहमङ्गलानि
कीर्त्तिप्रसादान्यवजीतमनोहराणि ।
पूर्व्वं प्रजन्मसु मुनेश्चरितानि भक्त्या
भक्त्या स्वकाव्यकुसुमाञ्जलिनार्चयिष्ये ॥

End. जग्मुर्देवा सुमेरौ त्रिभुवननमितं शाक्यसिंहं प्रणम्य
गन्धर्व्वा मण्डलाग्रेऽथ दितिसुतगरुड़ा ब्रह्म रुद्रेन्द्रकल्पाः ।
कैलासे सिद्धविद्याधरहयवदना मारुता यक्षवर्गा
नागाः पातालभूमौ प्रमुदितमनसो वीतरागादिदोषाः ॥

No. B. 15.

BODHISATTVÁVADÁNA-KALPALATÁ.

बोधिसत्त्वावदानकल्पलता ।

Substance, yellow paper, 10¼ × 4½ inches. Folia, 152. Lines on a page, 10. Extent in s'lokas, 3,705. Character, Devanágarí. Appearance, old. Verse. Very incorrect.

A store-house of legends regarding Buddha's former existences. It seems to be partly a sequel to, and partly a poetical amplification of, the work noticed under the last preceding No. It is called a 'tree yielding whatever is wanted of it,' (kalpalatá) and the metaphor is kept up in the generic name of its subdivisions, which are called *pallava* or "leaves," and not *adhyáyas* or "chapters." The codex under notice is obviously incomplete, as it commences from the 51st chapter or pallava. It appears, however, from the presence of an invocatory verse at the beginning of the chapter, and the absence of all such invocations at the beginnings of subsequent chapters, that the work was divided into two parts, of which the first included 50 chapters, and the second 58. Each chapter contains a distinct story, illustrating a particular moral maxim, or an incidence in the life of the saint. The author of the work was Kshemendra, who had the title of *Mahákavi* or "the great poet." He was probably the same with the author of the *Kathá-sarit-ságara*, the archetype of Somadeva Bhaṭṭa's *Vrihatkathá*. If this identification be tenable, the date of the work would be the 5th century of the Christian era.

LI.—*Ten Sufferings.* Lord Buddha, during his sojourn by the side of the tank Anavatapta, while giving an account of the former lives of

S'áriputra and Maudgalyáyana, illustrated the maxim that "every creature must suffer from the effects of his works" by adverting to the ten mundane pains which he suffered. He said:

(1). "In one of my previous existences, when I had the name of Kharvota, I killed my half-brother at the instigation of my wife, Káliká: I have an ulcer on the top of my right toe as a consequence.

(2). "As Arthadatta, a merchant, I killed one of my own calling, who was much opposed to my interests. The consequence is, that I have suffered from a sore caused by the prick of a catechu thorn.

(3). "In another existence, as Chapala I threw away, with my own hand, the contents of Upárishya's alms-bowl. This Upárishya was a Pratyeka Buddha. I have my alms-bowl always empty for that outrageous conduct.

(4). "As Bharadvája, I falsely charged my elder brother Vas'ishṭha with holding criminal intercourse with a maid-servant, who was an anchorite; and that is why Sundarí has published a similar scandal against me in my present existence.

(5). "As a Vaisya, Mriṇála by name, I wanted to live with Bhadrá, a public prostitute, on the condition that she should not allow any body else to have connection with her. Finding her one day in the company of another, in a fit of anger, I killed her. Consequently a Bhikshuṇí has brought a false charge against me in this life.

(6). "As Manthara, a Bráhmaṇa, finding one day my neighbours giving a splendid feast to Vipashyí, I railed at them, saying, 'these stupid bald-heads should be fed with barley and weavelled kodra; they do not deserve rich viands.' I have now to live upon kodra and barley in consequence of these irreverent words.

(7). "Born in ancient days as Uttara, I spoke ill of one Pudgala. I have suffered greatly for it, and had to lead a vicious life for six years in the present existence.

(8). "There was a rich patriarch, Dhanaván by name, in the country called Karpaṭa. He had a son named S'rímán. Tiktamukha, 'bitter-faced,' a medical practitioner of the place, cured S'rímán of various diseases, but obtained nothing for his remuneration. When S'rímán fell ill again, Tiktamukha put a period to his life by administering a strong poison to him. I was that medical man, and for my treacherous conduct to S'rímán, I suffer from spermatorrhœa in this life.

(9). "In another existence, as a fisherman, I took great delight at the sight of a large fish under convulsions of death from repeated strokes of the axe. I suffer from cephalgia in consequence of that demoniac conduct.

(10). "Born as an athlete, I treacherously put one of my antagonists to death. I suffer from rheumatism for that deadly sin."

Rukmavatí Avadána. The saint then related the following story: S'achípati, or Indra, once came to pay his respects to the saint, and, finding him smile, enquired after its reason. The Lord, recalling to his memory some ancient events, said: "There was one Rukmavatí in the city of Utpalávatí; she found a young woman, ravenously hungry after delivery, just on the point of eating up her new-born baby; immediately Rukmavatí cut her breast with a sharp knife, and offered it to the hungry mother. When news of this event reached the heavens, Indra presented himself before that wonderful woman, and asked her if she had any agitation in her mind at the time of performing that superhuman deed? She replied in the negative, which was of course true. Indra granted her a boon by which she was transformed into a man. Soon after, the king of the city breathed his last, and the crown was offered to Rukmavatí, the newly made man. His reign was the happiest ever recorded in the annals of Utpalávatí.

"In her next life Rukmavatí was born in the family of a rich banker. The banker's son always thought deeply of the miserable condition of birds. Finding no other way of relieving them, he proceeded to a cremation ground, cut his own flesh into minute pieces, and distributed them to the winged animals. A big bird plucked out his eyes. The pain was excruciating, but Sattvavara, the banker's son, was all firmness. He discoursed with perfect composure on the evanescent character of everything human, and on the great merit of charity.

"He was again born as a great Bráhmaṇa. In a short time he got the reputation of a wise man. Finding a tigress on the point of devouring her new-born whelp, he offered his own body, which saved the young tiger's life."

LII.—The story of *Adínapuṇya;* to be found in the Avadána of that name.

LIII.—The story of *Subháshitagaveshi;* to be found in the Avadána S'ataka, S. 38, p. 29.

LIV.—*Sattvaushadha Avadána.* When the Lord converted Pushyilá, a female ogre, a smile was seen on his lips. Indra, who was near, enquired after the cause of his smile. The Lord said he was thinking of some ancient events. In the days of yore, there was a king named Mahendra Sena in the city of Mahendravatí. He had a son Sattvaushadha by name. Diseased people from different quarters of the globe used to come to him. They were invariably cured by his touch. After his death, wise people in the neighbourhood kept his çorpse exposed near the border of a forest, where it was miraculously preserved from rotting. People still recovered their health by touching his corpse.

The Lord said to Indra, "a future king As'oka will erect a chaitya at the spot where Sattvaushadha's body was preserved. I am that Sattvaushadha."

LV.—The story of *Sarvandada ;* to be found in the As'oka Avadána.

LVI.—*Páshána-sarpa Avadána.* The Lord was living at Hingumardana, the king of which place had a great veneration for him. One day the ministers of the king complained of a terrible snake, which lived on mount Páshána, and destroyed a large number of people every day. The Lord undertook to quiet the serpent. He was perfectly successful. The serpent became a rigid Buddhist from that time.

LVII.—*Bálokshí Avadána.* There were four stúpas at Páshána. The Lord erected a fifth one himself. At Bálokshí he induced a rich banker to erect a stúpa, celebrated afterwards as Bálokshíya stúpa. The Lord converted Dambara, a Yaksha of the village Dambara, and Mallíká, a Chandalí of Bhandálagráma. At Pátala he made Potala, a follower of his creed, to erect a splendid stúpa on his hair and nails. The Lord said to Indra a king Millinda will erect a stúpa at Pátala.

LVIII.—*Punyabala Avadána.* The Lord was seen smiling at Pushkalávatí. Indra asked the reason of his smiling. The Lord said there was a king, Punyabala by name, at Punyavat. One day when going to his villa he found by the road-side a miserable diseased old man, suffering greatly. Touched with pity the king established a hospital in his city. He used to inspect the cures effected by the physicians in his service. One day, on coming to superintend the hospital he found a blind old man complaining the loss of his sight. On being apprised of the King's presence, the old man approached him and said, "O king, if you could grant me your right eye I would recover my sight."

Instantly the king plucked out his eye. This old man was Indra. He threw off his disguise, replaced the king's eye, and granted him several boons.

LIX.—*Kuṇála Avadána.* King As'oka of Páṭaliputra had many wives. His son Kuṇála, by Padmávatí, had peculiarly graceful eyes. His eyes attracted the attention of Tishyarakshá, one of his numerous step-mothers: she became enamoured of him. But Kuṇála was true to his wife Káṉchanamálá. He rejected with scorn the offers of a vicious step-mother's love. Tishyarakshá determined to destroy his eyes, the causes of her shame. Kuṇála proceeded by order of his father to Takshas'ilá to war against its rebellious governor. Anxiety on account of the absence of a dear son produced serious illness in the king. He suffered greatly, and it was only Tishyarakshá's care that cured him. As a reward she was allowed to reign supreme for seven days. During these seven days, she wrote to the Governor of Taksha-s'ilá to pull out the eyes of Kuṇála. That letter was intercepted. It fell into the hands of Kuṇála, who, honoring the command of the reigning empress, caused his own eyes to be destroyed. Káṇchanamálá, his wife, brought him back to the capital. As'oka, who knew nothing of what had transpired, was all in tears at the piteous condition of his son. People asked Kuṇála if he bore any grudge against her who was the cause of his misfortune. He said "No. I am quite satisfied with my step-mother's conduct." His professions were all true, and because they were true, he got his eyes back, and they were even more charming than before.*

LX.—The story of *Nágakumára;* see Avadána S'ataka, S. 59, p. 34.

LXI.—The story of Karshaka, vide As'oka Avadána.

LXII.—The story of *Yas'odhará*, see Bhadrakalpa Avadána, S. 1, p. 42.

LXIII.—*Pippaláyana Avadána.* In the town of Magadha there lived a Bráhmaṇ named Nyagrodhakalpa. His wife Surúpá gave birth to a beautiful son under a pippala tree. This son was named Pippaláyana, or the son of a pippala tree. Averse to the pleasures of the world, the son refused to marry. But on the urgent solicitations of his father,

* This version of the story is, in several respects, different from what has been given in the As'oka Avadána (*vide ante*, p. 11).

he produced a golden image, saying, if any one could procure him a girl as fair as the image, he would marry, well knowing no terrestrial being could equal the image in beauty. After a long search, a friend of his father found Bhadrá, the daughter of Kapila, possessed of the necessary qualification. Her colour was as bright as that of gold; but she too was much against marriage, a circumstance which led Pippaláyana to accept her as his bride, because he knew full well that the duties of married life will never have to be endured by him. Pippaláyana obtained Bodhi knowledge from the instructions of Kás'yapa, then dwelling under the shade of a sacred tree, Bahupatra by name. Pippaláyana was afterwards celebrated under his patronymic as Mahá Kás'yapa. Bhadrá too obtained the highest bliss by renouncing the world.

On being asked the reasons of their rapid advancement, the lord said, Pippaláyana, in one of his former existences, was a poor man; he nevertheless feasted S'ikhí, a Buddha, when he was almost dying from want of food. In another existence, he endowed a splendid stúpa, erected by his father King of Kriki, with a rich golden parasol.

LXIV.—*Kinnari Avadána.* Vidyádhara, a serpent-catcher, attempted to capture the king of serpents, and drag him out from his abode by means of drugs and mystic incantations. The king, greatly terrified, took shelter with a hunter, named Padmaka. This man killed Vidyádhara with poisoned arrows, and obtained from his protegè a charmed noose of wonderful power. On his death he bequeathed the noose to his son Utpala, who dwelt at Hastinápura in the vicinity of Valkaláyana's hermitage. Once upon a time Utpala heard a charming song resounding in the air. Learning it was being sung by an exceedingly beautiful Kinnarí,* he captured her by means of his noose. The Kinnarí, to regain her liberty, offered to give him her crown-jewel, which could lend the power of traversing the universe at pleasure. When the two were settling their bargain, in came Sudhana, a young prince of Hastiná, on a hunting excursion. Utpala gave him the crown-jewel, and the Kinnarí married him, and the married couple proceeded to the palace.

At this time, there lived in the royal household two Bráhmaṇas, Kapila and Pushkara, the former serving as priest to the king, and the

* The Kinnaras are a fabled race of demi-gods with human bodies and equine heads. They were noted for their musical accomplishments, and held the rank of heavenly choristers and followers of Kuvera, the god of wealth.

latter, in the same capacity to the prince. They were vain of their learning, and always quarrelled with each other. One of the fuditories of the king rebelling, the king directed his son to lead an army against the rebellious vassal. Sudhana left his wife with her crown-jewel under the care of his mother. The king, after his son's departure, dreamt an inauspicious dream, and Kapila his priest advised him to offer a Kinnarí as a burnt-offering to propitiate the enraged divinity who had caused the dream. Kapila was a shrewd man who took this opportunity of humbling his rival, for he knew full well that the prince was sure to die if the Kinnarí were killed in a sacrifice. But he was disappointed. The queen privately warned her daughter-in-law, and sent her away with the crown-jewel, to Kinnarapura.

The Kinnarí left a ring and some charmed butter with Valkaláyana, requesting him to hand the two things over to Sudhana.

Sudhana returned victorious from the war. But his joy was damped by the loss of his wife. He determined to proceed to Kinnarapura, and immediately set forth in a northerly direction. On his way he obtained the ring and the butter from Valkaláyana which helped him immensely in overcoming the fatigues of his journey. He crossed the mountains Himálaya, Kuladu, Ajapatha, Kámarúpa, Ekadhara, Vajraka, and Khadira, one after another, and encountered many adventures. Beyond mount Khadira he found two great mountains turning on a wheel which made that road impassable. He destroyed the axle of the wheel, and fixed the mountains in their proper places. After this adventure, he had to ford the Guhá, Patangá, Rodiní, Hasiní and several other furious mountain streams before he reached Kinnarapura. There he met his wife, and the two wept tears of joy.

The Lord said "I am that Kinnarí and I am that Sudhana."

LXV.—*Naliní Avadána.* Asked by his audience to give an account of the preceding existence of his parents, the Lord said: King Kás'yapa had a daughter named Naliní. When she was of a marriageable age, she was placed by her father near the hermitage of a sage named Kás'yapa, who had a youthful son of great beauty, begot by a deer. The youth was named Ekas'riñgí, because he had a short horn on his head. Naliní met the youth, brought him to her father's house, and was married to him. Ekas'riñgí afterwards took other wives, and had by them a thousand sons. The sage Kás'yapa afterwards became Suddhodana; the deer, Gautamí; King Kás'yapa, Daṇḍapáni; Ekas'ringi, myself; Naliní, Yasodhará; and the thousand sons, my S'rávakas and followers.

LXVI.—The story of *Kavikumára*; *vide* Avadána of that name.

LXVII.—*Sangharakshita Avadána.* Sangharakshita, the son of Buddha-rakshita, was intended, from his conception, by his father to be a disciple of S'áriputra. Acting according to the instructions of that great teacher, Sangharakshita renounced the world. A few of his friends invited him to accompany them on a voyage. He accepted their invitation. When their ship was far away from land, it was overtaken by a sudden storm. Every one feared that his end was come. But a voice from heaven quieted their mind. It said, "Cast Sangharakshita overboard and save yourselves." They threw him overboard, and he was carried to the Nágaloka. The Nágas, unable to bear the pure refulgence of his person, managed to throw him into the ship again. But the unfortunate Bhikshu, while sleeping, was again cast overboard, and left alone on a desert shore by his inhuman companions. Unmoved by sufferings, Sangharakshita resolved to travel through the whole length and breadth of the earth. He passed through many viháras, witnessing various extraordinary scenes, each testifying to the truth of the great principle that the merits of a work are never destroyed. Once he lodged at a vihára where he found the Bhikshus to be very simple and well-behaved people. They collected their vegetables, dressed their curries, and prepared their food. But as soon as the viands were placed on the plates, each grain of rice became transformed into a large wooden club. The Bhikshus took the clubs up, and began to strike at one another. They continued fighting in this way till the ground was all covered over with blood. At the end of the fight, they quietly sat down, talking as old friends. On enquiry, Sangharakshita came to learn that in a previous existence they had fought at a vihára where the Bhikshus were eating, and this was a daily punishment for that great misconduct.

At another vihára Sangharakshita obtained, with much difficulty, an empty room on condition that he was to keep strict silence. But there, the presiding divinity of the place appeared before him, complained of the criminal and unnatured conduct of the Bhikshus, and requested him to reform them. He instantly began to preach, and was in a short time master of the place. The five hundred Bhikshus who dwelt there were all corrected, and converted. With these he proceeded through the sky to the place where the Lord Buddha was then residing. Buddha preached to the new converts, and they returned home well pleased. Finding the Lord alone Sangharakshita said, "O Lord, on my way back I have seen animals of the shape of pillars, walls &c. What are they? In consequence of what sin have they got such unnatural shapes?" The Lord said, "they were all S'rávakas to the Lord Kás'yapa. They had spat on the walls of the monastery or Sanghagriha, and therefore they now suffer."

Sangharakshita easily obtained Arhatship. The Lord said the reason of his high and rapid advancement was that in one of his previous existences, he had made a samádhi under the instruction of Lord Kás'yapa.

LXVIII.—*Padmávatí Avadána.* The Bhikshus asked the Lord why and for what sin, on the part of Yas'odhará was she, on her first delivery, ordered by Suddhodana to be put to death. The Lord said, there was a king Brahmadatta by name, at Kampilla. He picked up in the forest a destitute girl, Padmávatí, who scattered lotuses at every step she moved, and made her his favorite queen. This girl was born of a hind, who had drunk of a portion of S'ándilya's seed. She was very simple-minded. Other queens, envious of her position, used to play tricks upon her, and at the time of her first delivery cheated her most shamefully. These wicked ladies, on the occasion, told her, "Dear Padmá, you are a rustic girl, you do not know how to give birth to a royal child. Let us help you." She yielded. They covered her eyes, threw into the river the twin boys she brought forth, and decked her face with gore. They deceived her by telling that it was only a lump of flesh that she had given birth to, and it had been thrown into the river. At the same time they informed her husband that Padmá had eaten up her two new-born sons. The king, enraged at her inhuman conduct, ordered her to instant execution. But there were shrewd men in the court, who privately saved her life.

The divinity presiding over S'ándilya's hermitage appeared to the king in a dream, and revealed the whole truth to him. The king made a strict investigation in the harem, and found that Padmávatí had been perfectly innocent. He became disconsolate, and gave vent to loud lamentations.

Soon after some fishermen appeared at the court, and presented the king with two infants who betrayed their royal lineage by the resemblance of their features with those of the king. They were reported to have been found in a vessel floating on the river. The courtier who saved Padmá's life now wished to produce her before the king. But she refused to return, and proceeded to her father's hermitage. After the death of her father, she travelled through various places in the habit of a Parivrájiká. In the course of her peregrinations she stopped at Benares. Brahmadatta conducted her with great honour to his capital from that place.

"In a previous existence Padmávatí, while yet a girl, had given a lotus with which she was playing to a Pratyeka Buddha, but wantonly had taken it back. Because she had given a lotus, therefore at every step she produced a lotus; because she had taken it back, therefore she was ordered to execution. This Padmávatí is Yas'odhará."

LXIX.—*Buddha-prasádiní Avadána.* King As'oka lived at Páṭaliputra. He erected chaityas and raised stúpas over Sugata's relics collected from various quarters, even from Nágaloka, and always feasted the Buddhist Sangha. The stúpas raised by him numbered eighty-four thousand. He used to feast the Sangha every day. One day a vain Bhikshu, told an illiterate old man : "Do you, old man, know why the king feeds you? He will ask you some questions on the mysteries of our religion." The old man felt very much distressed, for he was perfectly innocent of all learning, and greatly disliked being exposed. But the goddess Buddha-prasádhiní appeared before him, encouraged him, and instructed him by saying "Tell the king in reply, 'hear O King, the sum and substance of all religion. The deposits in a treasury are but fuels to the fire of greed. The meritorious works performed with wealth, spread all over the earth. Eating and sleeping are for the satisfaction of those only that are blinded by ignorance.' "

As'oka presented the old man a common piece of cloth interwoven with golden threads. This old man obtained Arhatship after performing a samádhi, under the instruction of the gods. On another occasion king As'oka, finding the vestment of a Bhikshu highly perfumed, asked him the reason. The Bhikshu said, "I lived a month in heaven under a Párijáta tree; and thence the odour." From the time of this conversation As'oka undertook to dedicate holy gardens to the three Ratnas.

LXX.—*Mádhyantika Avadána.* Mádhyantika, a Bhikshu, was sent to Káshmir as a missionary by his spiritual guide A'nanda. Káshmir was at that time peopled solely by the Nágas. The Nágas poured a shower of arrows upon him. But these weapons formed a splendid parasol over his head. The Nágas, wondering at this miraculous result, granted him an uninhabited site, and he very soon converted that place into a Vihára.

LXXI.—*S'oṇavásí Avadána.* S'oṇavásí was a propagator of the Buddhist faith at Mathurá. He was asked by two athletes the meaning of the term S'oṇavásí. He said: "Finding an old man not willing to exchange his s'oṇa or ochre-colored vestment even for a royal robe, I panted for a similar ochre-colored cloth, hence I am called Soṅavásí."

At Urumuṇḍa a hill in Mathurá he converted Naṭa and Bhaṭa, two Nágas, and erected two Viháras of the same name in commemoration of their conversion.

LXXII.—*Upagupta Avadána.* Upagupta was intended by his father, Gupta of Mathurá, to be a disciple of S'oṇavásí. Upagupta had deep reverence for S'oṇavásí. Vásavadattá, a prostitute, finding Upagupta very handsome, desired him to call it hers. Upagupta said, "This is not the proper time for going to a prostitute; I shall call at the proper time." Some time after this, Vásavadattá poisoned one of her paramours at the instigation of another. She was sentenced to be killed with torture. The executioner cut her nose, her ears, her hair, and took away her clothes. Upagupta, thinking that to be a proper time for seeing a prostitute, appeared before Vásavadattá, and instructed her in his faith, which gave her great consolation. Upagupta became an Arhat; he conquered Káma and commanded him to exhibit Sugata's beauty. Káma transformed himself into Sugata, assuming a brilliant form, with large eyes shut in meditation, and still eye-brows. Upagupta converted eighteen lacs of the people of Mathurá.

LXXIII.—*Nágadosha Avadána.* See As'okávadána.

LXXIV.—*Sampádí Avadána.* As'oka was a Kalpavriksha to all beggars. He gave away ninety-six lacs of gold pieces in thirty-six years. At the time of his death his grand-nephew Sampádí prevented his treasurers from obeying the orders of the old king. As'oka, having nothing else at hand, gave away one-half of the pill he was desired to use, and at last, by the advice of Rádhagupta his minister, granted the whole kingdom to the Sangha. Sampádí bought it back at the cost of four crores of golden dinars.

LXXV.—*Svastimán Avadána.* Svastimán, a Jina, who lived at S'rávastí, told the Bhikshus, that ignorance is at the root of all the vices of the world.

LXXVI.—*Vidura Avadána.* Jina found a large animal suffering excruciating torture from the bite of innumerable worms subsisting on its ulcers. Jina said, "This animal was in the course of the transmigration of his soul, a king, named Vidura; and he beat a Pratyeka Buddha who had entered his seraglio, though the person had entered it only to teach his wives the true religion. He will have to suffer the tortures of hell-fire, to be born in the Chaṇḍála caste, to kill a holy man, and again to suffer in hell. Born a man he will have to take ordination as a monk from the teacher Uttara, and to be punished by Kás'íràja for being honored by his wives."

LXXVII.—*Alpasvása-Mahásvása Avadána.* Four serpents, Dhritaráshṭra, Virúrha, Virúpáksha, Dhanádhipa, and two men, Kaiṇakeya and his nephew S'aila, all obtained the highest bliss from Jina's instructions. They all lived in or about the forest Aḍumáya. The Lord Jina said, they all had been attentive to the lectures of Kás'yapa Buddha in their previous existences, under the names of Alpasvása and Mahásvása.

LXXVIII.—*Sakra chyavana Avadána.* See As'oka Avadána, *ante*, p. 15.

LXXIX.—*Jívas'armá Avadána.* Jívas'ármá was a learned Bráhmaṇa of S'rávastí; he married at an advanced age at the request of his friends. His young wife thought the old man intolerable. To satisfy her wicked cravings, she wanted to have him away from home, and induced him to travel from court to court in quest of alms. The Bráhmaṇa collected a large amount of money; but he was robbed of all he had got by a gang of thieves on his way home. He was lamenting over his loss when Lord Bhútabhávana gave him a treasure with which he returned to his wife. Finding her not satisfied still, he renounced the world, and soon obtained the rank of an Arhat. The Lord related the story of Mahendra Sena to explain the merits of Jívásarmá.

LXXX.—*Supriya and Subhadra.* Lord Buddha, while lying on his death-bed at Kus'í, remembered two persons who were greatly puffed up with vanity. He resolved on humbling them. One was Supriya, a king of the Gandharvas, who, being requested by Indra to accompany him on a philanthropic journey, told him, "I cannot go because I have to play on my flute." To humble him Buddha employed a master musician created by himself. Unable to surpass this man, Supriya humbly prayed the Lord, and obtained the highest bliss from the Lord's instruction.

The Lord said, "this Supriya was a worshipper of Kás'yapa who performed a Samádhi with a view to be the king of the Gandharvas. The other supremely vain man was Subhadra, a *Yati*, who, seeing a fig tree covered with blossoms, thought the blossoms proceeded from the merits of his good works. When the blossoms withered, he thought it was from his own sinfulness. But the nymph who dwelt on the fig tree said, 'It is neither from your merit nor from your sin that the blossoms have grown and withered, but for the birth and death of a Buddha in the vicinity.'" Subhadra, humbled in his pride, proceeded to the dying Buddha, became his disciple, and died before him.

The Lord said, Subhadra had been in his previous existence As'oka, a disciple of Kás'yapa, who prayed for dying before the eyes of his spiritual guide.

The Lord said, "We never feel any pain in doing things liked by others. There was in days of yore a king named Vijayanta in the city of Ajitodaya. His subjects were all virtuous men. They filled the heaven by proceeding thither in crowds after death. Indra, to test the virtue of the king sent a cruel beggar to him. This relentless man asked bits of flesh from the king's body. The king granting, he went on asking continually till the king was literally reduced to a skeleton."

LXXXI.—*Hetúpama Avadána.* See As'oka Avadána, *ante*, p. 14.

LXXXII.—*Bhavasarmá Avadána.* See As'oka Avadána, *ante*, p. 14.

LXXXIII.—*Chandra Súrya Avadána.* Suddhodana once asked Buddha why was it, that Ráhula remained for six years in the womb; and why was Yas'odhará so long oppressed with the heavy load? The Lord replied, "a king of Mithilá had two sons, Chandra and Súrya. Súrya, the eldest, renounced the world. One day he drank water from a rishi's water-pot without his permission. But immediately after he repented of his using the property of another person without his consent, and went directly to king Chandra to obtain instruction as to the proper course of expiation. Chandra made him tarry at his capital for six days and then gave the proper instructions, after consulting with the Bráhmans of his court. I was that Súrya, and my son Ráhula was the king Chandra. A milkmaid went to sell butter-milk in company with her young daughter. The daughter gave the heavier vessel to her own mother, and took the light one herself. The daughter is now Yas'odhará who feels the consequence of her selfishness."*

LXXXIV.—*Madhurasvará Avadána.* See As'oka Avadána, *ante*, p. 15.

LXXXV.—*Upananda and Kuhana.* The Bhikshus asked the Lord why was the Lord so fond of the diseased. The Lord said, there were no pains more unbearable than those that affect the body.

Sivi, king of S'ikhi-ghosha, had a charitable dispensary. A patient sought relief thereat. The physicians in the king's employ advised him to use the blood of one who had never been angry since his birth. The king, considering himself to be such a one, gave his own blood, and the patient recovered in six months. Once on a time, the king's son felt unwell. The physicians prescribed for him a butter named sarvasára, the ingredients of which should be the extracts from every drug known, and especially from the nerves of a bird called Jívanjíva. It had to be prepared in twelve years, and by boiling the ingredients four thousand times. The drug was prepared, but no sooner had the king's son raised the cup of butter to his mouth, than a Pratyeka Buddha, who had been suffering from the same disease, demanded it of him. The king's son immediately relinquished the cup; but he was cured by the healing power of the holy man.

The Lord said, "That king's son was myself." The Bikshus asked, why did those two suffer from the same disease? The Lord replied, "Upananda the younger son of Brahmadatta of Benares conspired with Kuhana, the younger brother of the royal priest, to deprive the heir-apparent Nanda of a limb. He succeeded, but afterwards repenting restored the kingdom to his brother. Upananda and Kuhana raised several Viháras before their death. Upananda was Sivi's son, and Kuhana was the Pratyeka Buddha."

LXXXVI.—*Kalinja-s'as'aka Avadána.* Some Bhikshus asked the Lord what claims an elder person had to the veneration of a younger.

* The story has been given at length in the Rev. S. Beal's translation of the oldest Chinese version of the Legend of S'ákyá Buddha, pp. 361 *et seq.*

The Lord said during the reign of Brahmadatta there lived at Benares four animals: a francoline partridge, a hare, a monkey and an elephant, who all honoured an elderly banyan tree. On account of the merits of this good work there was always abundance of rain and plenty of every thing. "I am, oh Bhikshus, that partridge, Sáriputra is the hare, Maudgaláyana is that monkey, and Ananda is the elephant."

LXXXVII.—*Padmaka Avadána.* See As'oka Avadána, (*ante*, p. 15).

LXXXVIII.—*Chitra Avadána.* Chitra, the son of Bimbisara, king of Rájagriha, became a Bhikshu at an early age. But his wife managed to bring him back to his house. When Lord Buddha came to hear of this, he appeared before Chitra and dispelled the darkness from his mind. In a short time Chitra became an Arhat. The Lord said, "Chitra in one of his previous existences was similarly deceived by his wife; he was in that existence Haris'ikha, the son of a priest to the king Brahmadatta. Haris'ikha entered a monastery in company with his elder brother Hariháyana. He subsequently fell in love with Lávanyavatí, the daughter of a king. The lady spared no pains to ingratiate herself in Haris'ikha's favor, and was successful. Hariháyana, deeply mortified at this sudden change in his brother, came to him and led him back to the monastery. I am that Hariháyana, and Chitra is Haris'ikha."

LXXXIX.—*Dharmaruchi* or *Timingila Avadána.* Some merchants of S'rávastí were returning from a prosperous voyage, when they fell within the tremendous jaws of a whale (timingila) of huge bulk. In utter helplessness they cried, "salutation to Buddha, salutation to Buddha, salutation to Buddha," and they were saved. They obtained Arhatship by worshipping Lord Buddha who then resided at S'rávastí. Beholding the miraculous deliverance of the merchants' ship, the whale ceased to be a carnivorous animal, and died from want of proper food. The Nágas, unable to bear the putrid smell of the whale's carcass, threw it upon the sea-shore, where the bones formed a hill of no small height.

After the death of the whale its soul was born in the family of a Bráhman, and was named Dharmaruchi. The new-born babe was so voracious that his hunger could not be appeased with the milk of a hundred women. When grown up, he became a Bhikshu with the sole object of getting plenty of food. But his appetite was nowhere satisfied. One day he ate up alone a feast prepared for a whole Buddhist congregation (sangha). The host, alarmed at his voraciousness, fled with his family to where lord Buddha dwelt. The Lord said, "fear not; he is neither a Yaksha, nor a Rákshasa; he is Dharmauchi, a Bhikshu destined one day to obtain Arhatship." The Lord then took Dharmaruchi to the above-mentioned bone-hill, and reminded him of his doings in his previous existence, which excited in his mind a feeling of resignation. He obtained Arhatship from the Lord Buddha.

The Bhikshus asked the Lord what were the merits that raised Dharmaruchi to such an eminence. The Lord said, "in a previous kalpa, there was a patriarch, Dhamas'ila by name. He raised a stúpa in honor of Khemaṅkara, a Buddha, in spite of strong opposition from an anti-buddhist party. He had for his ally only one man, named, Sahasrayodhi. I am that patriarch Dharmaṣila, and Sahasrayodhi is Dharmaruchi. In another kalpa two Bráhmaṇa brothers, Mati and Sumati, appeared at the sacrifice of Vásava, king of Benares. They obtained whatever they sought from the king. The king's daughter, named Sundarí became enamoured of Sumati; but her suit was rejected by the stern Bráhmaṇa. Thus deeply mortified, she resigned the world, and became a Bhikshuṇí. Sumati dreamt a strange dream, for the explanation of which he repaired, by the advice of rishi Parṇáda, to Lord Dvípankara, who lived at Dvípávatí. There he met Sundarí, and asked flowers from her. When offering him the flowers Sundarí prayed that he be her husband in the next existence. Sumati fell prostrate before the lord with his clotted hair scattered all over the ground. Lord Dvípankara trod them down, exclaiming, 'you shall become a great Buddha, S'ákyamuni by name.' Mati, who was standing by, felt his Bráhmanic pride scandalized by the unbrahmanly conduct of his brother; but Sumati induced him to revere the Lord. I am that Sumati, Yas'odhará is Sundarí, and Mati is Dharmaruchi."

In another kalpa, during the advent of Krakuchchanda, a great Buddha, there lived, at Ujjayiní, a merchant's wife, named Kámabalá. During her husband's absence she accepted her son As'vadatta for her paramour, and poisoned her husband on his return home. To evade punishment she fled with her son to some foreign country, where As'vadatta finding her in the embrace of another, put a period to her guilty existence. As'vadatta afterwards became a Buddhist, and was fond of repeating the formula 'namo buddháya, namo buddháya.' As'vadatta is the same person as Dharmaruchi.

XC.—*Dhanika Avadána.* The Bráhmans of Vais'ali passed a

decree, banishing from the town every one who invited Buddha to his house. The householder Dhanika, unmindful of the decree, invited Buddha who had been dwelling at Kúṭágára by the side of lake Markaṭa. Dhanika, his wife, his son, and his daughter-in-law were all staunch Buddhists. They feasted him for four days. When the Bráhmans tried to enforce their decree, Dhanika succeeded in appeasing them.

The Lord said—"During a terrible famine, Dhanika, in his previous existence, had granted the only piece of cloth his family had to a Pratyeka Buddha, and hence his prosperity and influence."

XCI.—*Subháshitá Avadána.* The great city of Kús'i was celebrated for its Gymnasium. The athletes of the place had all been converted and raised to the rank of Arhats by Lord Buddha. They were very fond of religious talk. The Lord was one day greatly delighted by their conversation. He said, he was, in all his previous existences fond of religious discourse. In course of one of these, he gave his own flesh to a Rákshasa for a moral saying. The monster at last proved to be Indra in disguise, come to test his character. The purport of the saying was, that all the impressions of the human mind are momentary like the flash of lightning.

XCII.—*Maitrakanyaka Avadána, vide* Avadána S'ataka.

XCIII.—*Sumágadhá Avadána.* Sumágadhá, daughter of Anáthapiṇḍada, was married to a person at Pauṇḍravardhana. Her father-in-law, on one occasion, invited some Jinas to his house. They were all naked, and without the least sense of propriety. Shocked at their complete nudity and their want of good breeding, Sumágadhá exclaimed, "Oh how infinitely superior is our Lord to these boorish wretches." On her mother-in-law expressing a desire to see the Lord. Sumágadhá, ascending the highest roof of the house, worshipped Buddha with flowers and incense. The flowers fell at the Lord's feet at the Jetavana grove. Through his omniscience the Lord knew from what direction the flowers had come. Instantly he presented himself at Pauṇḍravardhana, where he was received with the highest honor.

"Sumágadhá once was," said the Lord, "Kánchanamálá, the daughter of Kriki; she had accepted the ascetic condition with five hundred handmaids under the instructions of Kás'yapa."

In another existence she honored a stúpa with a garland of orange flowers.

XCIV.—*Yas'omitra* or *Sundara Avadána.* Yas'omitra, son of Punyamitra, had a fountain of pure limpid water at the root of each of his incisor teeth, so he was perfectly ignorant of what thirst was.

The Bhikshus enquiring after the origin of this strange phenomenon, the Lord replied: "Sundara, son of a banker of Benares, acting under the instruction of Lord Kás'yapa, became a hermit. Suffering intensely from thirst he could not anywhere find water; wells, tanks and even rivers dried up at his sight. When he was on the point of death for want of water, Lord Kás'yapa compassionately filled his vessel up, and made its contents inexhaustible. The Lord took a palmful of water from the waterpot, which conferred so great a merit on Sundara that he never lost his supply of water."

XCV.—*Sanku-Sandhidatta Avadána.* Sanku and Sandhidatta, two brothers, lost their father Arthadatta, a merchant of Rájagriha, when they were very young. Their mother brought them up with great difficulty, and, when they grew up, employed them in pilfering. The thieves were detected by the vigilant police of Ajátaṣatru, and sentenced capitally. At the place of their execution Buddha interposed in their favor, rescued them from the gallows, and carried them to his hermitage, where they soon rose to the exalted rank of Arhats.

The Lord said, "In one of their former existences, they were the cubs of a hungry tigress from whose jaws I preserved their lives by offering my own."

XCVI.—*Kunjara Avadána.* King Udayana of Avantí was taking a walk in one of his gardens with five hundred of his wives, when five hundred holy men entered the garden to gather flowers. Some of them cast sidelong glances at the royal wives. The king took umbrage at their conduct, and ordered their hands and legs to be cut off. The order was instantly executed. The holy men screamed loudly from excruciating pain. Buddha, who was near, heard their groans with compassion, and looked at them with an eye of grace. They got their legs and hands back by a miracle.

The Lord said "Five hundred ministers of Brahmadatta, king of Benares, afraid of the effects of the king's anger at their neglect of duty, fled through the desert. They were entertained with water and fruits by an elephant which lived there. They settled in the neighbourhood of the elephant's dwelling, and, when it died, gave it a grand funeral. I am that elephant."

XCVII.—*Kachchhapa Avadána.* When the Lord lived at the Venuvana grove at Rájagriha, the envious Devadatta sent five hundred well-armed hermits to put an end to Buddha's existence. They all made the Lord their aim at one and the same time. Thousands of weapons were simultaneously poured on him from all quarters. But in passing through space these were transformed into so many garlands of sweet-scented flowers. The hermits on their knees begged his pardon, which was instantly granted. They gradually rose to the rank of Arhats.

The Lord said, "These hermits had been, in one of their previous existences, merchants at Benares. On a sea voyage their ships had all wrecked. But they were all saved by myself in the shape of a tortoise. But when I was fast asleep they wanted to eat my flesh. I awaked, and, having found them extremely hungry, offered them my own body and obtained the highest merit."

XCVIII.—*Kus'alas'ilá Avadána.* The Lord entertained a large number of famine-stricken hungry athletes, converted them to his own faith, and raised them to the rank of Arhats.

He said "The athletes of Koṭá obtained the highest knowledge from the preaching of Kus'álas'íla, a hermit. I am that holy hermit."

XCIX.—*Pàdmaka Avadána.* To be found in the As'oka Avadána, *ante*, p. 15.

C.—*Prabhása Avadána.* Prasenajit, king of Kos'ala, asked the Lord, saying, "O Lord, tell me truly in what existence did the desire for Sambodhi first arise in your mind?"

The Lord replied, "When I was Prabhása, king of Prabhávatí, I had an elephant who went to the forest out of his love to a female consort, and returned to my stable again. My elephant-driver, who was very proud of his skill in training elephants, boasted before me, saying, 'Sire, you see my skill, the elephant comes to the stable again.' I asked him, 'Was there any man who was superior to all temptations?' He said, 'Yes, there are Tathágatas. It is by their glory that the earth is enlightened.' From that day I felt a craving for Bodhi knowledge."

CI.—*Syámáka Avadána.*

CII.—*Siñha-kunjara Avadána.* One evening the Lord was conversing familiarly with all his Bhikshus at the Jetavana grove. The conversation turned on an inquiry about the origin of philanthropy. Is it a natural propensity, the result of accumulated deeds of merit, or of constant practice? The Lord said, " even ferocious animals, like lions, are susceptible to that feeling. For instance, a company of merchants were on the point of being devoured by a large venomous serpent, on the seashore. They screamed aloud at the prospect of instant death; their screams were heard by a lion and an elephant. They fell from a high hill on the serpent and crushed him to death. But they themselves lost their lives from the poisonous breath of the dying reptile. I am that lion, Sáriputra is the elephant, and Devadatta is the reptile."

CIII.—*Priyapiṇḍa Avadána.* Priyapiṇḍa, son of Vajrapiṇḍa, king of Vajravatí, by Rohiní, daughter of Meru, king of Gangádhípatya, was born with a grand jewelled parasol over his head. On his coming to the throne he gave away his whole property for the good of the animal creation. Durmati, his minister, to get the throne for himself, instigated Meru, maternal grandfather to the king, to war. Always averse to bloodshed, Priyapiṇḍa proceeded to his grandfather's capital to appease him. There by his own fiat he created a rich banquet for all his men. At this the grandfather thought him to be a god, and honored him as such.

The Lord said " Priyapiṇḍa had been in a former life, Mulika, a physician practising at Benares; he had cured a Pratyeka Buddha of a mortal disease, and given him a painted umbrella. I am that Priyapiṇḍa, and Devadatta is that wicked Durmati."

CIV.—*S'as'aka Avadána.* See p. 50.

CV.—*Raivataka Avadána.* Raivataka, a bhikshu of S'aila Vihára at Kás'míra, was boiling water in order to dye his cloth at a retired spot, when there came in a Bráhmaṇa who had lost his cow. He asked the Bhikshu what was he about. On receiving the Bhíkshu's reply the Bráhmaṇa came to the boiling vessel, and to the utter ruin of the Bhikshu found it full of blood and beef. The Bráhmaṇa brought a criminal suit against the Bhikshu, who was sentenced to 12 years' imprisonment for theft. On his release, at the expiration of the term, he gave the following explanation of his suffering. He was, in a previous existence, a cattle-lifter; once on a time having stolen and killed a cow, he had pointed to a Pratyeka Buddha as the real culprit; he suffered imprisonment for that sin.

CVI.—*Kaṇakavarṇá Avadána.* Kaṇaka was king of the city of Káṇakavatí. A minister's son was found guilty of carrying on an intrigue with the king's daughter, Kaṇakavarṇá. They were both ordered by the king to the place of execution. But the king's son, Kaṇakavarmá, who was very fond of his sister, exerted in their favour, and succeeded in sending them away from Kaṇakavatí. The king enraged at the disobedience of his son, banished him from the city. The banished prince travelled through various cities, and arrived at last at the deserted city where his sister dwelt. Being apprised that the city was depopulated by the destructive ravages of 60,000 Yakshas, he destroyed them all single-handed (except one that sought his protection), took the administration of the city in his own hands, and appointed the minister's banished son as his prime-minister. The Lord said, "I am that Prince."

CVII.—*Suddhodana Avadána.* Suddhodana, a merchant of Benares, received the benefit of hearing a good saying at the sacrifice of all his wealth which he bestowed on Bálasarasvatí, the daughter of Brahmadatta. The Lord was that Suddhodana, who was the speaker of it.

CVIII.—*Jímútaváhana Avadána.* Jímútaketu, the king of Kánchanapura, according to the custom of ancient Hindu Rájás, abdicated the throne in favor of his son Jímútaváhana, and proceeded to the mount Malaya to seek salvation. His son used to go there to pay his respect to his old father. One day he found on the mount a beautiful girl, whom he married. She was the daughter of Vís'vavasu, king of the Siddhas. The married couple took a long walk in the hills, when they suddenly met a female Nága sobbing aloud. According to an agreement with Garuḍa, her son was that day to offer himself up as food to that bird-king. Jímútaváhana offered to go in his stead, and soothed the weeping mother's mind. He sat at the place agreed upon, when Garuḍa in a long swoop struck his monstrous bill on the crown of the prince's head. His wife, supposing him dead, kindled a funeral pyre, and exclaimed when on the point of ascending it, "O Haravallabhá, (the favorite of Hara) you promised me a bridegroom who was to have empire over the Vidyádharas. But you see my widowhood commences before a week is past, after our happy union. How can the words of a chaste one like thee be false?" Instantly

Haravallabhá sent a nectareous shower and resuscitated Jímútaváhana. This story has been dramatised in the Nágánanda of S'ríharsha.

Beginning. नमो रत्नत्रयाय । ये हेलोच्छलितप्रभावलहरीजाताद्भुतश्रेणयः
सत्त्वोत्साहभुवः स्वभावविमलज्ञानप्रकाशाश्रयाः ।
आज्ञालेख्यलिपिं विधातृनृपतेः संसक्तकर्मावलीं
चित्रं तेऽपि न लङ्घयन्ति कुटिलां वेलामिवाम्भोधयः ॥

End. या च भू भूरिभूष्टत्वतसलिलवलन्मालिका शेषशीर्षे
मायूरच्छत्रशोभामनुभवति फणारश्मिरत्नप्रतानैः ।
धत्ते यावत् सुमेरुः क्षितितलकमले कर्णिकाकारकान्तिं
शास्तुस्तावत् कथेयं कलयतु जगतां कर्णिकारप्रतिष्ठां ॥

Colophon. समाप्ता बोधिसत्त्वावदानकल्पलता । कृतिरियं महाकवेः क्षेमेन्द्रस्य ।

BUDDHA-CHARITRA.

बुद्धचरित्रम् ।

Substance, paper, 10 × 6½ inches. Folia, 81. Lines on a page, 23. Extent in s'lokas, 2445. Character, Newári. Samvat 1878. Prose and verse. Incorrect.

An episode in the story of the wars between the gods and the demons, in which a girl named Ánandá, deputed by the Lord Buddha, overcame many she-demons. By Nathamala *alias* Náthuráma Brahmachárí. In the portion of the earth called Ilávrata-khaṇḍa there reigned a powerful king of the demons, Buddha by name. He had eleven great marshals. The gods trembled at his name. Once on a time, the gods and the demons had an encounter in the way leading to the southern country. After the slaughter of many thousand demons, Brahmá ordered Vis'vakarmá to prepare a battle-field at the foot of the Himálaya, and requested Súrasena, king of Udyota, to come to his aid. Súrasena came with a well-appointed army led by his sons Jayasena and Kálasena. There were several battles fought, in many of which the female demons took part. Lord Buddha sent a girl, named Ánandá, who vanquished the heroines on the side of the Daityas. The book ends with the description of the heroic achievements of Gangá on the Buddhist, and Raktabhakshá on the enemy's side.

This codex contains a dictionary of the Mátrikás, or such mystic terms as Om, An, &c.

Beginning. ॐ नमो गणेशाय। अतः परं प्रवक्ष्यामि उत्तरं स च युद्धादि तच्चेदमभवि-
ष्यत्कारणा बुधाभिधानं महादैत्यः तेन पराक्रमं महत्तं कृतं युद्धानां नगसहु-
चरकैरपि युद्धसमयस्तच कृतं युद्धं महत्तरं नानास्त्रप्रहारास्त्रयुद्धं चैव दुर्मद-
कृतं तेन च दैत्येन बुधेन च दुरात्मना। नगनगसहुचरकै अत्यते पराक्रम-
हतस्तेन नानावाणैः प्रहारणैर्महावीरो महाधीर यथा पूर्व्वकृतयुद्ध तथा तेन
कृतं महत् नानाशास्त्रप्रहारणैश्च कृतं तेन दुरात्मना देवैश्च दानवैस्तन युद्ध
तत्र महद्भुतां।

End. महायोद्धा महावीर आगतो तद्रणे शुभे अत्यत शुरो बलवान् शतवाणाश्च
प्रेरिश्चात्ततं युद्धे च तचैव दशवाणै हता खटा पञ्चवाणै छिता स खरथस्य
वधता कथा बहवशैस्ततास्तस्य खण्डखण्डनसंशयकृतं तत्र महादिव्यं धकयस
मचमदा पञ्चाशद्वाणकैस्तम सारथिताडिता च पश्चिणि वाणै ताडितं चैव
कपोले दैत्ययुग च महाघोराश्च दैत्याश्च मूर्च्छागतमानया पश्चादुत्थाय दैत्योऽसौ
रथभ्रष्टो दुरात्मन जग्राह परिघं घोरं धावितो घन्तु वै यदा तदा च कालचक्रेण
चक्रे +त्वा शिरश्छिनत् मस्तकं पतितं भूमौ हाहाकारं तदाऽभूत्।

Colophon. इति श्रीबुद्धचरित्रे श्रीनखमलब्रह्मचारिविरचिते पिशाचकालचक्रयुद्धवर्णनं ।

CHHANDOMṚITALATA.

छन्दोऽमृतलता।

Substance, paper, 10¾ × 4 inches. Folia, 47. Lines on a page, 8. Extent in s'lokas, 758. Character, Nágara. Prose and verse. Old. Incorrect.

This work is divided into six Manjaris, and lays down rules regarding Sanskrit metres. The metres noticed are what are used in ordinary Sanskrit compositions. None of the Vedic metres has been noticed. By Amritánanda.

Beginning. ॐ नमो रत्नत्रयाय। देवं प्रणम्य शाक्येन्द्रं जयलक्ष्मीसमुद्भवः।
श्रीरामानन्दनन्दनयोऽमृतानन्दोऽतनोदिमां ॥
बहूनि विदुषां सन्ति छन्दःशास्त्राणि यद्यपि।
सारमाहृत्य सर्व्वेभ्यश्छेदनार्थोऽयमुद्यमः ॥

शाक्यमाहात्म्यकुसुमा गद्यपद्याखिलसङ्कुला ।
इयं छन्दोऽमृतलता विद्वत्कण्ठे लगिष्यति ॥
पद्यं चतुर्भिश्चरणैः समेतं इत्तं तथा जात्यभिधानमेतत् ।
इत्ताभिधानस्याचरसङ्ख्ययुक्तं(?) मात्राकृतं जात्यभिधं द्विधा तत् ॥

End. व्यवहारोदितं प्रायो मया छन्दोऽत्र कीर्त्तितं ।
प्रस्तारा हि पुनर्मोक्षं केवलं कौतुकं हि तत् ॥

Colophon. इति छन्दोऽमृतलतायां गद्यप्रभेदा षष्ठी मञ्जरी समाप्ता ।

DHARANI-MANTRA-SANGRAHA.

धरणीमन्त्रसङ्ग्रहः ।

Substance, paper, 10¼ × 3¾ inches. Folia, 171. Lines on a page, 6. Extent in s'lokas, 2180. Character, Newári. Prose and verse. Incorrect. Old.

This work treats of the A'ryaharáhara, A'ryábhayakári and other Dharaṇí mantras, and gives the rules for the meditation of those mantras.

Beginning. ॐ नमो वज्रसत्त्वाय । ॐ नमो बुद्धाय गुरवे । ॐ नमः सङ्घाय महत्तमाय ।
विहरति कनकाद्रौ शाक्यसिंहो मुनीन्द्रोऽपरिमितसुरसङ्घैः सेव्यमानो जनौघैः ।
कुवलयदलनेत्रो लक्षणैर्युक्तगात्रः स भवधिततष्ट(?) सर्व्वलोकहितार्थः ॥
ये देवाः सन्ति मेरौ वरकनकमये मन्दिरे ये भुजङ्गा-
+++++++स्फणिमणिकिरणा ध्वस्तसर्व्वान्धकाराः ।
कैलासे स्त्रीविलासैः प्रमुदितहृदया ये च विद्याधरेन्द्रा-
स्ते मोक्षद्वारभूतं मुनिवरवचनं श्रोतुमायान्ति सर्व्वे ॥
आयान्ति श्रोतुकामा असुरसुरगणाः सिद्धगन्धर्व्वनागाः
कुष्माण्डाः किन्नरेन्द्रा गरुडहरिहराः शक्रब्रह्मादिदेवाः ।
पूजां पञ्चोपचारैस्त्रिभुवननमितं मेदिनीदुर्लभोऽयं
भक्त्याहं रचयामि प्रणमितशिरसा तं महायानसूत्रं ॥
ॐ नमः श्रीआर्य्यावलोकितेश्वराय । अथ खलु मैत्रेयो बोधिसत्त्वो महासत्त्वः भगवन्तं शाक्यमुनिं तथागतं अर्हन्तं सम्यग्बुद्धं प्रणम्यैवमाह । अभिज्ञानाम्यहं रत्नकेतोस्तथागतस्य सम्मुखं श्रुतं । आर्य्यावलोकितेश्वरस्य बोधिसत्त्वस्य महासत्त्वस्य हराहरानामकहृदयमन्त्रं ।

End. राजा उत्फुल्लहृदयो भूत्वा ससम्भ्रमं श्रीवसुधारापादाम्बुजे शिरसा प्रणम्य सन्तोष्य उक्तश्च यथा देवी प्रसन्ना भूयात् तथा करोमि व्रतसम्पूर्णं कृत्वा राजा प्रभृतिसर्व्वसत्त्वास्तुसिभवने नीयन्ते। राजपुत्रमेकं यौवराज्ये स्थापयित्वा धर्म्म-देशनार्थं तेन पौरजनेन सर्व्वमर्त्यमण्डले प्रकाशयित्वा सुखेन तिष्ठति।

Colophon. इति श्रीवसुधाराव्रतपूर्व्वमर्त्यमण्डलगतकथा समाप्ता।

No. B. 42.

DAS'ABHU'MI'S'VARA.

दशभूमीश्वरः।

Substance, paper $10\frac{1}{2} \times 3\frac{3}{4}$. Folia, 221. Lines on a page, 6. Extent in s'lokas, 3,397. Prose and verse. Old. · Incorrect.

A treatise on the ten different stages which a person must pass through, before he can attain Buddhahood. These stages are technically called *Bhúmis*, and thence the codex derives its specific name. It forms one of the nine Dharmas or sacred scriptures of the Nepalese Buddhists, and is held in high esteem. It must also be of considerable antiquity as it was carried to China at an early age. It was translated into Chinese under the name of *Shi-chu-king*, by Kumárajíva and another.

Like most of the Maháyána Sútras, it is narrative in form, and professes to have been related by Buddha himself. The scene is laid in the heaven of Indra, where the Lord was residing amidst the gods, who were very obedient to him in the expectation of obtaining the highest bliss through his favour. During the second week of his residence in the celestial palace, in company of the recently converted Devarája and a large company of Bodhisattvas, one of the latter, Vajragarbha by name, performed, by his permission, the meditation named *Maháyánaprabháva*, or 'the glory of the great Translation.' Ten Buddhas, resplendent in brilliant beams of light, manifested their divine presence on all sides of Vajragarbha by their superhuman power. They touched Vajragarbha with their hands without stirring from their seats. This touch interrupted the meditations of the Bodhisattva. On awaking he enumerated the names of the ten *Bhúmis* or progressive conditions of Bodhisattvas. *Viz.*, Pramuditá, Vimalá, Prabhákarí, Archishmatí, Sudurjayá, Abhimukhí, Dúrangamá, Achalá, Sádhumatí and Dharmamedhyá. He then addressed the Buddhas, saying, "O sons of Jinas, you know all the stages of knowledge of the Buddhas, past, present and future." At the mention of the ten *bhúmis* the curiosity of the other Bodhisattvas was awakened, and they solicited, through Muktichandra as their mouthpiece, an account of what those *Bhúmis* were. Vajragarbha replied, " a person of honest resolution should expel from his mind all doubts and disbelief by his unswerving devotion to hundreds of thousands and millions of Buddhas." He was proceeding further, when rays of light issued forth from the pores of Buddha's body, brightly illuminating the persons and seats of the Devas, Buddhas and others. Vajragarbha then continued ; " the condition in which a person meditates upon the Lord of religion, the immeasurable Buddha pervading all space, formed of the essence of Dharma, introducer of all knowledge and wisdom, is called *Pramuditá*. He who enters this stage rises superior to all the rules that bind the *Bodhisattvas*, and elevates himself far above ordinary men. He is taken in the family of Tathágatas, and is not contaminated by his intercourse with people of any low caste." The mental tendencies which are characteristic of this Bhúmi are—disinterested mercy, disinterested love for created beings, charity, resignation, knowledge of the S'ástras, knowledge of the world, suppression of fear, patience, worship of Buddha and devotion to him. These are the ten Dharmas or qualities attainable in this stage.

He who has acquired all these qualities becomes desirous of rising up to the stage called *Vimalá*. The characteristics of this stage are,—desire for simplicity, for tender-heartedness, for activity, for consulting others' for equality, for doing good, for purity, for impartiality, for large-heartedness and for magnanimity. These are generically called the ten *Ásayas* or ' desires,' and they tend to show him the way to good works.

When these desires are well established and purified, men rise to the third stage called *Prabhákarí*. The mental condition of the person who has attained this stage is characterised by ten tendencies or *chittásaya-namaskáráh*. These are—1, purity of mind ; 2, tranquillity of mind ; 3, faith ; 4, immovableness of mind ; 5, firmness ; 6, ardency of mind ; 7, retentiveness of mind ; 8, frankness of mind ; 9, magnanimity of mind (the tenth is omitted). In this stage men have their essence purified and their heart freed from grief.

In the next, the 4th stage, or that of *Archishmatí*, the aspirant to perfection is enlightened by ten different sorts of religious lights, *viz.*, (1), the light that shows the movements or workings of existence ; (2), that which shows the movements of regions; (3), that which shows the movements or workings of qualities; (4), that which shows the working of Ákás'a or space; (5), that which shows the movements of cognition; (6), that which shows the movements of desire; (7), that which shows the movements of form; (8), that which shows the movements of formlessness; (9), that which shows the movements which lead to separation from all ambition; (10), that which shows the movements that lead to separation from magnanimity. When he has acquired these lights, he acquires ten different powers which are calculated to fit him for the reception of true knowledge. These are: (1), the desire of remaining undistinguishable; (2), the vision of the three jewels and their equal favor; (3), the thought of the rise and cessation of the impressions; (4), the thought of the non-creation of nature; (5), the thought of men's inclinations; (6), the thought of the performance of work; (7), the thought of the annihilation of the world; (8), the thought of works under all circumstances; (9), the thought of the beginning and the end; (10), the thought of non-existence.

From this stage the devotee passes to the fifth or *Durjayá* stage. In this he acquires the ten-fold purifications of his mind. (*Chittásaya-vissuddhimatá.*) These are: (1), the purity of the past of Buddhadharma; (2), that of the future of the same; (3), that of the present of the same; (4), that of the discipline; (5), that of the mind; (6), that of sight; (7), that of means proper and improper; (8), that of imagiuation; (9), that of reflection of the future of true knowledge; (10), that of capacity for assimilating the truth. In this stage a Bodhisattva obtains a variety of transcendental powers, and his memory, his judgment, his modesty and his patience all become strengthened.

The sixth stage is called *Abhimukhí.* In this stage the devotee acquires the idea of ten religious equalities, namely: (1), equality in the causes of all Dharmas; (2), equality in the definition of all Dharmas; (3), equality of the non-origin of all Dharmas; (4), equality in all Dharmas; (5), equality in the diversion of all Dharmas; (6), equality in the purity of all Dharmas; (7), equality in the absoluteness of all Dharmas; (8), that of Niryuha; (9), equality in the reflection of these Dharmas in one another, like the reflection of the moon in transparent water; (10), equality in the lustre of two different Dharmas. In this stage man acquires the power of discrimination, or the power of judging things aright, understands the world to be mere delusion, and alleviates the mundane pains of himself and others.

Dúrañgamá is the seventh stage. In this stage the man acquires the power of chalking out a way for acquiring Bodhi knowledge by wisdom and other means. Under no circumstance does his mind go astray from the right path. He devotes his whole soul to Tathágata.

The eighth stage is *Achalá*. One well established in this stage, understands all truth about physical organization.

In the ninth or *Sádhumatí* stage a man can look through the minds of others. He always has goodness in a bodily form by him, and Lord Buddha presents himself before the vision of his mental eye.

A Bodhisattva, having received the full development attainable in the ninth stage, invades the tenth or Dharmamedhyá bhúmi. When he has performed, to his complete satisfaction, all the duties of this stage, he becomes endowed with manifold attributes of wonderful power. These ten stages of perfection are similar to the four stages of the Vaishṇavas and the Sufis.

Beginning. ॐ नमः श्रीवज्रसत्त्वाय । ॐ नमः सर्व्वबुद्धबोधिसत्त्वेभ्यः ।
यस्मिन् पारमिता दशोत्तरगुणा तैस्तैर्नयैः सूचिता
सर्व्वज्ञेन जगद्धिताय दश च प्रख्यापिता भूमयः ।
उच्छेदध्रुवनिर्ज्जिता च विमला प्राप्ता गतिर्मध्यमा
तत् सर्वं दशभूमिकं निगदितं शृण्वन्तु बोध्यर्थिनः ॥

End. सर्व्वावती पर्षत् भगवतो वज्रगर्भस्य भाषितमभ्यनन्दन् ।

Colophon. इति श्रीबोधिसत्त्वचर्य्याप्रस्थानो नाम महायानसूत्ररत्नराजः समाप्तः ।

No. B. 30.

DURGATI-PARIS'ODHANA.

दुर्गतिपरिशोधनम् ।

Substance, paper, 14 × 4 inches. Folia, 22. Lines on a page, 10. Extent in s'lokas, 1,196. Date, Samvat 734. Character, Newári. Appearance, old. Prose and verse. Incorrect.

Descriptions of certain forms of meditations inculcated by the Lord Vajrapáṇi during his sojourn in the Nandana grove of Indra, the audience being composed of Devas. The yogas taught were Durgati-parishodhana-rája, A'diyoga, Karma-rájas'rí, Akálamrityuharaṇa, and so on. The work extends to eleven chapters.

Beginning. ॐ नमः श्रीवज्रसत्त्वाय । एवं मया श्रुतमेकस्मिन् समये भगवान् सर्व्वदेवोत्तमो नन्दनवने विहरति स्म । मणिसुवर्णशाखालताबद्धवनस्पतिगुल्मौषधिकमलो-त्पलकर्णिकारवकुलतिलकाशोकमन्दारमहामन्दारादिभिर्नानाविधैः पुष्पैरुप-शोभिते कल्पवृक्षसमलङ्कृते नानालङ्कारभूषिते नानापक्षिगणकूजिते तूर्य्य-मकुन्दवेणुभेरीप्रभृतिप्रणादिते शक्रब्रह्मादिदेवासुरैर्भिर्नानाविधाभिः क्रीड़िते सर्व्वबुद्धबोधिसत्त्वाधिष्ठिते सर्व्वशक्रब्रह्मादिविद्याधरदेवासुरःपञ्चकोटिनियुत-शतसहस्रैरनेकयक्षराक्षसासुरगन्धर्व्वकिन्नरमहोरगनागादिपर्षद्भिर्नानाविधाभिर्म-हाबोधिसत्त्वकोटिशतसहस्रैरष्टाभिः ।

End. इदमवोचद्भगवानात्तमनाः शक्रब्रह्मादिदेवपर्षत् सदेवमानुषासुरगन्धर्व्वयक्ष-राक्षसादिश्चितसुखावाप्तये भगवतो भाषितमभ्यनन्दद्विति ।

Colophon. इति सर्व्वदुर्गतिपरिशोधनतेजोराजस्य तथागतस्यार्हतः सम्यक्सम्बुद्धस्य कल्पैका-दशः समाप्तः ।

No. B. 41.

DVA'VIÑS'A AVADA'NA.

द्वाविंशावदानं ।

Substance, paper, 15 × 4½ inches. Folia, 94. Lines on a page, 6. Extent in s'lokas, 2,500. Date, ? Character, Newárí. Appearance, new. Verse. Incorrect.

A collection of twenty-two stories illustrating the merits of devotion to Buddhism and to the duties enjoined by it. The author's name is not given; but from the form of salutation at the beginning of the work, it is evident that the work is accepted by the Buddhists to be due to a private person. The codex professes to be complete; but owing to errors in numbering the stories, or some other cause, only nineteen stories have been found in it. The scene is laid at the Kukkuṭa Vihára near Rájagriha, where As'oka expressed a wish to hear the stories, and his spiritual instructor, Upa Gupta, narrated them, alleging them to have been originally related at that place by Buddha himself to his disciples.

I.—*Ratnavyúha Avadána.* The first story is intended to illustrate the merit of devoting money for the repairs of Buddhist monuments.

While the Lord was lecturing his disciples on the merits of alms-giving, in came a prince named Ratnavyúha, dazzling the eyes of the beholders by the splendour of his jewels. After paying his respects to the Lord, he departed. The Bhikshus enquired what were the high merits which had raised the visitor to such a dizzy eminence?

The Lord said in one of his previous existences the Rájá was a boatman. But he repaired a broken dilapidated stúpa situated at the village of Kús'í in the country of Malla, and from the merit thereof had been born a prince and owner of profuse wealth.

II.—*S'ántamati Avadána.* The second story (numbered IV in the codex) illustrates the merits of charity.

To show a miracle, Buddha produced a heavenly light from his woollen garment. The light delighted a banker so much that he immediately gathered some flowers, and threw them over the Lord's head. These formed a splendid parasol. The S'reshṭhí, dying in a short time, was born in the heaven of Indra. There he remembered what had made him a Devaputra; he descended on earth, worshipped Buddha, heard his discourses, acquired the Bodhi knowledge, and obtained nirváṇa. The Bhikshus asked what was the cause of this banker's speedy elevation. The Lord said, "Sántamati, a poor banker of Kus'í, always attended the lectures of the Buddhist preachers. One day he gave his own food (having nothing else to spare) to a Bhikshu. The Bhikshu's benediction was, that he should be a rich man and a sincere Buddhist. In a month, while pouring water on a neighbouring stúpa, he found that he was pouring hot water and rubies and diamonds; he went to the ghât whence he had drawn the water, and found there a heap of jewels. He took them up, but instead of enjoying them, devoted them to charity, and always prayed for nirváṇa. This S'ántamati," added the Lord, "was the present banker who obtained the *summum bonum* of Buddhist faith."

III.—*Uttírṇa Avadána.* A merchant, named Uttírṇa died in a ship-wreck. He went to heaven, and there became a Devaputra. His young wife prayed the Lord to show her in a dream where her husband then was. In a dream her husband appeared before her, and informed her what had happened. She kept a fast for eight days in a "love-circle" (प्रणयचक्र), and, after death, was transformed into a Devakanyá. She lived in peace with her husband.

The Bhikshus enquired what had raised the couple so high?

The Lord gave the following history of their previous existence: "King Prádes'ika-maṇḍalina was taught in the doctrine of Ahiñs'á, or non-injury to created beings, by Dharmaruchi, a Rishi, but, forgetting his precepts, Prádes'ika killed a hind. The animal cursed him saying that he should die in a shipwreck. Uttírṇa is that cursed king."

IV.—*Kshatríyarája Avadána.* One day while Buddha was preaching, Indra came down to worship him. The Bhikshus asked why should the king of the Devas honor a mortal? Buddha replied, "In one of my transmigrations I was a Kshatríya king; I honored Kshemañkara in every way, and erected a large stúpa to his honor, and hence my greatness."

V.—*Dhátustejá Avadána.* Dhatustejá, son of Dharmakalpa, a king of Dakshiṇápatha, came to visit the Lord, and was immediately sanctified. The Bhikshus enquired what the youth had done to deserve such honor. The Lord said: "In the 91st kalpa, Lord Vipas'yí lived in the metropolis of king Bandhumati. When the lord departed from this world, the king caused to be erected on his remains a stúpa, a mile high, and a merchant's son decorated it with jewels. That king is now Dharmakalpa, and the merchant's son is the prince.

VI.—*Chandraprabha Avadána.* Chandraprabha, coming by the aerial way, asked the Lord how the series of transmigrations can be put a stop to. Receiving the proper answer from Buddha, he returned home. The resplendent brightness of Chandraprabha's person struck the beholders with wonder; they became inquisitive about the cause of his good fortune. His merit consisted in bestowing a golden circle in the Great Víhára of Vípas'yí, who flourished in the 91st kalpa in the metropolis of king Bandhumati. That grantor of the golden circle was subsequently born in the Kuru family and named Chandraprabha.

VII.—*Divyananda Avadána.* While Buddha was residing at Rájagriha, a householder invited him, feasted him, honored him, and desired Buddhahood from him. Buddha complied with his request. "I was that householder."

VIII.—*Purṇa Avadána.* The Bhikshus asked "O Lord, in what way did you get this power of working miracles?" Lord said, "as a Kshatríya king I feasted Buddha Purṇa for three months. That piece of good work has made me great."

IX.—*Dváriká Avadána.* While Kás'yapa preached at Benares, a girl, being asked for pure water, gave to eight Bhikshus a quantity of delicious sherbet. She was borne to heaven, where she never feels thirsty.

X.—*S'ukla Avadána.*

XI.—*S'reshṭhikanyá Avadána.*

XII.—*Mátsaryayukta Avadána.* A troop of Bráhmans, having made their obeisance to Buddha, expressed their desire to enter Pravrajyá or itinerancy. Instantly all were, by a miracle, shaved, and their clothes transformed into rags, except one who remained as he was. The Lord said, the cause of this exception was, that the person was full of Bráhmaṇic pride. On his solicitations, the Lord changed his clothes into rags, but these rags were all dirty. Being asked the cause of this, the Lord said, "that Bráhmaṇ, in one of his former existences, did not make his obeisance to Buddha Padmottara, disdaining to bow to a S'ramaṇa."

XIII.—*Vihára Avadána.* During Buddha's lifetime, the inhabitants of the city of Vihára were noted for their profligacy. Buddha sent some of his Bhikshus to chant a gáthá there. This simple expedient cured the citizens of their shameful immorality.

XIV.—*Kushṭhi Avadána.* A leper, without hands and without feet, circumambulated the famous stúpa of Vipas'yí several times. He was restored to his former health and vigour. A voice from heaven then recited the following :—

"He sat before the stúpa of Vipas'yí, covered his body with a heap of white cloth, plastered his body with all sorts of perfumes, and then set the whole on fire; the merit of his great deed raised him to the rank of a Pratyeka Buddha in one existence; in another he obtained nirváṇa."

XV.—*Surendradamana Avadána.*

XVI.—*Suvarnábha Avadána.*

XVII.—*Vapusmataḥ Avadána.*

XVIII.—*Chandana Avadána.*

XIX.—*Surúpa Avadána.*

Beginning. ॐ नमो भगवते श्रीगुणसागराय ।

नत्वा श्रीशाक्यकेतुं सुरगणसहितं देवदेवाधिदेवं
संसाराब्धेः स्रवन्तं सकलगुणनिधिं गौतमं बुद्धनाथं ।
संसारे सिंहनादं सकलभयहरं धर्म्मच्छत्रं मुनीन्द्रं
वक्ष्येऽहं धर्म्मरत्नं मुनिवरकथितं सर्व्वलोकाभिलाषं ॥
तद्यथाऽशोकभूमीन्द्रः कुक्कुटारामसंश्रितं ।
उपगुप्तं पुनः प्राह द्वाविंशतिकथोत्सुकः ॥

भदन्त श्रोतुमिच्छामि चैत्यसेवाकथां शुभां ।
श्रण्येवं धर्म्मपीयूषं त्वन्मुखाम्बुजनिर्गतं ॥
इति विज्ञप्तिमाकर्ण्य उपगुप्तः समादिशत् ।
शृणुश्लोक प्रवक्ष्यामि द्वाविंशत्यवदानकं ॥ तद्यथा,
विहरति भगवान् शास्ता सम्बुद्धो लोकनायकः
राजगृहे महोद्भासे गृध्रकूटे सुखालये ।
महता भिक्षुसङ्घेन सार्द्धं द्वादशभिः शतैः ॥

End. इत्यादिष्टं मुनीन्द्रेण श्रुत्वा सर्व्वेऽपि भिक्षवः ।
एवमस्त्विति प्राभाष्य प्रत्यनन्दन् प्रबोधिताः ॥
सभा सर्व्ववती सापि श्रुत्वैतत् सम्प्रसादिता ।
तथेति प्रतिवन्दित्वा प्रत्यनन्दन् प्रबोधिताः ॥

Colophon. इति श्रीद्वाविंशतिपुण्योत्साहावदानसूत्रं समाप्तं ।

No. 816 A.

GAṆAPATI-HRIDAYA.

गणपतिहृदयः ।

Substance, Nepalese yellow paper, 7½ × 3. Folia, 2. Lines on a page, 5. Extent in s'lokas, 10. Character, Newári. Date, ? Prose. Incorrect.

Mantras for an amulet in praise of Gaṇapati. The mantras are alleged to have been disclosed to A'nanda by Buddha himself when sojourning at Rájagriha. Whoever wears or recites them, or hears them recited, attains whatever he wishes. The mantras are of the usual mystic character common in Tántric works. They include such phrases as *Om namastu te Gaṇapataye sváháh*, *Om Gaṇapataye sváháh &c.* The most remarkable fact in connexion with this little work is the proof it affords of the Buddhists having adopted the adoration of Gaṇes'a, a purely Hindu deity.

Beginning. ॐ नमो भगवते आर्य्यगणपतिहृदयाय । ॐ नमो रत्नत्रयाय । एवं मया श्रुतमेकस्मिन् समये राजगृहे विहरति स्म । गृध्रकूटपर्व्वते महता भिक्षुसङ्घेन सार्द्धं त्रयोदशभिक्षुशतैः सम्बहुलैश्च बोधिसत्त्वमहासत्त्वैः तेन खलु पुनः समये भगवान् आयुष्मान्तमानन्दमामन्त्रयते स्म । यः कश्चित् कुलपुत्र आनन्द इमानि गणपतिहृदयानि धारयिष्यति वाचयिष्यति पर्य्यवाप्स्यन्ति ते प्रवर्त्तयिष्यन्ति तस्य

सर्व्वाणि कार्य्याणि सिद्धानि भविष्यन्ति । तद्यथा, ॐ नमोऽस्तु ते गणपतये स्वाहा इत्यादि ।

End. इदमवोचद् भगवानात्तमनाः ते च बोधिसत्त्वास्स सर्व्वावती पर्षत् सदेवमानुषासुरगरुड़गन्धर्व्वास्स लोका भगवतो भाषितमभ्यनन्दन्निति ।

Colophon. आर्य्यगणपतिहृदयनामधारणी समाप्ता ।

No. A. 9.

GAṆḌA-VYU'HA.

गण्डव्यूहः ।

Substance, paper, 17 × $6\frac{3}{4}$. Folia, 232. Lines on a page, 12. Extent in s'lokas, 13,929. Character, Newári. Appearance, old. Prose and verse. Incorrect.

The history of Sudhana in search of the perfect knowledge. The work is reckoned as one of the nine principal scriptures of the Buddhists, and held in high esteem. It was taken to China in the 7th century, and was translated into the Chinese language by Amoghavajra during the reign of the Tang dynasty. Its Chinese name is Ta-shing-mi-yen-king.

Once upon a time, while residing with Samantabhadra, Manjus'rí and others, lord Buddha showed them the marvellous workings of a certain mystic position called Siñha-vijrimbhita. As soon as the lord assumed that meditative position, the interior of the room expanded to an indefinite extent, the floor became thickly studded with sapphires and other precious stones, and gigantic pillars of solid emeralds supported the roof. A Bodhisattva, named Ras'miprabha, decorated the sky with clouds of various kinds, some showing heavenly flora, some raining nectarous perfumes.

Then Sáriputra, approaching Manjus'rí, made him acquainted with the presence of a host of holy Bhikshus. With them Manjus'rí started on a journey to the southern regions, and settled himself in a grove where stood the Víhára of Máladhvajavyúha, where he had formerly held his meditations. On this the people of the neighbouring town of Danyakára came in crowds to receive his instruction and his benediction. The lord taught them, and singled out one young man to be the object of his special favour.

This young man was named Sudhana from the fact that immediately after his birth his father had suddenly become very rich. Manjus'rí narrated to him the marvellous deeds of Lord Buddha. Sudhana chanted the praise of Manjus'rí in sweet and melodious verses, and declared himself a candidate for Bodhi knowledge.

Manjus'rí advised him to have the benefit of instruction from Meghas'rí, who resided at Mount Sugríva in the country called Rámavarta. Meghas'rí shifted the burden of instructing Sudhana to Ságaramegha of Ságaramukha, who on his turn advised Sudhana to repair to Supratisṭhita of Ságara on the way to Lanká. Sudhana was again disappointed. He was directed to proceed to Vajapura, a city of Draviḍa, to receive instructions from a Drávidian named Megha. Megha professed his ignorance of Bodhi knowledge.

By his advice Sudhana repaired to Sáradhvaja at Milanapuraṇa, the land's end of Jambudvípa; thence to the Bhikshuṇí Ás'á, the wife of Suprabha of Samudravelatí to the east of Maháprabhu; thence to Bhishmottarasanghesha of Nalapúra; thence to Jayashínáyatana in the country of Ís'asha; thence to Maitráyaní, the daughter of Siñhaketu, at the city of Siñhavijrimbhita; thence to Sudars'ana of Trinánjana; thence to a boy named Indriyas'vara of the city of Sumukha in the country called S'ramaṇa Maṇḍala; thence to the Upásika Prabhúta of Samudraprasthána: thence to the patriarch Vidvan of Mahásambhava; thence to the banker Ratnachúḍa of Siñhapotí; thence to Samantanetra, a manufacturer of perfumery, at the city of Samantamukha in Múlaka; thence to Nala of Náladhvaja; thence to the king Maháprabha of Suprabha; thence to the Upás'iká Achalasthirá; thence to Sarvagráma of Toshala in Mitatoshala; thence to Utpalabhúti in Prithuráshṭra; thence to the slave Paisa of Kulágára; thence to the banker Jayottama of Nánuhara; thence to the Bhikshuṇí Siñhavyasambhitá of Kalingavana in S'roṇapasanta; thence to Bhagavatí Sumitrá of Ratnabhijjiha in Durga; thence to the patriarch Vesṭhila of Subhapárangama; thence to the Bodhisattva Avalokites'vara of Poṭalaka; thence to Ananyagámí of Pashatmaṇḍala, and finally to Mahádeva of Dváravatí. All the places mentioned above belong to the region called Dakshiṇápatha or southern India.

Leaving Dekkan in the south, Sudhana directed his steps by the advice of Mahádeva towards Magadha. In that country he paid his devotion to eight Rátridevatás, or goddesses of night. These had different names, and dwelt in different localities, two of which Kapilavastu and Bidhimaṇda are well known in the history of the Buddhist religion.

But none could afford full satisfaction to Sudhana, and he remained unpossessed of perfect knowledge. He then entreated Gopá, the wife, and Máyá the mother, of the great Buddha for instruction, and here he was partially successful. They recommended him to Surendrábhá at the house of Indra, and she, to a young teacher Vis'vámitra of Kapilavastu. At every change of teacher, the amount of his knowledge increased, and with redoubled zeal he applied himself to the acquisition and perfection of knowledge. He received several valuable lectures from the patriarch Surendra and the goldsmith Muktasára of Varukutcha, from a Bráhman Sivirátra of Dharmagráma in Dekkan, from a boy S'rísambhava, and a girl S'rímatí of Sumukha. From Sumukha he travelled to Samudrakatíha where Maitreya told him plainly that none but Manjus'rí himself would be able to make his knowledge perfect. Thus after passing through a hundred austerities he went back to Manjus'rí, who was living in the vicinity of Sumaná. Sudhana, by the favor of Manjus'rí at last obtained full and perfect knowledge from the holy Samantabhadra.*

Beginning. ॐ नमः सर्व्वबुद्धबोधिसत्त्वेभ्यः। गण्डव्यूहमहार्णवस्रोतनिनादि मो जिनसुतानां।
पर्षण्मण्डलसागरनाम्ना व्यूहादिकं प्रोक्तं। सुगतसमाध्यवतारणा अचिन्त्य-
बुद्धनिदर्शनञ्च। धीमत्सङ्क्रागमनं श्रावकविषयानुगमनञ्च। स्तुतिमेघाचिन्त्य-
महद्बुद्धोत्पादप्रकाशनं सुधियां। सद्धर्म्मरत्नसागरसमन्तभद्रार्थनिर्द्देशं॥ सर्व्व-
तथागतसुचरितसमाधिसागरपरम्परागमाज्जिनसुतसमाधिसागरपरम्पराश्चानुगन्त-
व्याः। इति सुगतसमाधिशतैर्विमोक्षसागरपरम्पराभिश्च सुगतात्मजेन सुधिया
मञ्जुश्रीनामधेयेन। निर्द्दिशता सुगतानां व्यूहमचिन्त्यं तथा जिनसुतानां विक्री-
डितैर्बहुविधैः स्फुटं जगदनन्तपर्य्यन्तं। तस्यैवं निर्द्दिशतो दशबलतनयस्य
बोधिवरसत्त्वा अवतेरुर्विषयोदधिमथ सुगतानां निरवशेषं। तेषां समाधिसागर-
सङ्क्रामदशबलानुभावेन विक्रीडितैरचिन्त्यैश्चरन्ति यस्यानुभावेन एवं समाहित-
धियस्ते वशिनः सत्त्वसागरमनन्तं प्रविचेरुर्विनयशतैर्विविधैरात्मप्रभावनयैः। न
च सुगतपादमूलात् केचिदपि उपजग्मुस्ते महासत्त्वा विविधैर्विमोक्षविषयैर्विह-
रन्तश्चाप्रमेयैस्ते। प्राक्रामन् दक्षिणापथमध्वचर्य्यां जिनसुतस्य मञ्जुश्रीबोधि-
सत्त्वलालितैर्विनयन् सत्त्वान् परमबोधौ। धन्याकरान् पुरवरादनुपूर्व्वेणाथ

* *Vide passim* the Introduction to my edition of the Lalita Vistara, pp. 8 f.

सोविनयवशाद्विनयामास महानजमचिन्त्यनिर्द्देशवशिताभिः। तत्र सुधनं कृपालुर्धर्म्मधनो बोधयेत् समादाय कल्याणमित्रसागरवर्त्मन्यवतार्य्य कारुण्यात्। विजहार सत्त्वविनयैर्बहुभिः सेचार्थैर्वेप्यमितकायः। एवंविधैरुपायैरभिविनयं भाव्यजनकायं। सुधनोऽपि मदनुशास्त्या मेघश्रीसागराम्बुदप्रमुखं कल्याणमित्रसागरमारोग्यसमन्तभद्रार्थं। विनयन् सत्त्वसङ्घान् तत्कायान्तर्गतः समाधिश्रुतैः। विजहारानन्तधियः समन्तभद्रचर्य्याभिमुखं। एवं मया श्रुतमेकस्मिन् समये भगवान् श्रावस्त्यां विहरति स्म। जेतवनेऽनाथपिण्डदस्यारामे महाव्यूहे कूटागारे। सार्द्धं पञ्चमात्रैर्बोधिसत्त्वसहस्रैः समन्तभद्रमञ्जुश्रीबोधिसत्त्वपूर्व्वङ्गमैः।

End. इदमवोचद्भगवानात्तमनाः सुधनः श्रेष्ठिदारकस्ते च बोधिसत्त्वा आर्य्यमञ्जुश्रीपूर्व्वङ्गमास्ते च भिक्षव आर्य्यमञ्जुश्रीपरिपाचितास्ते चार्य्यमैत्रेयपूर्व्वङ्गमाः सर्व्वभद्रकल्पिका बोधिसत्त्वास्ते चार्य्यसमन्तभद्रबोधिसत्त्वप्रमुखा यौवराज्याभिषिक्ताः परमाणुरजःसमा महाबोधिसत्त्वा नानालोकधातुसन्निपतितास्ते चार्य्यशारीपुत्रमौद्गल्यायनप्रमुखा महाश्रावकाः सा च सर्व्वावती पर्षत् सदेवमानुषासुरगन्धर्व्वाश्च लोका भगवतः समन्तभद्रस्य बोधिसत्त्वस्य भाषितमभ्यनन्दन्निति।

Colophon. आर्य्यव्यूहो महाधर्म्मपर्य्यायात् यथा लब्धः सुधनकल्याणमित्रपर्य्युपासितचर्य्यैकादश आर्य्यगण्डव्यूहो महायानसूत्ररत्नराजः समाप्तः।

No. 816 B.

GRAHAMÁTṚIKÁ DHÁRAṆÍ.

ग्रहमातृकाधारणी।

Substance, Nepalese paper, $6\frac{3}{4} \times 2\frac{1}{2}$. Folia, 17. Lines on a page, 5. Character, Newári. Date, ? Appearance, old. Prose. Incorrect.

Mystic mantras for the adoration of the nine planets. The mantras were disclosed to a congregation of gods by Buddha himself when residing in the Alakavati mansion of Indra. The mantras are of the Tántric type, full of mystic particles. It is enjoined that, after worshipping the planets in certain mystic diagrams drawn on the floor of a room, the mantras should be recited seven times daily, from the 7th to the 14th of the waxing moon in Kártika, and the rite should be concluded on the 15th at midnight. The rite insures longevity to ninety-nine years, prevents all evils resulting from adverse planets, and makes the adorer capable of remembering the history of his former existences. This Hindu ritual must be of a comparatively modern date.

Beginning. ॐ नमो भगवत्यै आर्य्यमातृकायै। एवं मया श्रुतमेकस्मिन् समये भगवान् अलकवत्यां महानगर्य्यां विहरति स्म। अनेकदेव-नाग-यक्ष-राक्षस-गन्धर्व्वासुर-गरुड़-किन्नर-महोरगापस्मारादित्य-सोमाङ्गार-बुद्ध-बृहस्पति-शुक्र-शनैश्वर-राहु-केतुभिः अष्टाविंशतिभिश्च नक्षत्रादिभिस्तूर्य्यमाणो महावज्रमयालङ्कारेण व्यूहाधिष्ठानाधिष्ठिते सिंहासने विहरति स्म अनेकबोधिसत्त्वशतसहस्रसार्द्धं। तद्यथा। ॐ वज्रपाणिना च नाम बोधिसत्त्वेन महासत्त्वेन। ॐ वज्रचन्द्रेण च नाम बोधिसत्त्वेन महासत्त्वेन। ॐ वज्रसत्त्वेन च नाम बोधिसत्त्वेन महात्त्वेन। वज्रवेगेण च नाम बोधिसत्त्वेन महासत्त्वेन। वज्रसेनेन च नाम बोधिसत्त्वेन महासत्त्वेन। वज्रविनायकेन च नाम बोधिसत्त्वेन महासत्त्वेन। वज्रचापहस्तेन च नाम बोधिसत्त्वेन महासत्त्वेन। वज्रविकुर्व्वितेन च नाम बोधिसत्त्वेन महासत्त्वेन। वज्राधिपेन च नाम बोधिसत्त्वेन महासत्त्वेन। वज्रालङ्कारेण च नाम बोधिसत्त्वेन महासत्त्वेन। वज्रविक्रमणेन च नाम बोधिसत्त्वेन महासत्त्वेन। ज्ञातिवज्रेण च नाम बोधिसत्त्वेन महासत्त्वेन। पद्मकेतुना च नाम बोधिसत्त्वेन महासत्त्वेन। अवलोकितेश्वरेण च नाम बोधिसत्त्वेन महासत्त्वेन। समन्तभद्रेण च नाम बोधिसत्त्वेन महासत्त्वेन। समन्तावलोकितेश्वरेण च नाम बोधिसत्त्वेन महासत्त्वेन। लोकश्रियायेण च नाम बोधिसत्त्वेन महासत्त्वेन। रत्नकेतुना च नाम बोधिसत्त्वेन महासत्त्वेन। विकम्पितवज्रेण च नाम बोधिसत्त्वेन महासत्त्वेन। पद्मगर्भेण च बोधिसत्त्वेन महासत्त्वेन। पद्मनेत्रेण च नाम बोधिसत्त्वेन महासत्त्वेन। मञ्जुश्रियायेण च बोधिसत्त्वेन महासत्त्वेन। मैत्रेयेण च बोधिसत्त्वेन महासत्त्वेन। एवं प्रमुखैर्म्महाबोधिसत्त्वसङ्घशतसहस्रैः सार्द्धं परिवृतः पुरस्कृतो भगवान् धर्म्मन्देशयति स्म। आदौ कल्याणं मध्ये कल्याणं पर्य्यवसाने कल्याणं। स्वर्थं सुव्यञ्जनकेवलं परिपुर्णं परिशुद्धम्पर्य्यवदातं ब्रह्मचर्य्यं सम्प्रकाशयति स्म। चिन्तामणिमहाव्यूहालङ्कारो नाम धर्म्मपर्य्यायं देशयति स्म। अथ खलु वज्रपाणिः बोधिसत्त्वो महासत्त्वस्तत्पर्षन्मण्डलमवलोक्यासनादुत्थाय स्वच्छन्द्याधिष्ठानेन भगवन्तमनेकशतसहस्रं प्रदक्षिणीकृत्य प्रणम्य पुरतो निषद्य। समर्सेण वज्रपर्य्यङ्कमायुषं लीलया तत् पर्षन्मण्डलमवलोक्य वज्राञ्जलिं कृत्वा स्वहृदये प्रतिष्ठाप्य। भगवन्तमेतदवोचत्। गताश्च भगवन् उग्रा उग्ररूपाश्च रौद्राः क्रूराः क्रुररूपाश्च ते चाहयन्ति उपद्रवांश्च कुर्व्वन्ति ते सत्त्वान्विठयन्ति। केषाञ्चित् प्राणमपहरन्ति। केषाञ्चित् प्राणमपहरन्ति। केषाञ्चिद्दीर्घायुष्काणां। सत्त्वानामप्रायुः कुर्व्वन्ति। एवं सर्व्वसत्त्वान् सर्व्वोपद्रवाहयन्ति(?)। तद्देशयतु भगवन् तादृशं धर्म्मपर्य्यायं। येन सर्व्वसत्त्वानां सर्व्वोपद्रवेभ्यो रक्षा भविष्यति।

End. अथ ते सर्व्वे ब्रह्मा आदित्यादयः साधु साधु भगवन्निति कृत्वा प्रणम्यान्तर्हिता अभूवन् । इदमवोचद्भगवानात्तमनास्ते च भिक्षवस्ते च बोधिसत्त्वा महासत्त्वाः सा च सर्व्वावती पर्षत् सदेवमानुषासुरगरुडकिन्नरगन्धर्व्वाश्च लोका भगवतो भाषितमभ्यनन्दन्निति ।

Colophon. आर्य्यग्रहमातृकानामधारणी समाप्ता ।

No. B. 27.

GUṆAKAŔAṆḌA-VYU'HA.

गुणकारण्डव्यूहः ।

Substance, paper, 17½ × 5½. Folia, 120. Lines on a page, 8. Extent in s'lokas, 4,740. Character, Newári. Appearance, old. Incorrect.

An account of the character, religious teachings, and miracles of Árya Avalokites'vara, a Bodhisattva. Avalokites'vara refused to enter Buddhahood until all living creatures would be in possession of the Bodhi knowledge. He had a long life. He had seen three or four Buddhas pass through their mundane cáreer during his lifetime. He had been a friend to Vipas'yí, to S'ikhi, to Jina, and to Sákya Muni who had held him in high esteem. His principal occupation was to provide salvation to sufferers in hell; but he felt equally for all. In one of his philanthropic tours he passed through Ceylon or Siñhala, Benares, and Magadha, granting salvation, and preaching the gospel of Buddha's religion even to worms and insects. Even the gods of heaven were not beyond the range of his benevolence. He granted one Sukuṇḍala, a poor god, immense wealth, and above all showed him the way to nirváṇa by sending him to the Jetavana grove. Reclaiming the wicked, relieving sufferers, providing food for the famine-stricken, curing the diseased, were the daily routine of his duties. He attained to such high distinction by his noble deeds that he was called the *Sangha-ratna* or the "jewel of the Buddhist Church."

The work opens with a request from Jinas'rí to Jayas'rí, the great preacher of Bodhimaṇḍa at Buddha Gayá, to give an account of the origin of the "three jewels." This most secret and most mysterious subject was first divulged by Upa Gupta to As'oka at the Kukkuṭáráma Vihára in Páṭaliputra. According to Upa Gupta, Lord Jina, the destroyer of Mára's pride, is the *Buddha-ratna* or "Buddha jewel." Others who will hereafter rise to Buddhahood by Bodhi knowledge will likewise be Buddha-ratnas. The all-powerful intelligence that impels men towards Bodhi knowledge is *Dharma-ratna* or "the jewel of religion." A'rya Avalokites'vara, the son of Jina, resplendent in his knowledge of Buddhism, and firm in his faith, is the *Sangha-ratna* or "jewel of the Church." Other Bodhisattvas, and Arhats who revel in the four Brahmas, and have a thorough command over their ownselves, are, also jewels of the Church.

Having thus explained the mystic trinity of Buddha, Dharma and Sangha, Upa Gupta, at the request of As'oka, instructed him in the practice of Poshadhavrata, and gave an account of the Sangha-ratna in the following manner :—

Once on a time Lord Buddha performed an ecstatic meditation named *sarvasañs'odhana* or "the purifier of every thing." No sooner he sat in that posture, than golden rays illuminating the whole province were seen proceeding from some unknown region to that place. Suvarnávaraṇa Vishkambhí a saint, struck with wonder at this miracle, asked the Lord whence did the rays proceed? The Lord said "from A'rya Avalokites'vara who, by the command of Jina, is now preaching the doctrine of Nirváṇa at Avíchí, the stygian lake of fire. These rays, after having purified the wretched people of that hell, are come here to enlighten the ignorant and the sinful." At the request of Vishkambhí, the Lord gave several stories illustrating the power and the goodness of Avalokites'vara.

The Lord said, once on a time when Vipas'yí was preaching on earth, Avalokites'vara shot forth his holy light for the spiritual benefit of the residents of hell. Vipas'yí gave an account of the importance of Buddha-ratna. Before the creation of the world, the first Buddha, who was pure effulgence of light without a speck, held a samádhi named *Lokasanjanana* or "creation." Forthwith S'iva, Brahmá, Vishṇu, Súrya, Chandra &c. were generated. The first Buddha allotted distinct works of creation to these.

Vishkambhí solicited the Lord to tell him by what samádhi Avalokites'vara had acquired the power of saving the souls of the sinful. The Lord said "by thousands of samádhis." He said, even he himself was once benefitted by Avalokites'vara's power of saving men.

The Lord said, "in one of my previous existences, I was Siñhala, son of Siñha, a merchant of the capital of Siñhakalpa. Siñhala led a nautical expedition. His vessels were overtaken by a storm, and wrecked off the island called Támradvípa or copper island; but fortunately no life was lost. By the grace of the Lord to whom Siñhala was very much devoted, the passengers safely reached the shores of Támradvípa. That island was inhabited by Rákshasís, who could assume any form they wished. On seeing the ship-wrecked people, they assumed the charming forms of celestial nymphs, expressed their concern at their distress, accepted them as husbands, and led them home. One night when all were asleep, Siñhala saw the lamp in his room *laugh.* Siñhala asked the lamp the reason for its laughter. The lamp said, "the nymphs with whom you live here are Rákshasís in disguise. You are in imminent danger for your lives. If you want to save yourselves, there stands a horse named Baláha on the sea-shore ready at your service. Mount on his back, but do not open your eyes until you land safely on the other side of the ocean." Siñhala assembled all his companions, and induced them to follow the lamp's advice. They all mounted the horse. The horse rose to the sky. The Rákshasís, seeing their prey, which they had thought was most secure in their grasp, flying away, raised loud lamentations. Their husbands were touched with pity, opened their eyes contrary to their promise, and dropped down into the ocean, where they were devoured by their wives. Siñhala alone escaped safe. The Rákshasí who had fallen to his lot, came to Siñhala's father in all her bewitching beauty, and complained that she had been forsaken by Siñhala who had married her. But Siñhala was successful in making his father understand what she really was. The female ogre then proceeded to the king of the country to proffer a complaint against Siñhala. The king was convinced by her that her story was true, and, on Siñhala's refusal to take her back, accepted her as his own queen. In a short time, however, he with all his family was devoured by her. Siñhala was, by the unanimous consent of the citizens, raised to the throne. He expelled the Rákshasís from Támradvípa, and named it Siñhala after himself.

"I am, O Vishkambhí, that Siñhala; Avalokites'vara is the horse Baláha, Mahallaka the Bodhisattva is the king, and Anupañsá is that Rákshasí. The merits of Avalokites'vara may be counted by myriads. In one of the pores of his body there are thousands of heavenly choristers, in another millions of Ṛishis."

Vishkambhí then heard from the Lord the benefits of repeating the formula of six letters or Shaḍaksharí Mantra, and obtained that mantra at Benares.

The work was translated into Chinese, according to the Rev. S. Beal's Trípíṭhaka, (p. 35) under the name of Mau-chu-pa'o-ts'ang-to-lo-ni-king, its Sanskrit equivalent being Ratna-karandaka-vyúha-sútra. It is reckoned among the Maháyána Sútras.

Beginning. ॐ नमः श्रीरत्नत्रयाय । नमः सर्व्वबुद्धबोधिसत्त्वेभ्यः ।

यः श्रीघनो महाबुद्धः सर्व्वलोकाधिपो जिनः ।
तं नाथं शरणं गत्वा वक्ष्ये लोकेश सत्कथां ॥
या श्रीभगवती देवी सर्व्वधर्म्माधिपेश्वरी ।
तस्या भक्तिप्रसादेन वक्ष्यामि बोधिसाधनं ॥
येन सम्पालितं सर्व्वं त्रैधातुकमिदं जगत् ।
तस्य लोकेश्वरस्याहं वन्दे सर्व्वार्थसाधनं ॥
तद्यथाऽभून्महासत्त्वो जिनः श्रीराज आत्मवित् ।
त्रिरत्नशरणं गत्वा यतिरर्हन् जिनात्मजः ॥
एकस्मिन् समये सोऽर्हन् बोधिमण्डे जिनाश्रमे ।
बोधिचर्य्याव्रतं धृत्वा जगद्धिते समाश्रयत् ॥
तदा तत्र महाभिज्ञो जयश्रीर्यतिरात्मवित् ।
सद्धर्म्मं समुपादेष्टुं सभासनमथाश्रयत् ॥
तं दृष्ट्वा श्रावकाः सर्व्वे भिक्षवो ब्रह्मचारिणः ।
तत् सद्धर्म्मामृतं पातुमुपेत्य समुपाश्रयन् ॥
तथान्य बोधिसत्त्वाश्च सर्व्वे बोधिव्रतसाधिनः ।
सुभाषितामृतं पातुं तत्सभां समुपाश्रयन् ॥
भिक्षुण्यश्चैलकाश्चैवमुपासका उपासिकाः ।
व्रतिनोऽपि महासत्त्वाः सम्बुद्धभक्तिचारिकाः ॥
ब्राह्मणाः क्षत्रियाश्चापि राजानो मन्त्रिणो जनाः ।
अमात्यः श्रेष्ठिनः पौराः सार्थवाहा महाजनाः ॥
तथा जानपदा ग्राम्याः पार्व्वतिकाश्च नैगमाः ।
तथान्यदेशिका लोकाः सद्धर्म्मगुणवाञ्छिनः ॥
सर्व्वे ते समुपागत्य तमर्हन्तं जयश्रियं ।
यथाक्रमं समभ्यर्च्य प्रणम्य समुपाश्रिताः ॥
तत् सद्धर्म्मामृतं पातुकृताञ्जलिपुटा मुदा ।

साक्षारं तं समालोक्य परिवृत्य निषेदिरे ॥
तदा सोऽर्हन् महासत्त्वो बोधिसत्त्वो जिनात्मजः ।
जिनः श्रीराजमालोक्य सर्व्वान् लोकान् सभागतान् ॥
चिरलगुणमाहात्म्यं श्रोतुं समभिलाषिणः ।
समुत्थायासनात्तस्य जयश्रियः पुरोगतः ॥
उद्वहन्नुत्तरासङ्गं जानुभूमितलाश्रितः ।
पादाब्जे साञ्जलिं नत्वा प्रार्थयद्देवमादरात् ॥
भदन्त श्रोतुमिच्छामि चिरलोत्पत्तिसत्कथां ।
तद्भवान् समुपादिश्य सम्बोधयतु मां गुरो ॥

End. इति जयश्रियाख्यातं श्रुत्वा सर्व्वेऽपि साङ्घिकाः ।
एवमस्त्विति विज्ञाप्य प्रत्यनन्दन् प्रमोदिताः ॥

Colophon. इति जिनश्रीराजपरिपृष्टजयश्रीसम्भाषितश्रीमदार्य्यावलोकितेश्वरगुणकारण्डव्यूह-
सूत्रराजः समाप्तः ।

No. B. 36.

KALYA'NA-PANCHAVINS'ATIKA'.

कल्याणपञ्चविंशतिका ।

Substance, yellow paper. Folia, 14. Lines on each page, 6. Extent in s'lokas, 250. Character, Newári. Appearance, old. Verse. Incorrect.

A hymn in praise of Buddha in twenty-five sragdhará verses. Each verse ensures a particular blessing, and so the twenty-five are called 'twenty-five blessings.' By Amritánanda.

Beginning. श्रीमानाद्यः स्वयम्भूरमितरुचिरमोघाभिधो ++बुद्धः
श्रीमान् वैरोचनाख्यो मुनिभवमुनिराट् वज्रसत्त्वः सुसत्त्वः ।
श्रीप्रज्ञावज्रधारी सकलशुभकरो आर्य्यतारादिकाश्च
कल्याणं वः क्रियात् स क्वचिदपि सततं तिष्ठतां नौमहे तं ॥

End. स श्रीमानब्जपाणिः स जटधरहयग्रीवपार्षद्गणेशः
कल्याणं वः क्रियात् स क्वचिदपि सततं तिष्ठतां नौमहे तं ।

Colophon. इति नैपालिदेवता कल्याणपञ्चविंशतिका अमृतानन्दविरचिता समाप्ता ।

No.

KAPIS'A' AVADA'NAM.

कपिशावदानम् ।

Substance, paper, 10½ × 3. Folia, 35. Lines on each page, 6. Extent in s'lokas, 590. Character, Newári. Appearance, old. Incorrect. Prose and verse.

A story in illustration of Beneficence. Lord Buddha held a large assembly of his followers. S'aripatra requested the Lord to pronounce an eulogium on charity. The Lord gave them the following story, said to have been first told by Vipas'yí long before the lord's advent.

Once on a time Tatavísuta was born a monkey, Jnánákara by name. In consequence of his sinful character the whole forest was beset with darkness at the time of his birth, and famine raged on all sides. Some time after, Dípankara's presence in the forest restored it to light, and there was plenty of everything. Jnánákara, wondering at this sudden change, gave a jack-fruit to the worker of the miracle. Dípankara gave him instruction in the philosophy of Buddhism, and promised him transformation into a man. He learned the character of man from a friend, and, dying, was born a merchant's son at Kámarthí. He was named Dharmas'rí. When Dharmas'rí was very young, Dípankara, who was passing by, asked him to give the applicant anything that he could afford with good will. Dharmas'rí gave a handful of dust, which was instantly changed into gold. He gave another handful of dust, which was changed into dainties for the Sangha. Dípankara granted him a boon, saying, "for this good conduct, you are to become Sarvananda, the king of Dípávatí. Sarvananda always used to please Dípankara with food, and raiment."

Then the Lord gave the assembled multitude a lecture on morals, diversifying it with a description of the Satya Yuga and the duties which appertained to that Yuga.

Beginning. ॐ श्रीरत्नत्रयाय नमः ।

कन्दर्पदर्पशमनं प्रणिपत्य मूर्द्धा शौद्धोदनिं सुरनरार्च्चितपादपद्मं ।
श्रुत्वा गुरोः सुगतसूत्रसतत्त्वविज्ञं सूत्रं तदर्थसमनुस्मरणं करिष्ये ॥
यथैव गङ्गा· यमुनाप्रसङ्गे गोदावरी तीर्थसरस्वती च ।
सर्व्वाणि तीर्थानि वसन्ति तत्र यत्रार्कबन्धोस्य कथाप्रसङ्गः ॥

तथैव पुण्यं भवतीति भावात् स्नानाच्च गात्रस्य यथो पवित्रं ।
अनादिकल्पार्चितकल्मषाणि निहन्ति तस्मादिह मानवानां ॥
यद्दुर्लभं कल्पशतैरनेकैर्मानुष्यजन्मोऽपि च वान्यकेषु ।
तत् साम्प्रतं प्राप्तमतो भवद्भिः कार्य्यो हि धर्मश्रवणाय यत्नः ॥
एवं मया श्रुतमेकस्मिन् समये भगवान् श्रावस्त्यां महानगर्य्यां विहरति स्म । तत्र भगवान् शाक्यमुनिस्तथागतोऽर्हन् सम्यक् सम्बुद्धोऽनेकैर्भिक्षुशतसहस्रैः सार्द्धं जेतवने महाविहारे सभां कारितवान् । अथ खल्वायुष्मान् शारीपुत्रो धर्म्मसेनापतिर्भिक्षुरुत्थायासनादेकांसमुत्तरासङ्गं कृत्वा दक्षिणजानुमण्डलं भूमौ पातयित्वा येन भगवान् बोधिमण्डवराग्रतलेनोपसङ्क्रमति स्म । उपसङ्क्रम्य च कृताञ्जलिर्भगवन्तं त्रिःप्रदक्षिणीकृत्य प्रणम्यैतदवोचत् । पूर्व्वजन्मानं शुभकर्म्मफलं वदस्व ॥

End जले स्थले तथा शैले वनेऽरण्ये गृहाश्रमे ।
जापयेन्मौनयोगेन सदा एकाग्रमानसः ॥
ऋद्धिसिद्धिं महाप्राज्ञः प्राप्तो भवेन्मुनीश्वरः ।
इति श्रुत्वा शारिपुत्रो भिक्षुः सर्व्वगणैः सह ॥
शाक्यसिंहं मुनिं नत्वा प्रक्रान्तोऽतिसुखालयम् ।

Colophon. इति श्रीकपिशावदाने चर्य्याव्रतनिर्द्देशो नाम नवमोऽध्यायः । इति कपिशावदानं समाप्तं ।

No. 815.

KA'RAṆḌAVYU'HA.

कारण्डव्यूहः ।

Substance, Nepalese yellow paper, 13 × 3. Folia, 82. Lines on a page, 5. Extent in s'lokas, 1600. Character, Newári. Date, ? Prose. Incorrect.

A highly amplied version of the work noticed under the name of Guṇakáraṇḍavyúha. The work is in prose, but it has obviously been amplified from the poetical version abovenamed. The names and incidents have been in some cases modified or changed, and many new incidents and stories have been worked in. But the purport remains the same—the glorification of the great Bodhisattva Árya Avalokites'vara. The differences are not of such a character as to need detailed specification. The work belongs to the class Maháyána Sútra, and, as usual in that class of writings, does not bear the name of its author. Its name does not occur in the Rev. S. Beal's Tripíṭhaka.

Beginning. ॐ नमो भगवते आर्य्यावलोकितेश्वराय । एवं मया श्रुतं एकस्मिन् समये भगवान् श्रावस्त्यां विहरति स्म । जेतवने अनाथपिण्डदस्यारामे महता भिक्षुसङ्घेन सार्द्धमर्द्धत्रयोदशभिर्भिक्षुशतैः सम्बहुलैश्च बोधिसत्त्वैर्महासत्त्वैः ।

End. अथ खल्वायुष्मानानन्दो भगवतः पादौ शिरसा वन्दित्वा प्रक्रान्तः । अथ ते महाश्रावकाः स्वकस्वकेषु बुद्धक्षेत्रेषु प्रक्रान्ताः । ते देवनागयक्षगन्धर्व्वासुरगरुडकिन्नरमहोरगमनुष्यामनुष्याः प्रक्रान्ताः । इदमवोचद्भगवान् आत्तमनास्ते च बोधिसत्त्वा महासत्त्वाः सा च सर्व्ववती पर्षत् सदेवमानुषासुरगरुडकिन्नरमहोरगगन्धर्व्वाश्च लोका भगवतो भाषितमभ्यनन्दन्निति ।

Colophon. इति आर्य्यकारण्डव्यूहं नाम महायानसूत्ररत्नराजं समाप्तं ।

No. 816 C.

KAVIKUMÁRA KATHÁ.

कविकुमारकथा ।

Substance, yellow paper, 10 × 4. Folia, 18. Lines on a page, 8. Character, Newári. Appearance, old. Prose and verse. Incorrect.

A story of one of Buddha's former existences. It was related by Upa Gupta to As'oka as a narrative which had been originally told by Buddha himself to his followers at Gridhrakúṭa to account for an incurable sore on his toe. The occasion for the recital was offered by a S'ákya youth having at early dawn pelted a large stone at Buddha to kill him, and the stone falling on his toe caused a deep wound. The followers enquired why such an accident had happened, and Buddha in reply gave the story. Formerly there lived in the city of Kámpilya a king named Satyarata. His chief queen Lakshmaṇá was for a time childless, but on the king's taking a second wife named Sudharmá, the former bore a son, who was named Lolamantra. On the death of the king, Lolamantra succeeded to the kingdom, but soon after Sudharmá bore a posthumous child who, at the time of birth, had a jewelled coronet on his head. The boy was named Kavikumára. When the news of his birth was brought to the king, astrologers informed him that the boy would for certain set him aside. The king thereupon deputed a person to kill the child, but the news of this had already been communicated to Sudharmá by Govisháná, a favourite of the king, and so she deposited her child with a fisherman (Kaivarta), and, taking his new-born daughter, sent her to the king as the child she had borne. A few years after, the king's astrologer, seeing the boy playing at king in a field, knew that it was the son of Sudharmá, and informed the king of the imposition that had been practised on him. The king was greatly incensed, and deputed a large army to kill the boy; but the boy had timely information, and, taking the jewelled coronet from his mother, ran away, and, hiding first in the house of a potter, then in that of a hatter, then in a forest, at last fell into a river. The king's messenger, thinking that would put an end to the life of the boy, came back, and reported the circumstance to the king. The boy, however, was saved from death by a Yaksha. From the Yaksha he repaired to a forest where he was attacked by a hunter, but a Vidyádhara interposed, and cut off the head of the assailant, and taught the youth the science of magic. By the power of this magic the youth assumed the form of a beautiful damsel, and returned to the dominion of his brother. The king Lolamantra was enchanted by the beauty and the musical accomplishments of the damsel, and invited her to his bed-chamber, but, when he attempted to embrace her, Kavikumára assumed his masculine form, and killed him. Buddha said, "I am that Kavikumára, and because I had killed my brother, I was doomed to hell for many thousand years, and now a small remnant of my sin has given me this sore."

The work professes to form a part of a large work named *Vratávadána-málá.*

Beginning. ॐ नमो रत्नत्रयाय ।

विचरति कनकाद्रौ शाक्यसिंहो मुनीन्द्रोऽपरिमितसुरसङ्घैः सेव्यमानो जनौघैः ।
कुवलयदलनेत्रो लक्षणैर्युक्तगात्रः समभवदधितिष्ठन् सर्व्वलोके हितार्थः ॥ १ ॥
ये देवाः सन्ति मेरौ वरकनकमये मण्डले ये च यक्षाः
पाताले ये भुजङ्गाः फणिमणिकिरणैः ध्वस्तसर्व्वान्धकाराः ।
कैलासे श्रीविलासे प्रमुदितहृदया ये च विद्याधरेन्द्रा-
स्ते मोक्षद्वारभूतं मुनिवरवचनं श्रोतुमायान्ति सर्व्वे ॥ २ ॥
गन्धर्व्वा मण्डलाग्रे सुरचितललिते स्वासने ये लसन्ति
दिव्यै देव्यन्ततोयैस्सलकुचकलशैः सिच्यमानाप्सरोभिः ।

भूता ये सागरान्ते मलयगिरितटे ये च सिद्धाः सुरेन्द्रा-
स्ते मोक्षद्वारभूतं मुनिवरवचनं श्रोतुमायान्ति सर्व्वे ॥ ३ ॥
ब्रह्मेन्द्रा दिव्यरूपाः समसुखनिरताः सुप्रभाः शुद्धरूपाः
यक्षाश्चादित्यवर्गाः सुरनरगरुड़ा राक्षसाः किन्नरेन्द्राः ।
गन्धर्वादिप्रमुख्या विलसितहृदयाः श्रोतुमायान्ति सर्व्वे ॥ ४ ॥
मन्दारके वै कुवलयचम्पकनागपुष्पैर्गन्धोत्तमैरगुरुचन्दनकुङ्कुमाद्यैः ।
रत्नोत्तमैः कनकरागनिबद्धकाया आयान्ति युद्ध(?)नियमश्रवणाय धर्म्मं ॥ ५ ॥
आयान्ति देवभुजगाः सुरकिन्नरेन्द्राः शक्रादयः प्रबलधर्म्मकृताधिकाराः ।
बौद्धं वचः प्रथमसौख्यनिमित्तभूतमेतत् प्रकाशितमिह श्रवणाय धर्म्मे ॥ ६ ॥
यद्दुर्लभं कल्पने(?)रन्यकैर्मानुष्यमष्टाक्षरदोषयुक्तं ।
तस्मात्त्वतं प्राप्तमतो भवद्भिः कार्य्यो हि धर्म्मश्रवणाय यत्नः ॥ ७ ॥
अस्मिंश्च लोके करुणात्मकानां निर्व्वाणमार्गोत्तमदेशकानां ।
सुदुर्लभं जन्म तथागतानामतो हि धर्म्मश्रवणेन सिद्धिः ॥ ८ ॥
आयान्ति श्रोतुकामा असुरसुरनराः सिद्धगन्धर्व्वयक्षाः
कुम्भाण्डाः किन्नरेन्द्रा गरुड़हरिहराः शक्रब्रह्मादिदेवाः ।
पूताः पञ्चोपचारैस्त्रिभुवननमितं मेदिनीदुर्लभं यत्
भक्त्याहं वाचयामि प्रणमति शिरसा तं महायानसूत्रं ॥ ९ ॥

नमो बुद्धाय । नमः सङ्घाय नमो नमः । नमो रत्नत्रयाय । श्रीमत् उपगुप्तमशोकः पुनर्व्यजिज्ञपत् । पुनः श्रोतुमिच्छाम्यष्टमीमहिमानं । उपगुप्तोऽवदत् । एकस्मिन् समये शाक्यकेशरी राजगृहे गृध्रकूटे करण्डकनिवापाख्ये वेणुवने विजहार ससङ्घः ।

End. सुगतोदितं यथोदितं श्रुत्वाऽशोकनृपेश्वरः स्वयं समुपास्य प्रमुदितः प्रजाश्चारथ । तस्यानुभावात् क्रमात् बोधिचरीः समाप्य सम्बोधिपदमाप्नुयात् ।

Colophon. इति व्रतावदानमालायां कविकुमारकथा समाप्ता ।

No. B. 23.

KRIYÁSAṆGRAHA-PANJIKÁ.

क्रियासङ्ग्रहपञ्जिका ।

Substance, palm-leaf, 12½ × 2. Folia, 166. Lines on a page, 7. Extent in s'lokas, 4,285. Character, Newári. Appearance, old. Prose and verse. Incorrect.

No. B 10. Substance, Nepalese yellow paper, 12 × 3. Folia, 220. Lines on a page, 7. Extent in s'lokas, 4,285. Character, Newári. Appearance, fresh. Date, Samvat 1859. Incorrect.

A collection of rituals. By Kuladatta. In its general character the work bears a close relation to the Hindu Tántric digests. The codex begins with the definitions of a spiritual guide and his disciple. Then comes the ceremony for erecting and consecrating a Vihára. One desirous of erecting a Vihára should proceed to his spiritual guide on an auspicious day and under an auspicious asterism, and, after paying something in the shape of Dakshiṇá, thrice ask his permission to erect a Vihàra. The request should be made in the following terms: "I am, Sir, an Upásaka. I am desirous of building a Vihára; I solicit your permission." From the time of serving this notice, the spiritual guide should employ himself in such ceremonies as are required previous to the erection, particularly relating to those for producing materials and for removing obstructions, and he should count his beads one hundred thousand times, repeating the mystic formula of Chakres'a, or of the divinity he usually worships. When the number of repetitions is complete, he should proceed to the examination of a site for the building. A piece of land covered by inauspicious trees is unsuitable for a Vihára. Land with pippala trees on the east, *pentaptera Arjuna* on the south-east, *Butea frondosa* on the south, fig trees on the south-west, silk-cotton trees on the west, Vakula *(Mimosops elengi)* on the north-west, glomorous fig trees on the north, and thorny trees on the north-east, is pronounced inauspicious. A triangular piece of ground, or one with uneven surface and full of pits is to be avoided. Land situated on the south-east, the south, the south-west, the west, and the north-west sides of a town or corner is unsuitable. Soil mixed with broken pots, grease, oil or milk, and sacrificial grounds, and cremation ghauts, are impure. But hills, and places where there are Chaityas, As'ramas, penance groves and temples are pure. Viháras should be erected on these. A square plot of ground stretching towards the east, or the north, is the most auspicious. The site for a Vihára should have tanks full of white, red or blue lotuses on the north; mango, jáma and kadamba groves interspersed with large flowering trees on the east; punnága, párijáta, and other trees with sweet-scented flowers, and with the underground covered with jasmines &c. on the south; and shady trees like pippala, jack &c. and juicy plants, on the west. The sound of Biṇa, flute, tom-tom &c. are auspicious. For Bráhmaṇas earth of a white colour, and having the smell of curdled milk, ghi &c. and a sweet taste is auspicious; for Kshatriyas, that of a red colour, having the scent of lotus, champaka &c., and astringent taste; for Vais'yas, that of yellow colour, and having the flavour of wine and of the exudation from the temples of elephants, and sour taste; for S'údras, that of a black colour, no smell and bitter and pungent taste is preferable.

There are several different modes for finding out what land is suitable for what caste, and also what land is suitable for a Vihára. Dig a pit one or two cubits square, place white flowers on the east, red on the west, yellow on the north, and blue on the south sides of the pit. The colour of the flower that withers the latest will indicate the caste for which the land is fitted for a Vihára. Again, pour a quantity of water into the selfsame pit, light a lamp on an earthen pot. If it produces a white flame on the east, it is fit for Bráhmaṇas, if a red flame on the west, it is for the warrior caste, and so forth. There are other modes for finding the same thing out. Some say the city in which a Vihára is to be erected should be situated on the northern, some say on the southern bank of a river.

When the Vihára is to be consecrated by sacrifice, the A'chárya, thoroughly versed in the three *samádhis*, should sit in the evening on a square diagram well cleansed with cow-dung; he should first worship the three jewels and praise the ten Dikpálas by chanting gáthás, and then, with the left knee touching the ground, and the hands folded, ask them for land by uttering certain gáthás.

Then turning towards the south and placing before him an earthen pot shaped like a crescent, he should scatter over it charcoal dust from a cremation ground, and also blue flowers. The next ceremony is that of lighting the Kopágni—a fire taken from the hearth of the Chaṇḍála who guards the cremation ground. In this fire, burning with full blaze, the A'chárya should pour forth libations with the sound of hum bursting from his throat and with the chant of the awful formula "Níla-varṇam Nílámbharaṇa bhúshitam" &c. Then he should employ himself in removing 'salyas' or such evil working bones as may be underground. Then follow the ceremonies of Vástu worship, worship of Viháradevatá, measurement of the ground with a string, observation of omens, examination of the Vástu serpent, laying of the foundation stone, division of the Vihára into rooms, felling of trees for the Vihára, different measures of these trees according to the difference of caste, &c.

The work then lays down rules for building a dwelling-house. The table of measurement is as follows:—

7 atoms	make	1 aṇda (egg).
7 aṇḍas	"	1 sukshmaraja or minute powder.
7 sukshmarajas	"	1 s'as'araja.
7 s'as'arajas	"	1 ekáḍharaja.
7 ekáḍharajas	"	1 sáraja.
7 sárajas	"	1 yúka.
7 yúkas	"	1 yava or barley.
6 yavas	"	1 kaniyas'anguli.
7 yavas	"	1 madhyamánguli.
8 yavas	"	1 jyeshṭhánguli.
11 angulis	"	1 vitasti.
1 vitasti	"	1 cubit.

The room of a Vihára in which the Lord's image is to be placed should be painted with the representations of Tathágatas, Bodhisattvas, the goddess of knowledge and Vidyádharas. A pair of eyes and a pair of water-pots are to be painted on every door, on the outer face of the door the ten figures of a water-pot, an ear &c.; at the top of the windows Tathágatas, chosen Bodhisattvas, and various decorations. In the interior of the room, just against the image, should the Bodhi tree be painted, with Varuṇa and Lokádhipas on the right and left of the image. Varuṇa should be painted white, with two hands holding a terrible noose. On the right side of the door, should be painted the two fierce images of Mahábala, and Mahákála,—Mahábala black with two hands, one face, and three eyes at once red and circular, his hairs brown and raised upwards, his face fierce with protuberant teeth, with tiger skin for clothes and eight serpents for ornaments, touching the right shoulders with the four fingers of the left, and the left shoulder with those of the right hand.

The figure of Mahákála is nearly the same but made fiercer by a garland of skulls.

On the left side of the door should be painted the king and the queen of Hareta birds facing each other, the queen seated on an emerald throne, white, exceedingly beautiful, with jewelled staff in hand, and ever engaged in one of her five hundred frolics. The king should be represented as sitting on a throne of rubies. The painted figures are to be consecrated by ceremonies peculiar to each.

The work then enters upon the subject of ordination. A disciple desirous of renouncing the world should take a solemn vow, with folded hands, before his spiritual guide, in the following words:

"I such and such a person, take shelter with Dharma, take shelter with Buddha, take shelter with the Sangha for ever." The spiritual guide should then communicate to him the five S'ikshápadas or Primary Lessons. The disciple should promise to take nothing not given to him, to renounce double-dealing, falsehood, and the use of wine, during the course of his whole life, and solicit his spiritual guide to grant him the light of the Five Lessons in the following words:—"Grant me, O Lord, the protection of the three, grant all that an Upásaka wants, such as the Five Lessons &c.; my name is such and such, I solicit the favour of my A'chárya in investing me as a Bhikshu." After this, his head should be shaved, leaving only the coronal hair. Then the Guru should try the firmness of his disciple's determination by questions, and, having satisfied himself of his sincerity, should anoint him with waters brought from the four oceans, and make him put on a piece of ochre-colored cloth. The Neophite should announce his entrance into the order by repeating the following word three times: "I, of such and such a name, throw away the signs of a householder's state for ever, and receive those of a hermit." Then he should place himself entirely under the protection of the 'three jewels' by reciting the formula —"I take refuge with Dharma, I take refuge with Buddha, I take refuge with Sangha." After having received the ten commandments from the Guru, he should have recourse to the following formula—"As my Lord never neglects the duties of life, so I too promise never to deviate from the path of duty in my life." Then he should request his *guru* to favour him with an alms-bowl and a piece of ochre-colored cloth. He should call the whole congregation around him, place his right knee on the ground, and with folded hands, say, "I am named such and such, bring that piece of cloth to me, let it remain here that the congregation may have confidence in me, and delight to see me. Bring that piece of cloth, Upádhyáya, I request you, let it remain here for the satisfaction of the congregation. Bring that piece of cloth, O Lord, that I may inspire confidence." On the Ácharya's handing him over the consecrated cloth, he should wear it, and thenceforth be one of the Bhikshus.

The text is full of technical terms, and not always intelligible.

Beginning. ॐ नमः श्रीवज्रसत्त्वाय।

महागमात् सदाम्नायात् सच्छिष्याध्येषणावशात्।

वज्रसत्त्वं जगन्नाथं नत्वेयं क्रियते मया॥

सेवादिभूशोधनभूपरिग्रहाः पादस्य संस्थापनदारुकर्म्मणी।

देवप्रतिष्ठा च तथैव गण्डीध्वजोच्छ्रयः शेषत एव कार्य्यः

परीक्षा गुरुशिष्याणां गुरोरध्येषणा ततः।

मन्त्रसेवां गुरुः कुर्य्यात् ततो भूमेः परीक्षणं॥

तत्र विहारादिकर्म्म विधातुकामो यजमान आदावाचार्य्यं परीक्षेत। यः सत्त्वेषु दयारहितः परमर्म्मभेदकः सत्त्वविद्वेषी। छद्मनरचितः कुलप्रमतमदोरमर्य्य-भ(?) आत्मप्रशंसी परदोषोद्भावकस्तमाचार्य्यं परित्यजेत्। गुरुरपि एवंविधं शिष्यं परित्यजेत्। यः पुनः श्रद्धाप्रज्ञाकृपावान् अक्रोधः वीर्य्यसत्त्वाविसंवादकः पूज्यो गुरुपरीक्षकस्तमेवंविधं शिष्यमनुकूले यद्गुरुः।

End. निरीक्षतन्त(?) निखिलं मयेयं संधृता चारुतरा विशुद्धा।

नापूर्व्व+++++भनेन तथापि सन्तः सुपीयं(?) क्षमध्वं॥

सारसरलमनर्थं श्रीकुलदत्तेन योजितं ग्रन्थं।

यजमानमनोहरणं निखिलाचार्य्यस्य परमाभरणं॥

पञ्जीविपापविपिनी यदवाप्य गुरुं मया।

वज्रसत्त्वोऽस्तु लोकोऽयं ते नीवद्ध(?) मया वरः॥

Colophon. इति महापण्डितनिःसङ्गाचार्य्यश्रीकुलदत्तविरचितक्रियासङ्ग्रहनामपञ्जिकाष्टम-प्रकरणं समाप्तं।

No. B. 32.

KUS'A JATAKA.

कुशजातकं ।

Substance, paper, 16¾ × 4⅝. Folia, 73. Lines on a page, 8. Extent in s'lokas, 2,153. Character, Newári. Date, ? Appearance, old. Verse. Incorrect.

An account of a fast called Poshadhavrata, illustrated by a tale regarding the origin of the Ikshḥáku race, and the miraculous transformation of one of the descendants of Ikshákn. This descendant, named Kus'a, was no other than Buddha himself in a former life. The work professes to be a part of a large collection of tales, which bears the title of 'Mahavasvávadána-Kathá.' The story in question is said to have been first related to Rájá As'oka by Upa Gupta who had heard it from Buddha himself. The occasion for it was given by the story of Bodhisattva's destroying the wicked Mára by the sound of a hiccough. The Bhikshus all expressed their wonder at the tale of so great a miracle, and S'ákya Muni related to them a story of which the following is an abstract:

Subandhu of Benares was the lord of sixty thousand cities. In the bed-chamber of the royal palace, there sprang up, all of a sudden, a large number of sugarcane trees. From one of these, a boy was produced, who was named Ikshváku after his birth-place. On the demise of Subandhu, Iks'hváku ascended the throne. He had five hundred wives of whom Avúdá was the chief. Avúdá obtained from Indra a pill which promoted pregnancy. This she dissolved in water, and took a small quantity of the mixture, distributing the rest of it to her rivals. Every one of them gave birth to a son of whom Avúdá's child was the most ugly; but it had on its person all the signs of a royal personage. All the children had the cognomen of Kus'a, such as, Indrakus'a, Devakus'a &c., after the kus'a grass at the extremity of which their mothers had partaken of the medicinal water. Kus'a, the son of Avúdá, was, as the eldest and born of the chief queen, raised to the throne, and he married Sudars'aná, the daughter of the king of Kányakubja in Súrasena. Sudars'aná finding her husband very ugly, left his house, and went over to her father's. Kus'a too proceeded to Kanyakubja, and there displayed his skill in various arts to win the heart of his consort. By the advice of his father-in-law, he placed a valuable jewel (Jyotirasa) on his head. Instantly his ugliness was changed into the most charming beauty, and his wife had no more objection in accepting him.

Beginning. ॐ नमः सर्व्वबुद्धबोधिसत्त्वेभ्यः ।

अथाशोको महीपालः प्राञ्जलिः प्रणमे मुदा ।
उपगुप्तं यतिं नत्वा प्रार्थयद्देवमादरात् ॥
श्रुतं मया भगवता कथितं पोषधव्रतं ।
उपोषधाभिधानेन देवपुत्रेण सञ्चितं ॥
व्रतराजमिदं शास्त्रिन्निद्या लयवासिना ।
श्रुतं पुनरजातादिशत्रुणाऽकृतपापना ॥
पापरोगवतो रोगमुक्तये रचितं गुरो ।
धर्म्मपालाभिधेनापि राज्ञा प्राप्तं महोत्तमं ॥
त्रैलोक्यमोहनं रत्नं पोषधव्रतपुण्यतः ।
तेन रत्नेन दारिद्र्यं शान्तीभूतं श्रुतं मया ॥
वशिष्ठेनर्षिणा भाषोपवासकृतवर्म्मणा ।
चतुर्वर्गफलप्राप्त्यै चीर्णं श्रुतं मयादरात् ॥
मणिचूडेन राज्ञापि पोषधव्रतपुण्यतः ।
चूडारत्नं प्रदत्वा वै दुःप्रसहस्य भूपतेः ॥
राज्यशाला महामानी श्रुतो भवन्मुखाङ्कुरो ।
पुनश्चेच्छाम्यहं श्रोतुं निःप्रजानां जगद्गुरो ॥
केन पुण्येन पुत्राप्तिः स्यात्तद्वृद्धिर्भवेत् कथं ।
दीर्घायुष्ट्वं सुरूपत्वं कुलीनत्वं विवेकिता ॥
सौभाग्यं योषिताञ्चैवमवैधव्यकरं व्रतं ।
गृहस्थानां गृहैश्वर्य्यकरं पुण्यं यतीश्वर ॥
इत्येवं नृपराजेनाशोकेन प्रार्थितस्तदा ।
उपगुप्तस्ततः प्राह राजेन्द्रं व्रतमानसं ॥
शृणु राजन् प्रवक्ष्यामि यथागुरूपदेशतः
पवदं धनदं श्रीदं आयुरारोग्यकारकं ॥
ज्ञानानां ज्ञानिशमनं महापातकनाशनं ।
विरूपाणां रूपकरं सकलाधिकसिद्धिदं ॥

तदिदानीं प्रवक्ष्यामि निरपत्येन भूभुजा ।
सुबन्धनाकं वंशेन व्रतं चीर्णमुपोषधं ॥
तद्यथा गुरुणा शोणवासिना कथितं मम ।
तेनापि श्रुतपूर्व्वं तद् गुरुवक्त्राद्यतिः पुनः ॥
तद्गुरुणा बोधिद्रुममूले श्रुतं मनीश्वरात् ।
शाक्यसिंहान्मानजेतुर्जातकावलिदर्शितुः ॥
कथ्यते तन्महाराज समाहितमनाः शृणु ।
श्रुत्वा सर्व्वत्र लोकेषु बोधयित्वा प्रचारय ॥ भूतपूर्व्वं भिक्षवः ।

End. स्यात् खलु पुनर्भिक्षवोऽस्माकमेवमस्मादन्यः स तेन कालेन तेन समयेन कम्पिल्ल-नगरे पुरुषोऽतोषि येन भार्य्यायै दैर्ष्यप्रकृतेन दुष्टचित्तेन प्रत्येकबुद्धोऽत्यारक्षितः कुशो राजा तेन कालेन तेन समयेन कम्पिल्लनगरे स पुरुषोऽतोषि । यन्या सा भार्य्या यतोषि । सा सुदर्शना महेन्द्रेणाथ धीमता । तस्य भिक्षवः कर्म्मणो विपाकेन कुशराजो विरूपोऽतोषि ।

Colophon. इति श्रीमहावस्तवदानकथायां कुशजातकं समाप्तं ।

No. B. 14.

LOKES'VARA S'ATAKA.

लोकेश्वरशतकः ।

Substance, yellow paper. Folia, 30. Lines on a page, 5. Extent in s'lokas, 250. Character, Newári. Appearance, old. Verse. Incorrect.

A hymn in praise of Lokes'vara in a hundred stanzas. By Vajradatta.

Beginning. ॐ नमो लोकनाथाय ।
भास्वन्माणिक्यभासो मुकुटभ्रतिनमन्नाकनाथोत्तमाङ्गे
भक्तिप्रह्वे सरोजासनशिरसि हसन्मालतीमालिकाभाः ।
सौख्ये शीलस्मृगाङ्कामलकमकपिशितां शाश्वते शान्तयन्त्यो
लोके लोकेशपादामलनखशशभृत्कान्तयः सन्तु शान्त्यै ॥

End. कविरपि जन्मनि जन्मनि भक्तश्चरणेऽवलोकेशस्य ।
प्रकृतिशरणगोऽतरलधीः पराहितगुरुकार्य्यकार्य्यस्यां(?) ॥

Colophon. इति महाचपतलिकश्रीवज्रदत्तकविविरचितं श्रीलोकेश्वरशतकं समाप्तं ।

No. 785.

LALITA VISTARA.

ललितविस्तरः ।

Substance, yellow paper. Folia, 246. Lines on a page, 7 to 9. Character, Newári. Appearance, old. Prose and verse. Correct.

The early life of Buddha. See Introduction to my edition of the Lalita Vistara, 'Asiatic Researches', XX, and Foucaux's 'Rgya-cher-rol-pa.'

No. B. 12.

LANKA'VATA'RA.

लङ्कावतारः ।

Substance, paper, 14¼ × 4. Folia, 198. Lines on a page, 7. Extent in s'lokas, 3,000. Character, Newári. Date, ? Prose and verse. Appearance old. Very incorrect.

An account of a visit paid by S'ákya to the king of Lanká (Ceylon), and of his preachings in that island. It is reckoned as one of the nine principal texts of Nepalese Buddhism, and held in high esteem. In common with the other eight works, it is called a "*Mahávaipulya Maháyána Sútra.*" Three different translations of it exist in the Chinese, one under the name of *Tarshing-jih-ling-kia-king*, another under *Lang-kia-o-po-ta-lo-pao-king*, and the third under *Jih-leng-kia-king*, the last by Bodhiruchi of the Wei Dynasty (circa 168—190.)

Abstract. Buddha had been on a visit to the capital of the serpents (Nágaloka) in the ocean, but returned thence in a week, and settled on the mount Malaya in Lanká. Rávana came to pay his respects to the great personage, and prayed him to give the definitions of virtue and vice. When Rávaṇa was satisfied, a Bodhisattva, Mahámati by name, asked Buddha several questions, and received satisfactory answers. The questions were 1st, From what principle of human nature ratiocination has its origin? 2nd, How an argument can be made pure, *i. e.*, how to detect fallacies? What is the nature of fallacies? From what principle in human nature do fallacies proceed? Where do the emancipated go? How could one in bondage be emancipated?

What object do holy men meditate upon? What effect is produced by belief? What is a cause? What an effect? What are the hundred and eight padas or select sentences? What are the different ways in which Vijnánas or ideas are generated? In how many ways are they retained, and how are they lost? What are the grounds of a belief in the fact of universal causation? What is ambiguity in speech? How and from what source is it produced? What is Nirváṇa? How do Arhats and Tathágatas hold the meditation of Bodhisattvas? What are the different definitions of obtaining attention and of moving it? What are fixed as the five in succession? What are the definitions of entity and non-entity? What are the definitions of teaching, doctrine, and regulation or rule? What are the eight different sorts of transitoriness? What are Bodhisattvas, S'rávakas, Pratyeka Buddhas, Nirodhakramas and Amesandhis? Whether Tathágata is eternal? When all these questions were answered, the Lord delivered a lecture on the Saugata philosophy, and explained the nature of a mystic formula which wards Rákshasas off.

Beginning. ॐ नमः श्रीआर्य्यसर्व्वज्ञाय। समाप्ता वस्तुविक्रान्त विक्रमि इच्छा(?) प्रज्ञापार-
मितानिर्द्देशः सर्व्वसत्त्वसन्तोषाद्बोधिसत्त्वपिटकान्तं।
नैरात्म्यं यत्र धर्म्मा हि धर्म्मराजेन भाषितं।
लङ्कावतारे तत्सूत्रमिदं यत्नेन लिख्यते॥
एवं मया श्रुतमेकस्मिन् समये भगवान् लङ्कापुरे समुद्रमलयशिखरे विहरति स्म। नानारत्नगोत्रपुष्पप्रतिमण्डिते महता भिक्षुसङ्घेन सार्द्धं महता च बोधिसत्त्वगणेन नानाबुद्धक्षेत्रसन्निपतितैर्बोधिसत्त्वैर्महासत्त्वैरनेकसमाधिवशिताबलाभिज्ञाविक्रीड़ितैर्महामतिबोधिसत्त्वमहासत्त्व पूर्व्वङ्गमैः सर्व्वबुद्धपाण्यभिषिक्ताभिषिक्तैः स्वचित्तगोचरपरिज्ञानकुशलैर्नानासत्त्वचित्तचरित्रनिरूपणविनयधारिभिः पञ्चध(?)स्वभावविज्ञाननैरात्म्याद्वयगतिङ्गतैः।

End. शशरोममणिप्रख्यं मुक्तानां देशयेन्नयं।
यथा हि ग्रन्थो गङ्गेन युक्तो युक्तिस्तया यदि॥
अतो मुक्तिर्भवेद्युक्तिमन्यथा तु न कल्पयेत्।
चक्षुः कर्म्म च तृष्णा च अविद्या योगिनस्तथा॥
चक्षूरूपे समस्तापि आविलस्य मनस्तथेति।

Colophon. आर्य्यसद्धर्म्मलङ्कावतारो नाम महायानसूत्रं सगाथकं समाप्तं।

No A. 11.

MAHA'VASTU-AVADA'NA.

महावस्तवादानः ।

Substance, paper 18¾ × 5¼. Folia, 334. Lines on a page, 11. Extent in s'lokas, 18,370. Character, Newari. Date, Newári Samvat 822. Appearance, old. Prose and verse. Incorrect.

A cyclopædia of Buddhist legends and doctrines. It gives an elaborate history of Buddha's life and preachings, explaining every incident of his life by references to his past existences. It also gives a simple and popular exposition of many abstruse doctrines of the Buddhist faith.

When Lord Buddha was at the Jetavana grove, Maudgaláyana visited eight principal places of torture in hell. They were—(1) Saujíva, (2) Kálasútra, (3) Saugháta, (4) 1st Raurava, (5) 2nd Raurava, (6) Mahávíchi, (7) Tapana, (8) Pratapana. On his return from the infernal regions, he delivered four different speeches before four different assemblies, painting in glowing colours, the tortures, the convulsions, the insufferable pain of the nether world. After the conclusion of each lecture, he enjoined, in forcible language, the necessity of Bráhmacharya and of abstinence.

When the Lord lived at Gṛidhrakuṭa in Rájagṛiha, Maudgaláyana chanced to meet a Suddhávása Devaputra. From him he learned of the great merits of one Uttíya, a banker, the disciple of Sarvávibhú. Maudgaláyana immediately changed his destination, and directed his steps towards Vasumati, where Uttíya lived. On his way he happened to meet Abhaya and Nanda, two Bhikshus. He cultivated Abhaya's friendship, but tried to annoy Nanda by calling him a Brahmachárí, but in vain. They all proceeded to Sarvávibhú before whom Maudgaláyana made a confession of his wicked design of annoying Nanda. He feasted the Lord with rich viands obtained from Uttíya and some perfumers. The Lord said to Abhaya, who had betaken himself to meditation, "You are to become a Buddha in future, in the hundred thousandth Kalpa—your name will be S'ákya Muni, and these perfumers with Maudgaláyana will be your first S'rávakas." Lord Sarvávibhú then taught them the four Charyás or practices. The first refers to the conduct of those who love their parents, live in their families, revere Bráhmaṇas, beg in their own quarters, never neglect the ten duties, instruct others, relieve the poor, perform good works, worship the lord, and train the mind for the reception of the highest Sambodhi knowledge : this Charyá is called Prakriti. 2nd, The conduct of those who hope for Buddhahood in one of the innumerable Kalpas to come, who want to be perfect in knowledge and in good conduct, to be the lord and governor of gods and men : it is called Praṇidhána Charyá. 3rd, Those who hopefor Bodhi knowledge by gradation, are said to be in Anuloma Charyá. 4th, The endeavours of men to put a period to future transmigration are included in the last or Vivarttana Charyá.

At the request of Maudgaláyana, Kás'yapa gave him a description of the ten Bhúmis or stages, they are : (1) Durárohá, (2) Barddhamáná, (3) Pushpamaṇḍitá, (4) Ruchirá, (5) Chittavichitrá, (6) Rúpavatí, (7) Durjayá, (8) Janmánudes'á, (9) Jauvará, (10) Abhisheká. A Bhúmi means the ground-work of Bodhisattva knowledge. The names, however, here given do not correspond with what occur in the Das'abhúmís'vara, *ante*, p. 86. The characteristics of the first Bhúmi are alms-giving, mercy, indefatigableness, want of arrogance, knowledge of the S'ás'tras, progress, the power of pleasing men, and patience.

The characteristics of the 2nd stage are twenty Adhyás'ayas or intentions. They are, (1) intention for doing good, called Kalyáṇádhyás'aya ; (2) Snigdhádhyás'aya, or that state of mind in which the man is never moved by anger ; (3) Madhurádhyás'aya, or that state of the mind in which people are disposed to please women by service ; (4) Tíkshnádhyás'aya, or the knowledge of this world and the world to come ; (5) Vipuládhyás'aya, or the desire resulting in the active exertion for doing good to all creatures ; (6) Vichitrádhyás'aya, or charity without pride ; (7) Aparyyádánádhyás'aya, open-handedness ; (8) Anupahatádhyas'aya, or the power of resisting the temptations of the wicked ; (9) Asádháraṇádhyás'aya, or uncommon diligence for the happiness of the whole animal creation ; (10) Unnatádhyás'aya, or contempt for the doctrines of Tirthikas ; (11) Ahripanádhyás'aya, or pursuit of virtue for other than enjoyment ; (12) Anivartyádhyás'aya, or firmness in the belief in Buddha in spite of strong temptations ; (13) Akritrimádhyás'aya, or aversion to the state of merchants, Pratyeka Buddhas, and others ; (14) S'uddhás'aya, or desire for supreme good and contempt for all gains ; (15) Driḍhádhyásáya, or determination in spite of opposition ; (16) Svabhávádhyás'ya, or contempt for gifts not given with a good will ; (17) Triptádhyás'aya, contentment or aversion to earthly enjoyment; (18) Pungaládhyás'aya, ambition for omniscience; (19) Anantádhyás'aya, or charity without the expectation of celestial enjoyments in return. The 20th is not given.

The principal characteristic of the third stage is the passion for alms-giving. The following is a list of the duties to be performed in gradually passing from the fourth to the eighth stage. Reverence to parents; firm belief in the identity of the Stûpa with the Sangha or Buddhist congregation; aversion to all hostile criticism against Tathágata's character; aversion to sin; accumulation of meritorious deeds; exertion for virtue; aversion to slaughter; dislike of grievous hurts in a burst of passion; close adherence to the ten ways to virtue; unwillingness to mix in counsels for murder; performance of good work without vulgar curiosity; cheerfulness in times of danger; absence of a sense of exaltation in times of prosperity; purity of heart; holiness of desires, and pious works. In the eighth stage the mind becomes all-mercy. The Bodhisattvas, who passing the ninth enter the tenth stage, become the means of doing an immense amount of good to others. On receiving the full development of the tenth stage the Bodhisattva, who pants for human abode and longs to receive an earthly form, is a Sambuddha. He enters the womb, remains in the womb, obtains his caste, renounces the world: heroism and knowledge become his characteristic virtues.

The last is explained by references to the history of S'ákya Muni. He entered Máyá's womb, that is, his Garbhákránti. His son remained for years in Yas'odhará's womb. He renounced the world and so forth. The Sannibaddha, who dwells at the root of the Bodhi tree and obtains omniscience, gets five eyes, *viz.*, the animal eye, the celestial eye, the eye of knowledge, that of religion, and that of Buddha. The animal eye sees by the help of light. It sees real objects and minute objects. The celestial eye is superior to the eyes of Devas and Yakshas—larger, brighter and more powerful. The eye of Dharma produces ten different powers; 1st the power of appreciating; 2nd, that of appreciating the merits of men of different kinds; 3rd, that of knowing the different essences which lead to mukti; 4th, that of knowing the characters of other people; 5th, that of knowing the consequences of good or bad actions; 6th, that of evading mundane pains; 7th, the knowledge of the importance of meditation; 8th, the power of recalling to mind the events of former existences; 9th, the purity of the celestial eye; 10th, the destruction of all mundane pains.

The Buddha's eye sees eighteen things: It gives unrestricted view of the present; (2) the remembrance of the past; (3) prescience of the future; (4) perfect knowledge following delusions *i. e.*, false knowledge, false work &c.; (5) of all previous perfect knowledge following the delusions of mind, karma &c.; (6) of all perfect knowledge consequent on delusions produced by words; (7) the belief that ideas or opinions cannot be destroyed; (8) strength; (9) memory; (10) deep meditation; (11) perfect knowledge; (12) the knowledge that emancipation can be injured; (13) there is no falling off; (14) no creation; (15) permanence of devotion to memory; (16) permanence of the faculties of the mind; (17) fearlessness; (18) unity of determination.

Lord Buddha delivered a long discourse on the greatness of the Jinas, and on their duties and excellences. They give instruction to the congregation; and, though possessing superhuman powers and abilities, still conform to the ways of man. They wash their faces, though these smell sweetly. They take baths, though ever so pure. They take meal, though they never feel hungry. The voice of a Sugata sounds like music, and is as delightful as the distant rolling of clouds.

Dípañkara.—Kás'yapa gave the following account of Dípañkara to Maudgaláyana. In one of the innumerable past kalpas there was a king named Archchishṭa in the royal city of Dípavatí. Dípavatí was a large city, extending over an area of 84 square Yojanas. Bodhisattva Dipañkara, while descending from the Tushita heaven, thought Archchishṭa to be a suitable father for him, and accordingly entered the womb of his queen, the virtuous Sus'ílá. This was done on the occasion when the full-moon was in conjunction with the auspicious asterism Pushyá. The mother was in a state of sound health, neither affected by bilious nor by phlegmatic humour. She saw the Bodhisattva in her womb, and the Bodhisattva saw her from it. When in the throes of childbirth, she requested the king to send her to a tank where lotus grows. When she arrived at the side of the tank, lo! an island sprang up in the midst of it. The Bodhisattva was born on that island. At the moment of his birth there was a miraculous manifestation of a large number of bright lamps, hence his name Dípañkara. On the second day of his birth Dípañkara commenced his philanthropic tour round the earth, equally useful to gods and men. For the benefit of his relations he returned to Dípavatí with eighty thousand Bhikshus in his company. The king, his father, accorded him a magnificent reception. He employed five hundred Bráhmaṇs to recite Vedic hymns. Megha, one of these, offered five lotus flowers to Dípañkara, and asked a boon to the effect that he might become in one of his future existences equal to Dípañkara in power, in knowledge, and in every good quality. His request was granted. It was foretold on the occasion that Megha would become Buddha S'ákya Muni of Kapilavastu.

Mañgala Vastu.—The Lord said to Maudgaláyana that he obtained a similar boon from Mañgala the next Buddha after Dípañkara. Mañgala had three several congregations consisting of a hundred thousand, ninety thousand and eighty thousand S'rávakas respectively. His two favourite disciples were Sudeva and Dharmadeva and two principal Bhikshunís, S'ívá and Rochaná. Sudeva and S'ívá were celebrated for their knowledge, and the other two for their power of working miracles (ṛiddhi). Mañgala's father was Sundara, and his mother S'rí. The future S'ákya Muni was then an elephant, Atula by name, a resident of the city of Uttara. He gave Mañgala a hearty welcome and got his benediction.

Chhattra Vastu.—In the Sub-Himalayan regions there lived a female Yaksha, named Kaṇḍala, who had one thousand sons, some being twins. They proceeded to Vais'áli and stole the vital power of the inhabitants. Labouring under various diseases, people forgot to propagate their species. The Lichchhavas, the royal Kshatríyas of Vais'ali, were then the most influential men. To remedy this evil Tomala, their headman, undertook a journey to Rájagṛiha where Lord Buddha had been dwelling for some time.

On the solicitation of Tomala, Buddha consented to grace the city with his presence. Vimbisára the king of Rájagṛiha begged permission to follow him, and it was easily granted. The Lichchhavas came a long way to receive the Lord.

When they reached the banks of the Ganges, a parrot, a messenger from Gosṛ'iñga came, humbly bowed to the Lord, invited him in human voice to Gosṛ'iñga, and went away. Every one wondered at the human voice of the bird; but the Lord said, that was nothing new; Brahmadatta king of Benares had three sons, the first an owl, the second a starling, the third a parrot. Up to an advanced age he had no sons. He went to the Himálayas to receive the blessings of the Ṛishis. They advised him to pick up three eggs which he had seen on the way, and to nurse the young ones as his sons. He placed those eggs in vessels filled with honey and clarified butter. The eggs produced young ones in due time. The young chicks were equally intelligent, each had a strong retentive memory, and each spoke just as men do. They were all trained in state-craft. When asked by the king, they gave very intelligent answers with regard to the first principles in politics. The owl said, "Strong passions are unworthy of a king, for when he restrains his passions, his wealth increases, his virtues and his intelligence have free scope for development." The starling (s'álika) said, "There are three cardinal points in political economy, acquisition of wealth, accumulation of wealth, and proper investment of the accumulated hoards." The parrot said, "There are five sources of a king's strength, 1st prowess, (2) children, (3) relatives, (4) army consisting of elephants, horse, foot and chariots, (5) prudence, the most important of all."

As soon as the Lord touched the boundary of the city all the inhabitants regained their health. Every one was astonished at this miracle. The Lord said, "Do not wonder, this is not the first time that epidemic diseases have been cured by my presence. In one of my former existences, I was Rakshita, the son of Brahmadatta's priest; this Brahmadatta was the king of Kampillya in Pánchála. Rakshita, deeply sensible of the miseries of the worldly life, betook himself to the forest at the foot of the Himálayas, and there practised austerities. In a short time he acquired considerable power of working miracles. He could touch the sun and the moon with his hands. At this time the people of Kampillya contracted a contagious disease which defied the skill of experienced physicians. But as soon as Rakshita entered the outskirts of the city at the request of the king, all the sufferers were reported to be convalescent.

"Similarly, when I had been born as Mahes'a, the renowned elephant of the king of Benares, I was invited by the people of Mithilá to cure them of an epidemic (Amánusha-vyádhi): my presence was enough for the attainment of their end.

"In the same manner, I saved the citizens of Rájagṛiha by my presence, when I had been Rishava, a bull, in the kingdom of Anga."

Thus saying, and taking a meal, the Lord directed his steps towards the lake Markaṭa.

Story of Málini.—A Pratyeka Buddha entered the city of Váráṇasí for alms, but got nothing. A girl, finding his alms-bowl empty, brought him home, and gave him a hearty meal. When he died a stúpa was erected on his remains, and the girl decorated the stúpa every day with flowers and aromatics. She desired that she may be born with a garland of flowers in every one of her future existences ; her desire was fulfilled. In her next existence she was born a Devakanyá with a garland of flowers round her neck. From heaven she descended on earth, and was born in the same way as Máliní, the daughter of Kriki, king of Váráṇasí. Máliní invited lord Kás'yapa and his retinue, and entertained them with a sumptuous meal. The Bráhmans, numerous and influential at the court of her father, taking umbrage at her conduct, induced the king to order her banishment. Máliní humbly begged for a week's respite, which was granted. During those seven days, five hundred of her brothers, the ministers and officers of the Bhaṭṭa army, and the citizens were all converted to the A'rya Dharma. The converts regarded Máliní as the saviour of their souls. Angry at the wicked machinations of the Bráhmans, they proceeded in a body to remonstrate with them. The Bráhmans took refuge with the king. They revoked the sentence of Máliní's banishment ; but induced the king to send ten armed men to kill Kás'yapa, the root of all their woes. These armed men were easily converted by the great Sage. They next deputed a larger number of men, but with the same result. They saw that by sending armed men they only added to the already overwhelming number of the perverts. They, therefore, determined to despatch the business themselves. Armed with clubs, maces and other weapons they marched in martial array to the hermitage of Kás'yapa. Kás'yapa invoked the goddess Prithví, and desired her to show her powers against these Bráhmans. She rooted up a stout palm tree, hurled it at the Bráhmans, and crushed them to death.

Story of Jyotipála.—Márakáraṇḍa was a place in the kingdom of Kos'ala. Buddha dwelt there for some time with all his congregation. One day, just on the breaking up of his meditation, his eyes fell on a piece of grassy plain of wide extent. He smiled. A'nanda, who stood near, asked " O Lord, why do you smile ?" The Lord said, " This plain had been the dwelling place of Kás'yapa. He had his hut here. Krakachchhanda, Kaṇaka and Kás'yapa all sat at this spot." He added, " This Márakáraṇḍa had been at one time Veruḍiṅga, a village principally inhabited by Bráhmaṇs. Kás'yapa had here only one disciple, named Ghaṭíkára, a maker of earthenwares. Jyotipála was one of the young sons of Ghaṭikára. The disciple heard one day that his Lord was dwelling in a forest close to Veruḍiñga. With great difficulty he dragged his unwilling son, fond of idle play, to the presence of the sage, who gave the youth "the five lessons." In a short time Jyotipála entered a hermitage. When Kás'yapa, in the course of his perambulations, returned to Ghaṭikára from Váráṇasí, for to him Ghaṭikára was dearer than the king of that place, Jyotipála asked him for a boon, praying to be raised to the list of Buddhas in a future existence. This boon was granted, and it was also foretold that Jyotipála would practise Brahmacharya in the Bhadrakalpa at Kapilavastu, and, then rising to the Tushita heaven, should become a Devaputra named Svetaketu, and afterwards S'ákya Siñha.

Origin of the Kauliya tribe.—Kalyáṇa was the son of the king Mahásammata. Kalyáṇa begat Ráva. Ráva begat Uposhadha. Uposhadha begat Mándhátá. The descendants of Mándhátá were all kings for several generations. One of them, Sujáta, became king of the Ikshváku in the great city of Sáketa. He had six children. The five legitimate children were, Upura, Nipura, Kalakaṇḍaka, Ulkámukha, and Hastikas'írsha. The illegitimate son was Jeta, the son of a concubine named Jetí. The king was so very fond of her that, in compliance with her wishes, he disinherited his legitimate sons, and nominated Jeta to the throne. The disinherited sons proceeded towards the north, followed by a large retinue of loyal citizens and soldiers. They were at first hospitably entertained by the king of Kos'ala. But their popularity with his own subjects displeased the king. He dismissed them from his presence, and ordered them to quit his city. They entered a forest at the foot of the Himálaya, where Ṛishi Kapila had his dwelling-place. They built a city there, the city was named Kapilavastu from the vicinity of the Ṛishi. U'pura, the eldest of the brothers, was elected king. He was succeeded by Nipura. Karakaṇḍa succeeded Nipura, and was himself succeeded by Ulkámukha. Ulkámukha had Hastinikas'írsha for his son, and Siñhatanu for his grandson. Siñhatanu had four sons and one daughter. The sons were S'uddhodana, Dhautodana, S'uklodana, Amṛitodana, and the daughter was Amitá. Amitá was a leper. All the skill of the royal physicians was employed in vain to cure her. The loathsome disease made her an object of general hatred. Her brothers carried her to a hill named Utsañga-parvata, where they placed her in a subterranean room stored with provisions which would last for years. The entrance to the room was closed for ever. The only door by which the interior could be approached was covered with planks; and a heap of earth, placed on those planks, concealed everything. The new mode of living had its effects on Amitá's constitution. She, in a short time, recovered from the dreadful disease. A tiger caught the scent of a human being, and scratching the earth away laid the planks bare. Kola, a Rishi, who lived close by, happened to come near the planks. He removed them, and discovered Amitá blooming with all the freshness of youth. The charming maid made an impression on his mind. He married her. The marriage was blessed with an issue of 32 children. These were sent to Kapilavastu, where they were received with open arms, because Kola was no unworthy relation to the S'ákyas, having himself reigned for a long time as the king of Váráṇasí. Amitá's sons were known either by their patronymic Kauliya, or by the name of Vyághrapádyá, from the circumstance of their mother having been discovered by a tiger. The S'ákyas and Kauliyas were afterwards connected by innumerable matrimonial ties.

Birth and Marriage of Máyá Deví.—There was in the country of Devaüha a great S'ákya named Subhúti. He married in the family of the Kauliyas, and had seven daughters, *viz.*, (1) Máyá; (2) Mahámáyá; (3) Atimáyá; (4) Anantamáyá; (5) Chúlímáyá, (6) Kolísábá and (7) Mahéprajávatí. Máyá was the most lovely, the most beautiful and the most accomplished of them all. When Siñhahanu died, and was succeeded by his son S'uddhodana, the first measure of the new king was the celebration of his own marriage with Máyá and Maháprajávatí, and that of his brothers with the other daughters of Subhútí. All the Pratyeka Buddhas were delighted in giving their respective forecasts (Vyákaraṇáni) to the effect that the Bodhisattva would descend from the Tushita heaven in the twelfth year after this marriage.

Story of the Deer Kings.—There were five hundred Pratyeka Buddhas at Rishipaṭṭana in Váráṇasí. They too gave their own Vyákaraṇánis. At that time there were two lords of the deer at Váráṇasí; they were named Nyagrodha and Vis'ákha, sons of Ráhaka. Each of them had a flock of 500 deer under him. Brahmadatta, king of Váráṇasí, was in the habit of hunting and killing the deer. The deer kings, unable to stop this slaughter of their subjects, made a treaty with the king on the condition of sending one deer every day to the royal kitchen. Years rolled on. No party had any reason for complaint. The king, secure in the enjoyment of the tribute of venison, discontinued his hunting excursions. The deer, too, after having spared one of themselves for the king every day, jumped, frisked and ran about just as they liked. At last an event occurred which put a stop to the tribute altogether. It was on the occasion when a doe was in her turn to be sent to the king. She was *enceinte*. She applied to the deer-king Vis'ákha under whom she lived, for a change of her turn on the score of her being big with two fawns. Her death, so pleaded she, would cause the death of three animals. But none of the flock volunteered to go in her stead. When the deer kings found their efforts to be of no avail, Nyagrodha, one of them, nobly resolved to sacrifice himself at the altar of charity. He proceeded forthwith to the royal presence, and explained to him the circumstances under which he had taken the resolution. The king was struck with wonder at the generosity of the poor animal, and immediately issued a proclamation freeing the deer-kings from their contract.

Exactly at the time of this proclamation Bodhisattva was descending from the Tushita heaven. He was thinking of a family which he could grace with his birth. Vimbisára and Udayana requested the Lord to honor Rájagriha or Kaus'ámbí by making it his birth-place. But he preferred S'uddhodana, because Máyá, his would-be mother, was virtuous, kind-hearted, and honorable, and she had only seven days to live after the birth of her son.

Birth of Buddha.—Actuated by a divine impulse Máyá requested her husband to send her alone to the Dhritaráshṭra palace. There she intended to practise the eleven virtues of Ahiṇs'á, Brahmacharyya &c. S'uddhodana complied with her request. On the night of the full moon, when the moon was in the Pushyá constellation, the Bodhisattva entered the left side of his mother while she was reclining after sunset on a milk-white sofa. When in labours Máyá remained leaning on the branch of a tree in the *Lumbiní* garden. In that posture she gave birth to Sarvárthas'iddha. On that day the S'ákyas had born unto them five hundred sons, including Sundarananda and others, five hundred daughters including Yas'odhará &c., five hundred horses, the same number of slaves and elephants; they also obtained the same number of diamonds and hoards. S'uddhodana sent a palankin made by the hands of Vis'vakarmá to bring the mother and the son to the palace.

When Buddha was born, all creatures obtained what they wanted, from which circumstance he was called Sarvárthas'iddha "the gratifier of every wish." No sooner was the prince brought to the palace, than the king sent for learned astrologers to cast his nativity. They unanimously declared the child would be a 'great man,' a Mahápurusha. He, they declared, had all the thirty-two signs of greatness, such as Samá or symmetry, Hrishṭá or stoutness, Dirghá, tallness, A'yatá or broad-chestedness, Upasakha &c. The astrologers assured the king that at the time of the prince's birth the diadems of the gods had fallen from their heads.

Asita, a Bráhman of Ujjayiní in Dakshiṇápatha, who was well versed in the mysteries of the Vedas, who had renounced the world, who had lived long on the Vindhya mountain, practising austerities as a hermit, came from the Himálaya, his recent lodge, to see the Bodhisattva. He descended before the boy from the aerial regions, and began to weep. "O, what a wretch am I," cried the old man, "I shall not be able to avail myself of the sublime teaching of this boy! So old am I, that I am sure to perish before he commences preaching the doctrine of Nirváṇa. I am sure he will become a great Buddha. The signs are clear and distinct; the marks deep and indubitable. There are eighty characteristics which indicate a future Buddha, and I discern them all on this little boy. Unfortunate that I am, I shall not see the miracles wrought, the austerities practised, and the difficulties surmounted by him on his way to Nirváṇa!"

First Meditation of Sarvárthas'iddha.—Once on a time king S'uddhodana went to one of his parks with his family. The prince took a walk beyond the park, and entered a village inhabited by husbandmen. He saw a serpent and a frog. He startled the serpent, and it devoured the frog. This convinced the prince of the evanescent character of everything mundane. Under the shadow of a rose-apple tree he fell into a deep meditation. Five Ṛishis, who were passing through the air, were suddenly stopped in their course as soon as they came over his head. They could not proceed further in spite of all their endeavours. They were quite at a loss as to the reason of this strange phenomenon. But they soon came to learn that a Bodhisattva was in meditation below. They chanted a gáthá, turned round, and went another way.

The king at his meal enquired after Sarvárthas'iddha. He was no where to be found. The chamberlain searched after him from grove to grove, but to no purpose. At last he was discovered holding a meditation under the rose-apple tree, and the most strange sight was, that the shadow of the tree had not forsaken him though the sun had gone from the east to the west. The king, when this was reported to him, ran to the spot, fell on his knees, and praised his son in hymns.

Yas'odhará's Blushing.—But he entertained an apprehension that his son would take the first opportunity to renounce the world. The best means to provide against that contingency would be, he thought, to marry him as soon as possible. From this motive, he invited all the S'ákya girls to his park. Among the rest came Yas'odhará, the accomplished daughter of Mahánámá *alias* Subhúti. The king appointed his son to receive these girls, and to offer them presents of rich dresses. Yas'odhará, when the prince came to him, blushed. Her blushing was explained in the following way:

There lived in former times Nárada, a Bráhmaṇa of the family of Kaus'ika, at Váráṇasí. Having found by bitter experience that the thirst for temporal enjoyment would never come to an end, he entered the monastic life, and practised Yogas at the foot of the Himálaya. He succeeded so far as to work miracles, and to learn the "five experiences." But he was still found deficient in "the art of apportioning" (Sañvibhája). To teach him this, Indra came from heaven, with the sun, the moon and Mátuli in his company. They demanded victuals from Kaus'ika Nárada, telling at the same time that heaven is gained by alms, and hell by withholding the same. Kaus'ika promised to set every day, without fail, a portion of his food for the needy. Hirí, the daughter of Indra, fell in love with Nárada, and her cheeks reddened at the sight of the Ṛishi. Hirí was Yas'odhará and Nárada, Buddha.

Yas'odhará's Revenge.—At the grand party aforesaid, prince Sarvárthas'iddha presented rich clothes to all the assembled girls. He gave a ring and many valuables to Yas'odhará, but still she was not satisfied. Why? Because in one of their former existences, he and she were the banished prince and princess of Kás'í. The prince caught a guana, and asked his wife to cook it. She declined. The prince was obliged to dress it for himself. But when it was ready, the princess expressed her desire to partake of the dish, and her husband managed to deprive her of her share by swallowing it while she had been away to fetch some water. The princess, in her subsequent existence, as Yas'odhará, avenged her wrong.

Yas'odhará's Choice.—Though she was certain that the prince would renounce the world, yet Yas'odhará rejected the hands of Sundarananda and Devadatta. The reason is, that once on a time the beasts, in a large assembly at the foot of the snowy range, wanted to elect a king to govern them. It was settled that, whoever should reach the mountain in seven days should be their king. All ran towards the mountain. But a tigress won the prize. A female on the throne was an idea repugnant to the beasts, and so they requested her to choose a husband who should rule them. A bull wooed her in vain; an elephant courted her with no better success; but a lion married her. The tigress was Yas'odhará, the bull Sundarananda, the elephant Devadatta, and the lion Buddha.

Trial of Strength.—When the girls had been dismissed, S'uddhodana learned from his ministers that Yas'odhará had made a deep impression on the prince's mind. A negotiation for marriage was immediately set on foot with Yas'odhará's father. But Mahánámá declined their offer on the score of Sarvárthas'iddha's ignorance of the science of war, and also on the score of his want of artistic skill. S'uddhodana was greatly mortified at this repulse. The prince, being apprised of the reason of the king's distress, caused a proclamation to be made throughout the city inviting youths to show their excellence in feats of strength. There was a large gathering on the day appointed. A furious elephant entered that day one of the gates of Kapilavastu. Devadatta killed it by a slap with his open hand; but, unable to remove the carcass, he had to double it. Sundarananda could only drag it a few paces to clear the way. But Sarvárthas'iddha threw it beyond the seven walls of Kapilavastu. In another trial Devadatta's arrow pierced two palm trees, and reached the third. Sundarananda's arrow pierced three trees and reached the fourth, while the prince's arrow not only pierced through seven trunks, but passed on to the nether world. Moreover he made use of a certain Siñhadhanu's bow, which none of his contemporaries could string.

Story of Dharmapála.—Certain Bhikshus requested the Lord to kindly explain to them how he came to recognize the long lost descendants of the S'ákyas, or S'ákiyamushṭís. The Lord said there was nothing new in it to wonder at. Brahmáyuh was a priest to the king of Váráṇasí, and Dharmapála was his son. He placed his son under the tuition of an Áchárya on the Himálaya. At a short distance from the school there was a large tank inhabited by a dragon. When Dharmapála plunged into the tank for bathing, the monster dragged him in. Dharmapála cultivated the friendship of a serpent prince who dwelt at the bottom of the tank, and instructed his subjects in the ten Karmapáṭhas. The monster, when dragging in Dharmapála, had killed another boy whose remains lay floating upon the water. The tutor, supposing the remains to be those of Dharmapála, carefully collected them, and forthwith proceeded to Váráṇasí to inform Dharmapála's father of the sad accident. Brahmáyuh assured the tutor that Dharmapála was alive, and that the remains were those of another. He feasted the tutor with every care, and sent him back to the Himálaya, where, to his great surprise, the tutor saw Dharmapála sitting in his hermitage. "I am that priest, and Ráhula was Dharmapála," said the Lord.

Proficiency in Archery.—The Bhikshus enquired how the lord could shoot his arrow to so great distance, as adverted to above. The Lord said 'This is not the first time I have done so. I had been, in one of my previous existences, a king of Váráṇasí. My empire extended to Takshas'ílá. Once on a time I appointed my brother as my lieutenant at Váráṇasí, and marched to Takshas'ílá to suppress a revolt there. While absent from my capital it was besieged by a neighbouring prince. Instead of hastening to the relief of the capital, I aimed an arrow at my enemy who had his left foot pierced by it. I also contrived to attach a letter to the arrow threatening his life unless he instantly quitted my territories. He did not stop a moment after the perusal of my letter, but immediately broke up his encampment. It is not, therefore, at all extraordinary that I should be able to send an arrow to the nether region in my present existence."

Proficiency in Art. Story of Mahaushadha and Amará.—In reply to the query why Yas'odhará was gained by a display of skill in manual arts, the Lord remarked that he had done so before, and illustrated the fact by the following story. Two miles from Mithilá, there was a village named Javakachchha, where Mahaushadha, a Bráhmaṇ, had his residence. He wanted to obtain the hand of a blacksmith's daughter, named Amará. But the blacksmith would not consent to marry his daughter to one not acquainted with any manual art. The Bráhmaṇ, thereupon, tried hard to acquire an art, and subsequently exhibited so much dexterity in needle-work that the blacksmith was glad to give his daughter in marriage to him. That Bráhmaṇ was Sarvárthas'iddha, and Amará, his wife Yas'odhará in a former life.

Proficiency in Prowess. Story of a Vedic Student and S'irí.—To the question why Yas'odhará had to be gained by prowess, the following story was related to furnish a reply. A learned Bráhmaṇ of Váravárí got an invitation from Samudrapaṭṭana. After the perusal of the letter he told his five hundred disciples that any one of them who could go to Samudrapaṭṭana would be rewarded with the hand of S'irí, his daughter. One of the students, who was in love with S'irí, determined not to lose this golden opportunity. He volunteered to go, reached Samudrapaṭṭana, obtained valuable presents; but on his voyage back to Váravárí, his travelling bag, containing the presents, fell into the ocean. Unable to bear the idea of losing such a magnificent prize as S'irí, he determined to recover his bag by draining the sea, and set with all his might and main to the work. This induced the Devas, the Nágas, the Yakshas and the Rákshasas of the ocean to restore him his bag. Buddha was that bold and persevering student, and S'irí Yas'odhará.

Story of Suchandrima and a Kinnarí.—In illustration of the fact that Sarvárthas'iddha had always to submit to great difficulty in obtaining the hands of Yas'odhará, he related the following story. Once on a time, Suchandrima, a king of Siñhapura, undertook, by the advice of a Bráhmaṇ, the celebration of a grand sacrifice, in which he intended to immolate one of every species of animal. Several hundreds of huntsmen were employed to catch wild beasts. When everything was ready, he invited learned Ṛishis, who travelled by the aerial way, to superintend the arrangement of the materials. They unanimously declared that a Kinnarí was wanting. The hunters were ordered to fetch a Kinnarí. One of them went to the Himálaya in search, and lodged in the hermitage of the Ṛishi Kás'yapa.

All of a sudden he heard a tiny note of celestial music. He enquired of the Ṛishi whence it came. Being told that a Kinnara Princess, named Manohará, came every day to a lotus tank close by, and being advised that she could be caught only by means of truth, the wily hunter proceeded to the tank, and, by telling a truth, managed to capture the maiden. Rájá Suchandrima, now furnished with the full complement of animals, invited his friend Subáhu, the Lord of Hastiná, to the sacrifice. Subáhu deputed his youthful son Sudhanusha to the sacrifice. The young prince, at the very first sight, fell in love with the Kinnarí, and found to his great satisfaction that his feelings were reciprocated. He repaired to the king Suchandrima, and represented to him the sin and impiety of slaughtering so many thousands of innocent animals. He discoursed long on the merits of Ahiñs'á, and, at last, succeeded in inducing the king to set the animals at liberty, and to put an end to the sacrifice. The king dismissed the assembled Bráhmaṇs with valuable presents. The prince returned in company of Manohará, the Kinnarí, to Hastinápura, where he had long been associated by his father in the government of the kingdom. But the prince, in the company of the beautiful lady, neglected his official duties. This being reported to the aged king, he quietly dismissed the Kinnarí from the palace. She directed her steps towards the Himálaya. On the banks of the S'atadrú she cultivated the friendship of Utpalaka and Mánavaka, two hunter boys, put in their hands a precious ring and a garland with fragrant earth as tokens, and requested them, if the prince ever came after her, to tell him the way she had taken.

In the absence of his beloved one, the prince languished, and pined away. The palace, the city, the harem, pleased him not. The king tried to afford consolation, but failed. One night the prince stole away from the royal residence, and, attended only by one servant, directed his course to Kinnarapura. He met the hunter boys on the S'atadrú; and they handed over to him the Kinnarí's mementos. Unmindful of their remonstrance he proceeded through the hills and forests, his guide on the way being the tokens which had been left here and there by Manohará for the purpose. After much difficulty he safely reached

Kás'yapa's As'rama. Kás'yapa ordered a huge monkey to convey him to Nirati, the capital of Manohará's father. The monkey placed him on its shoulders, and, jumping from peak to peak, from mountain to mountain, carried him safe to the capital. There the prince contrived to put his ring into the water-pot of one of Manohará's handmaids. The ring happened to fall before Monohará's eyes. She instantly concluded the prince's appearance in the city, and apprised her father of it. The king gave a hearty welcome to the prince, his son-in-law. After some time, the prince expressed his desire of returning to his own country. On awaking one morning he found himself in Hastinápura with his wife. Yambhaka, one of his father-in-law's messengers, had conveyed them while asleep through the region of air. There were no bounds to the joys of the people of Hastiná at the reappearance of their lost prince. Subáhu was Suddhodana,; his wife, Máyá; Utpala, the hunter boy; Ráhula, Mánavaka the other hunter; Ananda, the monkey As'varája; Druma, Manohará's father Mahánámá; Manohará, Yásodhará; and Sudhanusha, Sarvárthasiddha himself.*

S'ákya's Early Life.—During his residence in S'rávasti the Lord, one day, recalled to his mind what his mission on earth was, and addressed his Bhikshus on the subject of his early life.

When he was young his father erected for him three buildings, and supplied them with the richest furniture. They were suited to the three seasons of the year—places for wantonness, pastime and pleasure. But Sarvárthasiddha's firm conviction was that the householder's state was a state of sinfulness, without a break. He who would prepare himself for hermitage or pravrajyá should not stay in his family; knowing this he renounced the world, severing all ties of relationship, and leaving behind him the inheritance of a mighty empire. His parents wept, but could not make any impression on a mind bent on religious excellence, or the attainment of Bodhi knowledge. From Kapilavastu he proceeded to Vais'álí. There lived a Jina, named Arádhakáláma, who had three hundred S'rávakas. His doctrine was "abandon whatever you see" [*lit.* "see, see, and abandon, abandon"]. Sarvárthasiddha conceived a high opinion of the doctrine, and applied to the teacher for admission as a pupil. But his pupilage was short. The Jina said "my religion is such

* This version of the story differs in many material points from the one given on p. 62.

that a faithful, noble-hearted man might practice Brahmacharya, and at the same time learn to honor the holy ways to bliss." This did not satisfy the inward cravings of the prince for a complete and absolute destruction of all mundane pains. He left Vais'álí for Rájagriha, where Rudraka, son of Ráma, dwelt. He had seven hundred S'rávakas under him. His doctrines too did not please the prince, who next went to the mount Gayás'irsha. There three ideas struck him, *viz.*, 1st, that a Bráhmaṇ, or a S'ramaṇa, who wants to attain the Bodhi knowledge by the exertion of his body and mind, both impure, is like one who wants to produce fire by the rubbing of two bits of wood immersed in water: both are equally doomed to experience the acute pangs of disappointment. 2nd, As a man cannot produce fire by rubbing a dry piece of wood against a wet piece, so a Bráhman cannot attain the highest knowledge by purifying his body, when his heart remains impure. 3rd, Even as fire can be produced by rubbing two dry pieces of wood, so is the Bodhi knowledge attainable by the union of the body and the mind, both equally stainless. Contemplating over these analogies he reached the village of Uruvilvá. There in solitude flowed the pure and limpid stream of Nairanjaná. The scenery delighted the hermit greatly. He determined to make that place his abode, and the scene of his salvation.

Having taken this resolution he attempted to restrain his *káya*[8] or sensations, and also his *chitta* or mind, by means of meditation. Then he commenced the most difficult meditation called Ásphánaka-dhyána, *i. e.*, meditation by restraining his breath from escaping through the nostrils and the mouth. Having no other outlet his breath passed through the ears, making a sound like that of bellows. When he restrained his breath through those passages also, it rushed upwards, and, breaking open his scalp, escaped. Some advised him to live on one plum a day. It weakened him greatly. Some advised him to live on a single grain of rice a day, some on a grain of sesamum, some advised him absolute fast, and so on. He found that by these austerities he was getting emaciated; that his strength was departing; his beauty fading; his complexion growing pale and haggard. He concluded, that was not the right way to gain the Bodhi knowledge. He had felt, he thought, far greater delight at home when he fell into a deep meditation under the rose-apple tree. That, he believed, was the right method of obtaining the highest bliss. So he took a bath in the pure and cooling stream of the Nairanjaná; regained his health by wholesome diet; obtained, by begging, a handful of hay from a dealer in corn; scattered it round the Bodhi Tree; turned thrice round the Tree from the right; and sat below it, recalling to mind every thing in the world.

On that very day, in the still awful moments of midnight, S'uddhodana saw, in a dream, his darling son in the form of an elephant, riding on a brilliant fig tree resplendent with jewels. Pearls, rubies and precious stones covered him from head to foot. He stood in the middle of a broad street of the city, where people flocked from all quarters, even at that dead of night, to anoint him.

Yas'ódhará dreamt of a bright piece of cloud, glowing like lightning with tremulous light, pouring a refreshing shower over the three regions, and delighting the whole animal creation with the music of its roar. She dreamt also that Brahmá was explaining the dream to her.

Bodhisattva himself saw five visions: in one of them he saw that the whole earth was his couch; Sumeru, red like the Vimba fruit, his pillow; his right hand resting on the eastern, his left on the western, and his legs on the southern, ocean. In a second he saw S'thirikás, a kind of grass, shooting from his navel, covered the whole face of the heavens.

Suddenly the events of his householder life recurred to his memory. He remembered his asking the permission of his father to enter the hermitage, and the affectionate tears of that aged father, imploring him to stay at home, at least, to the end of his own life. He remembered, also, that at the time of this conversation S'uddhodana thought of placing him in a magnificent palace in the midst of bewitching beauties, fascinating girls, charming celestial damsels. S'uddhodhana actually performed what he thought. But nothing could tempt the virtuous soul, bent only upon the final and complete deliverence of himself. The prince only longed for that sort of delight which he had experienced under the rose-apple tree. Neither music, nor dance, nor the beauty of youth could, in his estimation, produce such a thrilling delight as that deep meditation afforded. The deity presiding over the Lumbiní forest, in an invisible shape, gave the first intimation to the king of the mental distress of his beloved son. The heart of the aged monarch melted away at the sight of the lifeless emaciated complexion of Sarvárthasiddha. With tears at the sight of the lack-lustre countenance, the aged man asked him, if there was anything wrong with him, if he entertained any fear of the loss of his wealth, or of an invasion from an enemy. The prince replied, he saw everything wrong with him; "because", said he, "I constantly find that disease creeps upon health, and death steals away life. Life passes away, and death comes nearer every year. There is loss of wealth, because all the religions of the world are false, foolish, contradictory. They are a stumbling-block to the accumulation of our wealth, *viz.*, spiritual wealth. There is fear of the enemy, for false reformation in religion produces misery, and that reformation is our enemy. I can stay at home if you can guarantee that youth should not be followed by imbecility, health ruined by disease, life destroyed by death."

S'uddhodana again thought of quieting his son's mind by agreeable female company. But the prince expressed his desire to proceed to a park. Immediately the streets were strewn with flowers, and the prince, in a gorgeous procession, proceeded to the park. Every care was taken to keep away the blind, the maimed, the lame, the old, and the dead, from his sight; but a potter, the son of Ghaṭikára, a Suddhábása Devaputtra, placed in the way an extremely old man, weak, pale, and tottering, leaning for support upon a crutch.

At the sight of this miserable creature, Sarvárthasiddha fell into a melancholy vein of thought. Old age and misery, thought he, are inseparable from the state of man. The sufferings of the old man made so deep an impression on his mind that he could not proceed on his journey; he ordered his charioteer to drive homewards. On another occasion, the sight of a man labouring under various diseases made him stop his journey to another park, and return home. The sight of a dead body was enough, on another day, to send him back from his way to a third park. On the fourth time, when he attempted to go to a fourth park, he fell in with a Bhikshu. The prince asked him the reason of his renouncing the world. The reply was "for the restraint, quietude, and annihilation of the soul." The prince was greatly delighted at the answer. Just at this moment a Chakraváka cried aloud—"blessed is your father, blessed your mother, and blessed the girl whom you have married." This Chakraváka afterwards became Mṛigí, the mother of Ánanda.

The king prepared for anointing his son as second king, under the auspicious star Pushyá; but the prince thought that was the most auspicious moment for entering the hermitage. The gods and the Devaputras encouraged him in his purpose. At the moment of midnight, when Ráhula descended from his mother's womb, the prince surveyed his seraglio, got disgusted at the indecent picture it presented, and finally took leave of the world. At a retired place (Anáseyasthána), 96 miles from Kapilavastu, in the kingdom of the Mallas, in the vicinity of the As'rama of Vas'ishṭha, the prince dismissed his servant Chaṇḍaka with Kaṇṭaka, his horse. He exchanged his silken robe for an ochre-colored vestment, and cut off his crown-lock (chúḍá).

Story of Syámá and Vajrasena.—The reason why Buddha abandoned his faithful wife Yas'odhará is given in the following story.

There was in times of yore a horse-dealer at Taks'hasilá, named Vajrasena; on his way to the fair at Váráṇasí, his horses were stolen, and he was severely wounded. As he slept in a deserted house in the suburbs of Váráṇasí, he was caught by policemen as a thief. He was ordered to the place of execution. But his manly beauty attracted the attention of Syámá, the first public woman in Váránasí. She grew enamoured of the man, and requested one of her handmaids to rescue the criminal at any hazard. By offering large sums of money, she succeeded in inducing the executioners to set Vajrasena free, and execute the orders of the king on another, a banker's son, who was an admirer of Syámá. The latter, not knowing his fate, approached the place of execution with victuals for the criminal, and was severed in two by the executioners.

The woman was devotedly attached to Vajrasena. But her inhuman conduct to the banker's son made a deep impression on his mind. He could not reconcile himself to the idea of being in love with the perpetrator of such a crime. On an occasion when they both set on a pluvial excursion, Vajrasena plied her with wine, and, when she was almost senseless, smothered and drowned her. When he thought she was quite dead, he dragged her to the steps of the ghat and fled, leaving her in that helpless condition. Her mother, who was at hand, came to her rescue, and by great assiduity resuscitated her. Syámá's first measure, after recovery, was to find out a Bhikshuṇí of Takshas'ilá, and to send through her a message to Vajrasena, inviting him to her loving embrace. Buddha was that Vajrasena, and Syámá, Yas'odhará.

Story of a Serpent-catcher.—The Lord said he was at another time saved by Yas'odhará. He was then a king of the serpents, living at

Váráṇasí. On the eighth, the fourteenth and the fifteenth day of the moon, he used to fast and remain motionless at a place where four roads met. On one of these occasions he was caught by a serpent-catcher. He had many wives, but none succeeded in rescuing him. The chief of them proceeded boldly to the king of Váráṇasí. Her pathetic appeals and eloquent description of her husband's virtues moved the king, who immediately ordered the serpent-catcher, on pain of death, to set the serpent-king free; that chief queen was Yas'odhará.

Sequel to the visions.—After the vision Buddha went to beg his food in Uruvilvá, where Sujátá, who was his mother in five hundred previous existences, feasted him with milk and honey. Rájá S'uddhodana, after the vision of the elephant, sent a man to the Uruvilvá grove to enquire after his son's health. The man saw him motionless in a trance, with his breath stopped, and concluded that he was dead. But the Rájá did not believe his report. The messenger, being sent again to the grove, found Buddha in perfect repose.

Story of Syámaka.—It struck some of the audience as strange that the king should, from so great a distance, know better about his son's health than those who were around him. But this was explained by a reference to his previous history. He was, once on a time, a Bráhmaṇ who entered the third stage with his wife in company. At his hermitage on the banks of the Subhánjaní, in the neighbourhood of Gotama's hermitage, he had a child born unto him. The boy, named Syámaka, was always dutiful to his parents. In fact he was the principal support in their old age. His filial love was so great that he could never take rest until after his parents had been properly served. The king of Váráṇasí was very fond of hunting in Gotama's forest. In one of his hunting excursions he aimed an arrow at what appeared to him to be a stag, drinking in a river, but when it was too late he found out his error. It was the Bráhman's son, who had come to fetch water for his blind parents, that fell pierced by his weapon. The king hastened to his rescue. But the young man was on the point of death. He had time only to acquaint the king with the precarious position in which this unforeseen circumstance would reduce his beloved parents. In compliance with his dying request, the king carried his parents to his corpse, laid it before them, confessed his crime, and tried in various ways to afford them consolation. They wept bitterly for their affectionate child. At last the old Bráhmaṇ said he would revivify his son by telling the truth. His action was as good as his word. In a short time S'yámáka revived. S'uddhodana was formerly the father of Syámáka.*

Story of S'iriprabha.—Buddha practised austerities at Uruvilvá; his ardour was so great that he lived eighteen months on one plum a day, eighteen on one sessamum seed a day, eighteen on one grain of rice a day, and for eighteen months he took no food at all. His eyes sunk in their sockets, the sound of his breath was like that of bellows, his head became bare and white like an autumnal bottlegourd. Every member of his family grew anxious for his life. Yas'odhará, though at home, made it a point to lead an ascetic life. Henceforth she lived on simple food, and slept on the bare ground. Nor did she do this, said the Lord, in this life alone, but also in a previous existence. Yas'odhará always followed in the wake of her husband. She was then the fond hind to a loving stag who was named S'iriprabha. Her husband fell into the snare of one Lubdhaka, a hunter. The hind placed herself before the hunter, and requested him to kill her before killing her husband. Her fidelity saved her husband, for the hunter was too chivalrous to turn a deaf ear to the request of a chaste wife.

Story of S'akuntika, the fowler.—When holding deep meditation with austere fervour for final emancipation, Buddha had to resist strong temptations thrown in his way by Mára to seduce him. But the resolute devotee did not swerve in the least from the path he had selected. The love of emancipation was almost a part of his existence. Nor was this remarkable, said the Lord to his audience, for in his previous existences too he had hated bondage as he hated the devil. In one of these he was a fowl, and Mára a fowler. The fowler used carefully to rear his fowls, and, as soon as they grew fat, to kill them, and sell their flesh. Buddha, as the fowl, having observed this, carefully avoided eating anything, so he waxed weaker and weaker every day, so much so, that he could well slip down through the interstices of the cage in which he was confined. The fowler did not notice this incidence. In a short time, the fowl gained his master's confidence by appearing very tame and attached to him, and, when wholesome food restored him to strength, fled away.

* This story forms a part of the Das'aratha Játaka of Ceylon, and is there called Syáma Játaka. The names and details are slightly different. The story is also told of the Hindu king Das'aratha in the Rámáyaṇa. *Antiquities of Orissa*, I. p. 90.

Story of a Tortoise.—In another existence Buddha was a tortoise and Mára a florist. When gathering flowers, Mára espied the tortoise, and succeeded in catching it. The tortoise, with unusual presence of mind, turned the florist's flower-basket upside down, and as soon as the florist hastened to collect his flowers, jumped into the water and escaped.

Story of a Porpoise.—Mára, in a third existence, was a porpoise in the sea, and Buddha a lord of monkeys living in a forest close to the sea-shore. Whenever the porpoise came on the shore the monkey-king kindly supplied him with fresh fruits from a glomorous fig tree. Thus close intimacy was formed between them. But their intimacy was an eyesore to the wife of the porpoise. She, on one occasion, feigned illness, and demanded from her husband, the heart of a monkey, alleging that a monkey's heart alone could cure her of her illness. The porpoise urged, how could an aquatic animal get the heart of a beast? She then pointed to his friend the monkey-king. The porpoise induced his friend, by telling stories of rich gardens on the other side of the sea, to cross it on his back. But in the midway he plunged into the water, dragging the monkey with him. The monkey, in alarm, asked his friend "what are you about?" The porpoise replied "my wife demands a monkey's heart." "You are mistaken, friend," said the monkey with the presence of mind characteristic of his species, "I have left my heart hanging on the figtree on the sea-shore." The foolish porpoise believed what he said, and carried the monkey back to the forest, where he easily escaped from the murderous hand of his friend.

Story of a fowler and his prey.—Mára watched Buddha very closely for years, but could not discover a single flaw in his conduct. At last, to his great mortification, the wicked one had to desist from his attempts of tempting the staunch ascetic. In a former existence too Buddha, as a learned king of the fowls, frustrated, by his prudence, all the attempts to catch the birds living under his authority, which the fowler Mára made by scattering grains and by spreading his net.

Story of Surúpa, the deer king.—The Bhikshus asked the Lord why did he offer his flesh and blood for a Subháshita, or good saying? The Lord replied, once on a time he lived, under the name of Surúpa, in a forest beyond the Himaláya, as the leader of a herd of wild deer. Indra, to try him, approached him in the guise of a hunter, and offered to recite a good saying if he could offer his life for it. He consented. The Subhásbita was—

वरं रेवं रूपाणां सत्पुरुषाणां
पाद पांशु रजो न सौवर्णो पर्वतः ।

"The dust of a good man's feet is preferable to a mountain of gold." The former destroys while the latter increases our grief. Buddha kept his promise, and gave his body to the disguised hunter.

Character of Avolokita Vyákarana.—The Lord, while sojourning on the Gridharakuṭa hill near Rájagriha, was requested by Nanda, a Devaputra, to recount what becomes manifest at the time when is attained true knowledge, technically the Avalokita Vyákaraṇa. Nanda was seconded by Sunanda, Sumata, Is'vara, Mahes'vara and other Devaputras of pure inclinations and holy abode.

The purport of what Buddha said on this occasion is this :—

When a Bodhisattva sees the finite from the shore of infinity, the Devaputras of pure abode acquire eighteen pleasing qualities, such as association of the past, reproduction of the past, production of the Yuga, production of the auspicious, production of the excellent, production of the ancient, production of the commendable, &c. The piece of ground whereon sitting a Bodhisattva kills great Yakshas, defeats large armies, saves the souls of multitudes of men, governs the hearts of men as a charioteer does his horses, should possess sixteen qualities. It should be purified by burning, provided with a seat at the centre. It should be situated far away from the haunts of men, in a country not governed by Mlechchas, and within the limits of Áryávartta. It should be level, dry, full of flowering plants, well known, well protected, unconquered, no birth-place for an avatára, unfrequented by Mára, like a throne in the earth, hard as adamant four fingers deep, a place where soft grass, green as a pigeon's neck, grows in circles.

*Story of Jyotishpála.**—Jyotishpála of Jyotishpa was Ananga, son of Baudhuma, who reigned at Baudhumati in the 91st Kalpa. Baudhuma, son of Vipas'yí, became a great Buddha. Once on a time the king invited his enlightened son to his capital to receive Buddha. But Ananga advanced several miles in a different direction to wel-

* This story seems to be out of place, for it breaks the narrative of the Avalokita knowledge.

come the Lord, fell prostrate at his feet, and requested him to dine at his house for three months. The Lord signified his consent by his silence. The king was greatly annoyed by Ananga's taking advantage of him. He remonstrated with him, but in vain. At last it was settled that they should feed the Lord with his whole congregation on alternate days for three months. When only two days of the fixed period remained, the king prohibited his subjects to sell anything to Ananga, on pain of death. Ananga had still one day to feed the Lord. He grew very anxious. But his anxiety was soon removed by Indra, who came in person to him, and offered to supply him with everything. Then he miraculously brought into existence wells of ghi and curds, he created a golden palm tree with silver leaves by the aid of Visvakarmá. The boon Ananga obtained for thus entertaining the Lord was proficiency in the knowledge of Buddha.

Avalokita Vyákaraṇa, continued.—Bodhisattva made use of thirty-two different standards of morality, and manifested five different smiles. He looked like a lion in five sorts of frowns. He gaped in five different ways; coughed in five different styles. Then he held the first meditation, greatly delightful on account of the dispassion it produced. In this meditation he had doubts. In the second, he had no doubt. It was delightful to him through *samádhi*, or because it made his mind intent on his own emancipation. The third meditation afforded him great delight by recalling to his mind the contempt with which he had renounced the world The fourth destroyed both pleasure and pain. It gave him equanimity of mind by doing away with mirth and melancholy consequent on pleasure and pain.

In the first *prahara* or watch of the night he concentrated his mind for the conception of knowledge with the aid of the celestial eye. He saw all, high caste or low caste people, the rich and the poor, in short he saw men of all denominations. In the second watch, he directed his thoughts to recal to mind his ancient abodes; and in the last watch he reached his goal. He obtained perfect *sambodhi*, to which there is nothing superior in the world. It showed him what is misery, how it is produced, and in what way we can get rid of it. It pointed out to him what are the mùndane pains, how produced, and how healed. It produced in his mind the impression that those who blindly believe that existence is only an evolution of the existent, suffer from misery and mundane pains. It held out before his mind's eye, as it were in a mirror, the process how these are produced and repressed. The delusion that existence is an evolution of the existent produces false intuitions, or those which give the conceptions of hunger, sleep &c. False intuitions are the causes of perceptions. From perceptions we arrive at the ideas of name and form, whence the sins of the senses have their rise. From these we have the sensation of touch (all other sensations being subordinate to touch). From sensation are produced the feelings of pain, and from these desire and will. From will proceeds materials. From these results the connection of the soul with body, birth, imbecility, death, grief, lamentation, misery and melancholy. Thus the long category of pains has its rise.* But he, who has faith in the doctrine of non-existence, *i. e.*, existence is evolved from non-existence, from what the Naiyáyikas call Abhába, has no delusion, and consequently no false intuition. The extensive fabric of misery, thus having its foundation undermined, falls to the ground. Bodhisattva remained for a week under the Bodhi tree during which millions of gods came to honor him.

Story of Bodhisattva's descent as a Nága.—The Lord lived for a long time with a large congregation at the park Ámrapálí in Vais'álí. There Vis'uddhamati, a Bhikshu, requested him to explain the Nágávalokita. The Lord said a Jina, named Himas'así, descended from the Tushita heaven in the form of a Nága, and was born heir to the king Shaḍváshāṇa. In the 29th year of his age, he renounced the world. After 12 years of asceticism he entered the kingdom of Magadha where the daughter of a general honored him. He soon after became Buddha. After obtaining the Bodhi knowledge, he went to the banks of the Nairañjaná. The whole earth trembled under his steps. Then he returned to the Bodhi tree. The gods, who came to pay their respects to the Lord, saw the Bodhi tree. Some conceived it was 16 miles high, some thought it was thousands of miles high. Some thought it was decorated with pearls, some with rubies. Some saw a siṇhásana upon it, others saw the siṇhásana two hundred yojanas high.

After this follows a panegyric on virtuous conduct and then the story is continued thus :

When the serpent Kála visited Buddha on the banks of the Nairanjaná, the lord exhibited his skill in working marvels for the deity Amritás'ána. When he assumed the form of a lion rampant, five

* The arguments are given at length in the Lalita Vistara, see my Buddha Gayá, pp. 41ff.

hundred lions turned round him in reverence. In this way he successively assumed the forms of a serpent, an ox, and a cuckoo. The serpent praised the Lord in loud hymns. The Lord coughed. The sound killed Mára with all his attendants. He penetrated into the depth of Bodhi knowledge, and set the august wheel of virtue in motion.

Story of Kus'a.—When he appeared at Rájagrihá, the Bhikshus asked him why the wicked Mára was destroyed by the coughing of the Lord. The following story of Kus'a was related in reply.*

Once on a time, there reigned at Váráṇasi, a king named Subandhu. All of a sudden his bed-chamber miraculously turned into a sugarcane plantation. One cane among the rest was so refreshing to the eye that the king called some astrologer in, to ascertain what was in it. They predicted that a son was to be born to the king from the cane. In time the cane swelled to the size of a bamboo. One morning a boy issued forth from the sugarcane tree, and he was named Ikshâku, or the sugarcane-born. The boy was nourished by the chief lady of the royal seraglio. On the death of S'ubandu, Ikshâku became king. He had many queens, of whom Alindá was the chief. Even to an advanced age the king was childless. He consulted holy men for getting a child. Their advice was to open the seraglio thrice every fortnight to the public use. All, except Alindá, took advantage of this liberty, and, leaving the palace at night, went wherever they liked. One of Subandhu's near relations held the post of Indra in the thirty-third heaven. Indignant at the unworthy and shameful conduct of Ikshâku, he transformed himself into an old decrepit dirty Bráhmaṇ suffering from a loathsome cough. He managed to throw himself at the royal presence, and begged to have a queen for dalliance. The king gave him the choice of his seraglio, and he selected Alindá. The Bráhmaṇ dragged the chief Queen of the palace, in spite of her stubborn opposition, to an old dilapidated building in the suburb. Alindá had to wash his feet, and to stand before him in complete nudity. But she would never consent to prostitute her body. In the morning Indra threw off his disguise, expressed his satisfaction at her conduct, and rewarded her firmness by placing some drugs in her hands. "This will," said he, "remove your barrenness. I grant this boon in accordance with your own desire.

* The substance of the story is the same as given in the Kus'a Játaka, (*ante*, p. 100).

Dissolve this powder into water, and take the solution. Your son will be active and energetic, but since you did not respond to my loving call, he will be like ugliness personified." Alindá gave a full account of this incident to her husband, and he made the whole seraglio use the medicine. The quantity of solution was so small and the number of ladies so great that they had to take it in homœopathic doses by using the sharp end of a kus'a blade for their measure-glass. Five hundred children were born to the king. He named them after the kus'a grass Indrakus'a, Devakus'a &c. The ugly child of Alindá was named simply Kus'a or, as some say, S'uddhakus'a. He was no favourite with the king, who made several attempts to disinherit him. All the king's endeavours were defeated by the activity and energy of Kus'a. On one occasion, the king concealed a small ball of sweetmeat under a big heap of large ones, and declared that any one of his sons who could discover the small ball would be made king. Kus'a was given the last chance, but that only served to make the work easier to him. On another occasion the king promised to nominate him his successor who could eat the fastest. All waited for dishes to be brought to them, but Kus'a took his meal on the bare ground, and was, in spite of the king's reluctance, nominated his successor. Finding that Kus'a had on him the signs of royalty, the king determined to frustrate his hopes of ascending the throne by concealing his wealth, and by declaring in enigmatic terms at the time of his death where he had concealed them. The king thought Kus'a would not be able to solve the enigmas, and that any other son who could get the wealth would get the kingdom also. On his accession Kus'a collected all the wealth by solving the enigmas. One of these enigmas, for instance, was Yojananidhi or eight-mile hoard. But Kus'a dug a portion of the stable where horses were harnessed, guessing from the word Yuj "to yoke" that the stables were meant, and got the wealth.

Mahendraka, the tribal king of Bhadrakasat in Kányakubja, had a very beautiful daughter. Alindá immediately after Kus'a's accession, set a negotiation on foot for her son's marriage to that princess. The match was soon settled. The nuptials were celebrated with great pomp by proxy at Kányakubja. But Alindá was apprehensive lest her fair daughter-in-law would commit suicide at the sight of so deformed a husband. She, therefore, prepared rooms underground where, under the plea of family customs, she placed the young couple. No light was admitted into the rooms. The couple enjoyed their honey-moon in the dark. But Sudars'aná, the princess, grew impatient to see her beloved husband, and urged her mother-in-law to bring about an interview in the light. Alindá, to avoid Sudars'aná's seeing the ugly husband, made one of her step-sons personate Kus'a on the throne, while the real Kus'a with his thick lips, corpulent belly, deformed head, held the royal umbrella. Sudars'aná was well pleased with her supposed husband, but she expressed her indignation at so black and ugly a person being allowed to hold the parasol. On one occasion when walking in the royal park she fled from him as from a monster.

But in a short time, her mistake was corrected. At a great conflagration of the city the elephant park was saved, simply by the activity of the king. He was for some time in every body's mouth. They described him as very black, with large red eyes, &c. Sudars'aná then found out her error. She learned, to her great surprise and grief, that the monster at the park was her real husband. She instantly begged the permission of her mother-in-law to proceed to Kányakubja. The permission was granted, and she set out for Kányakubja to hide her shame.

The king, unable to bear the separation, appointed one of his half-brothers as regent, and proceeded himself to the north with a Víná in his hand. On his arrival at Kánykubja his first measure was to apprise Sudars'aná of his presence in the city. By his skill in the culinary art, he soon got himself appointed at the royal kitchen. There in private he tried to persuade his refractory wife, but to no purpose. She was inexorable.

In the meanwhile, the scandal of Sudars'aná's leaving, and in a way divorcing, her husband spread far and wide. Seven feudatories of the king of Kánykubja offered to marry her. But their offers were indignantly rejected by the king. They made a common cause with one another, and advanced to seize the capital. The king, in wrath scolded his refractory daughter, and threatened to cut her into seven pieces for these seven rebels, if he got worsted in the coming conflict. Sudars'aná, trembling with fear at so terrible a threat, had now recourse to her almost divorced husband at the kitchen. He promised to save her, and to fight her father's cause. The king was now told of his son-in-law's appointment as a cook. He hastened to receive him, and, heaping honors upon honors on him, made up for all his former neglect. The hero advanced on an elephant towards his enemies, and by a shout at the onset so quailed their spirit that they surrendered themselves his captives. The king gave them each a daughter at the request of Kus'a. After enjoying his triumph for a few days at Kányakubja, Kus'a set out in the company of his humbled wife for his own kingdom. On his way, he looked at his own image reflected in a glassy brook, and was so much disgusted at his deformity that he wanted to drown himself. But just at that time Indra manifested himself before him, and presented him a garland set with the rare jewel called Jyotírasa. "Put this on, and it will make you," said Indra, "the most beautiful man on earth. When you wish to assume your own form, cover this with your clothes and your beauty will be hidden." Kus'a put on the jewel, and Sudarsaná was transported with delight, when she found her husband blessed with a celestial form.

Buddha was Kus'a; Mahendraka, the king of Kányakubja, was Mahánámá; Máyá was Alindá; Sudars'aná was Yas'odhará; Mára and his companions were the seven rebel kings.

At the request of the Bhikshus the Lord explained to them why Kus'a was born so ugly. He said, in one of his previous existences, he was Sudars'ana, and had a very loving wife. In his absence, she entertained a Pratyeka Buddha with dainty food. Vexed at the sight of a young man in his wife's company, he railed at them. His wife told him to put a stop to his railleries, adverting to the holy character of the guest, and called heaven to witness that there was nothing wrong in her. The Pratyeka Buddha, too, to convince the householder of his sacred character, fled like a flamingo through the sky. This set at rest the suspicions of Sudars'ana; he begged his wife's pardon, fell into a profound meditation, and wished to have the faithful lady for his wife in the next existence. Sudars'aná was that faithful wife. Her husband was ugly, because he had entertained unbecoming suspicions against a Pratyeka Buddha.

Stories of Mára's attempts to seduce Buddha.—The question was asked, Why could not Mára find a single flaw in the Lord's conduct, though he watched carefully for several years? The Lord said, this was not the only time he had so failed; once on a time the leader of a wild herd of cattle was followed long by a wily jackal who wanted to have the ox's flesh, but the ox proved more cunning than the jackal, and escaped. The ox was Buddha and the jackal Mára. This story is called *Vrishabha Játaka.*

Buddha was at another time a leader of a troop of monkeys and Mára a marine monster who devoured every one of the monkey troop which happened to come to the water side. The gradual decrease of the number of his troop attracted the attention of the leader. After a careful investigation he found the footprints of monkeys leading to the water side were far greater than those returning from it. He immediately published a mandate prohibiting his troop from going to the water side, and thus saved all further destruction. This story is called *Vánara Játaka.*

In another existence the Lord escaped from the snares of Mára, and made him experience a sad disappointment in the following manner. Mára was a serpent, and Buddha a leader of monkeys. The monkey-chief fell once into the lake where the serpent dwelt. The serpent, to devour him, raised his head high above the water. The subtle monkey instantly addressed the serpent, saying, "I would be no adequate food for you, but see yonder there is a large troop of monkeys." As soon as the stupid serpent turned his head to see the troop, the monkey put one of his legs on his head and at one leap reached the shore. This story is also called *Vánara Játaka.*

Story of Punyavanta and his friends.—For several successive existences the Lord was a lover of virtue. In one of these he was Punyavanta, son of Anjana, a king of Váránasí. He had four friends, all sons of high officials. They were Víryyavanta, S'ilpavanta, Rúpavanta, and Prajņávanta; their names showing their peculiar excellences. The five friends set out on a journey to Kámpilya in order to test the usefulness of their respective excellences. They found a block of timber floating on the river. Víryyavanta, or he who was possessed of great strength, volunteered to bring it to the bank. He succeeded. The timber, to his great advantage, proved to be sandal-wood. The proceeds from its sale, a hundred thousand pieces of gold, were distributed among the friends. They were very glad, and they loudly praised the advantages of strength.

S'ilpavanta, or he who was skilled in the fine arts, then took up a Víná or harp, and sitting in a corner of the city, began to play upon it. The charm of his performance drew crowds around him. It was soon found that he had no match in the city. The Víná had seven cords, but such was the dexterity of S'ilpavanta that when one of these was broken, the same melting music proceeded from the remaining six cords. He managed to perform the same tune even when there was only one cord left in the instrument. He obtained large rewards for his skill. These he shared with his friends, who were all loud in the praise of artistic skill.

The charm of Rúpavanta's beauty captivated the heart of the first public woman at Kámpilya. At the bidding of her fascinating paramour, the woman gave large sums of money to his friends, and they all acknowledged the excellence of beauty.

It was now the turn for Prajñávanta, or wise man, to show his worth. He went to a market place where he found a banker's son quarrelling with a public woman for a sum of money, a hundred thousand karaṇdas. The banker's son had called in the woman the night before, and had offered her the sum of money in question as her fee for the night. But she had other engagements, and therefore had to decline the offer, promising to come in the morning. In the morning she was told that the banker's son was in no want of her company as he had enjoyed it in a dream. The woman then laid her claim to the money on the ground that it was with her that he had passed the night. The quarrel grew, and there was none who could bring it to an amicable conclusion. Prajñávanta offered his mediation. He ordered the money to be brought in, placed a mirror before it, and commanded the public woman to take the money from within the mirror. "It is your shadow" said the subtle arbitrator, "that he enjoyed in a dream, and you are entitled to a shadow ; how can you expect real and tangible money in return. Take the money reflected in the mirror." The woman was put out of countenance, and the banker's son, flushed with success, gave a heap of gold to Prajṇávanta, who called in his friends to partake of his gains.

The meek and virtuous Punyavanta planted himself before the royal palace. A minister's son, charmed with his simplicity, sought his friendship. Punyavanta was lodged in a part of the king's residence. When he slept there, he was waited upon by the king's daughter, who felt an affection for him. The royal officers, having discovered the princess in the company of a stranger brought the stranger to the king. On investigation Punyavanta proved innocent. His high lineage too remained no longer concealed. He was married to the Princess of Kámpilya, and was appointed heir to the kingdom.

S'oṇaka was Víryyavanta in his previous existence. Ráshṭrapála was S'ilpavanta. Surendra was Rúpavanta. S'áriputra was Prajñávanta.

Story of Vijitári.—In another existence the Lord suffered greatly for his love of virtue. He was then the open-handed munificent king Vijitárí of Mithilá. His ministers and friends combined to banish him from the kingdom in order to prevent the drain on the royal treasury on account of his reckless donations. He lived in the midst of a forest in the Himálaya, where Indra came to try his sincerity. In a long speech, Indra pointed out to the ex-king the disadvantages of reckless munificence. He produced a hell before the king where all the sufferers were extravagant donors. But all these could not produce the least change in the king's mind, and he declared that it was better to suffer in hell than to see people suffering in the world. Well pleased at the declaration, Indra went to heaven, where he commanded the clouds never to let a drop of water fall on Mithilá. The famine-stricken Maithilese restored their banished king to the throne, and the drought was at an end.

Story of Kás'yapa's retirement from home.—When the lord was living on the bank of the tank Karaṇḍaka, Mahákás'yapa gave a complete history of the state of his mind before taking the Pravrajyá. The state of a householder appeared to him to be a state of sinfulness and bondage, Bráhmacharya appeared to be pure and stainless. He renounced the world, and an accident brought him in contact with Buddha, who gave him instruction. Buddha taught him to carefully guard his mind from the allurements of the senses. He told him to see with his eyes, to smell with his nose, to taste with his tongue, to touch with his skin, but never to consider the objects of the senses to be realities, for belief in the reality of sensuous objects brought forth misery, pain and melancholy.

Story of Sáriputra.—Four miles from Rajagrihá there was a small hamlet named Alanda. A rich Bráhmaṇ of that village had seven sons by his wife Sárí. One of them only survived. His name was Upatishya *alias* Sáríputra. He had a friend, named Kolita, of the Mudgala clan; he was named Maudgaláyana after the name of his clan. They studied together under the same preceptor. Once on a time on mounting the Agrasamája hill, they fell in with five hundred Yatis resident there. The state of perfect contentment in which they lived, the consideration they enjoyed, the music and dance of their establishment, stimulated the young friends to enter the hermitage. They were admitted into the fraternity by Sanjayí, son of Raivatí. Upatishya, known in history as Sáríputra, learned all the scriptures relating to asceticism in a week, and his companion did the same in two weeks. By chance they met Upasena, a disciple of Buddha. Upasena was on his usual begging excursion. They asked him in private what sort of lessons did he receive from his preceptor? Upasena replied that the cardinal doctrine of their faith was that the world is a creation of *pratyaya* or false notion. The subtle and penetrating intellect of Sáríputra could not fail to perceive the fundamental difference and vast superiority of this doctrine. He resolved to throw himself, a humble student, at the feet of the Lord, and persuaded Maudgalyáyana and the five hundred Yatis to adopt the same resolution. The Lord was then living in the same city. In the first conference with the Lord, S'áríputra enquired of him as to who was subject to birth and death, to life and bondage, and what were the causes of these four phenomena? The Lord replied, "a union of the four substances lead to all these. The causes of birth are ignorance, insatiable desire for enjoyment and work. The causes of death are the loss of longevity, loss of work and want of appetite. The causes of life are longevity, work and form. The cause of bondage is one, *viz.* work; and work cannot be destroyed until ignorance is dispelled, and thirst after enjoyment is quenched." By lessons and precepts like these, the Lord emancipated S'áríputra and others from birth, death and bondage.

The Lord said, this was not the first time that he had saved Sáríputra and five hundred of his companions. In one of his former existences, he was Kés'í, a powerful horse who crossed over the sea with five hundred merchants on his back, and thereby saved their lives from the snares of the female ogres of the Rákshashídvípa. Excepting the incident of the laughing lamp, the present story is substantially the same as that given in the (Bhadrakalpávadána).

Story of Udáyí, or Káka Játaka.—When the fame of Buddha for his sanctity spread far and wide, the inhabitants of both sexes of Kapilavastu clamorously demanded that he should be invited from Rájagriha to their city. S'uddhodana, to please them, sent a deputation to invite him. The deputation consisted of Buddha's youthful companion Udáyí and his favourite groom Chhandaka. They were, on their arrival at Rájagriha, converted to the new faith by the Lord. The S'ákyas who had been raised to divine rank by their merits, descended from heaven and urged the Lord to bless their relatives by his lectures.

Following the example of S'ikhí, an elder Buddha, the Lord undertook the journey to Kapilavastu on foot. Blessed were the lands through which he passed. Health and plenty followed in his train. Nature wore a smiling appearance wherever he presented himself. Barren fields became fertile, and ruined cities rose into sudden prosperity. Celestial music filled the air. Heavenly flowers were showered on the road. Gods smeared the roads with unearthly sandal paste. His journey resembled a royal progress. It took him fifteen days to reach the environs of Kapilavastu. The grove, called Nyagrodhárâma, was fitted out for his reception. He was attended by eighteen hundred Bhikshus. In the morning this whole army of beggars entered the city to collect alms. Rájá S'uddhodana, while on his way to Nyagrodhárâma, happened to fall in with some of these bald-headed, half-starved, emaciated men. He immediately fell into a melancholy vein of thought. "O what a change! What a great misfortune. My imperial son is reduced to the most degraded condition of human life!" These thoughts were too much for him. Tears trickled down his aged cheeks. He ordered his coachman to turn back, and determined never to see his wayward boy. The news of the king's strange conduct reached Nyagrodhárâma in a short time. Udáyí, at the Lord's bidding, passed to the royal presence through the air, showed some miracles, praised Buddha in hymns, convinced the king of his son's great power, and induced him to give up his former resolution.

When the king came to Buddha's residence, Buddha showed him many miracles. S'uddhodana fell on his knees before his son. Buddha delighted him with an affectionate and interesting conversation.

"How was it" asked the Bhikshus "that S'uddhodana was persuaded by Udáyí?" The Lord's reply was that in times of yore there was a king, named Brahmadatta, at Váráṇasí, and a chief of the crows, named Supátra, was his neighbour. Supárs'vá, the wife of the crow-king, was big with child. She longed for princely food. The minister of the crow-king was immediately ordered to supply royal dishes. None of the eighty thousand of the king's subjects volunteered to steal viands from Brahmadatta's kitchen. The minister set himself resolutely to meet the queen's wishes. On the first day he succeeded very easily. On the second day, the men employed in the kitchen spread a net all round the cook-sheds; but the cunning crow snatched a portion of the food from the cook's hand as he was carrying it to the dining-room. The food also was, on the third day, covered with a net. The crow struck at the cook's nose with his beak; but the man dexterously managed to catch hold of him. He complained to the king of the injury done by the wretched crow to his nose. The crow too gave a true history of his mission. The history surprised the king. He admired the zeal and fidelity of the crow, and ordered a portion of the royal food to be set apart for the crow-queen every day. Buddha was the crow-king; Yasodhará, the queen; Brahmadatta, S'uddhodana; and the minister, Udáyí.

The story of Hastini Játaka was told in answer to the query why Maháprajávatí was blind with tears in his absence, (*vide* Bhadrakalpa Avadána, Story XXXII).

Story of three Asuras.—The Lord trained many thousands of creatures in his faith, by preaching, by precept, and also by working miracles. Ráhulu, Muchálinda and Sambara, three royal Asuras, honoured the Lord with flowers and salutations. They were, they said, candidates for the ranks of Arhat. They fell into a deep meditation. The Lord smiled at their over anxiety. Beautiful rays of variegated colours proceeded from his teeth. These turned round him and then disappeared. As'vaki asked the reason of his smiling, for he knew Buddha never smiled in vain. 'These Asuras' said the Lord, 'are sure to be in heaven. They will descend from that place and worship Jina, and, after some hundred thousands of years, become Jinas.'

Story of Yos'odhará's blandishments.—S'uddhodana invited the Lord with his whole congregation, and gave him a splendid treat. He was followed by Gautamí, Maháprajávatí. Yas'odhará too gave him an entertainment. She approached her long-lost husband in a most bewitching trim. She herself served him with dishes, and displayed all those female arts which delude and enslave the sterner sex. But her empire over the preacher's heart had been lost for ever. She sent some choice sweetmeats through her darling child Rāhula, who asked for his paternal estates. Buddha said that he could give him an immense amount of wealth if he would only enter the Pravrajyá. Buddha returned to Nyagrodhoáráma after delivering a long lecture on virtue.

Why did Yasodhará try to tempt Buddha? In reply to this interesting question, the story of Ekas'ringá was by the Lord narrated as related in a preceding page.

Padmávati Játaka follows next (see page 65). And after that *Chandra Súrya Játaka* [see page 69].

Story of Upyaka called Gangápála Játaka.—S'uddhodana issued a proclamation commanding all the S'ákyas who had more sons than one to send one son each to the hermitage for the service of the Lord. Five hundred S'ákya boys left their homes, resolved to enter the pravrajyá. A barber boy, who went to shave the Lord, obtained two Dhyánas from him. The razor was, at the command of the Lord, then taken away from his hand, and he obtained two others. The S'ákyas gave all their rich dresses to the barber boy. But the boy, Upáli, was then in a different mood. Disclaiming the rich gifts, he presented himself before the Lord as a candidate for pravrajyá. The S'ákyas and Upáli were made to accept pravrajyá on the same day. At the conclusion of the ceremony, the Lord said, that Upáli should be the chief of the S'ákya Bhikshus. The S'ákyas honored Upáli by falling prostrate at his feet.

The Bhikshus thought it strange that the proud S'ákyas should bring their heads low before a lowborn barber. "But" said the Lord, "this is not the first time that they have prostrated themselves before a lowborn man." He gave the following story in illustration :—

Two poor boys of Benares gave a few beans enclosed in leaf-packets to a Pratyeka Buddha. One of them desired to become a Bráhmaṇ in his next existence, and the other a Kshatríya. For that act of charity, they had what they wished. One was born, Brahmadatta, king of Benares; the other, Upyaka, a Bráhman. Upyaka lived for a time in intimate terms with a girl with whom he had fallen in love. She desired to have perfumery and flower wreaths. Upyaka proceeded to the banks of the Ganges to get alms wherewith to buy the needful. He got a másha (a bean). When he was bringing it it slipped from his hand, and was lost. He set to find it out. Brahmadatta, finding a Bráhmaṇ intent on the diligent search of something in the scorching meridian sun, sent for him, and asked him what he was about. On being told of the loss of the másha the king offered to give him one. "But," said Upyaka, "that would make two if I could successfully find out my lost bean." The King offered him a couple of máshas, but still the Bráhman would not give up his painful search. He only said if he could find his one out, that would certainly add one to all that the king could give. The king at last consented to give him half his possessions, when Upyaka gave up his search. The king sacrificed so much, only because he was disposed to love the Bráhmaṇ. On one occasion, putting his head on the lap of Upyaka, he fell into a sound sleep. Upyaka, who already possessed half the kingdom through the king's benevolence, now formed a project of obtaining the other half by putting him to death. But his conscience stung him, and he gave up the foul intent. When the king awoke, Upyaka plainly confessed his treasonable purposes, and asked his permission to renounce the world, saying, that ambition can never be satisfied. On the departure of Upyaka, the king composed a verse in which he denounced ambition, and quoted Upyaka's conduct in illustration. Gaṅgápála, the king's barber, hearing the gáthá, went over to Upyaka and became a Bhikshu. He soon attained the five experiences. [Panchábhijñá.]

The success and good fortune of Gaṅgápála induced the king to throw himself with his whole court at Upyaka's feet. This Gaṅgápála was Upáli, and the S'ákyas were Brahmadatta's followers.

Story of Mahágovinda.—The Bhikshus asked the Lord why so many renounced the world when the Lord himself entered the hermitage? The Lord gave them a legend of Vipas'yí. Pañchas'ikha, the son of a heavenly chorister, illuminating the four quarters of the globe with the lustre of his brilliant person, descended to where the Lord was, and begged him to explain the legend of Mahábrahmá. The Lord said, king Dis'ámpati had a son named Reṇu. His family-priest had a son named Jyotihpála who, having silenced all his opponents in a controversy, obtained the title of Mahágovinda. By the instigation of Mahágovinda six noble Kshatríyas demanded from Reṇu a share of his father's territories. Reṇu was compelled to dismember his father's empire, and cede the six provinces of Kalinga, Paṭṭana, Máhes'avatí, Váráṇasí, Roruka, and Mithilá to the refractory nobles.

Successful in their ambitious projects, the nobles proceeded to Mahágovinda to ask him what to do next. Govinda turned his face to the north, and fell into a deep meditation. Mahábrahmá appeared before him in the fulness of his glory, and stood over his head. The saintly priest, awed by the divine presence, chanted solemn hymns, and offered flowers and incense. The boon that he prayed to obtain was instruction how to obtain immortality and perfect beatitude. The great truth was revealed. Mahábrahmá uttered the following words and disappeared:

"Have affection for none; be merciful to all; seek solitude; discriminate truth from falsehood; have no ámagandha (raw smell); forsake the company of women; and you will obtain immortality." The ámagandhas are: anger, untruth, talkativeness, egotism, envy, cruelty, speaking ill of others, and wrath.

Mahágovinda, having the great truth revealed to him, continued no longer in the wicked course of the world, but with Reṇu, the six Kshatríya chiefs, and thousands of others, entered the blissful state of Pravrajyá. Buddha was that Mahágovinda.

Story of Bahubuddha.—The Lord said to Ánanda there lived in a certain Kalpa, Indradhvaja, a Tathágata and Árhat, in the beautiful city of Indratapana. He explained the Mahá Buddha to Mahádhvaja; Mahádhvaja did so to Dhvajottama, Dhvajottama to Dhvajaruchira, and so on, till it was imparted to Bahubuddha. Then come some verses in praise of Samyak Samádhi.

Ráhula's conversion.—S'uddhodana requested the Lord to take his meal at his palace as long as he would be at Kapilavastu. The lord was silent. Ráhula obtained the five lessons from his father, and renounced the world in spite of his mother's remonstrances. The five lessons are these: (1) "I take refuge with Buddha, I take refuge with Dharma, I take refuge with Sangha; Buddha is my only protector; I have none else to look after me; Dharma is my only protector, I have none else to look after me;

Sañgha is my only protector, I have none else to look after me. (2) I solemnly take a vow of seclusion for life. (3) I will not take anything not given me. (4) I will never tread the paths of a wrong-doer. (5) I will never tell an untruth. I will fly away from the haunts of pleasure."

Story of Dharmalabdha.—When the wicked Mára, discomfited and put to route by the Lord, was lamenting over his sad lot, his daughters, Tantrá, Rati and others, tried their wily arts to seduce the great ascetic from the path of virtue. But they too shared their father's fate. After this, the Lord set the wheel of his religion in motion, and became the great founder of a new creed. The Bhikshus, always bent on enquiring after the causes of their Lord's actions, asked him the reason of the discomfiture of the daughters of Mára. They were told that there was in the city of Benares a good man named Dharmalabdha, who grew rich by enterprising voyages by sea. A company of five hundred enterprising youths waited in a deputation on him to request him to show them the way to wealth. He received them graciously, but at the same time gave them fully to understand the dangers and difficulties of sea voyages. He told them that he traded with the people of the Rákshasídvípa. The Rákshasís of the place were adepts in all sorts of fascinations. Unless one was confident of rising superior to their temptation, it was not safe to transact business with them. One who fell into their snare had no hope of seeing the Jambudvípa any more. But still these worshippers of mammon persisted. Dharmalabdha set sail with these five hundred merchants in his company, and a few men-of-war to protect them. But the five hundred young men, unable to resist the temptation of sensual enjoyment placed before them by the Rákshasís, fell into their snare, and were lost. In a few days after their landing at the cannibal island the gross and material part of their body formed delicious dishes for the delectation of the female ogres. Dharmalabdha alone came back, laden with riches. Repeatedly baffled in their attempt to tempt Dharmalabdha, the wicked gang of demons held a solemn council. It was determined at that meeting that one of their number should go to tempt and ruin the innocent man. The chief of the mischievous crew—an incarnation of deception—undertook to proceed to Benares. Concealed in the form of a celestial damsel, and accompanied by an amiable and handsome child, she presented herself at the door of Dharmalabdha, demanding admission into his seraglio as his married wife. She was denied access by that firm and experienced merchant. But Brahmadatta, the king of Benares, ignorant of her wiles and impelled by a chivalric feeling, not only gave her protection, but took her as his wife. At the dead of night the Rákshasí left the royal bed, made a feast of the king, and then gorged her appetite with all that fell in her way. She did not even spare the elephants. Anarchy prevailed over the whole country. Next morning, at a great council, Dharmalabdha was elected king. The Rákshasís were the daughters of Mára, and Dharmalabdha was the Lord himself.*

Story of a Goatherd.—When the Lord was practising austerities at Nairanjaná in the burning heat of the meridian sun, a goatherd planted a pipal tree by his side to relieve him. In a short time it grew into a gigantic size, overshadowing an extensive tract of land. The goatherd saw with delight the sudden growth of his tree. For the cheerfulness of his heart, the source of all human bliss, the goatherd was, after his death, translated to the region of the gods of the class thirty-three. He came down from that high position to dedicate the tree to the Lord, who with silence accepted the offering.

Story of the Lord's Progress from Uruvilvá.—From Nairanjaṇá the Lord went to Kshíriká, and thence proceeded to a small hamlet named Ujjvala. There he remained for 49 days without touching human food. On the fiftieth day a small quantity of ghi and honey was offered to him by a merchant named Trapushabhallika.† The Lord gave a few of his hairs, the pairings of his nails, and a few pieces of stones brought from a great distance by his miraculous power, to the merchant and his companions. The merchant established a stupa over these nails at a place named Báluka, over the hairs at Keshasthalí, and over the stones at S'ilu. Indra gave the Lord a myrobalan. After eating the kernel, the Lord threw the stone on the ground. Instantly from that stone grew forth a tree of gigantic dimensions. This is the first time that the Lord's *Riddhi* or miraculous power was displayed. Then for six long years

* This is the third version of the story told on page 97. The second version appears on p. 149.

† In the *Lalita-Vistara*, chapter XXIV, there are two merchants named *Trapusha* and *Bhallika*.

the Lord practised severe penances at Uruvilvá. At this time a pious man brought a S'oṇapañshukula* before the Lord, and offered it to him on the express condition that he should not eat it until he brought his austerities to a successful termination. The offerer was translated to the region of the thirty-three gods. When the lord wanted to partake of the fruit, he needed water to wash his hands and feet. Indra excavated a river with his nails. The river is still called Páṇikhátá. When the lord wanted a vessel to wash the fruit, four great celestial kings offered him four stone vases. In one he washed the S'oṇapánsukula; in the second he purified it; the third he miraculously threw at Trapushbhallika's dwelling in the Gándhára country. In the fourth he ate. These four stone vases were afterwards consecrated by men. The Lord then bathed in the stream of Páṇikhátá. He then wished to cross it. The Devaputra Kakubha, who lived in a large shady tree named Kakubha, ferried him over to the other side of the river. There he sat under the pipal tree planted by the goatherd. There for the first time did the thought of preaching the true religion cross his mind. He should not, he thought, keep to himself, the truth, so subtle, so brilliant, so grand, and calculated to improve the condition of mankind so greatly. Mahábrahmá and other gods at the same time came down from the regions celestial, to confirm him in his resolution. He felt in him a strength produced by previous meditation and by an irreproachable character. He thought there were only five men of respectable antecedents who may receive the doctrines to be preached by him. They were at Benares. He directed his steps, accordingly, towards that holy city. His route lay through Gayá, Náhál, Bundadvira, Lohitavastuka, Gandhapura and Sárathipura. The last place was situated on the banks of the Ganges. In the form of a goose the Lord flew over the river, and reached the deer park at Váráṇasí. On his way from Gayá to Váráṇasí, he was entertained by Sudarsana and Kamaṇḍalu, two Nágarájas, and Gaudha and Bundha, two Yakshas. He had much talk with Nadi and Upaka. In these conversations he declared in unmistakable terms his own prophetship, and spoke in high terms of his great mission on earth. He claimed honors, superior to those of Brahmacháris, Jinas and Arhats, and gave out that he derived every doctrine of his creed by inspiration.†

* A kind of plum.

† This story of the Lord's last days at Uruvilvá and his progress to Benares differs

At Benares, the five youths of respectable antecedents, who were his first companions, were converted. They became Bhikshus. There were, they were told, two ends which a Bhikshu should always keep in view. There should be no ignorant hankering after external enjoyments which were mere delusions, and also there should be no blind faith in the existence of a soul as the source of suffering and distress. To attain these two ends it is necessary to meditate on the four Áryasatyas 'or noble truths.' These were that there were suffering, combination of sufferings, an annihilation of suffering, and a Pratipat or belief which leads to the end of all sufferings. Union with enemies and separation from friends &c., are sufferings. Social instincts, ambition, love, &c., are the combinations of different sufferings. The annihilation of these feelings constitutes the annihilation of suffering. The belief or Pratipat has eight subordinate parts: 1, true insight, 2, true resolve, 3, true speech, 4, true end of Karma, 5, pure living, 6, true exercise, 7, true recollection, and 8, true meditation. The sufferings and their combinations are to be shuned by all possible means, while their annihilation is to be sought with eagerness. These noble truths were twelve times thought over and mastered by the Lord.

External qualities, feelings of consciousness, beliefs and impressions.—Are these Átmá? The external qualities are not Átmá, for they produce misery, and do not tend towards the attainments of the highest bliss, the goal of human desires. For the same considerations neither feeling, nor consciousness, nor the others can be regarded as Átmá. Candidates for Pravrajyá should learn very carefully that the external qualities, feelings, consciousness, beliefs or impressions, either external or internal, subtle or gross, good or bad, past, present or future—these are neither one's own self, nor are belonging to him. Misery and melancholy have their root in these, therefore men should try to disdain them. They are transitory, subject to birth and death, therefore the sooner these are discarded the better it is for the hermit.

Story of Ajñátakauṇḍilya.—Ajñátakauṇḍilya thought over these noble truths for three times, and his eyes were opened. He was in one of his former existences a potter who cured a Pratyeka Buddha from a bilious disorder, and obtained from him the boon that he should be the first man to receive the religion of Sugata.

in many respects from what occurs in the *Lalita Vistara*, and seems to be a very corrupt version. See my *Buddha Gayá*, pp. 45 f.

Ájnatakaundilya was, in another existence, a merchant relieved by the amiable and virtuous king of Kos'ala, who, to avoid bloodshed in a war with the king of Kás'í, had abdicated his kingdom, and gone into a voluntary exile. While roaming in the Dakshiṇápatha, he happened to see a shipwrecked merchant who was on his way to the king of Kos'ala, on whose munificence he counted for repairing his fallen fortunes. Little did the poor man know that he was addressing the very king of Kos'ala whose fortunes were now no better than his own. The king instantly disabused him, gave him an account of his own misfortunes, and expressed his sorrow that he could no longer be useful to a man in distress. The poor merchant, disappointed at the last resort which hope had pointed out to him, fell into a swoon, and remained insensible for a long time.

But a glimpse of hope now shot through the heart of the good king. He remembered that a price had been set on his head; so he persuaded the distressed gentleman, now recovering from the effect of the swoon, to take him alive to the king of Benares. This spirit of self-sacrifice surprised the king of Kás'í, who now repented of what he had done, and not only gave the merchant a large sum of money, but reinstated the king on his throne.

Story of Five Disciples. Bhadravargiya Jataka.—The Bhíkshus enquired how it was that the five men of respectable antecedents, who were the followers of Tirthikas, and were therefore ill-disposed to the Lord's creed, were so easily converted? It was an indication of very great sagacity in the Lord that he made them his staunchest adherents first of all. In one of their previous existences they were cast into the sea together with the Lord, who was the captain of the merchantman. They were all floating on the raging surge without the faintest hope of being wafted to firm land. On a sudden they found the captain whom they all implored to save them. Equally distressed with the rest, the captain happened to remember an old saying, that the sea never drowns a corpse. He instantly commanded them to lay fast hold of him, which they did. He drew out a knife and plunged it in his breast. With his dead body they all were thrown upon the shore.

Stories of wicked kings.—There was, once on a time, a king named Kálabha, reigning at Benares. Walking about in his pleasure-garden in the company of the ladies of his zenana, he fell into a profound sleep under a tree. In the meanwhile a Ṛishi from the Uttara-kuru came to the garden, and began to deliver a lecture to the ladies. The king, when he left his bed, was greatly enraged at the conduct of the uncouth stranger who had violated the sanctity of his female quarters. He asked the Ṛishi who he was. The Ṛishi declared himself to be a Kshántívadí, one who pardons all injuries, whereupon the king drew his sword and cut off one of the Ṛishi's fingers. The Ṛishi remained unmoved; the king cut a second finger, and then a third. Gradually his body was cut to pieces; but he could not be made to show any signs of distress. Milk only issued forth from the wounds and no blood. The Ṛishi was Buddha in a former life.

King Arjuna of Hastinápura was in the habit of killing those holy men who were unable to satisfy him by answers to the questions put to them by him. He put to death Gautama, a most amiable old Ṛishi, only for failing to answer one of his questions.

Nálikela was the king of Dantapura in Kalinga, who offered to some Ṛishis for their repast a basketful of wild thorny berries called s'vanakha *(Flacourtea cotaphracta)*, and forbad them to laugh on pain of death.

Daṇḍaki was another of the wicked kings. He reigned at Gobardhana in the Dakshiṇápatha. Vatsa, a disciple of Kas'yapa, who came for a change from the Himálayan regions (for he was suffering from consumption) to Daṇḍaki's city, was buried under a heap of dust by that wicked monarch. He was, however, rescued by a virtuous minister of the king. On the seventh day after his rescue Vatsa died, and immediately after his death, there was a great conflagration which converted the whole city into a heap of ruins. The king perished with all his wicked followers, the rescuer of Vatsa alone escaping for the timely information afforded to him by the Ṛishi.

Another disciple of Kás'yapa, Sarabhanga by name, obtained great merit by his austerities and his prowess. He was present at a great sacrifice held at a place between the Ganges and the Yamuná. Ninety-eight thousands of Ṛishis, three kings of Hastina and Dantapura (*viz.* Udyaka, Ashṭamaka, Bhínsaratha), and Indra, along with many gods, honored the sacrifice by their presence. Before this assembled multitude of gods and men Sarabhanga revealed the terrible fate that had befallen these four wicked kings who dishonored the venerable sages. Daṇḍakí, he said, was hurled headlong into the abyss of a hell named Kukkura; Arjjuna, with head downwards, was placed upon the stake, Nálikela lived on all that was loathsome; and Kálabha was drowned in the hell Abíchi.

Buddha in one of his previous existences was Svarabhanga, therefore he preached to all.

Notable conversions.—During his short sojourn in the Mrigadáva, the great preacher converted 30 kings and Púrṇa, a young Bráhmaṇ of Droṇavastu in the Kos'ala country. On his way from Uruvilvá he also converted 700 Rishis with matted hairs.

When he was at Uruvilvá, Rájá Vimbisára desired to see him, and instantly heard of the saint's sudden appearance in the Shashṭivana of his own capital Rájagriha. The Lord preached the truth to him, and showed him the way to Nirváṇa. The reason of showing this extraordinary favour to the king was, that in one of his previous existences he was the Lord's playmate. His name then was Arindama, and that of the Lord S'reṇya. He was king while S'reṇya was a hermit. In that existence too the Lord, after 84,000 years of separation, had remembered his old friend, and brought him to a hermit's life.

M. Em. Senart has an edition of this work now in the press.

Beginning. ॐ नमः श्रीमहाबुद्धाय। अतीतानागतप्रत्युत्पन्नेभ्यः सर्व्वबुद्धेभ्यः। महावस्तुन-आदिवन्धानीमानि बोधिसत्त्वानां बोधिसत्त्वचर्य्याणि। कतमानि चत्वारि। प्रकृतिचर्य्या, प्रणिधानचर्य्या, अनुलोमचर्य्या, अनिवर्त्तनचर्य्या। नमः अपरिमितध्वजाय तथागतायार्हते सम्यक् सम्बुद्धाय। यस्यान्तिके अनेनैव भगवता शाक्यमुनिना प्रथमं कुशलमूलान्यवरोपितानि राज्ञा चक्रवर्त्तिभूतेनादौ प्रकृतिचर्य्यायां प्रवर्त्तमानेन। नमोऽतीताय शाक्यमुनये तथागतायार्हते सम्यक् सम्बुद्धाय। यस्यान्तिके अनेनैव भगवता शाक्यमुनिना प्रथमं कुशलमूलप्रणिधानं कृतम्। वणिक्श्रेष्ठिभूतेनादौ प्रणिधानचर्य्यायां प्रवर्त्तमानेनाहं, पुनरहमनागतेऽध्वनि बुद्धो भवेयं, तथागतार्हन् सम्यक् सम्बुद्धो यथायं भगवान् शाक्यमुनिरिति नामधेयं विस्तरेण यावत् ममापि कपिलवस्तुनगरं भवेदिति। नमः समिताविने तथागतायार्हते सम्यक् सम्बुद्धाय। यस्यान्तिके अनेनैव भगवता शाक्यमुनिना अनुलोमप्रणिधानं कृतम्। राज्ञा चक्रवर्त्तिभूतेन अनुलोमचर्य्यायां प्रतिष्ठितेन।

End. इदमवोचद्भगवान् आत्तमनास्ते च देवा नागासुरा गरुड़किन्नरा महोरगाः सा च सर्व्वावती पर्षत् ते च भिक्षवो भगवतो भाषितमभ्यनन्दन्निति॥

आर्य्यमहासाङ्घिकानां लोकोत्तरवासिनां पाठन।

Colophon. इति श्रीमहावस्त्ववदानं समाप्तम्॥

No. B. 28.

MAṆICHU'ḌA' AVADA'NA.

Substance, paper, 12 × 36. Folia, 50. Lines on a page, 6. Extent in s'lokas, 1800. Character, Newárí. Date, ? Appearance, old. Prose and verse. Incorrect.

Story of Maṇichúḍa, a pious king of Suketa, who had given his own body to a demon. It was related by the Lord himself when dwelling in the Jeta Grove of S'rávasti. The lord having exhibited some miracles, the audience greatly wondered, and enquired how he had acquired the power of working miracles. Thereupon he narrated many stories of miracles effected in his former existences, and then said: Brahmadatta, king of Suketa, had a son born unto him, who had on his head at the time of birth a crown more refulgent than the sun, and drops of moisture falling from it converted a mass of iron into gold. On account of these miraculous events the child was named Maṇichúḍa, *alias* Ratnachúḍa. When Maṇichúḍa succeeded his father, he caused many alms-houses to be established, and ruled the country with great energy and justice. He had an elephant named Bhadragríví and a horse named A'júneya, each of which could travel 400 miles a day. At the time there lived, in a cave in the Himálaya, a sage named Bhavabhúti. The sage once found a beautiful damsel seated on a lotus in a tank. He named her Padmávatí, and brought her up in his hermitage. When she was grown up, he made her over to Manichúḍa, who married her, and had by her a son named Padmottara. The king once celebrated the great rite of Nigada Maháyajṇa, and in course of it was asked by a fierce demon to give him some human blood for food. Rather than disappoint a beggar on such an occasion, and at the same time unwilling to shed human blood, he ripped open his own neck, and gave the blood flowing therefrom. The demon next asked for some meat, and the king gave his own body. Greatly pleased by this extraordinary munificence, the demon, who was no other than Indra in that shape, assumed his own shape, and offered him universal sovereignty, long life, or whatever else he wanted. Maṇichúḍa wished to be a Buddha, so that he may be able to effect the salvation of mankind. The boon was granted. On the conclusion of the rite, the king gave away to the Bráhmaṇs by way of alms his precious horse and elephaut, as well as his wife and son.

A neighbouring king, named Dusprasava, demanded the elephant, and threatened war unless his request was complied with. Rather than fight and bring on carnage, the king bought back the elephant, and gave it to Dusprasava. At this moment four Pratyeka Buddhas seized Maṇichúḍa, and carried him away to the top of the Himálaya, where they left him. The minister of Maṇichúḍa ransomed the prince, and placed him on the throne. The queen was ransomed, and brought back home, and the Dusprasava was overpowered in battle. Thereupon Dusprasava sent five Bráhmaṇs to buy of Maṇíchúḍa the crown which was on his head. The king immediately split open his head, and gave the jewel; but by a miracle his head was reunited, and a new jewel of even greater magnificence sprung on it. "This Maṇichúḍa" said the Lord, "was myself in a former birth, and on account of my munificence I am now able to work miracles." Asked what had Maṇichúḍa done to attain the jewel, the Lord said, in a preceding birth Maṇichúḍa was the son of Aruṇa, a king who had erected a jewelled stúpa on the remains of Buddha S'ikhí, and the son had placed on it his own crown, and decorated it with a jewelled parasol.

Beginning. ॐ नमो रत्नत्रयाय सर्व्वबुद्धबोधिसत्त्वेभ्यः। एवं मया श्रुतमेकस्मिन् समये भगवान् श्रावस्त्यां विहरति स्म जेतवनेऽनाथपिण्डदस्यारामे भिक्षुसङ्घेन सार्द्धं यदा भगवता प्रातिहार्य्यं विदर्शितं निर्भर्त्सितास्तीर्थ्या वन्दिता देवमनुष्यास्तोषितानि सज्जनहृदयानि तदा भिक्षव आश्चर्य्यजाता अद्भुतजाता भगवन्तमिदमवोचत्। आश्चर्य्यं भदन्त यद्भगवता इदमीदृशं महाप्रातिहार्य्यं विदर्शितं। निर्भर्त्सितास्तीर्थ्या वन्दिता देवमनुष्यास्तोषितानि सज्जनहृदयानीति। एवमेतद्भिक्षव एवमेतत्। यथापि तत्सुपरिपूर्णकृतत्वात् बोधिसम्भारस्य तथा हि भिक्षवो दीर्घरात्रं तथागतेन त्रिभिः कल्पसङ्ख्येय दुष्करशतसहस्रैर्बोधिसम्भारः पूरितः। अपि तु तिष्ठन्तु तावदन्ये कल्पा यन्मयास्मिन्नेव भद्रकल्पे बोधिभारपरिपूरणार्थं सुदुष्करं कर्म्म कृतं। तच्छ्रूयतां भूतपूर्व्वं भिक्षवोऽस्मिन्नेव भद्रकल्पे साकेतनगरे ब्रह्मदत्तो नाम राजा राज्यं करोति।

End. इति हि भिक्षव एकान्तकृष्णानामेकान्तकृष्णो विपाकः एकान्तशुक्लानां कर्म्मणामेकान्तशुक्लो विपाकः व्यतिमिश्राणां व्यतिमिश्रस्तस्मात्तर्हि भिक्षव एकान्तकृष्णानि कर्म्माण्यपास्य व्यतिमिश्राणि च शुक्लेष्वेव कर्म्मस्वाभोगः करणीयः। इत्येवं भिक्षवः शिक्षितव्यमिदमवोचद्भगवान् आत्तमनास्ते भिक्षवो भगवतो भाषितमभ्यनन्दन्निति॥

Colophon. इति श्रीमणिचूड़ावदानं परिसमाप्तं।

No. B 4.

MAHA'-S'I'TAVATI'.

Substance, Nepalese yellow paper, 12·6 × 3·6. Folia, 186 to 192. Lines on a page, 5. Extent in s'lokas, 42. Character, Newárí. Date, 944, Newárí. Prose and verse. Incorrect.

A charm for warding off evils likely to result from adverse planets, ferocious animals, and venomous insects.

It is said that on one occasion when Buddha was sojourning on the bank of a tank near a cremation ground at Rájágriha, his son Ráhula appeared before him, and complained of the sufferings to which he was subjected by adverse planets, ferocious animals, venomous insects, and diseases, and prayed for relief. Thereupon the Lord imparted to him a charm which, when heard, or recited, or borne on the person as an amulet, was calculated to keep such evils a hundred thousand miles away from one so protected. The charm begins with the words "*angá kalingá bhangá varangá sansára-tarangá,*" &c. This work, along with four others, *viz.*, Mahá-pratisará, Mahá-sahasra-pramardiní, Mahá-máyurí, and Mahá-rakshá-mantránusáriṇí, bears the common name of *Pancharakshá*, or the "five protectors."

The first page of each of the five works has on its middle a *vignette;* that on the Mahá-s'ítavatí, represents a green-coloured goddess with three heads and six hands, seated on two Garuḍas. Of the heads one is yellow, one red, and one of the colour of the body.

Beginning. ॐ नमो भगवत्यै आर्य्यमहाशीतवत्यै । एवं मया श्रुतमेकस्मिन् समये भगवान् राजगृहे विहरति स्म । शीतवने महाश्मशाने दृघधिकायतनप्रत्युद्देशे तत्रायुष्मान् राहुलोऽतीव विहेत्ये देवग्रहैर्नागग्रहैरसुरग्रहै राक्षसग्रहैः किन्नरग्रहैर्मरुतग्रहैर्गरुड़ग्रहैर्महोरगग्रहैर्मनुष्यग्रहैरमनुष्यग्रहैः प्रेतग्रहैर्भूतग्रहैः पिशाचग्रहैः कुष्माण्डग्रहैर्द्दीपिभिः काकैरुलूकैः कीटैः सरीसृपैरन्यैश्च सत्त्वैर्मनुष्यामनुष्यैः । अथायुष्मान् राहुलो येन भगवांस्तेनोपसङ्क्रान्त उपसङ्क्रम्य भगवतः पादौ शिरसा वन्दित्वा भगवन्तं त्रिः प्रदक्षिणीकृत्य भगवतः पुरतो रुदन्नश्रूणि प्रवर्त्तयति स्म । अथ खलु भगवान् जानन्नेव राहुलमामन्त्रयते स्म । किन्नु त्वं राहुल मम पुरतः स्थित्वा चाश्रूणि प्रवर्त्तयसि । एवमुक्ते आयुष्मान् राहुलो भगवन्तमेतदवोचत् । इहाहं भगवन् राजगृहे विहरामि । शीतवने महाश्मशाने दृघधिकायतनप्रत्युद्देशे । सोऽहं भगवंस्तत्र विहेत्याः ।

End. इदमवोचद्भगवान् आत्तमना आयुष्मान् राहुलः सा च सर्व्वावती सभा सदेव-मानुषासुर-गरुड़-गन्धर्व्वाश्च लोका भगवतो भाषितमभ्यनन्दन्निति ।

Colophon. आर्य्यमहाशीतवती नाम महाविद्या राज्ञी महानुशंसा रक्षासूत्रं समाप्तं । आर्य्यमहाप्रतिसरा आर्य्यमहासाहस्रप्रमर्द्दिनी आर्य्यमहामायूरी आर्य्यमन्त्रानु-सारिणी आर्य्यमहाशीतवती एतानि पञ्चरक्षासूत्राणि समाप्तानि ।

No. B 4.

MAHA'-RAKSHA'-MANTRA'NUSA'RINI'.

Substance, Nepalese yellow paper, 12·6 × 3·6. Folia, 169 to 1185. Lines on a page, 5. Extent in s'lokas, 108. Character, Newárí. Date, 944, Newárí. Prose and verse. Incorrect.

A charm for keeping off diseases. It was imparted by the Lord when he was dwelling in the Bamboo grove near the town of Vaís'álí. A'nanda, who was in his company, was directed to go and recite it in the city of Vais'álí, and it brought untold blessings on that city. The charm begins with the words, *visarata* (5 times repeated) *Buddha lokánukampaka ájnápayati, sarvabuddhánumatina sarva-pratyeka-buddhánumatiná*" &c.

The goddess represented in this codex is four-headed and ten-handed, and seated on two peacocks. The colour of the goddess is red, but her heads are successively white, red, blue and yellow.

Beginning. ॐ नमो भगवत्यै आर्य्यमहामन्त्रानुसारिण्यै । नमः समस्तबुद्धेभ्यः । एवं मया-श्रुतमेकस्मिन् समये भगवान् राजगृहे विहरति स्म । वेणुवने कलन्दकनिवापे तत्र भगवान् आयुष्मन्तमानन्दमामन्त्रयते स्म । आगमयानन्द येन वैशालीत्येवं भदन्तेत्यायुष्मानानन्दः भगवतः प्रत्यश्रौषीत् । अथ भगवान् वृजिषु जनपदेषु जनपदचारिकां चरन् वैशालीमनुप्राप्य वैशालीं विहरति स्म आम्रपालिवने । तत्र भगवान् आयुष्मन्तमानन्दमामन्त्रयते स्म । गच्छानन्द वैशालीं गत्वा इन्द्रकीले पादं स्थापयित्वा इमानि महामन्त्रानुसारिणीमन्त्रपदानि भाषस्व इमा गाथाश्च । विसरत ५ बुद्धो लोकानुकम्पक आज्ञापयति ।

End. यदि तत्र बुद्धानुभावेन देवतानां देवतानुभावेन महतीतिर्व्युपशान्तेति ।

Colophon. आर्य्यमहारक्षामन्त्रानुसारिणी नाम महायानसूत्रं समाप्तमिति ।

No. B. 4.

MAHÁ-SÁHASRA-PRAMARDINÍ.

Substance, Nepalese paper, 12½ × 3½. Folia, 43 to 93. Lines on a page, 5. Extent in s'lokas, 718. Character, Newárí. Date 944, Newárí. Prose and verse. Appearance, old. Incorrect.

A collection of mantras and rituals for overcoming the evils which wicked spirits cause to mankind.

The work opens, in common with the other four works with which it is associated, in the usual style of the Maháyána Sútras, with the words "thus has it been heard by me," and claims to be a work of that class. It is said that when the Lord was dwelling in the grove of Prabhásavana, on the Gṛidhrakúṭa hill, in Rájagríha, in the company of thirteen hundred and fifty followers, he perceived, by his transcendental knowleḍge, that the town of Vais'álí was then under great tribulation. Earthquakes, cyclones, prolonged cloudiness emersing everything into impermiable gloom, and the evil eye of Saturn were rendering everything desolate there. At this juncture all the principal gods, headed by Brahmá and Indra, appeared before the Lord, and prayed that the knowledge of the Mahásáhasra-pramardiní mantra may be revealed to them. Thereupon the Lord enquired what mantras they knew to overcome supernatural evils? The great king Vais'ravaṇa said, "when men are afflicted by Yakshas, they laugh, run about, talk wildly, get angry, tremble, knock about, &c., and for it this is my mantra." The words of the mantra are *siddhe susiddhe sattve ave araṇe bale tambhe stambhe jaṭile akhane sukhane khakhane kharate kharange halipingale timingale timingilini mangale siddhyantu mantra padá sváhá, mama saparivárasya sattvánáncha svastyastu, vais'ravaṇasya mahárájasya námná balenáis'varyádhipatyena cha sváhá.* It means "may such and such (evils, naming them) be overcome by the the name, might, majesty and supremacy of the great king Vais'ravaṇa." Similarly the great king Dhṛitaráshṭra gave his mantra for overcoming Gandharvas, the great king Viruḍhaka his charm for overcoming Kusmáṇḍa Preta, and the great king Virúpáksha his charm for overcoming Nágagṛihas. Thereupon the Lord, with the voice of a lion, declared before the audience: "I am possessed of the ten great powers; I possess the four great secrets. By me alone was Mára overcome with his mighty army." He then recited the great mantra, "the secret for overcoming endless thousands of evils" :—*Mahásáhasra-pramardiní-sandhi.* It runs thus: *asanga-khaḍgavate balanirghoshe súre súravate vajrasame vajrágame vajradhare sushthe jambhe dridhasaraviraje vighare vairágra-prápte araṇe araṇodharmayukte dis'í vighushṭe sváhá, svastyastu mama sarvasattvánáṇcha tathágatasya námná balenais'varyádhipatehs'cha sváhá.*

On hearing this all the wicked spirits of the earth dispersed far and wide; and the lord appointed some of the leading gods guardians of the different quarters of the universe, each of the guardians undertaking to keep the peace by an appropriate mantra which he recited. After this the Lord, out of mercy for the Lichchhavis of Vais'álí repaired to them, and blessed them, removing all their troubles by the great mantra which he had recited.

The remainder of the work describes the different symptoms which manifest themselves when a person is afflicted by particular wicked spirits, and the rituals which should be observed when the great mantra is to be recited, or worn on the person; the details varying under different circumstances. The Rev. S. Beal, in his Buddhist Tripiṭhaka, notices a Chinese work named Sheou-hu-ta-tsien-kwo-t'u-king or the Mahásáhasra Maṇḍala Sútra, which, I believe, is the same with the work here described. It was translated by Shi-hu during the Sung dynasty (Circa 960 to 1278), and is said to contain Dharaṇís.

The *vignette* in this case represents a fierce goddess with exposed teeth and blue colour, seated on two crouching men of a yellow colour. The heads are successively white, blue, red and yellow.

Beginning. ॐ नमो भगवत्यै आर्य्यमहासाहस्रप्रमर्द्दिन्यै। एवं मया श्रुतमेकस्मिन् समये भगवान् राजगृहे विहरति स्म । गृध्रकूटपर्व्वते द्रोणपार्श्वे(?) ह्रदगोचररत्नहर्ष प्रभासे वनषण्डे महता भिक्षुसङ्घेन सार्द्धमर्द्धत्रयोदशभिर्भिक्षुशतैः ।

End. इदमवोचद् भगवान् आत्तमनास्ते च भिक्षवो भगवतो भाषितमभ्यनन्दन्निति ।

Colophon. आर्य्यमहासाहस्रप्रमर्द्दिनी नाम महायानसूत्रं समाप्तं ॥

No. B. 4.

MAHA'-PRATISARA'-KALPA.

Substance, Nepalese paper, 12½ × 3½ inches. Folia, 1 to 42. Lines on a page, 5. Extent in s'lokas, 588. Character, Newárí. Date, 944, Newárí. Appearance, old. Incorrect.

A charm for destroying sin, disease, and all difficulties.

It was revealed by the Lord when he was ḍwelling under a kalpa tree near a tank on the crest of the Mahávajra Meru mountain. It runs thus: *Om vipula-garbhe vipula-vimale vimala-garbhe vipula-vimala-vimala-garbhe vimale jaya-garbhe vajrajvála-garbhe gatigahane gagana-vis'odhane sarva-pápa-vis'o-dhane. Om guṇavati gagana-vihariṇi gagana-vihariṇi gaga-riṇi gagariṇi giriṇi giriṇi gubhari gardhabhari gamari gahari gaha gaha gargari garghari gagari gagari gabhari gabhari gabhi gabhi gahi gahi gamani gamani gara gara guha guha guru guru guruvichale muchale sumu-chale sváhá.* The meaning of most of these words is unintellegible, but the sentences formed by them are said to be most effectual in overcoming evils of every kind. In illustration of their supreme power, several stories are recited. In one case a person, bitten by a cobra, was saved from impending death by reciting it. Brahmadatta, after bathing in the Ganges, put the charm on his head, and thereby overcame a powerful king with whom he was engaged in war. A Bráhmaṇ, suffering from leprosy, put it on his neck and was immediately cured. On his death he was carried away by the messengers of Yama to the dreadful hell called Abíchi. On his appearance there all the instruments of torture lost their power, and the dwellers of hell were restored to felicity. Yama was thereupon obliged to remove him from this place of confinement. A ship was once assailed by sea-monsters, fearful storms, thunder and lightning, and was on the point of being engulphed into the sea, when one of the passengers wrote the mantra on a piece of paper, and stuck the paper on the top of the mast. Thereupon all commotions subsided, and the ship safely reached its destination. A malefactor was sent to the place of execution; he put the charm on his head, and the instruments of the executioners could no longer hurt him; and he was allowed to go away. After these illustrations come the rituals for consecrating the charm for putting it on, and then the praises thereof. The name of this work does not occur in the Rev. S. Beal's Catalogue of the Chinese Tripiṭhaka.

The *vignette* on the first page of this codex represents a goddess with four heads and eight hands, and seated on two lions. The body of the goddess and that of the lions are white, but the heads of the goddess are successively green, white, red and yellow.

Beginning. ॐ नमो भगवत्यै आर्य्यमहाप्रतिसरायै। एवं मया श्रुतमेकस्मिन् समये भगवान् महावज्रमेरुशिखरे कूटागारे विहरति स्म। महावज्रसमाधिभूमिप्रतिष्ठाने महावज्रकल्पवृक्षसमलङ्कृते महावज्रपुष्करिणीरत्नपद्मप्रभोद्भासिते महावज्रवालिकासंस्कृतभागे महावज्राधिष्ठाने महावज्रमण्डलमध्ये शक्रस्य देवानामिन्द्रस्य भवने।

End. इदमवोचद् भगवानात्तमना आयुष्मानानन्दः स च महाब्राह्मणस्ते च भिक्षवस्ते च बोधिसत्त्वास्ते च महाश्रावकाः सा च सर्व्वावती पर्षत् सदेवमानुषासुरगरुड़गन्धर्व्वाश्च लोका भगवतो भाषितमभ्यनन्दन्निति।

Colophon. आर्य्यमहाप्रतिसरा महाविद्या राज्ञी रक्षाविधानकल्पा विद्याधरस्यायं समाप्तः।

No. B 2.

MADHYAMAKA-VṚITTI.

Substance, Nepalese yellow paper, 16 × 4 inches. Folia, 201. Lines, 7 on a page. Extent in ślokas, 3,200. Character, Newárí. Date, ? Prose and verse. Old. Correct.

A commentary on a work called *Vinaya Sútra.* By Chandrakírti Ácháryа. The text is not forthcoming, nor has it been noticed by M. Burnouf, nor in the Chinise Tripíṭhaka; but initial words and sometimes entire stanzas occur in the commentary. Though the name of the text is *Vínaya* or "discipline," to judge from the commentary, the work is throughout metaphysical, and describes the rationale or philosophy of mental phenomena. The commentary is divided, probably in accordance with the text, into 27 chapters. CONTENTS: I. On cognition of external objects. II. Perception of motion. III. The nature of the organs of sense. IV. Shape and colour. V. Animated beings. VI. Attraction and the attracted. VII. Consciousness. VIII. Cause of consciousness. IX. Conditions precedent of consciousness. X. Relation between cause and effect, or of fire and fuel. XI. Existence, or of those who suffer birth, pain, pleasure and death. XII. Pain, what is it? XIII. Residual impressions. XIV. Relation between agents, organs and objects, as the seer, the seeing and the object seen; the hearer, the hearing and the object heard, &c. XV. Nature of disposition. XVI. The free and the bound. XVII. Deserts, their cause and effect. XVIII. Enquiry into what is self. XIX. Times past, present and future, their relations. XX. Subsidiary causes of fruition. XXI. Thought, its origin and cessation. XXII. Existence of Tathágata. XXIII. Origin of love, enmity and delusion in relation to good and evil. XXIV. Áryasatya or afflictions. XXV. Final emancipation. XXVI. Five instruments of knowledge, consciousness. XXVII. Right and wrong consciousness.

The author of the work is a Sunyavádí or Nihilist, who does not admit the material existence of anything, and the object of the work is to prove that nothing exists. The way in which he works out his theory will be illustrated by the following extract. The subject being vision, an antagonist is supposed to remark: (Text) "vision, audition, smell, taste, touch and mind are the organs, and the objects of these six are what are to be seen &c." (Commentary.) "Hence it follows that vision &c., are natural powers. But vision cannot be a power. If you say to see is vision and it is the eye, and colour may be described as its object." (It is not so.) (Text) "The eye does not perceive the truth of its own self; and how can that which cannot see its own self perceive others?" (Commentary.) "Thus the eye does not see its own self, for to do so would be an impossible function. (If you say) Though the eye does not perceive itself, still it beholds others like fire, *i. e.*, even as fire burns the substance of others and yet not its own, so the eye sees others though not itself; it would not be consistent." (Text) "Because the example of fire is insufficient to establish vision." (Commentary.) "The example of fire which you have adduced is not 'sufficient' *i. e.*, it is not apposite and not applicable, because" (Text) "the eye-possessing (is applicable to) what has been said about going, gone, and not-gone." (Commentary.) "That which exists with an eye is eye-possessing. The example of fire which you have adduced to establish the eye, has been condemued along with the possessor of the eye. How so? By the words 'going, gone and not gone.' Thus, that which is gone cannot go, the not-going cannot go, nor can the going go, and so the fire does not burn the burnt, nor does it burn the unburnt, and these are parallel passages. Thus, as the gone, the not-gone or the going, does not go, so the seen does not see, nor the unseen see, and the seeing, which is neither seen nor not-seen, does not see. This is what is said. Even as the gone does not go, so, it is said, the burnt dees not burn, and this is what is meant. And since the example of the fire is condemned by the example of going, gone and not-gone, the example of fire cannot be of avail to establish the position about the eye; and hence the conclusion is that the eye does not see others as it does not see itself."

दर्शनं श्रवणं घ्राणं रसनं स्पर्शनं मनः ।
इन्द्रियाणि षडेतेषां द्रष्टव्यादीनि गोचरः ॥

तस्मात् शक्तिर्दर्शनादीनि स्वभावतः इत्युच्यते । न शक्तिः इह हि पश्यतीति दर्शनं चक्षुस्तस्य च रूपं विषयत्वेनोपदिश्यते । यथा दर्शनं रूपं न पश्यति तथा प्रतिपादयन्नाह ।

स्वमात्मानं दर्शनं हि तत्तमेव न पश्यति ।
न पश्यति यदात्मानं कथं द्रक्ष्यति तत्परान् ॥

तत्रेदमेव दर्शनं स्वात्मानं न पश्यति स्वात्मनि क्रियाविरोधात् । ततश्च स्वात्मादर्शनात् श्रोत्रादिवन्नीलादिकं न पश्यति । तस्मान्नास्ति दर्शनं । यद्यपि स्वात्मानं दर्शनं न पश्यति । तथापि अग्निवत् परान् द्रक्ष्यति । तथा हि अग्निः परात्मानमेव दहति न स्वात्मानं एवं दर्शनं परानेव द्रक्ष्यति न स्वात्मानं इति । एतदप्ययुक्तं । यस्मान्न पर्याप्तोऽग्निदृष्टान्तो दर्शनस्य प्रसिद्धये । योऽयमग्निदृष्टान्तो दर्शनस्य प्रसिद्धये भवतोपन्यस्तः स न पर्याप्तो नालं समर्थो न युज्यत इत्यर्थः । यस्मात् सदर्शनः स प्रत्युक्तो गम्यमानगतागतैः । सहदर्शनेन वर्त्तते इति सदर्शनः । योऽयमग्निदृष्टान्तो दर्शनप्रसिद्धये भवतोपदिष्टः । सोऽपि सह दर्शनेन दृष्टान्तिकार्थेन प्रत्युक्तो दूषितः । केन पुनरित्याह । गम्यमानगतागतैः । तथा हि गतं न गम्यते नागतं न गम्यमानं एवं अग्निनापि दग्धं न दह्यते नादग्धं दह्यते इत्यादिना समं वाच्यं । यथा च न गतं नागतं न गम्यमानं गम्यते । एवं न दृष्टं दृश्यते तावददृष्टं नैव दृश्यते दृष्टादृष्टविनिर्मुक्तं दृश्यमानं न दृश्यते इत्यादि वाच्यं । यथा च गन्ता न गच्छते तावदित्युक्तमेव न दग्धं दह्यते तावदित्यादि वाच्यं । एवं दर्शनं पश्यते तावदित्यादिना अग्निदृष्टान्तेन सह गम्यमानगतागतैर्यस्मात् समं दूषणं अतोऽग्निवद्दर्शनसिद्धिरिति न युज्यते । ततश्च सिद्धमेतद् स्वात्मवद्दर्शनं परानपि न पश्यतीति ॥

Beginning. ॐ नमः श्रीवज्रसत्त्वाय । ॐ नमो रत्नत्रयाय ।

योऽन्तर्द्वयावासविधूतवासः सम्बुद्धधीसागरलब्धजन्मा ।

सद्धर्मतो यस्य गभीरभावं यथानुबुद्धं कृपया जगाद ॥ १ ॥
यस्य दर्शनतेजांसि परवादिमतं धनं ।
दहन्त्यद्यापि लोकस्य मानसानि तमांसि च ॥ २ ॥
यस्यासमज्ञानवचःशरौघा निघ्नन्ति निःशेषभवारिसेनां ।
त्रिधातुराज्यश्रियमादधाना विनेयलोकस्य सदेवकस्य ॥ ३ ॥
नागार्जुनाय प्रणिपत्य तस्मै तत्का + + नां विद्यतिं करिष्ये ।
उत्तानसत्प्रक्रियवाक्यनद्धां तर्कानिलाव्याकुलितां प्रसन्नां ॥ ४ ॥
तत्र न स्वतो नापि परतो न द्वाभ्यामित्यादि वक्ष्यमाणं शास्त्रं । तस्य कानि सम्ब-
न्धाभिधेयप्रयोजनानि इति ॥

End. अथ खल्वायुष्मान् शालिपुत्रो मैत्रेयस्य बोधिसत्त्वस्य महासत्त्वस्य भाषितमभिन-
न्द्यासनादुत्थाय प्रक्रान्तः ते च भिक्षव इति ।

Colophon. इत्याचार्य्यचन्द्रकीर्त्तिपादोपरचितायां प्रसन्नपदायां मध्यमकवृत्तौ दृष्टिपरीक्षा
नाम सप्तविंशतितमं प्रकरणं समाप्तं । समाप्तश्चेदं मध्यमकशास्त्रं सकललौकिक-
लोकोत्तरप्रवरप्रणीतनयार्थव्याख्याननैपुण्यविशारदं श्रावकप्रत्येकबुद्धानुत्तरसम्यक्
सम्बुद्धबोधिमण्डासनदायकमिति ।

No. B 4.

MAHÁKÁLA TANTRA.

Substance, paper, 10″ × 2½.″ Folia, 74. Lines, 5 on a page. Extent in ślokas, 400. Character, Newárí. Appearance, old. Date, Newárí Samvat, 923. Prose. Incorrect.

A treatise on mystic rites. Anonymous. CONTENTS: Origin of the word Mahákála. Fire altars. Mantras for two-handed divinities. Mantras for killing, dementing, stupifying, and subjugating persons. Rules for the lustration called Vajrábhisheka. Ditto for bathing images of gods. Praise of the Mantra of Deví. Rules for worshipping Mahákála. Adoration of particular Devís for the attainment of special objects. Persons who have attained perfection in the above forms of worship. Attainment of transcendental powers by rites performed on corpses. Rites for winning others' affection. Ditto for causing obstruction in others' affairs. Ditto for causing stupefaction. Ditto for causing death. Ditto for preventing rain. Ditto for pacifying Saturn when irate. Ditto for removing all disturbances. Ditto for managing kingdoms.

There is a Hindu Tantra of this name, and the contents are closely similar, but it is a distinct work.

Beginning. ॐ नमः श्रीवज्रमहाकालाय। एवं मया श्रुतमेकस्मिन् समये भगवान् देवीनां भगेषु विजहार। देव्याह। भगवन् भवेषु पतिताः सत्त्वास्तेषां किमुपायः कर्त्तव्यः।

End. इति श्रीमहाकालतन्त्रराजे सर्व्वोदयकल्पे भगवद्देव्या भाषितमभ्यनन्दन्निति।

Colophon. इत्येवं महाकालतन्त्रराजे श्रीबुद्धभाषितं महाकालतन्त्रराजं समाप्तं।

No. B 4.

MAHA'MA'YU'RI'.

Substance, Nepalese paper, 12½ × 3½ inches. Folia, 74. Lines on a page, 5. Extent in ślokas, 1036. Character, Newárí. Date, 944 Newári. Appearance, old. Incorrect.

A collection of mantras for neutralising the effect of snake-poison.

When the Lord was in the Jeta grove at S'rávastí, A'nanda reported that a Bhikshu had been bitten by a black serpent, and was on the point of dying, and thereupon the Lord revealed the mantras. They are all of the same character, full of repetitions, and unintelligeble words. One of them runs thus:—*Iḍi viḍi kiḍi hiḍi piḍini mede do deinbá áḍe üáḍe ghaḍe durghaḍe hiriṇi chatudi hurivegáḍi vegáḍi paśupisáchiní aponiṇí sváhá.*—Another begins with the word *hu* repeated 36 times, then *putu* 9 times, then, *nágaleleke* &c. The mantras are said to have been originally known to a king of peacocks who dwelt on the southern scarp of the Himálaya, and thence their name 'Máyúrí' or relating to a peacock. Peacocks are well-known to destroy small snakes, but I have never heard of their attacking cobras. In the Rev. Mr. Beal's Catalogue of the Chinese Tripiṭhaka, this work occurs under two names, *viz.*, Fo-mon-ta-kong tsio-ming-wong king, and Suk-tung-Fo-muk-to-kou-tsio-ming-wang-king, with the Sanskrit name 'Mahá Máyúrí-vidyá-rádjṇí-dhāraṇí.'

Beginning. ॐ नमो भगवत्यै आर्य्यमहामायूर्य्यै॥
मृतसञ्जीवनीं देवीं दुष्टसत्त्वनिवारिणीं
विद्यां राज्ञीं महामानीं मयूरीं प्रणमाम्यहं॥
नमो बुद्धाय नमो धर्म्माय इत्यादि बुद्धप्रणामानन्तरं, कालि करालि कुम्भाण्डि इत्यादि विषहरं मन्त्रं ततः प्रारम्भः यथा। एवं मया श्रुतमेकस्मिन् समये

भगवान् श्रावस्त्यां महानगर्य्यां विहरति स्म ॥ जेतवने अनाथपिण्डदस्यारामे महता भिक्षुसङ्घेन सार्द्धं अनेकैर्बोधिसत्त्वैर्महासत्त्वैः ।

End. इदमवोचद् भगवान् आत्तमना आयुष्मानानन्दः ये च तस्यां पर्षदि सन्निपतिताः । देवासुर-मरुत-गरुड़-गन्धर्व्व-किन्नर-महोरगादयस्ते सर्व्वे भगवतो भाषितमभ्यनन्दन्निति ।

Colophon. आर्य्यमहामायूरीविद्या राज्ञी सर्व्वार्थसाधिनी समाप्ता ॥

No. B 4.

MA'RICHI NA'MA DHA'RAṆI.

Substance, paper, 7½ × 3 inches. Folia, 2. Lines on a page, 5. Extent in ślokas, 50. Appearance, old. Character, Newári. Prose. Incorrect.

A charm for self-preservation. It was imparted when the Lord was at the Jeta grove in S'rávastí. In the course of one of his lectures he said, "There is a goddess who travels before the sun and the moon; she is invisible, indestructible, incomprehensible, intractible, unblamable. and unassailable by weapons. Her name is Marichí (darkness-destroyer). Whoever hears her name becomes possessed of her qualities, and this is her mantra." The mantra begins with the words.—"*Om prákramasi, prákramasi, udayamasi, vairamasí,*" &c. The Chinese verson of this work bears the name of Fo-shwo-Ma-li-chi-tiea-to-lo-li-catan-king, which means 'Buddha recites the Dháraṇí of Marichí Deví. and extends to two pages. In this work we find an attempt made to render Úshá or the Dawn of the Hindus subservient to Buddhist worship.

Beginning. ॐ नमो भगवत्ये आर्य्यमहामारिचियै । एवं मया श्रुतमेकस्मिन् समये भगवान् श्रावस्त्यां विहरति स्म । जेतवनेऽनाथपिण्डदस्यारामे महता भिक्षुसङ्घेन सार्द्ध-मर्द्धत्रयोदशभिक्षुशतैः सम्बहुलैश्च महाश्रावकैः बोधिसत्त्वमहासत्त्वैः तत्र खलु भगवान् भिक्षूनामन्त्रयते स्म । अस्ति भिक्षवो मारिची देवता सा सूर्य्यचन्द्रमसामपुरतोऽनुगच्छन्ति । सा न दृश्यते न गृह्यते न बध्यते न निबध्य न मुच्यते न मुह्यते न दण्ड्यते न दह्यते न शस्त्रामुपगच्छति ।

End. ॐ वर्त्मवत्तारिवलाहमुखी सर्व्वदुष्टप्रदुष्टानाञ्च मुखं बन्धय स्वाहा ।

Colophon. आर्य्यमारिचीनामधारणी समाप्तः ।

No. B 39.

PARAMA'RTHANA'MA-SAÑGI'TI.

Substance, Nepalese paper, 7½ × 3 inches. Folia, 72. Lines, 6 on a page. Extent in ślokas, 100. Character, Newárí. Appearance, fresh. Date, ? Prose and verse. Incorrect.

A hymn in praise of Buddha, each letter of the alphabet forming a distinct epithet, and implying an attribute of the sage. It is said to have been imparted by Buddha himself at the request of certain Bodhisattvas headed by Vajradhara. This style of stringing together epithets to form names is common both to the Hindus and the Buddhists, and is not unknown to the Arabs, who have similar works. One of their works is named the "Handsome names of God."

Annexed to the codex there are eight other hymns; (1) to Manjuśrí, in eight stanzas; (2) to Vágíśvara; (3) to Buddha as Daśabala; (4) to Avalokiteśvara by Chandrakántá, a Bhikshuṇí; (5) to S'ákya by Yaśodhará; (6) in praise of the personal beauty of Avalokiteśvara; (7) to Avalokiteśvara, by Charapati; and (8) in praise of Sañgha.

Beginning. ॐ नमो बुद्धाय गुरवे । नमो धर्म्माय तारणे । नमः सङ्घाय । महत्तमे नमः ।

ये देवाः सन्ति मेरौ वरकनकमये मन्दरे ये च यक्षाः
पाताले ये भुजङ्गास्फणिमणिकिरणा ध्वस्तसर्व्वान्धकाराः ।
कैलासे स्त्रीविलासैः प्रमुदितहृदयाः ये च विद्याधरेन्द्रा-
स्ते मोक्षद्वारभूतं मुनिवरवचनं श्रोतुमायान्ति सर्व्वे ॥
आयान्तः श्रोतुकामा असुरसुरनराः सिद्धगन्धर्व्वनागाः
कुष्माण्डाः किन्नरेन्द्रा गरुडचरिचराः शक्रब्रह्मादिदेवाः ।
पूजां पञ्चोपचारैस्त्रिभुवननमितं मेदिनीदुर्लभं यत्
भक्त्याहं वाचयामि प्रणमितशिरसा तन्महायानसूत्रं ॥
अथ वज्रधरः श्रीमान् दुर्द्दान्तदमकः परः ।
त्रिलोकविजयी वीरो गुह्यराट् कुलिशेश्वरः ॥ १ ॥
विबुद्धपुण्डरीकाक्षप्रोत्फुल्लकमलाननः ।
प्रोल्लालयन् वज्रवरं स्वकरेण मुहुर्मुहुः ॥ २ ॥
भ्रुकुटीतरङ्गप्रमुखैरनन्तैर्वज्रपाणिभिः ।
दुर्द्दान्तदमकैर्धीरैर्वीरवीभत्सरूपिभिः ॥ ३ ॥
उल्लालयद्भिः स्वकरैः प्रस्फुरद्वज्रकोटिभिः ।
प्रज्ञापनाय करुणाजगदर्थकरैः परैः ॥ ४ ॥
हृष्टतुष्टाशयैर्मुदितैः क्रोधविग्रहरूपिभिः ।

बुद्धकृत्यकरैर्नाथैः सार्द्धं प्रणतविग्रहैः ॥ ५ ॥
प्रणम्य नाथं संबुद्धं भगवन्तं तथागतं ।
कृताञ्जलिपुटो भूत्वा इदमाह स्थितोऽग्रतः ॥ ६ ॥
मद्धिताय अनाथाय अनुकम्पाय ये विभो ।
मायाजालाभिसम्बोधिं यथालाभी भवाम्यहं ॥ ७ ॥

End. गम्भीरोदारवैपुल्यो महार्थो जगदर्थकृत् ।
बुद्धानां विषयो ह्येष सम्यक् संबुद्धभाषितः ।

Colophon. आर्य्यमायाजालात् षोडशसाहस्रिकात् महायोगतन्त्रोपासितसमाधिजालपटलात् भगवता श्रीशाक्यमुनितथागतभाषिता भगवतो मञ्जुश्रीज्ञानसत्त्वस्य परमार्था नाम संगीतिः समाप्ता ।

No. B 4.

PARṆAS'AVARÍNA'MA-DHA'RAṆÍ.

Substance, Nepalese paper, 7 × 3 inches. Folia, 2. Lines, 5 on a page. Extent in ślokas, 12. Character, Newári. Date, ? Appearance, old. Prose. Incorrect.

A charm bearing the name of A'rya Parṇaśavarí, a demi-goddess or she-demon who is said to dress herself in leaves. It is full of mystic and cabalistic terms, and is believed, if worn on the person, to protect one from all evils and accidents. If begins with the words *Om amṛita amṛita amṛita-bhava amṛita-bhava amṛita-sambhava,* and ends with *Om Piśáchi parṇasavari hrīñ hah húñ phaṭ piśáchi sváhá.*

Beginning. ॐ नमो भगवत्यै आर्य्यपर्णशवरीतारायै । नमोरत्नत्रयाय । नम अमिताभाय तथागतायाऽर्हते सम्यक् सम्बुद्धाय । नम आर्य्यावलोकितेश्वराय बोधिसत्त्वाय महासत्त्वाय महाकारुणिकाय । वामने त्वां नमस्यामि त्वां नमस्यामि वामन । भगवती पिशाची पर्णशवरी पाश-परशुधारणी । यानि कानिचिद्भयान्युपपद्यन्ते । यानि कानिचित् महामाया यानि कानिचिद्नया ये केचित् दुर्मोपद्रवा ये केचिदुपाया ये केचिदाध्यात्मिका ये केचिद् बाधा ये केचिदुपसर्गा उपसर्गसम्भूता वा उत्पद्यन्ते । सर्व्वाणीति सर्व्वतः सर्व्वत एवोपपद्यन्ते पण्डिताः । तदन्येन सत्येन सत्यवचनेन सत्यवाक्यरज्जुः । एभिः पण्डिताधिष्ठितमन्त्रपदैः । मम सर्व्वसत्त्वानाञ्च रक्षणं कुरु परित्राणं कुरु ।

End. ॐ पिशाचि पर्णशवरि ह्रीः हः हूँ फट् पिशाचि स्वाहा ।

Colophon. आर्य्यपर्णशवरी नाम धारणी समाप्ता ।

Nos. A 1 to A 4.

PRAJṈA'-PA'RAMITA', S'ATASA'HASRIKA'.

No. A 1. (volume I.) Substance, Nepalese paper of a yellow colour, pasted double, 9½ × 6 inches. Folia, 467. Lines on a page, 11. Extent in ślokas, 26,968. Character, Newárí. Date, N. E. 923. Appearance, old. Prose. Generally correct.

No A 2. (volume II.) Substance, Nepalese paper of a yellow colour, pasted double, 20½ × 6 inches. Folia, 511. Lines on a page, 10—12. Extent in ślokas, 35,259. Character, Newárí. Date, N. E. 924. Appearance, old. Prose. Generally correct.

A 3. (volume III.) Substance, Nepalese paper of a yellow colour, pasted double, 21 × 6 inches. Folia, 499. Lines on a page, 10. Extent in ślokas, 24,800. Character, Newárí. Date, N. E. 924. Appearance, old. Prose. Incorrect.

No. A 3½. (a second copy of volume III.) Substance, Nepalese paper of a yellow colour, 14½ × 4. Folia, 623. Lines on a page, 9 to 11. Extent, 24,800. Character, Newárí. Date, N. E. 871. Appearance, old. Prose. Generally correct.

No. A 4. (volume IV.) Substance, country-made yellow paper, 21 × 6 inches. Folia, 534. Lines on a page, 10. Extent in ślokas, 26,650. Character, Newárí. Date, 920. Appearànce, old. Prose. Incorrect.

The generic name *Prajṉá-páramitá* or "transcendental knowledge" includes five different works. The first of which is said to comprise matter sufficient to make up one hundred and twenty-five thousand octosyllabic verses. The second contains one hundred thousand similar verses; the third, twenty-five thousand verses; the fourth, ten thousand verses; and the fifth, eight thousand verses. Of these, the Asiatic Society's Library contains the 2nd, the 3rd, and the 5th. All these are in prose, and, roughly speaking, the extents traditionally assigned to them are nearly correct. The work under notice is the second; it is generally known under the name of *S'atasáhasriká*, or the recension of a hundred thousand verses. By my calculation of 132 letters to the śloka, the actual extent is 113,677 ślokas. The specific name of the work is *Rakshá-bhagavatí*. It comprises 72 chapters or *Parivartas*, divided into four parts or *khaṇḍas*. It is preëminently a work of the Maháyána class, and its main topic is the doctrine of *Sunyaváda* or the evolution of the universe from vacuity or nihility. This topic is developed in the form of discourses in which Buddha himself is the chief expounder; but some of his principle disciples also appear as teachers. In the course of the discussions, all topics of metaphysics which had engaged the attention of the Buddhists and the Hindus are expounded at length, adverse systems are refuted, and everything is made to accord with the doctrine of nihility. The system of Hínayána is especially noticed, and refuted repeatedly. True Buddhism is declared to be founded on the theory of nihility, and the attainment of the highest perfection is made to depend on the performance of meditations of which the object should be *sunyatá* or nihility. The meditations enjoined are the same which are described in the *Sáṅkhya Sútra* of Kapila, and in the *Yoga Sútra* of Patanjali, and most of the technical terms used are evidently borrowed from the Hindu systems. All the duties enjoined in the Vinaya are repeatedly advocated, and their philosophical bearing to the vacuous doctrine is expounded. With so unreal an ultimatum, the force and persistency with which are enjoined the duties of benevolence, charity, good conduct, and abstinence from evil, each called a *páramitá*, are remarkable.

The work opens with the description of a scene on the Gṛidhrakúṭa hill, near Rájagṛiha, where the Lord performed a Samádhi, whereupon flames issued forth from his body, and illumined the ten quarters of the globe. He then opened wide his mouth, wherein were seen thousands of thousand-petalled golden lotuses, amidst which his image was seen seated. The light from his body relieved mankind from all pains and troubles. The dwellers in hell were ransomed; the deaf regained their power of hearing; the blind were restored to sight. Gods and aerial spirits all came to the place to worship the sage. Thereupon a Bodhisattva, named Samantaraśmi, asked the cause of this light. This led to the sage's imparting to his audience the *Prajná-páramitá*. The different *páramitás* were then successively expounded; these include the hundred and eight *páramitás* noticed in chapter IV of the Lalita-Vistara and a great many others; the advantages of following these *páramitás* are also detailed. The subject of vacuity or nothingness, *sunyatá,* is next expounded. Then follow instructions on five kinds of instruction (*s'ikshá*), eight kinds of disposition of the body (*aṅgaramattva*), four kinds of meditation (*dhyána*), four kinds of proofs (*pramáṇa*), four kinds of bodilessness (*arúpya-samápatti*), five kinds of consciousness (*abhijná*), six kinds of memory (*anusmriti*), which result from a knowledge of the true import of vacuity. Varieties of vacuity. Contrarities. Exercise of six of the páramitás. Purification of the senses.

Chapter II. The second chapter is devoted to the exposition of the true character of the soul (*átmá*), and its relation to form, colour and other qualities, and to vacuity (*sunyatá*).

Chapter III. Chapter third treats of the necessity of Bodhisattvas abstaining from passion, envy and other mental perturbations, and the relation of those perturbations to calm contemplation of the truth, and to vacuity.

Chapter IV. Relation of form to reality, and the propriety of ascertaining its bearing to vacuity.

Chapter V. The ascertainment of the notion of greatness, agitation, pain, pleasure, dispassion &c. through knowledge. Various forms of Samádhi calculated to afford that knowledge.

Chapter VI. All qualities are illusive (*máyámaya*). How they are to be overcome. Yoga is pointed out as the means for it. The influence of Márasatan in frustrating the fruits of Yoga, how to be controlled?

Chapter VII. Bodhisattva defined, his supernatural powers how derived? Humanity and its characteristics, how they are to be overcome by a Bodhisattva? Purport of various epithets used to indicate a Bodhisattva. How a Bodhisattva merges all natural attributes into vacuity? The six páramitás.

Chapter VIII. Characteristics of various kinds of Samádhi, such as Suraṅgamá, Ratnamudrá, Siṅhavikṛiḍitá, Suchandrá, Chandradhvajá, Sarva-dharmasaṅgatá, Vilokitamúrdhá, Dharmadhátu-niyatá, Niyatadhvajaketu, Saṛvadharma-praves'a-mudrá, Samádhirája-supratishṭhitá, Rasmipramuktá, Chalavyúha-samudgatá, &c.

Chapter IX. Definitions and expositions of the Bodhisattva attributes noticed in chapter I, *viz.*, 4 Samyak-prahánas; 4 Ṛiddhipádas; 5 Indríyas; 5 Balas; 7 Sambaudhyaṅgas; 8 Aṅgamárgas; 3 Samádhis; 11 Jṉánas, or perceptions; 3 Indríyas; 10 Anusmṛitis; 4 Dhyánas; 3 Pramáṇas; 4 Arúpya-samápatti; 10 Tathágata-bala; 4 Vaísáradya; 4 Prítisammṛit; 18 Áveśika-bandha-dharma. Nature of Dháraṇís, relation of letters of the alphabet to them.

Chapter X. Duties of the 1st stage—Ten Parikarmas. Ditto of the 2nd stage—8 Dharma-abhikshrás. Ditto of the 3rd stage. Elaboration of the duties of these stages.

Chapter XI. The doctrine of Maháyána and its advantages derived, principally if not entirely, from its recognition of the greatness of Sunyaváda.

Chapter XII. The Prajná-páramitá includes descriptions of all qualities, and their nature and effects. The subject only begins and is carried over to the next volume.

Volume II.

Chapter XII (continued). On vacuity in relation to matter. The ether (*ákás'a*), the best illustration of vacuity. Vacuity not subject to destruction.

Chapter XIII. All qualities are unreal as a dream, an illusion, or a mirage. Knowing this, Bodhisattva never fears anything. Qualities do not affect him. To him there is nothing eternal, nothing transient, nothing painful, nothing pleasant. Transcendental powers derivable from the Prajná-páramitá. Páramitás of two kinds, worldly and transcendental. Their descriptions.

Chapters XIV—XVI. The principles of Prajná-páramitá as imparted by the Lord to Indra. The end sought is the attainment of vacuity.

Chapters XVII—XX. A summary method of attaining the end by practising the six páramitás, and by worshipping the relics of Buddha in chaityas.

Chapters XXI—XXV. Instructions of Subhúti to Ánanda, showing how all the páramitás are included in the Prajná-páramitá, and how the attainment of the latter accomplishes the attainment of everything.

Volume III.

Chapter XXVI. Bhagaván's instruction to the son of Sáradvatí, to the purport that Bhagaván is the thorough master of the Prajná-páramitá, and that those who, knowing the nature of duty, do not accept the páramitás, and revile Bhagaván are doomed to endless pain and suffering in hell, and are subjected to other punishments.

Chapter XXVII. On purification and purified knowledge.

Chapter XXVII. The mode of acquiring the Prajná-páramitá, and the advantages thereof. The fruits of reciting it on particular days in the presence of (an image of?) Bhagaván.

Chapter XXIX. On the vacuity of all qualities explained in detail.

Chapter XXX. On the attainment of Yoga by a Bodhisattva.

Chapter XXXI. On the Sútránta doctrine, its utter worthlessness compared to the vacuous doctrine. No Bodhisattva should accept it.

Chapter XXXII. Defects of the Sútránta doctrine; the influence of Mára, how to overcome the same.

Chapter XXXIII. The whole of the Prajná-páramitá was disclosed by the Lord himself, for the good of creation. No Deva, nor spirit, nor human being can teach it. True knowledge can be acquired solely through the Prajná-páramitá.

Chapter XXXIV. The falsity of all doctrines not founded on the Prajná-páramitá and their unfitness for the ultimate end of man. They should not therefore be accepted.

Chapter XXXV. All objects attainable by the study of the doctrine of Nihilism.

Chapter XXXVI. Training fit for the attainment of the doctrine of Nihilism.

Chapter XXXVII. Training for the purpose. Suppression of all worldly desires. Ascent from the first or Srávaka stage to that of Pratyeka-buddha stage. Longings and ideas. Power of assuming any form at will.

Volume IV.

Chapter XXXVIII. Omniformity of shape. Pain and other accidents. They should all be associated with vacuity. The relation of shape, pain &c. to vacuity is efferent not afferent. Derivation of Tathágata implying this efferent action. Tathágata knows the ultimate vacuity of all things. Nihilism should therefore be studied through the Prajná-páramitá.

Chapter XXXIX. Purification of the body, mind, speech; avoidance of false notions.

Chapter XL. All qualities mutable. The Lord alone immutable.

Chapter XLI. Praise of the Prajná-páramitá.

Chapter XLII. Purification of Buddhism by the suppression of sensuous wants and feelings.

Chapter XLIII. Visit of the River Ganges to the Lord. Miracles worked at the time.

Chapter XLIV. Attainment of the doctrine of Nihilism through Prajná-páramitá.

Chapter XLV. All qualities compared to dreams.

Chapter XLVI. Doubts and disbelief characterstise sinful men.

Chapter XLVII. The necessity of studying the Prajná-páramitá for the suppression of all qualities, thoughts and ideas through dispassion.

Chapter XLVIII. The way of making the mind immense in meditation.

Chapter XLIX. All qualities being vain, the necessity of the religion of Buddha established.

Chapter L. Through the Prajná-páramitá all qualities cease to be perceptible.

Chapter LI. Through it Mára becomes speared through, and friendliness for creation is promoted.

Chapter LII. The mode and advantage of practising the six páramitás.

Chapter LIII. The practice of S'íla-páramitá (good conduct).

Chapter LIV. Vacuity in relation to qualities explained.

Chapter LV. Vacuity defined.

Chapter LVI. Preliminary study of the elementary principles of good.

Chapter LVII. The necessity of constant attention to S'íla-páramitá.

Chapter LVIII Kshánti-páramitá explained.

Chapter LIX. Dhyána-páramitá, contemplation and its modifications.

Chapter LX. Vacuous nature of all qualities.

Chapter LXI. Detailed account of the six Páramitás.

Chapter LXII. Destruction of illusion though the Prajná-páramitá.

Chapter LXIII. The practice of the six Páramitás, and the advantages thereby derived by Bodhisattva.

Chapter LXIV. Samádhi and its varieties, how produced.

Chapter LXV. Falsehood, incoherence, wickedness explained.

Chapter LXVI. Fruits of knowledge, friendliness, benevolence and other good qualities.

Chapter LXVII. Essential unreality of all qualities.

Chapter LXVIII. The six Páramitás whereby Bodhisattvas rescue creation from pain and suffering.

Chapter LXIX. How Bodhisattvas attain the position of Tathágatas.

Chapter LXX. How and why Bodhisattvas act in accordance with the belief of the unreal being real.

Chapter LXXI. Unreality of qualities again explained.

Chapter LXXII. All qualities being unreal or vacuous, the conclusion follows that the world is essentially unreal.

The Daśasáhasriká is included in the Japanese Tripíṭhaka, and occurs under the nome of "Mo-no-pan-jo-po-lo-mi-king." It was translated into the Chinese by Chu-Fo-nien and others, of the Tsin dynasty, (*Circa*, 265-313). The Tripíṭhaka includes two other works, both very short, one entitled "Fo-moo-par-tih-tsong-pan-jo-po-lo-mi-king" or "the Prajná-páramitá sútra of the mother of Buddha," and the other "Fo-show-ti-shi-pau-jo-po-lo-mi-to-sin king," or "Buddha recites the sútra called the heart of the Prajná-páramitá of S'akrarájá." Of these I have met with no Sanskrit exemplar.

At the end of the first khaṇḍa there are some verses which give the names of the copyists and the dates when the four volumes were completed. According to these verses, the first volume was completed at the monastery of Chakravihára, in the town of Lalitápurí, in Nepal, by Dhanadatta Vajrivíra, on Thursday, the 10th of the waxing moon during the ascendancy of Ristaká constellation in the month of A'sháḍha, in the year 923. The second volume was completed on Friday, the 11th of the waxing moon, in the month of Chaitra, of the Nepalese year 924, by Víradatta Vajráchárya. The third volume was completed on the day dedicated to the worship of Lakshmí in the year 924, by Siñhadatta Vajradhṛik. The fourth volume was completed on Friday, the 9th of the moon, in the month of Agraháyana, in the year 920, by Vidyádatta Vajri. The Panchavimśati Sáhasri was completed on Thursday, the 4th of the waxing moon in the month of Phálguṇa of the year 926, by Dhanadatta and Víradatta. The dates being Nepalese must correspond with A. D. 1803, 1804, 1804 and 1801. The dates are repeated at the end of each volume.

There is in the Asiatic Society's Library a Nepalese version of this work in four volumes, but I have not been able to read it. It is numbered A 5 to A 8.

Beginning of volume I. ॐ नमः श्रीसर्व्वबुद्धबोधिसत्त्वाय श्रावकप्रत्येकबुद्धेभ्यः ।

या सर्व्वज्ञतया नयत्युपशमं शान्त्यैषिणः श्रावकान्
या मार्गज्ञतया जगद्धितकृता लोकार्थसम्पादिका ।
सर्व्वाकारमिदं वदन्ति मुनयो विश्वं यया सङ्गता
तस्यै श्रावकबोधिसत्त्वगणिनो बुद्धस्य मात्रे नमः ॥
यदसुलभमनन्तकल्पकोटिभिः प्रसरणशतैरपि हेतुवर्ज्जितानां ।
भवतु हि जिना भरि+भूतं तदिदमिदं प्रतिपचुरग्रयानं ॥
गम्भीरञ्च न चात्यन्तं दुर्लभञ्च मुनेरपि ।
नैव तेन विना मोक्षं तस्मात् श्रोतव्यमादरात् ॥

नमो भगवते भैषज्यगुरुवैदुर्य्यप्रभाय तथागताय । नमो भगवत्यै प्रज्ञापारमितायै । नम आर्य्यावलोकितेश्वराय । बोधिसत्त्वाय महासत्त्वाय महाकारुणिकाय नमश्चण्डवज्रपाणये । महायज्ञासनाय तथागताय नमः सर्व्वबोधिसत्त्वेभ्यो भगवद्भ्यश्च । निराश्रवाः सर्व्वसत्त्वानां कुशलसम्भवा योगैः सम्भवन्ति, सिद्धा+ताश्च तथागतप्रतिलम्भातां सर्व्वसत्त्वानां सुखसौमनस्यसद्भावोऽस्त्विति । नमो भगवते रश्मिचन्द्रप्रतिमण्डितविद्युत्तेजोघोषेश्वरराजाय तथागताय । नमो भगवते शाक्यमुनये तथागताय अर्हते सम्यक् सम्बुद्धाय । यस्येयं धर्म्म++लेति । एवं मया श्रुतमेकस्मिन् समये भगवान् राजगृहे विहरति स्म । गृध्रकूटपर्व्वते महता भिक्षुसङ्घेन सार्द्धमित्यादि ।

End. यस्य बोधिसत्त्वो यश्च पूर्व्वान्तो यश्चापरान्तो यश्च मध्यं सर्व्वमेतदद्वयमद्वैधीकारं शतसाहस्र्यां प्रज्ञापारमितायां प्रथमखण्डं समाप्तमिति ।

विनायकैर्लोकगतो हितोद्यमैर्विधारयन्ते जगतां हितोत्तमाः ।
तथैव यां प्राप्य कृपात्मकैः सदा नमाम्यहं तां जननीं कृपात्मनां ॥
सदेवलोकासुरमानवास्तथा फणीन्द्रसङ्घा गरुडेन्द्रकिन्नराः ।
उदारभक्त्या विविधैर्महात्मभिः सपुष्पदानाञ्जलिभिरनेकशः ॥
मुदा सदैनां जननीं कृपात्मनां गृणन्तु वदन्तु सगौरवेण वै ।
भजन्तु सर्व्वे खलु बोधिमानसैः सदार्थिनां तामनिशं लभन्तु ते ॥

Colophon. आर्य्यशतसाहस्र्या भगवत्याः प्रज्ञापारमितायाः प्रथमखण्डं समाप्तमिति ।
ये धर्म्मा हेतुप्रभवा हेतुस्तेषां तथागतो ह्यवदत् ।
तेषाञ्च यो निरोध एवं वादी महाश्रमणः ॥ शुभमस्तु मङ्गलं ।
मात्राक्षरं परिभ्रष्टं मम दोषं न कालयेत् ।

याद्दशं स्थितमादर्शं ताद्दशं लिखितं मया ॥
गणनेत्राङ्कयुग्मवर्षे आषाढ़े सितपक्षके ।
दशम्यां कृत्तिकायाश्च जीववारे शुभे दिने ॥
नेपाललक्षिताण्यां चक्रविहारसंस्थितः ।
धनदत्तो वज्रवीरोऽलिखत् प्रथमखण्डकं ॥
वेददोरत्नमितिखितवर्षे नेपालसम्भके ।
चैत्रे सिते कवौ वारे एकादश्यां महातिथौ ॥
वज्राचार्य्यवीरदत्तलिखितं पूर्णतामगात् ।
द्वितीयखण्डं श्रीरक्षाभगवत्याः सुपुस्तकं ॥
तृतीयखण्डमलिखत् सिंहदत्ताख्यवज्रधृक् ।
लक्ष्मीपूजादिने वर्षे वेदाचिरत्नसम्भिते ॥
वह्निविद्यादत्तहस्तलिखितं तुर्य्यखण्डकं ।
सम्पूर्णमगमद्रक्षाभगवत्याः सुपुस्तकं ॥
पृषत्कपाणिरन्ध्रयुक्+ वर्षे मासः सहोऽभिधः ।
भुजङ्गमा तिथिः कवेर्दिनं यदा समालिख्यर (?) ॥
ऋतुद्वन्द्वरत्नैर्मिते वत्सरेऽस्मिन् तपस्यतः शुक्लतिथौ व्रजसङ्घे ।
तथा सिद्धियोगे गुरुवासरे पञ्चविंशाधिकं तत् सहस्राख्यपुस्तं ॥
धनदत्त-वीरदत्तौ तल्लेखकौ बभूवतुः ।
वज्रालङ्कारभक्त्यादिदानादभिप्रसादितौ ॥

Beginning of volume II. नमः सर्व्वबुद्धबोधिसत्त्वेभ्यः । पृथिवीधातुमत्तया युष्मान् शारद्वतीपुत्र पूर्व्वान्ततो बोधिसत्त्वो नोपैति । पृथिवीधातुशून्यतया पूर्व्वान्ततो बोधिसत्त्वो नोपैति । पृथिवीधातुविविक्ततया पूर्व्वान्ततो बोधिसत्त्वो नोपैति । पृथिवीधातुस्वभावतया पूर्व्वान्ततो बोधिसत्त्वो नोपैति । पृथिवीधातुमत्तया अपरान्ततो बोधिसत्त्वो नोपैति । पृथिवीधातुशून्यतया अपरान्ततो बोधिसत्त्वो नोपैति । पृथिवीधातुविविक्ततया अपरान्ततो बोधिसत्त्वो नोपैति । पृथिवीधातुस्वभावतया अपरान्ततो बोधिसत्त्वो नोपैति । इत्यादि ।

End. षट्लबला(?) समुदागमतया प्रज्ञापारमित बला समुदागमता द्रष्टव्या । प्रत्येकबोधिबला समुदागमतया प्रज्ञापारमिताबला समुदागमता द्रष्टव्या । प्रत्येकबोधिबला समुदागमतया प्रज्ञापारमिता समुदागमता द्रष्टव्या । मार्गाकारप्रज्ञावत्ता समुदागमतया प्रज्ञापारमिताबला समुदागमता द्रष्टव्या । अनुत्तरा

सम्यक् सम्बोधिबला प्रज्ञापारमिताबला समुदागमसमुदागमता द्रष्टव्या। अनेनापि भगवत्पर्य्यायेण महापारमितेयं बोधिसत्त्वानां महासत्त्वानां यदुत प्रज्ञापारमितेति।

Colophon. शतसाहस्र्याः प्रज्ञापारमितायाः पञ्चविंशतितमः परिवर्त्तः। द्वितीयखण्डः समाप्तः।

Beginning of volume III. ॐ नमः श्रीभगवते मारबलप्रमथनाय। अथायुष्मान् शारद्वतीपुत्रो भगवन्तमेतदवोचत्। यो भगवन् बोधिसत्त्वो महासत्त्व इह गम्भीरायां प्रज्ञापारमितायामधिमोक्ष्यते। कुतः सच्युतेहागतं (?) कियच्चिर-संप्रस्थितो वा स कुलपुत्रो वा कुलदुहिता वा अनुत्तराय सम्यक् सम्बोधाय कियन्तस्तेन तथागता अर्हन्तः सम्यक्सम्बुद्धाः पर्य्युपासिताः कियच्चिरं वा स दानपारमितायां चीर्णः कियच्चिरं वा स शीलपारमितायां चीर्णः कियच्चिरं वा स क्षान्तिपारमितायां चीर्णः कियच्चिरं वा स वीर्य्यपारमितायां चीर्णः कियच्चिरं वा स ध्यानपारमितायां चीर्णः कियच्चिरं वा स प्रज्ञापारमितायां चीर्णः। य इमां गम्भीरां प्रज्ञापारमितामर्थतो वा नयतो वा। इत्यादि।

End. एकैवैषा तथता अद्वया अद्वैधीकारा या वा वेणिकबुद्धधर्म्माणां तथता या च सर्व्वाकारज्ञता यास्तथता एका एव एषा तथता अद्वया अद्वैधीकारा।

Colophon. शतसाहस्र्याः प्रज्ञापारमितायाः परिवर्त्तः सप्तत्रिंशत्तमः। समाप्तश्चायं तृतीयखण्डः ये धर्म्मा हेतुप्रभवा हेतुस्तेषां तथागतो ह्यवदत्।
तेषाञ्च यो निरोध एवं वादी महाश्रमणः॥

Beginning of volume IV. प्रज्ञापारमितामेव प्राप्तां प्रज्ञाश्रयोदयां।
प्रज्ञाप्रख्यातसत्कीर्त्तिं तां प्रज्ञां प्रणमाम्यहं॥
पितरं बोधिसत्त्वानां सुगतं गतकिल्बिषं।
प्रज्ञाप्राप्तप्रनिर्य्याणं नमामि करुणात्मकं॥
या सर्व्वज्ञतया नयत्युपशमं शान्त्येषिणः श्रावकान्
या मार्गज्ञतया जगद्धितकृता लोकार्थसम्पादिका।
सर्व्वाकारमिदं वदन्ति मुनयो विश्वं यया सङ्गता
तस्यै श्रावकबोधिसत्त्वगणिनो बुद्धस्य मात्रे नमः॥
अथ खलु कामावचरा रूपावचराश्च देवपुत्रा दिव्यानि चन्दनचूर्णानि दिव्यानि उत्पलकुमुदपुण्डली(री)काणि गृहीत्वा येन भगवांस्तेन चिपन्ति स्म।

End. न स्वभावो न परभावः कुर्व्वत एव स्वभावशून्यता भविष्यति। या परिजानीयादिति॥

Colophon. शतसाहस्रयाः प्रज्ञापारमितायां अकोप्यधर्म्मतानिर्द्देशः द्वासप्ततितमः परिवर्त्तः । इदमवोचत् भगवानात्तमनास्ते दशदिग्भ्यः निपतिताः बोधिसत्त्वास्ते च महाश्रावकाः सदेवमानुषासुरगन्धर्व्वलोका भगवतो भाषितमभ्यनन्दन्निति । समाप्ता चेयमार्य्यप्रज्ञापारमिता शतसाहस्रिका दशदिगनन्तपर्य्यन्तलोकधातुसमुद्रपर्य्यापन्नसर्व्वबुद्धबोधिसत्त्वप्रत्येकबुद्धार्य्यश्रावकाम् अतीतानागतप्रत्युत्पन्नानां माता जनयित्री धर्म्मसमुद्री धर्म्मात्मिका धर्म्मनाभिर्धर्म्मनिधाना धर्म्मकोषाक्षयता धर्म्मोद्भूता विचिन्त्यादर्शनचेतलोमा धर्म्मता परसुखहेतुभूता सर्व्वदेवनागयक्षगन्धर्व्वासुरकिन्नरमहोरगमनुष्यामनुष्यनमस्कृता ।

बुद्धैर्लोकहितैषिभिः प्रकृति (टि) ता मोक्षाय या वर्त्तनी
एता (षा) सा सुगतात्मभावजननी ——————— ।
प्रज्ञापारमिता त्रिलोकजननी + + समुत्तारिणी
या निश्चित्य जिनौरसैः सुकृतिभिर्दानोदयैः पारिता ॥
भूमेर्भूमिविधा विभावा दशविधा विद्यासमुत्पादिता
कारुण्याच्च जनाश्चिदुःखपतिता बोधित्रयस्थापिता ।
तां प्रज्ञां सुचिरं प्रशान्तहृदयैर्य्युष्मान्तु पापं (?) सदा
या नित्या सुगतात्मजेषु वत्सधा सेयं प्रवक्ष्यमाणा (?) ॥
यामाराध्य विमत्सरा विमनसो बोध्यब्धिपारे श्रिये (?)
सान्द्रज्ञानस्फुरदर्कदीधितिरिव प्रोद्भासयन्ती जगत् ।
भिद्यादाशु मनोगुहासु निहितं सान्द्रं तमो देहिनां
एनां बुद्धसुगतानुयातपदवीं सर्व्वज्ञधीगोचरां
गम्भीरां परितः प्रपञ्चरहितां वेणीमिवोदन्वतः ।
प्रज्ञापारमितां प्रलेख्य विपुलं यत् पुण्यमाप्तं मया
तेनामुक्ततनुस्स एव सततं भूयात् समाप्तो जनः ॥

PRAJṆÁPÁRAMITÁ, ASHṬASÁHASRIKÁ.

No. A, 15.

Substance, Palm-leaf, 23 × 2½ inches. Folia, 182. Lines on a page, 6. Extent in ślokas, 8,190. Character, Nepalese. Date, Nepalese Era, 191. = A. D. 1231. Appearance old. Prose. Correct.

Very old, very carefully and well written, and profusely illustrated. The boards were richly painted, but the paint on the outer side has blistered, cracked, and have been smeared over with dabs of sandal paste, the work having been worshipped for generations past. On the inside, each board shows four figures of Buddha in a seated position, in the attitude of lecturing, with a devotee, on each side. The first leaf has a vignette showing a Buddhist figure, as above, surrounded by a group of seven disciples. This vignette, slightly differing in detail, is repeated on the second leaf. On the 12th leaf, at the end of chapter 1st, there is a vignette showing a flesh-coloured female squatting on a white carpet, and expounding something to a group of four disciples, two of white and two of yellow complexion. On the 18th leaf, at the end of chapter 2nd, there is a red coloured female standing amidst lotuses, and four devotees white, yellow, green and red, kneeling before her. On tbe 34th leaf there is a flesh-coloured standing female, dressed in the Bengali style in a red sárí, and has on the left a yellow boat with a bull's head for a prow, and in it a white female holding an oar and a jar for load, and below the boat a blue female seated amidst lotuses. On the right there is a temple having in it a white male figure. Above the temple there are two fishes revolving about each other. On the 37th leaf there are figures of Buddha with two devotees with a red screen and two chowries hanging behind. On leaf 49th is depicted Padmapáṇi, with 4 devotees of 4 different colours. On leaf 62nd, there are a yellow female standing in a plantain grove, and celestial beings flying in the air. Some of the vignettes show monsters of different kinds. One is a white coloured ten-handed female, having over her head a second head of a blue colour. Others have four or six arms. Some are attended by hideous monsters. In one, Buddha is attended by two white elephants, each having eight heads. On the last page, there is a white female with six hands, dressed in a tiger skin, and having a two-handed female child on her lap. In two separate vignettes on this page there are two chaityas.

This is the shortest abridgment of the work noticed under the last preceding number. Its specific name is Ashṭasáhasriká, or "the work of 8,000 verses." As the handiest of the five redactions, it is held in the highest appreciation, and is included in the nine canonical works, or "Dharmas," of the Nepalese Buddhists. It is divided into 32 chapters or *Parivartas*. The salutation at its beginning is somewhat peculiar. Instead of the usual formula of salutation to the three Ratnas, or to Buddha, or to Bodhisattvas, adoration is paid to the subject of the work, *i. e.*, the work itself, the renowned *Prajná-páramitá*, as "the source of knowledge of Tathagátas." The name being in the feminine gender, the work is addressed throughout as a female. The scene is laid on the Vulture Peak, (*Gṛidhrakúṭa*), near Rájagṛiha. When Bhagaván S'ákya was once sojourning there in the company of a large number of disciples and followers, Sáriputra opened a discourse by asking Subhúti information on the principles of the *Prajna-páramitá*, and the replies and discussions which followed form the subject of the work.

Contents. I. On the knowledge of all forms or archetypes.

II. The conversion of S akra, the lord of the Devas, by the Bodhisattva through instruction in the *Prajná-páramitá*.

III—IV. On the merits of the Prajná-páramitá, as the means of salvation, and how the same should be appreciated.

V. The advantages of reciting, hearing, writing, wearing on one's person, or giving away the work to fit persons.

VI. On the modifications of impetus, or the advantages of virtuous actions as means of Bodhi knowledge, or the modifications of those actions ultimately resulting in knowledge.

VII. On retributions for worldly actions, and salvation therefrom through the Prajná-páramitá.

VIII. On the gradation of modifications, or progressive changes for the better, leading ultimately to perfection.

IX—X. Praise of *Prajná-páramitá*, and the advantages of hearing it, &c., as in chapter IV, but more detailed.

XI. The works of Mára which obstruct the light of the Prajná-páramitá in Bodhisattvas.

XII. Creation, welfare of created beings due to Prajná-páramitá.

XIII. On the inconceivable, showing that all qualities are inconceivable.

XIV. Those who have faith in Sambodhi can acquire the Prajná-páramitá, proved by examples.

XV. Instructions in the Prajná-páramitá, by proficient teachers.

XVI. On the origin and purport of the phrase *anuttarám-samyak sambodhimabhisambuti-dhyastatthágata.*

XVII. On the immutability of the form of the Bodhisattva.

XVIII. Nihilism (*sunyatá*) defined.

XIX. In the field of Buddhism there are no roads infested by villains, or thieves, or drink, or disease, or famine.

XX. On the accessibility of the Prajná-páramitá by an easy means.

XXI. On the mischievons works of Mára, obstructing progress of Bodhi knowledge and corrupting devout persons.

XXII. For the attainment of Samyak-sambodhi, virtuous actions are indispensable, and they are best attained through the Prajná-páramitá.

XXIII. On the merit of hearing &c. the Prajná-páramitá, and the invincibility thereby acquired against enemies, &c.

XXIV. On vanity or vain-gloriousness.

XXV. On instruction in Bodhi knowledge.

XXVI. The lord instructs Subhúti how the illusive unsteady mind can acquire Bodhi knowledge.

XXVII. Description of Mára and of his attempts to corrupt earnest enquirers.

XXVIII. On the merit of strewing flowers on Chaityas, &c.

XXIX. On following the doctrine of the Prajná-páramitá.

XXX—XXXI. Questions and answers on following the Bodhisattva and his instructions.

XXXII. On the merits of instruction in the Prajná-páramitá. Wherever it is learnt and encouraged, there the Bodhisattva imparts religious instruction.

Beginning. निर्व्विकल्पे नमस्तुभ्यं प्रज्ञापारमितेऽमिते ।

या त्वं सर्व्वानवद्याङ्गि निरवद्ये निरीक्ष्यसे ॥

आकाशमिव निर्लेपा निष्प्रपञ्चान्निरक्षरा ।

यस्त्वां पश्यति भावेन स पश्यति तथागतं ॥

नव + ये गुणाद्या + बुद्धस्य च जगद्गुरोः ।

न ——— सत्त्वसन्द्र कियोन्द्रव (?) ॥

कृपात्मकाः प्रपद्य त्वां बुद्धधर्म्मपुरःसरीं ।

सुखेनाथान्ति माहात्म्यमतुलं भक्तिवत्सले ॥
सकृद्याश्रये शुद्धे यस्त्वां विधिवदीक्षते ।
तेनापि नियतं सिद्धिः प्राप्यते मोक्षद+ने ॥
सर्व्वेषामपि वीराणां प्रबोधिनियतात्मनां ।
येषिका (?) जनयित्री च माता त्वमसि वत्सला ॥
यद्बुद्धलोकगुरवः पुत्रास्तव कृपालवः ।
तेन त्वमसि कल्याणि सर्व्वसत्त्वपितामही ॥
सर्व्वपारमिताभिस्त्वं निर्म्मलाभिरनिन्दिते ।
चन्द्रलेखेव ताराभिरनुजातासि सर्व्वदा ॥
विनेयं जनमासाद्य तत्र तत्र तथागतैः ।
बहुरूपा त्वमेवैका नानानामभिरीड्यसे ॥
प्रभां प्राप्येव दीप्तांशोरवश्यायोदबिन्दवः ।
त्वां प्राप्य प्रलयं यान्ति दोषा वादाश्च वादिनां ॥
त्वमेव त्रासजननी बालानाम्भीमदर्शना (?) ।
आश्वासजननी चासि विदुषां सौम्यदर्शना (?) ॥
यस्य त्वय्यभिष्वङ्गस्त्वन्नाथस्य न विद्यते ।
तस्याम्ब कथमन्यत्र रागद्वेषौ भविष्यतः ॥
नागच्छसि कुतश्चित्त्वन्न च क्वचन गच्छसि ।
स्थानेष्वपि च सर्व्वेषु विद्वद्भिर्नोपलभ्यसे ॥
ये त्वामेव न पश्यन्ति प्रपद्यन्ते च भावतः ।
प्रपद्य च विमुच्यन्ते तदिदं परमाद्भुतं ॥
त्वामेव बध्यते पश्यन्नपश्यन्नपि बध्यते ।
त्वामेव मुच्यते पश्यन्नपश्यन्नपि मुच्यते ॥
अहो विस्मयनीयासि गम्भीरासि यशस्विनी ।
सुदुर्बोधासि मायेव दृश्यसे न च दृश्यसे ॥
बुद्धैः प्रत्येकबुद्धैश्च श्रावकैश्च निषेविता ।
मार्गस्त्वमेको मोक्षस्य नास्त्यन्य इति निश्चयः ॥
व्यवहारं पुरस्कृत्य प्रज्ञप्त्यर्थं शरीरिणां ॥
कृपया लोकनाथैस्त्वमुच्यसे न च वाच्यसे ।
शक्तः कस्त्वामिह स्तोतुं निर्निमित्तां निरञ्जनां ॥

सत्यैवमपि संस्तुत्या चाक्षुषैर्व्वयमीदृशैः ।
त्वामस्तुत्यामपि सतीन्तुष्टुषन्तः सुनिर्वृताः ॥
प्रज्ञापारमितां स्तुत्वा यन्मयोपचितं शुभं ।
तेनास्त्वाशु जगत्कृत्स्नं प्रज्ञापारपरायणं ॥

एवं मया श्रुतमेकस्मिन् समये भगवान्राजगृहे विहरति स्म । गृध्रकूटे पर्व्वते महता भिक्षुसंघेन सार्द्धमर्द्धत्रयोदशभिर्भिक्षुशतैः । सर्व्वैरर्हद्भिः क्षीणास्रवैः निःक्लेशैः वशीभूतैः सुविमुक्तचित्तैः सुविमुक्तप्रज्ञैराजानेयैर्महानागैः कृतकृत्यैः कृतकरणीयैरपहृतभारैरनुप्राप्तस्वकार्थैः परिक्षीणभवसंयोजनैः सम्यगाज्ञासुविमुक्तचित्तैः सर्व्वचेतो वशि परमपारमितां प्राप्तैरेकपुद्गलं स्थापयित्वा यदुताआयुष्मन्तमानन्दं ॥ तत्र खलु भगवानायुष्मन्तं सुभूतिं स्थविरमामन्त्रयते स्म । प्रतिभातु ते सुभूते बोधिसत्त्वानां महासत्त्वानां प्रज्ञापारमितामारभ्य यथा बोधिसत्त्वा महासत्त्वाः प्रज्ञापारमितां निर्य्ययुरिति ॥ अथ खल्वायुष्मन्तः शारद्वतीपुत्रस्यैतदभवत् किमयमायुष्मान् सुभूतिः स्थविर आत्मीयेन स्वकेन प्रज्ञप्रतिभानबलाधानेन स्वकेन प्रज्ञप्रतिभानबलाधिष्ठानेन बोधिसत्त्वानां महासत्त्वानां प्रज्ञापारमितामुपदेक्ष्यत्युताहो बुद्धानुभावेनेति ॥ अथ खलु आयुष्मान् सुभूतिः बुद्धानुभावेनायुष्मतः शारिपुत्रस्य इममेवंरूपस्य तस्यैव चेतः परिचित्तकमाज्ञयायुष्मन्तं शारिपुत्रमेतदवोचत् ॥

End. इदमवोचद् भगवानात्तमनसो मैत्रेयप्रमुखा बोधिसत्त्वा महासत्त्वा आयुष्मांश्च सुभूतिरायुष्मांश्च शारिपुत्र आयुष्मांश्चानन्दः शक्रश्च देवानामिन्द्रः सदेवमानुषासुरगन्धर्व्वलोका भगवतो भाषितमभ्यनन्दन्निति ।

Colophon. अथाष्टसाहस्रिकायां प्रज्ञापारमितायां परीन्दनापरिवर्त्तो नाम द्वात्रिंशत्तमः ॥
एकाधिके नवति नुगते प्रयाते संवत्सृते तपसि मास तिथौ दशम्यां ॥
संवत् ९९१ । फाल्गुण शुक्लदशम्यां तिथौ ॥

No. A, 10.

PRAJNA'-PA'RAMITA', PANCHAVIÑS'ATI-SA'HASRIKA'.

पञ्चविंशतिसाहस्रिका प्रज्ञापारमिता ।

Substance, country-made yellow paper, 18 × 6 inches. Folia, 409. Lines on a page, 12. Extent in ślokas, 20,045. Character, Newárí. Date, N. S. 926. Appearance, old. Prose. Incorrect.

A digest of the large work on metaphysics described under the Nos. A 1 to A 4. Like it, it is in prose. Its extent is usually reckoned at 25,000 ślokas, but the codex under examination does not come up to that extent. Roughly calculated it is limited to 20,045 s'lokas, and this would suggest the idea that it is defective; but from its beginning and colophon it would seem that it is complete. It is divided into eight chapters, each called a *parivarta,* as in the larger work. Though professedly a digest, the arrangement of the work is not founded on the plan of the S'atasáhasriká, and the treatment of the subjects is generally different. In fact the work is an independent one on the subject of Nihilism bearing on the attributes of Buddha.

The first chapter is devoted to *sarvákárajnatá,* or the knowledge of all forms and qualities by the Bodhisattva through the medium of the *Prajná-páramitá.* The second is entitled *márgajnatá,* or the knowledge of all modes of salvation; it is based on various purifications of the intellect, mind, body, &c. The third is *sarvajnatá* or "omniscience," which is attainable by thoroughly understanding the nature of Nihilism in relation to charity, good conduct, and the other four *páramitás.* The fourth is *sarvákárábhisambodha,* or cognizance of all forms whereby the Bodhisattva acquires a right understanding of the various phases of the mind under different circumstances. The fifth is *múrdhapráptana-púrvabodha,* or the way in which the Bodhisattva stores every form of understanding and all knowledge in his head, so that he can know all and everything superhuman even in his dream without any actual perception. The sixth is *ekakshnávisambodha,* or knowledge of all times present, past and future. In treating of it the succession of the six *páramitás,* including charity, good conduct, mercy, vigour, meditation, and true knowledge, have been described at length. The 7th is *dharmakáya,* or qualities as affecting the conduct of the Bodhisattva. The 8th is *moksha,* or lessons on the means of attaining Nirváṇa.

The codex was copied as stated elsewhere, p. 183 in the Nepalese year = A. D. 1806.

Beginning. या सर्व्वज्ञतया नयत्युपशमं शान्त्यैषिणः श्रावकान्
या मार्गज्ञतया जगद्धितकृतां लोकार्थसम्पादिका ॥
सर्व्वाकारमिदं वद न्ति मुनयो विश्वं यया सङ्गतं
तस्यै श्रावकबोधिसत्त्वगणिनो बुद्धस्य मात्रे नमः ॥
सर्व्वाकारज्ञतामार्गः शासितो योऽत्र देशितः ।
धीमन्तो वीक्षयीरन्न(?) मनालीढं परैरिति ॥
स्मृतौ बोधाय सूत्रार्थधर्म्मचर्य्यान्दशात्मिकां ।
सुखिनः प्रतिपत्तीरभित्यारम्भप्रयोजनं ॥
प्रज्ञापारमिता शाभिः पदार्थैः समुदीरिता ।
सर्व्वाकारज्ञता मार्गज्ञता सर्व्वज्ञता ततः ।
सर्व्वाकाराभिसम्बोधो मूर्द्धप्राप्तानुपूर्व्विः (?) ।
एकक्षणाभिसम्बोधो धर्म्मकायश्च ते ऽष्टधा ॥

End. इदमवोचद्भगवान् ते सुमनसो मैत्रेयप्रमुखा बोधिसत्त्वा महासत्त्व आयुष्मांश्च सुभूतिः आयुष्मांश्च शारिपुत्र आयुष्मानानन्दः शक्रश्च देवानामिन्द्रः सदेवमानुषासुरगन्धर्व्वश्च लोको भगवतो भाषितमभ्यनन्दन्निति ॥

Colophon. आर्य्यपञ्चविंशतिसाहस्रिकायां भगवत्यां प्रज्ञापारमितायामभिसमयालङ्कारानुसारेण संशोधितायां धर्म्मकायाधिकारः शिक्षापरिवर्त्तो नामाष्टमः समाप्त इति ।

विषयः । ये धर्म्मा हेतुप्रभवा हेतुन्तेषां तथागतो ह्यवदत् ।
तेषाञ्च योनिरोध ए++दी महाश्रमणः ॥
अत्र लेखनसमये ग्र विद्यमानत्वेऽपि शतसाहस्रिकप्रज्ञापारमिताप्रथमखण्डे समाप्तिवाक्ये लिखितत्वात् पुनरनुल्लेखः ॥

No. A 17.

PRAJNA-PARAMITA-TIKA.

प्रज्ञापारमिता-टीका ।

Substance, Nepalese paper, 10 × 4 inches. Folia, 230. Lines on a page, 9. Extent in ślokas, 9,200. Character, Newárí. Date, ? Appearance, fresh. Prose. Incorrect.

A commentary on the Ashṭasáhasriká recension of the Prajná-páramitá noticed under No. A 15. By Maitreya.

Beginning. या सर्व्वज्ञतया नयत्युपशमं शान्त्येषिणः श्रावकान्

या मार्गज्ञतया जगद्धितकृतां लोकार्थसम्पादिका ।

सर्व्वाकारमिदं वदन्ति मुनयो विश्वं यया सङ्गतं

तस्यै श्रावकबोधिसत्त्वगणिनो बुद्धस्य मात्रे नमः ॥

मायारूपसमानभावविदुषाम्मुक्तिम्परां योगिनां

संसारोद्भवबन्धनविच्छेदैः सम्मूर्च्छितान देहिनः ।

मैत्रेयेण दयावता भगवता नेतुं स्वयं सर्व्वथा

प्रज्ञापारमितानये स्फुटतया टीका कृता कारिका ॥

End. सुभाषितमिदं युष्माकं वचनमित्यादिना अभ्यनन्दन्निति नन्दितवन्त इत्यर्थः ॥

Colophon. अभिसमयालङ्कारालोकायां प्रज्ञापारमिताव्याख्यायां परीन्दनापरिवर्त्तो नाम द्वात्रिंशतितमः ॥

No. B 53.
PINḌAPATRÁVADÁNA.
पिण्डपात्रावदानम् ।

Substance, yellow Nepalese paper, 13 × 4 inches. Folia, 5, first seven leaves wanting. Extent, 100 ślokas. Character, Newárí. Date, ? New. Prose and verse. Incorrect.

An Avadána in praise of giving alms-bowls to Buddhist mendicants. The story runs that Sarvánanda, king of the great city of Dípavatí, once visited the great Vihára of Prasannas'íla, and thence brought the Buddha Dípankara to his metropolis, and presented him an alms-bowl full of rice, and thereupon the Buddha expatiated on the merits of giving alms. The first seven folia of the work being missing, the history of the work cannot be ascertained.

Beginning. (प्रथमं सप्तपत्राणि न सन्ति) ततः परं । नमो दीपङ्कराय ॥

प्रत्येकबुद्धाय च संविधाय पांशुप्रदानाच्छिशुपूर्व्वजन्मनि ।

तस्मात् प्रदानाद्भुवि शक्रकल्पो दीपावतीभूमिपतिर्बभूव ॥

End. अथ खलु राजा सम्भावयित्वा भगवन्तमेतदवोचत् ।

अद्य मे सफलं जन्म सफलं जीवितञ्च मे ।

अद्य बुद्धकुले जातो (?) बुद्धपुत्रोऽस्मि साम्प्रतं ॥

Colophon. इति पिण्डपात्रावदानं समाप्तं ॥

No. A, 12.

PÚJÁPADDHATI.

पूजापद्धतिः ।

Substance, Nepalese paper, 13 × 5½ inches. Folia, 584. Lines on a page, 9. Extent, in ślokas, 5,800. Character, Newárí. Date, ? Prose. Incorrect, and incomplete—wanting both at the beginning and at the end.

This is a collection of manuals for the performance of Pújá to different divinities. The first folium and several folia at the end being lost, neither the name of the author, nor the history of the work, can be ascertained from the codex.

In the portion which has come under my examination I find rituals for the worship of the following divinities, *viz.*, (1), Kubjikáguhyes'varí, (the secret hunchbacked goddess); (2), Harabhairava; (3), Harasiddhideví; (4), Chaṇḍes'varí; (5), Naradurgá, (offering her oleander flowers—*karavírajapa)*; (6), presiding divinity of houses (on occupying a new house); (7), the discus of Pas'chimes'vara; (8), Násiká, the presiding divinity of the nostrils; (9), Gaṇes'a; (10), Brahmáṇí; (11), Mahes'varí; (12, Kaumárí; (13), Vaishṇaví; (14), Váráhí; (15), Indráṇí; (16), Chámuṇḍá; (17), Mahálakshmí, (Nos. 10 to 17 represent the Ashṭamátṛikás of the Tantras (see my 'Antiquities of Orissa,' II p. 140); (18), Kulachakres'varí; (19), Revanta Mahábhairava; (20), Mahálakshmí; (21), Jayavatsalá; (22), Púrṇávatí Brahmáṇí; (23), S'ikásachchhanda Mahábhairava; (24), Kaumárí and Chámuṇḍá together; (25), Nṛityes'vara Mahábhairava; (26), Bhímasena Mahábhairava; (27), Ugrachaṇḍá; (28), Martyeśvarí; (29), Jhaṅkes'varí; (30), minor divinities. The divinities noticed are all more or less known in the Hindu Tantras, and the work is more of a Tántric ritualistic character than that of a Buddhist manual.

The codex being defective both at the beginning and at the end the initial and the concluding words are not given here.

No. B, 54.

PRAYOGA-MUKHA.

प्रयोगमुखं ।

Substance, Nepalese paper, 10 × 3½ inches. Folia, 28. Lines on a page, 11. Extent in ślokas, 740. Character, Newárí. Date, N. 903. Appearance, old. Prose and verse. Incorrect.

A book of exercises in Sanskrit grammar. It is divided into five sections or *paṭalas,* and treats successively of the cases, (*káraka*) compound words (*samása*), derivative words (*taddhita*) conjugations, (*tip*) and participal and verbal affixes (*kṛitya*).

Beginning. ॐ नमः सर्व्वज्ञाय ।

विज्ञातसकलज्ञेयमुत्तीर्णभवसागरं ।
प्रणम्य सुगतं सम्यग्वक्ष्यते शब्दशासनं ॥
प्रयोगमिच्छता ज्ञातुं ज्ञेयं कारकमादितः ।
संज्ञया षड्विधं भेदात्त्रयोविंशति वा पुनः ॥
तत्र पञ्चविधः कर्त्ता कर्म्म सप्तविधं भवेत् ।
कारणं द्विविधञ्चैव सम्प्रदानं त्रिधा मतं ॥

End. कारकपटलैः समासपटलः तद्धितपटलः तिङन्तपटलः कृत्यपटल इति पञ्चपटला नियन्त्रिताः ॥

Colophon. इति प्रयोगमुखं समाप्तं ।

No. B, 11.

RATNAMA'LA' AVADA'NA.

रत्नमालावदानम् ।

Substance, Nepalese paper, 16½ × 3½ inches. Folia, 110. Lines on a page, 7. Extent in ślokas, 2,600. Character, Newárí. Date, ? Appearance, old. Verse. Incorrect.

A collection of stories regarding persons who in former times became Buddhas. The stories are said to have been related by a saint named Upagupta to the emperor Aśoka. As'oka, surrounded by a large assembly of pious citizens of Páṭaliputra, was eagerly awaiting to hear some religious discourse when Upugupta presented himself before him, and narrated the following stories to satisfy his intense thirst for religious knowledge.

1. *Story of Kauśigha—Kauśighavíryyasahanávadána.* Once on a time Lord Buddha was delivering a lecture on religion to a crowded congregation in the garden of Anáthapiṇḍada at S'rávastí. Gods, demons, and men, eager to receive his instructions, assembled round him in great numbers.

He discoursed on the religion which showers its blessings in all its stages,—at the beginning, in the middle, and at the end. All came except Putraka,—a man of consequence (Mahájana), proud of his wealth,—who was a disciple of a Tírthika, named Púraṇa. By worshipping Bráhmaṇic gods, Putraka had obtained a son named Nanda, who at the age of six fell ill of anæmia, which prostrated him so much that he could not rise from his bed. Though in such a pitiable state of health, he mastered all the sciences of his day, and became devoutly religious. Putraka, anxious to relieve the sufferings of his son, implored his preceptor for help. Púraṇa assured him that Nanda would miraculously recover his strength and rise up when six sages, Púraṇa included, would make their appearance before him. But his assurance proved false. Instead of rising up at their appearance, Nanda could not make up his mind to see them. The wise men were put out of countenance. The omniscient Lord, observing their confusion and the helplessness of the dejected family, desired to bless it with his presence. Golden rays issuing from his glorious person proceeded to Nanda, as the harbinger of the Lord, raised up his drooping spirit, and dispersed the gloom of his mind. At the most blessed appearance of the Lord, Nanda recovered his strength, got up from his bed, fell at the feet of the Lord, and welcomed him. The Lord gave him a sandal-wood stick and told him that whenever he would strike that stick he would get a profusion of wealth. He went once for commerce in a foreign country, gained much wealth, and, returning home, invited the Lord to a sumptuous repast. The Lord accepted the invitation, and, after the repast, smiled, whereupon A'nanda asked the Lord; "why do you smile?"

The Lord replied, Nanda is sure to become a great Sugata, Kaus'igha by name.

2. *Story of Chandana—Snátávadána.* When the lord was residing in the Jetavana grove, five hundred merchants, on their way back from the island of Ratnákara, lost their way in a desert. Wandering in the immeasurable waste of sand, scorched by the burning rays of the meridian

sun, they were in great need of water, to allay their intense thirst. They prayed S'iva, Varuṇa and the whole host of Bráhmaṇic gods, but in vain. But no sooner they prayed to Buddha than he (Buddha) desired in his mind "let Indra send them a shower," and Indra, without the least delay, sent them a refreshing shower, which relieved them from their sufferings. All of them became great Bodhisattvas afterwards. The Bhikshus asked the Lord why should Indra send a shower at the desire of the Lord. The Lord said :—" Once on a time a great Buddha, named Chandana, preached all over the world. On one occasion he resided for three months at the capital of a king who was one of his ardent disciples. During the period of the Lord's residence in the capital there was a great draught. The king ordered a great tank to be dug, poured all sorts of perfumes and flowers into it, and compelled all his subjects to pour the perfumed water, lifted in golden vases, over the Lord's head. Indra was so well pleased with the honour done to Sugata that he poured immediately a heavy shower of rain. The king raised perfumed stúpas over the nails and hairs of the Lord, and prayed that he may become a Buddha. I am, O bhikshus, that king."

3. *Story of the Discus—Chakrávadána.* When the lord was residing in the Bamboo grove at Rájgṛiha, there was a merchant in that city who had a wife devotedly attached to him. His income always fell short of his expenditure; so his hordes were on the point of being exhausted. On one occasion his wife gave him a lecture on the advantages of affluence, which induced him to undertake a distant expedition. In the absence of her dearly loved husband, the merchant's wife began to worship Vishṇu for his prosperity and safe return. She vowed to offer a golden discus to Vishṇu on the event of her husband's safe return. Her husband came back a rich man. True to her vow, she proceeded to the temple of Vishṇu to offer that god the promised discus. The Lord made his appearance before the devout lady in her way to the shrine. Finding the Lord S'ríghana with all the thirty-two signs of greatness and eighty minor indications on his person, she offered him the discus, heedless of all the remonstrances of her companions. Not content with offering the discus, she worshipped the Lord, fell into a profound meditation, and prayed from the inmost core of her heart that she may become a Buddha Sugata, free from all pains, and having complete control over the senses. The Lord blessed her saying, " she shall become Chakrántara, a great Patyeka Buddha." The discus remained for a time over the head of Buddha, and then, by his permission, adorned the heads of Hari and

Hara. The merchant, too, at the instance of his wife, became a worshipper of the "three jewels."

4. *Story of a ghost—Pretávadána.* When the lord was in the Bamboo grove, Maudgaláyana, one of his disciples, went to a cremation ground, and there saw a ghost covered over with coarse hair, with a belly swelling to a mountain's height, with a conical mouth tapering to a point, suffering intensely from excruciating pains and a thirst which could not be alleviated, and repeatedly falling insensible into hysteric fits. On his return he enquired of the Lord the cause of the ghost's suffering. The Lord said the ghost was that of a woman who, in one of her previous existences, had refused to give the Lord Kás'yapa a palmful of water when he was very thirsty, and had haughtily insulted her husband when he upbraided her for the refusal. The Lord added she was to be rescued from her pains by Lokes'vara, son of Jina.

5. *Story of a blossom—S'alipushpávadána, vide* Avadánaśataka, story No. 53.

6. *Story of the handsome body—Vapushmadavadána, vide* the same, story No. 63.

7. *Story of a Devaputra who had been cursed to become a hog—S'úkarávadána.* Once on a time a Devaputra came to know that he would fall from heaven and become a hog in his next existence. The idea of degradation proved too much for him; he fell insensible. Indra, by pouring on him a shower of nectar, restored him to his senses, and advised him to worship the three jewels whereby he may escape the dreaded fate. On account of his devotion to Buddha, Dharma, and Sańgha he was born in the region of Tushita. Indra knew from the Lord that his advice was the best that could have been given to the Devaputra.

8. *Story about questions asked by certain gods—Praśnottarávadána.* Once on a time the Lord, after imparting religious instructions to his hearers, retired to his chamber and, sitting on a sofa, fell into a vein of intense devotional feeling. Gods came down from heaven to receive his answers to the following recondite questions:

Question. Who attain a good hereafter?

Answer. Those who lay out gardens, span rivers with bridges, build reservoirs under water-falls; who are faithful, well-behaved, veracious, merciful and free from vanity.

Q. Who goes to hell?

A. The blasphemer.

Q. Who multiplies his sins?

A. The blasphemer.

Q. Who is strong among donors ?

A. One who distributes rice in charity.

Q Who shines most ?

A. One who distributes clothes to the poor.

Q. Who is happy ?

A. One who gives water to the thirsty.

Q. Who has the finest person ?

A. One who gives lamps.

Q. Which is the keenest dart ?

A. Malicious words.

Q. Which is the most fatal poison ?

A. Anger.

Q. Which is the most consuming fire ?

A. Envy.

Q. Which is the most impenetrable darkness ?

A. Ignorance. (*Avidyá.*)

Q. What is to be accepted ?

A. That which you want.

Q. What is to be rejected ?

A. That which you have.

Q. What is the best armour ?

A. Forgiveness.

Q. What is the sharpest weapon ?

A. A penetrating intellect.

Q. Who is the worst thief ?

A. One who is clever in sophistry.

Q. What is wealth to a good man ?

A. His character.

The gods returned to heaven well pleased with these answers.

9. *Story of S'uklá—S'uklávadána,* vide *Avadánas'ataka,* story No. 73.

10. *Story of the golden-handed—Hiraṇyapáṇi, vide* the same, story No 83.

11. *Story of Hastaka—Hastakávadána.* There lived in the city of S'rávasti a householder as rich as Kuvera. He had a child who remembered the events of his previous existences. The moment he was born he kissed his hands, saying "O my hands, I get thee back after a long time." He was named Hastaka, because he kissed his hands. When grown up, Hastaka became a disciple of the Lord, renounced

the world, and was raised to the rank of an Arhat. Lord Buddha narrated the following story to explain the strange circumstance at the birth of Hastaka. Lord Kás'yapa preached his religion at Benares. He had two Bhikshus under him. One learned and pious, the other ignorant. The learned Bhikshu used to take the ignorant one with him whenever he was invited to a feast. On a certain occasion Mahápúṇya, the learned Bhikshu, did not find his companion, and was obliged to take another with him. To his great surprise he found his old companion at the feast, and taunted him for coming to a feast without an invitation. The taunts enraged the ignorant Bhikshu, who cursed Mahápuṇya to be born without hands, so that we may not again enjoy a feast. On return home, Mahápuṇya engaged himself in a samádhi to wipe away the evil of the curse. The ignorant Bhikshu, seeing him so engaged and repenting of his hasty conduct, fell at his feet, and prayed forgiveness. Mahápuṇya readily granted this; and said, "Listen, my boy, I forgive you the offence you have committed through gross ignorance, but you must act according to the directions I give you. Injure no animated being; take nothing that is not given you; abstain from female society; tell no untruth; indulge not in wicked and scurrilous speech." He did so, but for the sin of cursing an innocent person he was doomed to be born without hands for five hundred births. Now through the merit of following Mahápuṇya's advice he re-got his hands.

12. *Story of Sárthaváha—Ratnottamávadána.* Sárthaváha, a rich merchant of S'rávarti, had twice gone to foreign countries on commercial speculations, and had twice been shipwrecked. Before proceeding a third time he invited a large number of Bráhmaṇs, whom he fed sumptuously, and promised rich rewards should he return safely from his venture. He joined a party of merchants and was so far successful that his transactions proved highly profitable; but in his way home his ship was overtaken by a storm and drowned in the middle of the sea. He escaped with his life by sticking to a plank. This unnerved him quite, and he was very desponding. His wife, a pious woman, thereupon advised him to seek the asylum of Buddha. He did so, and promised many gifts to Tathágatas in the event of his next venture proving successful. The blessings of the Lord had their fruit. Sárthaváha returned from his next voyage a very rich man. He redeemed his promise to the Lord, and gave the Lord a profusion of jewels which changed into a parasol and stood high over the Lord. The Lord was

greatly pleased and said, Sárthaváha would, in a future, life be a Buddha under the name of Ratnottama.

From the colophon it is obvious that the codex is incomplete.

Beginning. ॐ नमः श्रीसर्व्वबुद्धार्य्यसत्त्वेभ्यः ।

यः श्रीमान् सुगतोबुद्धः सद्धर्मदेशकः जिनः ।
श्रीयेणानि त्रिलोकेषु चरन्तु तस्य सर्व्वदा ॥
पुरासीत् पाटलीपुत्रे नगरे स्वर्गसन्निभे ।
अशोको नृपराजेन्द्र स्त्रिरत्नसेवकः सुधीः ॥
एकस्मिन् समये तत्र स राजा जनैः सह ।
पौरिकैश्च सतां कृत्वा तस्त्रोधर्म्म समुत्सुकः ॥
अथाशोः सौगतोभिक्षुरुपगुप्तो जिनात्मजः ।
लोकान् धर्म्मोत्सुकान् दृष्ट्वा समाधिः सहासेन्निनः ॥
सत्सभायां समुत्तीर्य्य सिंहासने शुभासने ।
भासयन् तत्सभालोका तस्थौ पूर्ण स्त्रुधांशुवत् ॥
अथाशोको महाराज समेत्य पौरिकैः सह ।
पूजाभिः पूजयित्वातं उपगुप्तमवन्दत ॥

End. एतन्मे गुरुणाख्यातः संश्रुतं + यथामया ।
तथाचैवतवप्रीत्या कथ्यते च समुश्रृतां ॥
महाराज त्वथात्मेव स्वयं धृत्वा व्रतं शुभं ।
बोधयित्वा प्रजाश्चापि स्थापनीयाः सद्'शुभे ।
एवं चैते सदाप्येवं प्रत्यनन्दन् प्रबोधिताः ॥

Colophon. इति रत्नमालावदानं द्वादशं ।

No. B, 7.

SADDHARMA-PUṆḌARÍKA.

सद्धर्मपुण्डरीकं ।

Substance, yellow-coloured Nepalese paper, 15 × 5¾ inches. Folia, 131. Lines on a page, 10. Extent in ślokas, 2,800. Character, Newárí. Appearance, old. Date, ? Prose and verse. Incorrect.

An exposition of the leading topics of the Buddhist religion, forming one of the nine works constituting the scriptures of the Nepalese Buddhists. Mr. Hodgson describes it as "a Vyákaraṇa of the sort called gáthá. It contains an account of the Mahá and other Dípa Dánas, or of the lights in honour of the Buddhas, and Bodhisattvas; with narrations of the lives of several former Buddhas, by S'ákya, as well as prophetic indications of the future eminence of some of his disciples. Speakers and hearers S'ákya, Maitreya, Manjuśrí; &c." The work was translated into Chinese by Che-yen of the Sung dynasty (960—1278), and issued under the name of *Fa-hwa-sun-mui-king*. An epitome of it appears among the books of the Western Tsin catalogue, and a commentary of it in select explanations under the name of *Fa-hwa-in-kia* (*Beal*, pp. 14, 104). M. Burnouf's translation of the work into French was published in 1852, under the name of *Le Lotus de la Bonne Loi*. The scene is laid on the Vulture Peak (*Gṛirdhrakúṭa*) in Behar, and the work is divided into 27 chapters.

CONTENTS: I. On one occasion when the Lord was sojourning on the Vulture Peak near Rájagṛiha with a retinue of twelve hundred Bhikshus, he felt a desire to expound the principles of *Mahánirdes'a*, or the great identification of all things. Thereupon he performed the Samádhi called *antarnirddeśa*, or "intellectual ascertainment." While he was so engaged, showers of flowers fell on the place, and all Buddhist sacred places quaked. The Devas, impelled by wonder, came to the place. They found rays of light issuing from between the eyebrows of the saint, and cast a blaze of light on all sacred places. Maitreya, beholding this, asked of Manjuśrí the cause thereof, and was informed in reply that the miracle indicated that the Lord was about to expound the work under notice on the great religion, and a summary is given of the entire work.

II. The Lord explains to S'áriputra how former Buddhas had come to know all that nobody else knew, and how they expounded the great religion.

III. S'áriputra enquires why had so many Buddhas expounded the same religion? The Lord assures S'áriputra that he would be in a distant future time a Buddha under the name of Padmaprabha, and that his place of enlightenment will be Viraja. Adverting to the three Yánas, he says they are but different methods of attaining the same end. This is illustrated by a parable. When a house is on fire, the father, to save his children from being burnt, says, "boys, there are in the field horses, elephants, goats, pigs and sheep; go there and I shall give them to you to play with;" they go out and are then carried away to the same haven of security. So do Buddhas provide the three Yánas to save mankind from the burning world. Nor do they thereby commit a falsehood, for whatever the Yâna adopted, the end is the same.

IV. The parable is elaborated by Subhúti, Kátyáyana, Mahákáśyapa, and Mahámaudgalyáyana, who illustrate the subject by adverting to the sons of rich and poor men, the sons of rich men gain wealth by inheritance, poor men become rich by commerce in foreign countries, and when all become rich, the result becomes the same.

V. The Lord illustrates the subject by adverting to the same rain promoting the growth of different kinds of plants, and the same sun and moon enlightening all objects, concluding by saying that though the Yánas were different, the religion taught was the same. The question is then asked by Mahákáśyapa as to whether Nirváṇa was the same, or were there different kinds of it? The Lord declares it to be one and the same, and illustrates it by the parable of the born blind, who does not admit that there are different forms and colours and such objects as the sun, the moon, and the stars, but, on being cured of his blindness by proper drugs administered by competent physicians, becomes conscious of the truth, so the blinded by ignorance have occasion for various remedies according to the nature of their ailments, and ultimately come to the same knowledge.

VI. The Lord predicts how and when and where the four questioners will become Buddhas in remote future times.

VII. Account of an ancient Buddha named Mahábhijṉájṉáná-bhibhu who had sixteen sons, and who first inculcated the three Yánas. His doctrines are also explained.

VIII. The Lord predicts how, when, and where Púrṇa and four others of his disciples would become Buddhas in future times.

IX. Similar predictions regarding Ánanda, Ráhula and others.

X. The Lord declares that whoever will listen with becoming faith and devotion to even one verse of the law as explained by him in the Yána-sútra will attain the perfect Buddha knowledge.

XI. An apparition of a Stúpa appears in the sky over the Lord, and heavenly voices proclaim the merits of the Lord of the Saddharma-puṇḍaríka. The Lord explains the meaning of the stúpa, and then enters it. Thence he expounds the law.

XII. In a large assembly of Bhikshus, the Lord predicts when and where Gautamí and Yaśodhará would become Buddhas.

XIII. Directions regarding the expounding of the Saddharma-puṇḍaríka, after the Nirváṇa of the Lord. Improper places and immoral persons denied the benefit of the Lord.

XIV. Permission granted to eight foreign Bodhisattvas to expound the Saddharma-puṇḍaríka, and prediction as to what would be the result thereof. Numerous Bodhisattvas spring up from under the earth, and this miracle is expounded. Maitreya asks how should these have expounded the perfect Bodhi when the same was first obtained by the Lord under the Bodhi tree.

XV. The Lord explains this paradox. He says that the fact of his acquiring the Bodhi knowledge under the fig-tree should not be borne in mind; the knowledge he acquired had existed from long before, and it should be looked upon as of remote antiquity.

XVI—XVIII. On the merits of the work and the advantages of hearing it read and expounded.

XIX. Story of Sadáparibhúta, a Bhikshu, who used to recite twenty Gáthás and thereby obtain alms. The merits of those gáthás. This Sadáparibhúta was no other than the Lord himself in a former birth.

XX. Directions to those who came from under the earth to preach the Saddharma-puṇḍaríka. A miracle produced by the Lord putting forth his tongue which touched the region of Brahmá.

XXI. Advantages of putting on the work and magic formulæ as charms.

XXII. Story of Sarvasattvapriyadarsana, a Bodhisattva, who wrapped his body in cloth steeped in aromatic oils, and set fire to it to worship a Buddha, named Chandra-vimala-suryaprabhásaśrí, for twelve hundred years, and, on the Nirváṇa of that Tathágata, caused to be erected 84,000 chaityas, which he worshipped for 72,000 years. The Lord was that Bodhisattva.

XXIII. Story of Gadgadas'vara, who worshipped stúpas with many precious offerings. He was the same with the Lord.

XXIV. Account of Bodhisattva Avalokiteśvara.

XXV. Story of Subhányaha, who with his two sons Vimala-garbha and Vimala-netra and his wife Vimala-datta, worshipped a Tathágata named Jaladharagarjita-ghosha-suśvara-nakshatra-sañkusumita, and studied the Saddharma-puṇḍarika. In the time of S'ákya these were born as Bodhisattvas of the names of Padmaśrí, Bhaisajya-ráya, Bhaishajya-samudyata, and Vairochana, respectively.

XXVI. Samantabhadra Bodhisattva promises that he will not only not subject to retributive punishment those who will wear the Saddharma-puṇḍaríka, but reward them.

XXVII. The Lord enjoins that his followers should teach, expound and promote the spread of the religion of the Saddharma-puṇḍaríka.

Beginning. ॐ नमः सर्व्वबुद्धबोधिसत्त्वेभ्यः। वैपुल्य सूत्रराजं परमावतारनिर्द्देशं सद्धर्मपुण्डरीकं सत्त्वाय महापथं वक्ष्ये। एवं मया श्रुतमेकस्मिन् समये भगवान् राजगृहे विहरति स्म। गृध्रकूटपर्व्वते महता भिक्षुसङ्घेन सार्द्धं द्वादशभिर्भिक्षुशतैः सर्व्वैरर्हद्भिः क्षीणास्रवैरित्यादि।

End. इदमवोचद्भगवानात्तमनसस्ते असंख्येयास्तथागता अर्हन्तः सम्यक्संबुद्धा अन्यलोकधात्वागता रत्नवृक्षमूले सिंहासनोपविष्टाः प्रभूतरत्नश्च तथा तातोऽर्हन् सम्यक् संबुद्धः स च सर्व्वावान् बोधिसत्त्वगणास्ते च विशिष्टचारित्र प्रमुखा अप्रमेया बोधिसत्त्वा महासत्त्वा ये पृथिवीविवरेभ्योऽभ्युद्गतास्ते च महाश्रावकाः स च चतुःपर्षत् स देवमानुषासुरगन्धर्व्वश्च लोका भगवतो भाषितमभ्यनन्दन्निति। अक्षारकष्टप्राप्तिलाद्दाघ्यस्य खलु सम्भवं। गन्तुवं कुलपुत्रेण यत्र सूत्रमिदं भवतु।

Colophon. समाप्तं सद्धर्म्मपुण्डरीकं धर्म्मपर्य्यायं सूत्रान्तं महावैपुल्यं बोधिसत्त्वाववादं सर्व्वबुद्धपरिग्रहं सर्व्वबुद्धरहस्यं सर्व्वबुद्धनिगूढं सर्व्वबुद्धजाति। सर्व्वबुद्धगुह्यस्थानं। सर्व्वबुद्धबोधिमण्डं। सर्व्वबुद्ध धर्म्मचक्रप्रवर्त्तनं सर्व्वबुद्धैकघनशरीरं। सर्व्वोपायकौशल्य मेकयाननिर्द्देशं परमार्थविहारनिर्द्देशमिति।

No. B, 3.

SAMÁDHIRÁJA.

समाधिराजः।

Substance, yellow Nepalese paper, 14½ × 3½ inches. Folia, 226. Lines on a page, 6. Extent in ślokas, 5,339. Character, Newári. Appearance, old. Prose and verse. Incorrect.

A work of the class called Vyákarana, or narrative, in which various forms of meditations are described at length, pre-eminence being given to a meditation or *Samádhi* called 'the king of Samádhis.' Its object is to show the process by which a votary of Buddha may rise to the highest eminence, each chapter showing a step in the gradual progress of the human mind in its moral condition, and reciting one or more stories on moral excellence in illustration of the different stages of that progress. The principal interlocutors are Buddha and Chandraprabha, and the scene is laid on the Gṛidhrakúṭa hill where Buddha expounded the principles of a religion which showers its blessings at all its stages, at the beginning, at the middle, and at the end.

CONTENTS: Chapter I. Chandraprabha asked the Lord how can the Buddha be known? How can a man become veracious? How can he become an object of reverence even to the gods? And how can he obtain intuitive perception of things?

The Lord replied, that a Bodhisattva can easily attain all these, by practising the king of Samádhis named Sarvadharmasvabhávasamatávipaśchita Samádhi. First of all a Bodhisattva should be even-tempered, indifferent to the pleasures and pains of the world. Then, he should try to shower benefits on others in spite of all the obstacles that may be thrown in his way. When he becomes thoroughly even-tempered, benevolent and persevering, he is fit to attain those conditions which prepare the mind for the great Samádhi. These conditions are Kárya-samvara, Vák-samvara &c.*

II. The lord said "When I was a Chakravarti, I placed myself under the guidance of many Arhats and young Tathágatas on this very hill Gṛidhrakúṭa. The last of my spiritual guides was S'álendra, a king, who lived for six hundred and seventy millions of years. I worshipped him for full one hundred thousand millions of years, and he blessed me with the knowledge of the great *Samádhi*. The worship of Tathágatas is one of the principal conditions of the Samádhi.

III. He only is fit to receive the knowledge of the Samádhi who is prepared to proclaim the merits of the Tathágatas who have preceded him. The merits of a Tathágata are, that he is perfectly enlightened, learned, well-conducted, well-bestowed; that he is perfectly conversant with the ways of men; he is without a superior; he has a complete control over the senses.

IV. The real nature of the Samádhi is that the mind, unclouded by ignorance, should be fixed on one point. The knowledge of restraint put upon by ignorance, removal of the burdens of the world, the control of passions, and the correction of faults,—these also are essential to the Samádhi.

V. In ancient times the Jambúdvípa was divided between two kings named Dṛiḍhabala and Mahábala. Ghoshadatta, one of the most ancient Tathágatas, made his appearance in the kingdom of Mahábala, induced him to enter the hermitage, and taught him the great Samádhi.

* For explanations of these terms, *vide* chapter, 38.

Mahábala imparted the knowledge of the Samádhi to innumerable creatures for a hundred million kalpas, and afterwards at the end of a hundred thousand full kalpas attained nirváṇa. The myriads, who had been present at the time the king received instruction from Ghoshadatta also, after a long time, attained the highest object of their wishes. "So" said the Lord "he who wants to receive the knowledge of the Samádhi must renounce the world, and rise superior to all terrestrial attractions."

VI. One of the principal conditions of receiving the knowledge of the Samádhi is, that the receiver should be always ready and eagar to honour all Tathágatas, whether "in flesh" or in the nirváṇa state, with offerings of cloth, alms-bowls, flowers, stúpas, &c.

VII. Three *kshántis* are indispensable to the Samádhi. The first kshánti is that one should not quarrel with another, and should not speak unnecessarily. He should be intent on the acquirement of merit, and should consider all phenomena as illusions. The second is that the mind should be full of goodness (Satvaguṇa); it should be persevering in doing good to others, and should consider all creatures as equal. The third is that the devotee should perceive the Lokanátha in all the quarters of the universe.

VIII. The Bodhisattva who seeks to attain the knowledge of the Samádhi learns to regard all phenomena as *abháva* or unsubstantial. For instance, the phenomena of colour, sound, smell, &c. are not produced by causes, nay they are not produced at all. They cannot be defined, cannot be restrained. They are transient, because they cannot be always found in the same substance. They are void. They were inert before their manifestation. A Bodhisattva should be thoroughly conversant with the *abhávasvabháva* or nihilistic character of all phenomena.

There lived, innumerable kalpas ago, a Tathágata, who, the moment he was born, rose to the height of seven palm trees placed one upon another in the sky, and proclaimed that all things are produced from nothing. His awful words were echoed from all mountain peaks, from all trees and leaves, and from all herbs and bushes. He taught a prince, named Mahákaruṇachitti, the great Samádhi. The prince became a Tathágata, Suvichintitártha by name.

IX. One who seeks to attain the highest bliss, one who wishes to ferry all creatures over the troublesome sea of the world (*bhavárṇava*), should be practised in, and proclaim, the great Samádhi taught by all Buddhas, for it is the way to bliss for all of them, and explains the true idea of the quality of all creatures. One who seeks to attain the

Samádhi should regard every substance as an illusion, a dream, a mirage. One who is convinced of the illusive character of things, *i. e.*, one who is *gambhíradhamakshántikuśala*, can never be led astray by temptations, by sins, and by fascinating charms of the external world, because he never regards them as entities. He is honest, unerring, unmoved by passions, and becomes indifferent to pleasure. He is said to be capable of intent attention to one object, to be free from illusions, clever, prosperous, blessed, of irreproachable character, and possessed of wisdom.

X. "Be wise," said the Lord to Chandraprabha, "for even the Sambodhi is not beyond the reach of a wise man, much less so is your Samádhi."

"I shall become wise," replied Chandraprabha, "I shall be regardless of life and health; I shall learn from the Tathágatas. I am determined to attain Bodhi knowledge, to destroy the evil genius Mára, to rescue millions from all suffering. Place, O Lord, your right hand on my head."

No sooner was the holy hand, impressed with all the signs of greatness, placed on Chandraphrabha's head than all the hundreds and thousands and millions of Samádhis known presented themselves before him. Chandraprabha invited the Lord to his own house at Rájagṛiha, and gave him a grand entertainment.

XI. After the entertainment Chandraprabha presented the Lord with a rich robe valued at 990,000,000,000,000 pieces of gold, and distributed raiments to all the Bhikshus. All this time Chandraprabha was pondering over the most abstruse points of the Buddhist creed. He could not understand how the Bodhisattva could be non-cognisant of the phenomena of nature, &c.

The omniscient, aware of Chandraprabha's doubts from the very beginning, took this opportunity of explaining them, so that in a short time Chandraprabha was convinced.

XII. The Bodhisattva, who knows the nature of all phenomena, *i. e.*, that they are only illusions, becomes an adept in recollecting past events, rises superior to the temptations of the senses, and becomes proof against the fascinations of Mára and his daughters.

XIII. The Bodhisattva who seeks for the relief of creatures from their pains should hear, receive, teach, promulgate, deliberate over, and spread the knowledge of the Samádhi, because it cures all maladies. Such a Bodhisattva is sure to attain the Sambodhi knowledge.

XIV. From the house of Chandraprabha the Lord returned to Gṛidhrakúṭa, and there graced a throne prepared for him by Maitreya, who, with his permission, had returned a little earlier. Chandraprabha came to honour the Lord with a train of 8,000,000,000,000,000,000 persons. He sat down, and in a humble manner asked the Lord, what were the necessary qualifications for receiving the Samádhi? The Lord said, "they are four in number. The Bodhisattva who is learned and has such a complete control over his passion as never to resent a wrong has the first qualification. One who is upright, modest, retiring, noted for the unswerving integrity of his character, and is lauded by Áryyas and wise men, has the second qualification. One who is contented, free from avarice, humble, fond of the three dhátus (jewels), who relieves the distressed, and eagarly thirsts for Sambodhi, has the third qualification. One who is satisfied with his own condition, who has heard the scriptures, who is experienced in religious duties, to whom Dharma is the only guide, and who gladly imparts his knowledge to others, has the fourth qualification."

The Lord continued, "listen to me, Chandraprabha, long, long ago, there was a Tathágata, Svaráṅgaghosha by name. In the same kalpa he was preceded by Jṉánaśvara, Tejassvara, and Matíśvara, all of whom had practised this Samádhi. Long, long before the earliest of these, the world was blessed with the advent of Narendraghosha. Standing in the sky he lectured on the great Samádhi. The earth shook under his awful voice. The king S'iribala renounced the world at the bidding of that lord, and he was followed by all his friends, relatives, ministers and subjects.

"After his death S'iribala was again born in the same family. His name then was Dṛiḍhabala. He still exists and knows my mission. He has published millions and tens of millions of aphorisms on the illusive character of substances. All Bodhisattvas still believe in those aphorisms. Now-a-days he sometimes lectures on that Samádhi which leads to the purity of speech, body, mind and sight, and which destroys the effects of human work. Sometimes he speaks of the Samádhi which leads to salvation, *lit.* the reflection of the eight membered passage अष्टाङ्गिकमार्ग-भावना, to the meditation of the subordinate parts of the communion with Tathágatas, to truth, which produces keenness of intelligence, restoration of sight to the blind, to independence, to the knowledge of the evancescent character of the world" (*lit.* the interview or knowledge of illusion which has no beginning).

The Lord added that he had in one of his previous existences obtained the knowledge of the Samádhi from Buddha Dṛiḍhabala, and the events of his former existence he still remembered.

XV. Not to be puffed up with pride for one's own good works, to be indefatigable in the service of others, to have a large stock of knowledge, and to have unfailing presence of mind, are the qualities indispensable to one who aspires to the great Samádhi. One who has a mind to attain the knowledge can hear it at any time from any one.

XVI. A Bodhisattva who is not frightened at the hard conditions of the great Samádhi, becomes expert in enquiring into, in investigating and in ascertaining, the laws and religion of Buddha. He also receives emancipation according to the laws of that religion. On hearing these laudations, Chandraprabha became very anxious to practice the Samádhi, and obtained the permission of the Lord to do so. While he was engaged in deep meditation, the prince of the celestial choristers came down with five hundred musicians to sing hymns of praise in honour of the Lord. At the will of the Lord these gave out only Gáthás. In causing the production of these Gáthás the Lord had two objects in view, 1st, teaching the Gandharvas the proper notes of solemn music, and confirming by charming music Chandraprabha's noble resolution to practise the Samádhi. And the Lord succeeded in accomplishing both these objects. The Gáthás chanted on this occasion are named *Achintya-buddha-darma-nidhyapti-gáthá* or that which confirms the mind in the doctrines of the Buddhist religion, which is hard to comprehend.

XVII. In times long since past, king Indraketudvaja proclaimed the doctrines of a religion which trains the mind in benevolence, and in doing good to all creatures. One who prepares himself to accept the doctrines of that religion must be of spotless character, a friend to goodness, and an enquirer after truth. He should never be tired in honouring, serving, and doing good to Buddhas. If he fulfils all these conditions, he can easily obtain Sambodhi knowledge.

XVIII. A Bodhisattva aspiring after the highest bliss should have a thorough grasp of the doctrines and teachings of the religion which showers its blessings on all. His character too should be irreproachable.

Two sons of a banker were induced to renounce the world by a Sugata. They lived in a lonely forest. The king of Jambudvípa, when out on a hunting excursion, entered the forest, and became their disciple. Many thousands of his followers embraced the religion of their king. The king's brother, enraged at the defection from the good old religion of the Tírthikas, ordered the hermits to be killed. In the next existence one of these hermits became Dípankara, and the Lord was the other brother. The king is Maitreya, and Devadatta the king's brother.

XIX. A Bodhisattva desirous of attaining the great Samádhi should be regardless of his life and health. Any attention paid to life is injurious to his spiritual welfare, for it breeds work.

In meditating on the form of a Tathágata, he should not think of a material form, because a Tathágata is composed purely of religion. The form of a Tathágata is not produced; it is an effect without a cause, solemn, of immeasurable virtue, the cause of all things, immovable, baseless, resembling the sky, invisible, the eye of the universe, without a beginning, beyond the reach of thought, pertaining to the nature of the mind, unmoved by pleasure or pain, beyond the universe, without abode, full of love, self-controlled, impenetrable, infallible, and properly characterised by the word nihility. There is no other way of comprehending the form of a Tathágata than the practice of the Samádhi.

XX. All the senses and their objects are the attributes of Tathágata, *i. e.*, they are the different manifestations of his qualities. Since the senses and their objects are infinite and inconceivable, the attributes of Tathágata are also infinite and inconceivable.

All the feelings are the attributes of Tathágata. Since these are infinite and incomprehensible, the attributes also are infinite and incomprehensible.

Similarly all the infinite perceptions, passions and impressions are the attributes of the lord.

The knowledge of the identity of all substances, qualities and actions with Tathágata is called the knowledge of Dharma, or *Dharma-samvit.*

The earnest desire produced for the knowledge of Dharma is called the *Nirukti-samvit.*

The precepts taught by one who has the knowledge of Dharma are called the *Pratibhaṇa-samvit.* There is another called *Artha-samvit.*

One who is desirous of acquiring the four Samvits given above, should practise the great Samádhi.

XXI. All Bodhisattvas should consider Tathágata as nothing but an embodiment, Rúpa, (senses and their objects). He should consider Tathágata as identical with the imperishable state of Rúpa, and he should believe in the thorough and complete identity of these two, Rúpa and Tathágata.

Similarly he should believe firmly in the identity of the Tathágata with feelings, perception, passions and impressions. So that he should believe that pentaform matter is nothing but the Tathágata.

XXII. A Bodhisattva should preach before all creatures the knowledge of salvation, and should point out to them that merit, the root of all prosperity is the only means for the attainment of salvation. He should also explain to them what that merit consisted of. After doing these things, he becomes expert in the ways and means, and in a short time successfully accomplishes the Samádhi to which there is nothing superior.

XXIII. A Bodhisattva should learn to be vigilant, and to conduct himself so as to acquire watchfulness. One who is thoroughly well-versed in the six *Páramitás* acquires these qualifications. The following ten qualifications are acquired by those who acquire the Páramitá of Dána or charity. (1) He subdues malice; (2) acquires a self-sacrificing spirit; (3) affords enjoyments to all; (4) is born in a rich family; (5) becomes large-hearted; (6) an object of affection to men; (7) the leader of the four assemblies; (8) enjoys pleasure without being addicted to it; (9) his hand and feet become soft; (10) the sole of his feet becomes smooth.

XXIV. Following are the ten qualifications acquired by a Bodhisattva who has acquired the second Páramita or S'ila, *i. e.*, good conduct. (1) He completes his education; (2) shapes his conduct according to the precepts of Buddha; (3) is not an object of censure to the wise; (4) never breaks his promise; (5) cultivates knowledge; (6) renounces the world; (7) endeavours to attain nirváṇa, 8 (?) (9) acquires Samádhi; (10) is never poor.

XXV. Following are the ten qualifications acquired by one who is well established in Kshánti. (1) He is not burnt by fire; (2) not wounded by weapons; (3) never drowned in water; (4) not affected by poison; (5) is protected by gods; (6) obtains the thirty-two signs of greatness;* (7) is never overtaken by misfortune; (8) has an easy access to Brahmaloka; (9) leads a happy life; (10) is always cheerful.

Then follow enumerations of the qualifications of Bodhisattvas who have acquired the Páramitás of Virya, Dhyána, Prajṇá, &c., strength, meditation, spiritual knowledge, scholarship, habit of teaching, the doctrine of S'únyatá or emptiness of the world, Samádhi, and the habit of living in forests.

The Bodhisattva who has acquired true knowledge and has shaken off all connection with mundane qualities acquires the five experiences in addition to the tenfold qualifications aforesaid.

The five experiences are called nidhánas or treasures: (1) of Buddha;

* See my translation of the Lalita-Vistara, p. 142.

(2) of Dharma; (3) of Jṉána; (4) of purvantáparánta pratyutpanna-jṉána; the fifth is wanting. Seeing innumerable Buddhas in all directions is called the treasure of Buddha. Hearing the preaching of these Buddhas is called the treasure of Dharma. The acquirement of that knowledge is called the treasury of Jṉána by the virtue of which a Bodhisattva retains all moral precepts, teaches them to all creatures, and knows their real import. That experience by which thinkers obtain insight into the events, past present and future, is called *purvantáparánta-pratyutpanna-jṉá-nidhána*, (*lit.*) treasure of present, past and future.

XXVI. The Lord said, "Chandraprabha, you should learn to long for entering the hermitage, leaving your empire and all your wealth behind. Then you should learn to shake off all connection with the guṇas, to acquire Viveka and Kshánti, *i. e.*, true knowledge and the mercies. You should hear of the great Samádhi, and sacrifice yourself for the benefit of others."

Some hundreds of kalpas ago, Dṛidhadanta, a king of Jambu-dvípa, heard the great Samádhi from Tejogaṇarája, a Buddha. He renounced the world and gave all that he had to the Sugata and to beggars.

XXVII. In this chapter are enumerated the fruits of hearing and of practising the great Samádhi.

XXVIII. In order that he may learn the nature of Dharma a Bodhisattva should listen to, practise, accept, teach and inculcate the great Samádhi. One who is convinced of the nihility of all qualities becomes the object of Sugata's affection.

XXIX. Not to perceive the purity of character, not to practice the Samádhi, not to inculcate knowledge, to scrutinize the doctrine of mukti, and to know as it is the doctrine of the soul's salvation is called *Apari-graha* or non-acceptance of all qualities.

The experience by which a Bodhisattva, after displaying the power of working miracles, inculcates all the moral precepts to all creatures is called *Parikarma* or decoration of the great experience. One who desires the acquirement of the Parikarma and the Aparigraha should listen to &c. the great Samádhi.

He only is Buddha who finds unity in the diversity of Dharma, inasmuch as in their character they are all Sunya or empty.

XXX. A Bodhisattva, eagarly longing for the great Samádhi and for Bodhi knowledge, should believe in the doctrine of S úuyatá or nibility, and should be careful in the worship of living or dead Tathágatas. A Bodhisattva longing for mukti should worship the Tathágatas. He should with a souorous voice and with a heart melting at the suffering of others, proclaim the great Samádhi, for it alone can fix the mind in the S'únya, the cause of all qualities. When the Bodhisattva does this he is happy in salvation. In such an enviable position he perceives nothing. Deeply engaged in Praṇidhánas and in the Anupalambha Samádhi, he delights himself and others with meditations.

Innumerable kalpas ago, Ghoshadatta, saving the souls of millions, obtained the highest object of his wishes, *viz.*, nirváṇa. When king of Jambudvípa he determined to worship the great Sugata in a manner worthy of such a great potentate. Kshemadatta, a Bodhisattva, in the presence of the multitude assembled at the royal palace, thrust his right hand into a blazing fire, first wrapping the hand with cloth saturated with oil. Unmoved by the excruciating pain the Bodhisattva began eloquently to preach the Samádhi.

XXXI. One who aspires after the great Samádhi and the Bodhi knowledge should act according to the following four moral injunctions. (1) He should distribute alms for acquiring the knowledge of "easy means" from Tathágatas who know it. (2) He should try to learn it from those that have the Bodhi knowledge. (3) He should be ready to sacrifice his own self for the good of those that love worldly enjoyments. (4) He should teach the knowledge of self to those that long for it.

Achintya-praṇidhána-viśesha-samudgatarája, a Tathágata, was the teacher of a religion which prevailed for millions of years. At last, the Bhikshus, the guardians of his faith, became hopelessly corrupt. With one noble exception, all of them cared only for their own worldly interests. They all died of loathsome diseases. But that honest Bhikshu became the preceptor of Jnánabala, king of Jambudvípa. In the course of time, an abscess formed on the Bhikshu's thigh. The disease was pronounced beyond the skill of medical men. Every one was sorry for the honest and faithful Bhikshu. The king and his family were in great distress at the prospect of losing their preceptor. It was then announced to the king in a dream that the only medicine which could cure the Bhikshu was human flesh and blood; the blood to be used as an ointment, and the flesh as diet. This the king caused to be proclaimed all over his wide empire. But no one could be found willing to offer his own flesh and blood to the holy man. At length Jnánavatí, the king's daughter, came forward, and cut out a portion of flesh from her own thigh for the use of the royal preceptor. But there was still a difficulty. The Bhikshu had scruples to take human flesh. So it was dressed privately, and served to him. He ate it unwittingly, and was cured.

XXXII. A'nanda asked the Lord why Bodhisattvas feel no pain even when their limbs are torn asunder. The Lord replied, as a worldly-minded man, every part of whose body is burning under the fire of sin, can feel pleasure without the fire being extinguished, he has no pleasure but in the pursuit of gain; so does a Bodhisattva, who is desirous of escaping from the burning fires of grief, birth and decrepitude, and longs to obtain nirváṇa, feel no pain from such trifling matters as the amputation of a hand, or a foot.

The following story was cited in illustration of the preceding. At the time when Ratnapadma-chandra-vis'uddhábhyudgatarája obtained nirváṇa, there lived a king named Suradatta, who reigned over the whole of Jambudvípa. His capital was at Ratnavatí. He had eighty thousand wives, a thousand sons, and five hundred daughters. At that time, the false faith in mantras and sacrifices of the Tírthikas prevailed. The Bodhisattvas, under the leadership of their great preacher Pushpachandra, withdrew to a forest named Samanta-khaṇḍa. (A leaf here is lost in the MS.)

Pushpachandra, by observing a fast of three days, converted millions to his faith. On the fourth day of his fasting he imparted Bodhi knowledge to millions at Ratnavatí. On the fifth day he brought the queens to his faith. On the sixth the princes were converted. On the seventh day he presented himself before the king, who was surrounded by his servants and the inmates of his seraglio. At the appearance of the Bodhisattva the king's followers fell prostrate at his feet. But other feelings were working in the king's mind. He was surprised to find a stranger honoured so much in his presence. The Bhikshu's comely person, his bewitching beauty, and his appearance before the inmates of the harem roused deep suspicion in the king, who, without any enquiry, ordered the Bhikshu to be killed by mutilation. His hands and feet were separated from his body, and his eyes were plucked out. A week later, the king happened to pass by the way where the murder had been committed. He found that putrefaction had not yet set in in the Bhikshu's corpse: it looked as fresh as ever. The king then became aware of his own folly.

He recognized in the Bhikshu some Tathágata, and became the prey of remorse.

"One who desires the great Samádhi, Ananda," added the Lord, "should preach the religion of Tathágata even at the risk of his life."

XXXIII. When a Bodhisattva wishes to attain the excellent Bodhi knowledge he should listen to, practise, and preach, the great Samádhi.

XXXIV. In order to obtain the knowledge of Bodhi, a Bodhisattva should sow the seeds of prosperity.

Unnumbered ages ago Gaṇes'vara was a great Jina, and Varapushpa a great king. The latter consecrated innumerable gardens to the honour of the Sugata. He used to distribute food to the followers of Gaṇes'vara. He fell in, one day, with the Tathágata, and learned from him the great Samádhi. With five hundred of his sons he renounced the world, and practised the religion of Tathágata. After the nirváṇa of Gaṇes'vara, people returned to their old superstition; but they were brought back to Buddha's religion by Yas'ahprabha.

XXXV. "You should," said the Lord, "learn to restrain your body. By so doing a Bodhisattva learns to be indifferent to all doctrines, is endowed with the thirty-two great signs and eighty subsidiary indications of greatness,* aquires the ten supernatural powers of a Tathágata, the four wisdoms, the eighteen Vaiṇikas, the doctrine of Buddha, the three delights of the Moksha, the four Viháras of Brahma, the four Pratisañvids, the thirty-seven inferences of Bodhi, forgiveness, doubt and discrimination. By restraining the body, a Bodhisattva shrinks with horror from slaughter, theft, incontinence, falsehood, malicious speech, harsh words, contradictions, incoherent speech, robbery, murder, false notions, error, vanity, drugging, confining, obstructing, beating, threatening, piercing, anger, and covetousness. His hands and feet cannot be separated from his body, and if they be separated, he never feels weakened thereby.

The three delights of Moksha are—the delight afforded by the knowledge of Nihility, the delight afforded by the knowledge that things are produced without a cause, and the delight that he has to perform no samádhis any more.

The four amusements (Viháras), or those of friendliness (*Maitrí*) of sympathy, (*Karuṇá*) of delight, and of indifference.

For the four Pratisañvits, *vide* chapter XX, p. 213.

The thirty-seven inferences are the four associations (causes of memory), four destructions, four powers of working miracles, five senses, five powers, seven subordinates of Bodhi, and the eight ways to these.

* Vide my translation of the Lalita Vistara, p. 142.

Vis'eshachailí, a king, obtained the knowledge of Káyasañvara or the restraint of the body, from Jṉánaprabha, a Tathágata. Káyasañvara is only the entrance to better and nobler conditions. The disciple must try to think that his body is as pure and brilliant as the sky, and then he should try to identify these two things, the sky and his body.

XXXVI. The next step to be taken by a Bodhisattva is to aim at the purity of physical actions, and at the restraint of speech (*Váksañvara*). The latter shows the inactivity of existence in Nihility, the illusive nature of all things created, and that annihilation is the only truth.

XXXVII. The restraint of mind, *Manah-sañvara,* shows that the mind is unreal like a dream, an illusion, a mirage. From it men become fearless, worship Buddha, and learn a samádhi named Jválántarábha.

XXXVIII. Explanations of the following technical terms:

The purity of action is aversion to the world which is merely an illusion.

Árambhanasamatikrama, or abandoning of works; it is the giving up of all actions from the knowledge that they are unreal.

Skandhaparijṉá, or indifference to the Skandhas, is related to the Skandhas produced by the knowledge of their unreality.

A'yatanápakarsha, or low estimate of the senses, is abandoning them from the conviction of their shadowy nature.

Trishṇá-prahána, or want of ambition, is the refraining from all Dharmas.

Anutpádaśákshátkriyá, or sight of things unborn, is the non-perception of the Dharmas.

Kṛiyávatára is not attempting the destruction of mundane pains arising from Vírya.

Hetudípaná is the non-cessation of the Skandhas.

Karmaphalábhipranáśa is the destruction of the consequences of works which are illusive like dreams.

Márgabhávaná is the perception of the way to salvation.

Tathágata-samabodhana is the knowledge of the teaching of all the Buddhas.

XXIX to XLI wanting.

XLII. The Lord having discoursed upon the innumerable benefits to be derived by the practice of the Great Samádhí, many millions of his hearers obtained the Bodhi knowledge, many resolved to obtain it, many longed to become Pratyeka Buddhas, and a change for the better was produced in all.

Beginning. ॐ नमो रत्नत्रयाय । नमश्चन्द्रप्रभाय महाबोधिसत्त्वाय।

अनिरोधमनुत्पन्नमनाविलमनक्षरं ।
महायानमहं स्तोष्ये बुद्धज्ञानाभिवाञ्छया ॥
तारकं सर्व्वसत्त्वानां घोरसंसारसागरात् ।
संस्थापकञ्च निर्व्वाणे शान्तक्षेमनिरुत्तरे ॥
आकाशकल्पमचलं गभीरं शान्तमव्ययं ।
तद्बुद्धज्ञानममलं भक्त्या वन्दे सदादरात् ॥
अरूपमनिमित्तञ्च लक्ष्यलक्षणवर्ज्जितं ।
प्रापकं बोधिमार्गस्य अग्रयानमहं नतः ॥
गभीरोदारविपुलो धर्म्मो यत्र प्रभाष्यते ।
तद्बोधिमण्डफलदं महायानं नमाम्यहं ॥
शाश्वतोच्छेदरहितमहं तद्द्वयवर्ज्जितं ।
शान्यताप्रभावां (?) शान्तं वन्देहं बुद्धवर्णितं ॥
अप्रपञ्चनिरालम्बबोधिसत्त्वैर्नमस्कृतं ।
नमामि शिरसा रत्नं महायानमसंस्कृतं ।
स्तुत्वा शानमनुत्तरं निरुपमं संसारसंतारकं
यत्पुण्यं प्रचितं विसारि विमलं तुङ्गं महन्निश्चलं ।
सर्व्वस्तेन जडः प्रयातु चपलं सम्प्राप्य यानाधिपं
निर्व्वाणं विरजाः पुरोतमवरं बुद्धो यथा सर्व्ववित् ॥
आर्य्यं चन्द्रप्रदीपं दशबलवृषभैर्येद्दिदं सूत्रराजं
संख्यातीतैः प्रतीतैः श्रुतिहृदयपरिप्रीणनत्वात्मभाजां ।
सप्तद्भिः सन्ति गूढवक्त्रभिरपमलस्याधनीभिः सदैव
स्माविन्यस्तात्मभावः प्रणतिमुपगतस्तानहं भक्तिनम्रः ॥
वर्णाद्यायस्य वक्तुर्मुनिवरवृषभात्तुन्युपायन्निसाद् (?)
सार्व्वज्ञेयावबोधप्रशमिततपसाप्यप्रमेयः सदैव ।
आर्य्यं चन्द्रप्रदीपं दशबलगदिता (?) शेषसूत्राधिराजं
तं भक्त्या सम्भ्रमात्मा क्षितिनिहितशिराः सर्व्वकालं नमामि ॥
येनानन्तसहस्रकल्पनयुता नारागिता नायकाः
यस्य ज्ञानविशेषधर्म्म उदितश्चन्द्रो यथा निर्म्मलः ।
तं चन्द्रप्रभनिष्प्रपञ्चमतुलं संवर्णितं नायकैः
वन्दे सर्व्वसमाधिधर्म्मकुशलं आर्य्यं सदा भक्तितः ॥
स्तुत्वा धर्म्मस्वभावां दशबलजननीं सर्व्वबुद्धाश्च वीरां

नार्य्यं चन्द्रप्रभञ्च जिनवरतनयं सर्व्वदेवाधिवन्द्यं ।
पुण्यं प्राप्तं मया यत् स्थिरगगनसमन्तेन चाकस्मशेषः
स्ताभीभूयात् समाधेः सततमखिलयाशाञ्च सिद्ध्यथैवं ॥
समस्त सुगतोद्गीर्णसर्व्वसूत्राधिराजतः
आर्य्यचन्द्रप्रदीपाडि यथालब्धा ब्रवीम्यहं ।
आयान्तु देवमनुजाः सद्धर्म्मजातगौरवा
दुर्लभं श्रवणं ह्यस्य कल्पकोटिशतैरपि ॥
एवं मया श्रुतमेकस्मिन् समये भगवान् राजगृहे विहरति स्म । गृद्धकूटपर्व्वते
महता भिक्षुसंघेन सार्द्धं भिक्षुणीशतसहस्रेण आशीत्याच वोधिसत्वैः सार्द्धं ।

End. इदमवोचद्भगवान् अत्तमानाश्चन्द्रप्रभः कुमारभूत आयुष्मानानन्दस्तास्तश्च पर्ष-
द्दोभिक्षुः भिक्षुण्युपासकोपासिका अनेकै च शुद्धावासकायिका देवपुत्राः सदेवमा-
नुषासुरगन्धर्व्वाश्च लोका भगवतोभाषितमभ्यनन्दन्निति ।

Colophon. आर्य्यसर्व्वधर्म्मस्वभाव समताविपञ्चितात्मसमाधेर्य्यथालब्धद्मपरिवर्त्तोनाम द्वाचत्वा-
रिंशत्तमः समाप्तः ॥

No. B, 24.

SAPTAKUMÁRIKÁ AVADÁNA ALIAS AHORÁTRAVRATÁNUS'AÑSÁ.

सप्तकुमारिकावदानं वा अहोरात्रव्रतानुशंसा ।

Substance, very inferior Nepalese paper, 10 × 4 inches. Folia, 34. Lines on a page, 10. Extent in ślokas, 850. Character, Nágarí. Date, Sm. 1885.= S'áka, 1750.=Nepalese Era, 949. Appearance, fresh. Verse. Generally correct.

Description of a fast called Ahorátravrata, in praise of which a story is told of seven Nága damsels who had been cursed to be born as univalve shells, *s'ambúka*. The description was given to Aśoka by Upa Gupta, who said it had been before related by S'ákya himself, who attributed it to Vasubandhu, a Jina, who had heard it from the ancient Buddha Vipaśyi. Vasubandhu taught the rite to Indraprishṭha, a king of Gandhavatí, in the Púrvavideha country. Although called *ahorátra* or ephemeral, the fast extended actually to two days and two nights. The proper place for performing it is the neighbourhood of a sacred pool, a river, an ocean, a chaitya, or a temple. On the 13th of the waxing moon a temporary room or *dharmás'álá* has to be erected, duly plastered with cow-dung, and decorated with four flags and an awning. On the flour of the room three diagrams of Dharmadhátu are to be traced with rice-meal of different colours, and the night is to be passed in a fast. On the 14th, at midday, the three jewels are to be worshipped with fivefold offerings and appropriate mantras; the worshipper to break his fast by partaking of simple food in the afternoon. At dusk the place and the Chaitya are to be illuminated, and the worship repeated. On the 15th, or the fullmoon day, the worship is to be again repeated and the day passed in rejoicings with music and singing.

King Indrapṛáshṭha was the first to perform the fast. Having observed it, he had the good fortune to rule his kingdom with great ease and splendour, and then to enter the house of Jina. On this, Indra and other deities came to observe the ceremony of Ahorátravrata. In illustration of the merits of the fast, Upagupta relates the following story:

There was a large tank, named Chaitragarbha, in Magadha, where Gandharvas and Ṛishis used to perform the ceremony of Ahorátravrata. Eight* Nága damsels went to them to see the performance. The Ṛishis fell down insensible by inhaling their poisonous breath. After a while, however, they regained their senses, and cursed the damsels by saying: "Ye shall be born as shells, (*śambúkas*) since you made us senseless by your poisonous breath." On hearing the imprecation, the damsels propitiated the Ṛishis, who became sad at heart.

The curse, however, was irrevocable, and the damsels, turned into shells, lived in a pond. After a long while, a fisherman visited the pond, and cast his net into the water to catch fish, but instead of fish he got only eight univalve shells. He brought the shells home, and gave them to his wife. The fisherman, having consumed all the eatables he had in his home, went out of the house. His wife, not having any other article of food at hand, had to live on these eight shells, which she got boiled. The shells were all vivified in her womb. She became pregnant, and brought forth eight daughters in due time. When they grew up she sent them to market to sell fish.

One day, on the way, the eldest told to her sisters, "Sisters, on account of the great sin we committed in our former life, we have been born in a low family; if we commit the crime of killing animals, we shall have again to suffer." On this, they threw all the live

* The text has the word ashṭa "eight," and gives the names of the eight in detail, but the name of the work is *saptakumári* or seven damsels. In the absence of a second MS. to compare I cannot reconcile the inconsistency.

fishes into the water, and purchased some dead fishes instead of them, and, having sold the latter, gave the price to their mother. On another occasion, the fisherman's wife, having killed some live fishes sent her daughters to sell them. On the way, the sisters were surprised to see the dead fishes become alive, and threw them into the water. They then began to offer up their devotions to Buddha, whose temple was on the bank of the pond. Buddha, being propitiated, appeared before them, and through his grace they died on the seventh day after his appearance, and took their birth as daughters to king Kṛika, of Benares. Their names then were:—The first, Vratí; the second Dharmavatí; the third, Shubhamanjarí; the fourth, Dhímatí; the fifth Netramanjarí; the sixth, S'rímatī; the seventh, Madanajahá; and the eighth, Vratamálá. Vratí, married to king Dharmadaksha, performed, in company of her hushand, the ceremony of Ahorátravrata, and at last retired to the house of Jina.

Beginning. ॐ नमो रत्नत्रयाय । श्रीमद्रत्नत्रयं नत्वा त्रिधातुभुवनाधिपं ।
अहोरात्रव्रतकथां वक्ष्ये गुरूपदेशतः ॥
कुक्कुटाराममासीनमुपगुप्तं यतीश्वरं ।
कृताञ्जलिपुटोऽशोकः प्रार्थयदेवमादरात् ॥

End. तं भुक्ताङ्गीरर्ध्दिं सकलहितकारा बोधिसत्त्वाः सुधीराः
प्रज्ञाब्धेः पारयाताजिनगुणनिरता यान्ति बुद्धालयन्ते ॥

Colophon. इति अहोरात्रव्रतानुशंसायां सप्तकुमारिकावदानं सम्पूर्णं ॥

No. B, 17.

S'A'RDU'LAKARṆA AVADA'NA.

शार्दूलकर्णावदानं ।

Substance, paper, 10 × 4. Folia, 87. Lines on a page, 10. Character, Nágara. Extent in ślokas, 1800. Date, Sm. 1886. Appearance, decayed. Prose. Incorrect.

Story of S'árdúlakarṇa, in narrating which opportunity is taken to point out in detail the utter fatuity of relying on caste distinctions.

The scene of the story is laid at S'rávastí. When the Lord was once sojourning there, in the garden of Anáthapiṇḍada, A'nanda, his favourite disciple, used daily to go to the city to collect alms. One day, after partaking of a repast in the residence of a householder, when he was returning to the hermitage, he felt thirsty. Seeing a girl, named Prakṛití, the daughter of a Chaṇḍálí, raising water from a well, he asked her for a drink, and was duly served. The girl was smitten by the appearance of the hermit, and as he could not be otherwise influenced, she besought her mother, who was proficient in charms and incantations, to bewitch him by her art. The mother prepared with cowdung, in the middle of the courtyard of her house, an altar, lighted a fire therein, and threw into it, one by one, 108 arka flowers (*Calotropis gigantea*), repeating a mantra each time. A'nanda could not resist the force of this charm, and in the evening came to her house, and took his seat on the altar, while Prakṛití, in delight, was engaged in preparing a bed for him. The conscience of A'nanda now smote him, and he began to cry, praying that the Lord may rescue him from his dangerous position. The Lord, perceiving by his miraculous power how his disciple was situated, recited a Buddha mantra, which immediately overpowered the incantations of the Chaṇḍálí, and A'nanda returned to the hermitage. The Lord, thereupon, taught him the potent mantra whereby he could always overcome such evils.

Matters, however, did not progress so satisfactorily as could be wished. The girl, disappointed at night, rose early the next morning, put on her finest apparel, and stood on the road by which A'nanda daily went to the city for alms. A'nanda came, and she followed him to every house he went for alms. This caused a great scandal, and A'nanda, followed by the girl, ran back to the hermitage, and reported the occurrence to the Lord. The Lord was then called upon to exercise diplomacy to save the character of his disciple. He said to Prakṛití, "you want to marry A'nanda. Have you got the permission of your parents? Go, and get their permission." This afforded but slight respite, for Prakṛití soon returned from the city with her parents' permission. The Lord then said, "Should you wish to marry A'nanda, you must put on the same kind of ochre-coloured vestment which he uses." She agreed, and thereupon her head was shaved, she was made to put on ochre-coloured cloth, divested of her vicious motives, and had all her former sins removed by the mantra called *sarvadúrgati-śodhana-dháraṇí*, the destroyer of all evils. Thus did the Lord convert her into a Bhikshuṇí.

This conversion created a serious commotion. Rájá Prasenajit and the Brahmáṇs and Kshatriyas of S'rávastí were greatly scandalised by it, and came to remonstrate with the Lord on his highly improper conduct. The Lord knew their object, and explained the former history of Prakṛití by reciting the following story:

In a forest on the banks of the Ganges there dwelt Trisañku, a Chaṇḍála, who was the chief of ten thousands of his caste men. He had, in a former term of existence, studied the Vedas, the Itihásas, the S'ástras and other branches of knowledge, and remembered them in his present life. He had a son named Sárdúlakarṇa, and to him he taught all that he remembered of his previous learning. The youth thereby became proficient in every accomplishment. Trisañku thought of a Bráhmaṇ, named Pushkarasárí, who had an only daughter, thoroughly accomplished, and in every way worthy of his son. Next morning, followed by a large retinue, he proceeded to the abode of this Bráhmaṇ, and was well received; but when he made his request his host upbraided him for his presumption in asking the hand of a Bráhmaṇ girl for a Chaṇḍála youth, and this led to a long discussion on caste distinctions.

Trisañku said: "There is a marked distinction between ashes and gold, but there is nothing of the kind between a Bráhmaṇ and a person of another caste. A Bráhmaṇ is not produced like fire by the friction of dry wood; he descends not from the sky, nor from the wind, nor does he arise, piercing the earth. The Bráhmaṇ is brought forth from the womb exactly in the same way as a Chaṇḍála. When he dies he causes impurity exactly as other castes do: there is not the least difference in the case. Bráhmaṇs, longing for flesh-meat, commit most cruel sacrifices. They say that goats and the like, by being sanctifeed by mantras, go to heaven after slaughter. If this be the way to heaven, why don't they send their fathers, mothers, sisters, and the rest to heaven by the same expeditious way? Bráhmaṇ, Kshatríya, Vaiśya and S'údra are mere names, and imply no specific distinctions. All human beings have feet, thighs, nails, flesh, sides, and back exactly alike; there is not the slightest difference in any respect, and therefore there cannot be four different species. Even as boys, playing on the highway, take a quantity of dust, and, dividing it into different parts, call one part water, another milk, another curds, another flesh-meat, another ghi, and so on, but the dust does not thereby become any of those articles, so Bráhmaṇ &c., are mere names, and do not imply four distinct species. In animals, like the cow, the horse, and the like, there are marked differences in shape, and thereby the cow, the horse and the rest constitute distinct species. In the same way mangoes, hog-plums (*Spondias magnifera*), rose-apples, dates and the rest belong to different species; but there being no difference of shape in Bráhmaṇs, Kshatríyas, &c., there can be no difference of species. Devas become Bráhmaṇs, Kshatríyas Yakshas, Vaiśyas Nágas,

S'údras Asuras. Had there been any truth in the doctrine of the S'ruti that Bráhmaṇs produce Bráhmaṇs, aud Vais'yas Vaiśyas, there would certainly have been some specific marks. Moreover, every member of the four castes can attain heaven by the merit of his own actions, and there is no let or hindrance with reference to particular castes; surely therefore there are no specific distinctions of castes. Among men those who plough paddy-fields, sow seeds, and raise crops are called Kshatriyas. Those who, giving up marriage, retire to the wilderness, build huts of leaves, and there pass their days in contemplation, are called Bráhmaṇs. Among Bráhmaṇs, those who go to the village and teach mantras are called Adhyápakas. Those men who, calculating upon profit, undertake commercial transactions, are called Vais'yas. Those who earn their livelihood by petty works are called S'údras. Those who feel disposed to conduct the work of chariots and of elephants get the name of Mátaṅgas. Those who plough are called Karshakas. Those who trade are named Vaṇiks. Those who retire from home and accept asceticism are named Pravrajitas. Those who by their good conduct gratify people are called kings (Rájá). In none of these is there any specific organic distinction." By these and other arguments he silenced the Bráhmaṇ, who, thereupon, asked him, "Do you know the Sávitri (Gáyatri)"?

Triśaṅku said, "Yes I do, and also the origin of it. A long time ago, a Ṛishi, named Vasu, married Kapilá, the daughter of a Nakshatra. By devotion to her he lost his vigour, aud to regain it he repeated the Sávitri: "*Bhur bhuvar yat savitur na kapiláyá bhargo devasya dhímahi.*" The Sávitri of the Kshatriyas is: "*Om! jaṭilastápaso-bhútá gahanam vanamáśritá, &c.*" That of the Vais'ya is "*Om chittamáhí sahite vaiśya kanyaká, &c.*" That of the S'údra is "*Om! atapah sutapah jívedaham varshaśatam paśyedaham s'aradám s'atam.*"

The Bráhmaṇ questioned Tris'aṅku about the Nakshatras, their positions, stars, &c., about the planets, and many recondite questions about astrology and interpretations of omens; to all which the interrogated gave very satisfactory replies. The Bráhmaṇ, thus overcome in every way, at last gave away, notwithstanding the opposition of his disciples and pupils, his daughter to S'árdúlakarṇa.

"Now Bhikshus" said the Lord, "he who was Triśaṅku then is myself now. My son is S'árdúlakarṇa. This Ánanda, son of Sáradvatí, is the Bráhmaṇ Pushkarasárí, and the daughter of that Bráhmaṇ is Prakṛiti, the Bhikshuṇí."

The work professes to be a part of the Divya Avadána. It was translated into Chinese by Tchu-ja-hu, of the Western Tsin dynasty in 265 A. D. Its Chinese name is *She-tau-keen-king*. M. Burnouf has givin an abstract of the story in his Introduction to Indian Buddhism, pp. 205*f*.

Beginning ॐ नमो रत्नत्रयाय। एवं मया श्रुतमेकस्मिन् समये भगवान् श्रावस्त्यां विहरति स्म। जेतवनेऽनाथपिण्डदस्यारामे। अथायुष्मान् पूर्व्वाह्णे निवास्य पात्रचीवरमादाय श्रावस्तीं महानगरीं पिण्डाय (प्रावेक्ष्यत्) प्राविशत्।

End. इदमवोचद्भगवान् आत्तमनसस्ते भिक्षवो भगवतो भाषितमभ्यनन्दन्निति।

Colophon. इति शार्दूलकर्णावदानं दिव्यावदानोद्धृतं समाप्तं।

No. B, 46.

SARVATATHÁGATOSHNÍSHA-SITÁTAPATRÁ, ALIAS PRATYAṄGIRÁ-KALPA.

सर्वतथागतोष्णीषसितातपत्रा नाम प्रत्यङ्गिरा।

Substance, Nepalese paper, $7\frac{1}{2} \times 3$. Folia, 18. Lines on a page, 5. Extent in ślokas, 200. Character, Newárí. Date, N. S. 886. Appearance, old. Prose. Incorrect.

A collection of mantras said to have issued forth from between the eyebrows of the Lord when he was sojourning in the heaven of Indra, and was being worshipped by a large host of Devas, and the merit of wearing them, reciting them, or hearing them recited. The mantras are of the type of the mystic Víja mantras of the Hindus.

Beginning. ॐ नमो भगवते आर्य्यमहाप्रत्यङ्गिरायै। एवं मया श्रुतमेकस्मिन् समये भगवान् देवेषु त्रयस्त्रिंशेषु देवेषु विहरति स्म। सुधर्म्मायां देवसभायां महता भिक्षुसङ्घेन सार्द्धं पञ्चमात्रैर्भिक्षुशतैः। महता बोधिसत्त्वगणेन सार्द्धं तस्मिन् समये संबहुलाश्च देवपुत्रा भगवन्तं पर्य्युपासते स्म। तत्र खलु भगवतः ऊर्णाकोशादिमानि मन्त्रपदानि चरति स्म। नमो भगवते अपरिमितगुणप्रतिभानव्यूहातीतकल्पाय तथागतायार्हते सम्यक् सम्बुद्धाय। नमो भगवते गुणरत्नश्रीव्यूहतेजोराशिकल्पाय तथागतायार्हते सम्यक् सम्बुद्धाय।

End. इदमवोचद् भगवानात्तमनास्ते च बोधिसत्त्वाः सा च सर्व्वावती पर्षत् सदेवमानुषासुरगरुड़गन्धर्व्वश्च लोका भगवतो भाषितमभ्यनन्दन्निति।

Colophon. आर्य्यसर्व्वतथागतोष्णीषसितातपत्रा नामापराजिता महाप्रत्यङ्गिरा महाविद्याराज्ञी परिसमाप्ता।

No.

SRAGDHARÁ-STOTRA.

स्रग्धरास्तोत्रं ।

Substance, Nepalese yellow paper, 8 × 3 inches. Folia, 12. Lines on a page, 8. Extent in ślokas, 120. Character, Nágara. Date, Sm. 1881. Appearance, decayed. Verse. Generally correct.

A hymn in praise of A'rya Tárá. By Sarvajna Mitra. The goddess appears to hold the same position among the Buddhists as she does among the Hindus. The name of the work is due to that of the measure in which it is written; the measure comprises twenty-one syllables to the foot, broken into three equal parts by two çæsuras. The author was a Buddhist monk of Káshmír. He was renowned for his unbounded charity. Having given away everything he possessed, he proceeded to king Vajramukuṭa. In the way he met a poor Bráhmaṇ, who enquired of him the way to the home of Sarvajna Mitra. He said, "Have you not heard that he has given away everything he possessed, and is now gone to the king?" The Bráhmaṇ, thereupon, heaved deep sighs in utter despair, and shed tears. Sarvajna Mitra consoled him, by saying, "Never mind, come along with me, and I shall help you." Subsequently he sold his own person for its weight in gold to the king, and gave the proceeds to the Bráhmaṇ.

Beginning. ॐ नमो भगवत्यै आर्य्यतारायै ।

बालार्कालोकताम्रप्रवरसुरशिरश्चारुचूड़ामणिश्री-
सम्पत् सम्पर्करागानतिचिररचिता लक्तकव्यक्तभक्ती ।
भक्त्या पादौ तवार्य्यै करपुटमुकुटाटोप भुग्नोत्तमाङ्ग-
स्तारिण्याः पञ्चरत्नैर्नवनुतिकुसुमस्रगभिरभ्यर्चयामि ॥ १ ॥
दुर्लङ्घे दुःखवह्नौ निपतितनु(?) दुर्भगः कान्दिसीकः
किं किं मूढः करोमीत्यसकृदपि कृतारम्भवैयर्थ्यखिन्नः ।
श्रुत्वा भूयः परेभ्यः च्युतनयन इव व्योम्नि चन्द्रार्कलक्ष्मी-
मालोकाभ्यानिबद्धः परगतिगमनस्त्वामये पापहन्त्रीं ॥ २ ॥

End. मंस्तुत्य त्वद्गुणौघावयवमनियते यत्तदाप्तं मया यत्
पुण्यं पुण्यार्थवाञ्छाफलमधुररसास्वादमामुक्तिभोग्यं ।
लोकस्तेनार्य्यलोकेश्वरचरणतलस्वस्तिकस्वस्तिचिह्ना-
मक्लायायं प्रयायात् सुगतसुतमहीं तां सुखावत्युपाख्यां ॥ २० ॥

Colophon. इत्यार्य्यतारायाः स्रग्धरास्तोत्रं परिसमाप्तं ।

No. .

SRAGDHARÁ-ṬI'KÁ.

स्रग्धरास्तोत्रटीका ।

Substance, Nepalese paper, 8 × 3 inches. Folia, 59. Lines on a page, 5. Extent in ślokas, 580. Character, Nágara. Date, Sм. 1881. Appearance, decayed. Prose. Generally correct.

A commentary on the hymn noticed under the next preceding No. By Jinarakshita, a Bhikshu of the Mahá Vihára of Vikramas'ila Deva and spiritual guide of the king.

Beginning. नत्वार्य्यतारां जगदर्थसारां धर्म्माकरान्वेषणया समासात् ।
बालार्कमात्रस्य करोमि टीकां स्फुटार्थ्यहं श्रीजिनरक्षितः कृती ॥ १ ॥
प्रभूतविद्वेषकृतामनान्तःस्फुरच्छिखादग्धमुखेन हन्त ।
खलु त्वया सत्सुखदामभेयं टीकां न दूष्येत्त्वयि मेञ्जलिरेषः ॥ २ ॥

End. विधाय टीकां यदलम्भि शम्भोर्गिरीशसङ्काशमसीमशोभं ।
शुभं मया तारिणि स्रग्धरायाः स्तुते जगत्तेन तवास्तु बुद्धं ।

Colophon. श्रीमद्विक्रमशीलदेवमहाविहारीय-राजगुरुपण्डितभिक्षु श्रीजिनरक्षितकृता बालार्कस्तुति टीका परिसमाप्ता ।

No. B, 38.

S'ṚIṄGABHERI'.

शृङ्गभेरी ।

Substance, Nepalese yellow paper, 14 × 4 inches. Folia, 18. Lines on a page, 6. Extent in ślokas, 540. Character, Newárí. Date, ? Appearance, old. Verse. Incorrect.

Descriptions of the *Chaityasañvara* and of the *S'riṅgabherí* rites. The descriptions were given to As'oka by Upagupta, who said they had been first narrated by the Lord himself at the request of S'áriputra. The first rite consists in dedicating one or more model chaityas daily, till the number comes up to a hundred thousand. The models may be of cow-dung, clay, sandstone, or metal according to the means of the dedicator. The direction for this rite had been originally given by Vipas'yí to a prince named Pradípaketu. When the above rite is performed for a month from the 1st of S'rávaṇa (July-August), with the accompaniment of the music from a golden horn and other musical instruments it is called S'riñgabherí.

The origin of the rite is thus described :—In the town of S'aśiprabhá there reigned a king named Siñhaketu. His wife, Sulakshaṇá, was greatly devoted to him, and frequently begged and prayed that he should abstain from hunting. The king did not listen to her advice, and on his death, was born a buffalo. His wife was born in a Bráhmaṇ family, and, through her previous virtuous deeds, remembered the history of her former life. Knowing the buffalo to be her husband, she followed him everywhere. Once she prayed to the Lord to retrieve her husband from his brutal condition, and the Lord advised, her what to do. One day the buffalo was destroyed and eaten up by some wild beasts, and a few bones and the horns were all that were left behind. The faithful wife cast the bones into the river, brought water in the horns to wash the spot where the buffalo had fallen, and, washing the spot, buried whatever fragments she found and the horns, and erected a chaitya over them with river sand. For thirty days successively she worshipped this chaitya with the utmost reverence and devotion. On the twenty-first day a crystal chaitya came down from heaven, and entered the sandy one. The place became surrounded by a moat and seven successive lines of ramparts. The horns were changed into gold. Within this crystal chaitya a chamber became manifest, and from the golden horns within it came out a handsome young man, Dharmaṣ'ila, who took the woman by the hand, and claimed her as his wife. He was subsequently elected by the people king of the country, when he assumed the name Bhadras'riñgí, and his devoted wife was known by the name of Rúpavatí.

The work professes to be a chapter of a work named Chitraviñs'ati Avadána.

Beginning. ॐ नमः श्रीसर्व्वबुद्धबोधिसत्त्वेभ्यः। ॐ नमः श्रीमहाबुद्धाय।

आकाशनिर्म्मलीभूतो निष्पपञ्चगुणाश्रयः।
पञ्चस्कन्धात्मकः शान्तस्तस्मै भूपात्मने नमः॥
अथाशोको महीपालः सद्व्रताचरणोत्सुकः।
उपगुप्तं गुरुं नत्वा भूयः प्राह कृताञ्जलिः॥
नानावाक्यं प्रजानासि श्रुधं तत् भगवन् प्रभो।
शृङ्गभेरीति नामेयं स्तूपचैत्यविधिं कथां॥

शृणु राजन् महाविज्ञ गुरुणा मे यथोदितं ।
शृङ्गभेर्य्याः फलञ्चापि लक्षचैत्यविधिं तथा ॥

End. शृङ्गभेर्य्यावदानं ये शृण्वन्ति श्रावयन्ति च ।
ते सर्व्वे सुखिनो भूत्वा प्रयान्ति सुगतालये ॥
तत्रापि सर्व्वेषां संबुद्धाः सकलाः सदा ।
कृपादृष्ट्या समालोक्य कुर्व्वन्तु भद्रमाभवं ॥

Colophon. इति श्रीचित्रविंशत्यवदाने लक्षचैत्यव्रतशृङ्गभेरीकथा समाप्ता ॥

No. B, 29.

S'RIṄGABHERI'VRATA'VADA'NA.

शृङ्गभेरीव्रतावदानं ।

Substance, Nepalese paper, 10 × 4½ inches. Folia, 19. Lines on a page, 10. Extent in ślokas, 450. Character, Newárí. Date, N. S. 848. Appearance, old. Prose and verse. Incorrect.

An amplified version of the story given in the last preceding notice. The work professes to be a part of the Vratávadána-málá.

Beginning. ॐ नमो रत्नत्रयाय । आकाशनिर्म्मलीभूतो निष्प्रपञ्चो निराश्रयः ।
पञ्चभूतात्मकः शान्तस्तस्मै भूपात्मने नमः ।
अशोको व्यजिज्ञपद् गुरुमुपगुप्तं । लक्षचैत्यव्रतकथा श्रुता शृङ्गभेरीकथा श्रव-णीयाधुना श्राव्या । इति विज्ञाप्यमानोपगुप्तोऽशोकमकथयत् । शृण्वशोक साधु च सुष्ठु च मनसि कुरु । बुद्धो भगवान् शाक्यसिंहो गृध्रकूटपर्व्वते विजहार एकस्मिन् समये सार्द्धमर्द्धत्रयोदशभिर्भिक्षुशतैः । ततस्तत्र चतुरार्य्यसत्यकथनानन्तरं शारी-पुत्रेण भिक्षुणा परिपृच्छ्यमानोऽभ्यकथयत् शृङ्गभेरीप्रशंसनं । समाकर्णयाशोक ।

End. शृण्वन्ति श्रावयन्ति प्रमुदितमनसः कायवाक्चित्तशुद्धाः कुर्व्वन्ति स्तूपबिम्बार्च्चन-मभिलषितं प्राप्नुयुस्त्वापवर्गं । यस्मात्शोकोपगुप्तोप्युपदिशति ; ततोऽशोकराजोपि-श्राद्धी यात्रां कर्त्तुं महार्घां कृतगुरुप्रणतिः पाटलीपुत्रमागात् ।

Colophon. इति व्रतावदानमालायामशोकोपगुप्तसम्भाषणायां शृङ्गभेरीव्रतावदानं समाप्तं ।

No. B, 21.

SUCHANDRA AVADÁNA.

सुचन्द्रावदानं ।

Substance, Nepalese paper, 11½ × 4 inches. Folia, 15. Lines on a page, 7. Extent in slokas, 300. Character, Néwárí. Date, N. S. 245. Appearance, old. Verse. Incorrect.

A story in praise of the Vasudhárá rite. Suchandra, a man of great wealth and numerous progeny, was engaged in commerce, and some of his children held high offices under government. His youngest son was very vicious; he lost his share of the patrimony by bad speculations in loans, and by the advice of a wicked man stole two bricks from a chaitya, and placed them at the entrance of his room. This was followed by fraternal feuds, loss of wealth, and total dispersion of the family. Suchandra wished to go and see the Lord, but he had nothing at home wherewith to buy fit offerings for him. His wife found a bit of iron chain at the mouth of a rat-hole. With this he bought a few flowers, and repaired to the Lord. The Lord, gratified by his devotion, directed him to perform the Vasudhárá rite, whereby he regained his former wealth and influence, and prospered in every way. The rite should be undertaken on the 3rd of the wane in the month of Bhádra, or of Mágha, and repeated every month for a year. The rite consists in bathing in a river, putting on clean clothes, filling a pitcher with pure water over which the mantra of Vasudhárá has been repeated, placing the pitcher on *kus'a* grass spread on a pure spot, and then worshipping in the pot the goddess Vasudhárá. At the same time the mantra of Vasudhárá should be worn as an amulet on the person, and reverentially repeated many times and duly worshipped every morning, noon and evening. The charm begins with the words *Om! namo bhagavate vajradhare ságaranirghosha tathágate, &c.*

Beginning. ॐ नमः श्रीवसुधारायै । कौशाम्बीति च विख्याता पुरी चासीन्मनोरमा ।

देवनागमनुष्यैश्च पूर्य्यमाणा महीयसी ।
तत्रादित्यकुलोद्भूतो धर्म्मपालो महीपतिः ।
महिषी महाश्रीनाम्ना रूपवती स्मृता ॥
तस्मिन्नेव पुरे रम्ये सुचन्द्रो गृहनायकः ।
दारा चन्द्रवती तस्य गुह्यकेश्वरसन्निभः ॥
महाधनी महाधान्यो महाभागो महामतिः ।

बहुपुत्रो बहुभृतो बहुजनपरावृतः ॥
सुवर्णमणिमुक्तादिसर्व्वरत्नसमन्वितः ।
सितपीतादिरक्तादिनानावस्त्रसमन्वितः ॥
हस्त्यश्वगोकुलापन्नो वणिजां वणिजोत्तमः ।
चतुराशासमुद्रान्तं प्रख्यातः स महामतिः ॥
देवाग्निगुरुसमातिथ्यं पितृयज्ञन्तथैव च ।
नित्यमेवार्च्चितं तेन चैत्यविम्बार्च्चनं पुनः ॥
क्रयविक्रयकार्य्येषु उदारोदानकर्म्मसु ।
वाणिज्यकृषिकार्य्येषु पाशुपाल्येषु सूत्तमः ॥
अथ खलु पुत्रान् नियोजयति ज्येष्ठपुत्रो महाशयः ।
मध्यमो गृहे दक्षो व्यवहारे कनिष्ठकः ॥
नियुज्य पुत्रपौत्रांश्च व्यापारेषु समन्ततः ।
किञ्चिद्वार्द्धातिसम्पन्नः सदारो निलयाश्रितः ॥

End. सुचन्द्रो गृहपतिः परिपृच्छत्यपि आनन्दावधारय। सर्व्वधनधान्यहिरण्यसुवर्णरत्न- निधानमित्यपि धारय ।

Colophon. इति सुचन्द्रो गृहपतिः पृच्छति श्रीवसुधाराव्रतसर्व्वविधानं भगवता शाक्यमुनिना तथागतेन भाषितं समाप्तं ॥

No. B, 31.

SUGATA AVADA'NA.

सुगतावदानं ।

Substance, Nepalese yellow paper, 13 × 3¾ inches. Folia, 54. Lines on a page, 6. Extent in ślokas, 550. Character, Newárí. Appearance, old. Verse. Incorrect.

Stories relating to an ancient Buddha named Vasubandhu.

CONTENTS: (I.) When Lord S'ákya Siṅha sojourned on the crest of a hill named Kaṇakagiri, he was, one day, seen engaged in the performance of the Samádhi called *Lokasandarsana* or survey of the universe, and in course of it a flame issued forth from between his eyebrows. This flame enlightened twenty-eight thousand Buddhist sacred places, and the inhabitants of hell all came up to behold the wonder. Greatly surprised at this, Maitreya enquired of Maṇjus'rí the cause of it.

Manjus'rí replied that in former times there lived a Tathágata, named Varaprabha, who first performed this Samádhi, and after it he bestowed the perfect Bodhi knowledge to millions, and converted king Ajita and his eight sons, and seeing that S'ákya now performed the same Samádhi, he too will expound the same religion. (II.) After performing the Samádhi, S'ákya invited Maitreya and related to him the story a king named Indraprishtha, who reigned at Gandhavatí, in the Uttara Videha country. This king once dreamed that Vasubandhu, a Bodhisattva, was seated on a throne in his court, and expounded the Buddha religion. Thereupon he invited that saint from the town of Vikrama, in the Vihára country. (III.) On the arrival of the saint, the king solicited of him the true means of salvation. The instruction given by the saint comprised mercy to creation, abstinence from theft, cruelty, concupiscence, &c. (IV.) The king then enquired how it was that some people became rich, others poor; some learned, others stupid; some healthy, others diseased; some went to heaven, others to hell; and so forth. The saint replied that these were the results of former works. It was through the deserts of former works that beings were born as gods, mammals, birds and insects, and experienced the fruits of their own actions. Those who, through ignorance, fear, cupidity, or enmity, kill animals go to the hell called sanjíva, while those who kill wild animals by setting fire to forests repair to the burning hell called *Tapana*. (V.) On the other hand those who, keeping the three jewels foremost before them, sow the seeds of virtue, never suffer from disease, decay, distress, and grief. The three jewels are the ever-felicitous, the undecaying, the all-pervading spiritual home of Jina. On the king enquiring how the three jewels could be kept foremost, the saint dilated on the merits of establishing Viháras and Chaityas, and consecrating therein the emblems of the jewels. (VI.) He then dwelt upon the characteristics of the Sañgha, and on the merit of employing well-born, well-behaved, well-disposed, intelligent youths to the service of the Sañgha. (VII.) The saint then repaired, along with the king, to Benares to establish Viháras there. (VIII.) The king invited Bodhisattvas and other saintly personages to be present at Benares on the occasion of his establishing Viháras. (IX.) The reception of the guests at Benares. (X.) The feast given to them. (XI.) On the merits of presenting particular articles to Tathágatas. (XII.) On prayers addressed by the king to the guests, and his return home.

Beginning. नमः श्रीशाक्यमुनये ।

विहरति कनकाङ्गो शाक्यसिंहो मुनीन्द्रो-

ऽपरिमितसुरसंघैः सेव्यमानो जनौघैः ।

कुवलयदलनेत्रो लक्षणैर्युक्तगात्रः

स भवनिधितटस्थः सर्व्वलोके हितस्थः ॥

सार्द्धं द्वादशभिर्भिक्षुशतैः पारमितां गतैः ।

कृतकृत्यैर्वशीभूतैः सर्व्वज्ञज्ञानकोविदैः ॥

निःक्लेशैराजनेयैस्तैः क्षीणास्रवजितेन्द्रियैः ।

तद्यथा ज्ञानकौण्डिल्यनदीकाश्यपनन्दनैः ॥

उपनन्द-सुनन्दाद्यैरन्यैश्च श्रावकैर्गणैः ।

अपरैर्बोधिसत्त्वैस्तु धर्म्मचक्रप्रवर्त्तकैः ॥

मैत्रेयप्रमुखैः सार्द्धमशीत्या च सहस्रकैः ।

विंशत्या देवपुत्रेण सहस्रेणाष्टवेन च ॥

सार्द्धं देवाधिपेनैव चन्द्रसूर्य्यादिना तथा ।

चतुर्भिश्च महाराजैरनेकैः परिचारकैः ॥

सार्द्धं द्वादशभिर्ब्रह्मकायिकैश्च सहस्रकैः ।

अष्टाभिश्चाधिराजेन्द्रैर्बहुलैः परिवारकैः ॥

किन्नरेन्द्रैश्चतुर्भिश्च बहुगन्धर्व्वमण्डितैः ।

अथ श्रीभगवान् तैस्तैः सुवीच्यमणिमण्डितैः ॥

सिंहासने समुच्छ्राये पूर्णेन्दुरिव भासयन् ।

पर्षद्भिर्भगवांस्तेन समयेन चतसृभिः ॥

पुनः पुरस्कृतस्ताभिः सत्कृतो मानितोऽर्चितः ।

लोकसन्दर्शनं नाम समाधिं विदधेऽथ सः ॥

End. देवा नागाश्चरोयक्षाः किन्नराश्च महोरगाः ।

गन्धर्व्वा गरुडश्चैव स्वस्थाने समागताः ॥

जग्मुर्द्देवाः सुमेरौ त्रिभुवननमितं शाक्यसिंहं प्रणम्य

गन्धर्व्वा मण्डलाग्रेऽथ दितिसुतगरुडा ब्रह्मशक्रेन्द्रकृष्णाः ।

कैलासं सिद्धविद्याधरहयवदना मानुषा यक्षवर्गा

नागा पातालभूमौ प्रमुदितमनसो वीतरागादिदोषाः ॥

No. B, 20.

SUKHA'VATÎ-VYU'HA.

सुखावतीव्यूहः ।

Substance, Nepalese paper, 13 × 4 inches. Folia, 37. Lines on a page, 7. Extent in ślokas, 500. Character, Newárí. Date, ? Appearance, old. Prose and verse. Incorrect.

Description of a transcendentally pure and auspicious region called Sukhávatí. When the lord was at Gṛidharakúṭa hill, near the town of Rájagṛiha, A'nanda asked the Lord for an account of the great Tathágatas who had, in former ages, acquired the most perfect organs. The Lord in reply said, one of the earliest was Dipaṅkara, next to him Pratápaván, next Gandha, and next Lokes'vara. During the ministry of the last a Bhikshu, named Dharmákara, expressed a desire that of should be a Tathágata in a region where life was long, where there was no hell, no suffering, no disease, no ignorance, and no evil of any kind. This prayer was fulfilled, he attained perfection, and lived in the region of Sukhávatí, where the presiding Buddha was Amitábha, so named because there was no limit to his effulgence. The region is full of gardens, flowers, singing birds, lakes and everything that could make up the beau-ideal of perfection in the estimation of the Buddhists.

This work was translated into Chinese by Hiouen Thsang of the Tang dynasty; its Chinese name is Tching-tsan-seng-t'o-fo-shih-shau-king. Beal's Catalogue, p. 24.

Beginning. ॐ नमः श्रीसर्व्वबुद्धबोधिसत्त्वेभ्यः ।

नमो दशदिगनन्तापर्य्यन्तलोकधातुप्रतिप्रतिष्ठितेभ्यः । सर्व्वबुद्धबोधिसत्वार्य्यश्रावक-बुद्धेभ्योऽतीतानागतप्रत्युत्पन्नेभ्यः ॥

नमोऽमितान्ताय नमोऽचिन्त्यगुणोत्तरात्मने ।

नमोऽमितप्रभाय जिनाय ते मुने ।

सुखावतीं यामि तवानुकम्पया ॥

सुखावतीं कनकविचित्रकाननां ।

मनोरमां सुगतसुतैरलङ्कृतां ।

तथा चाश्रयां प्रथितयशस्यधीमतः ॥

प्रयामि तां बहुमणिसञ्चयां ।

एवं मया श्रुतमेकस्मिन् समये भगवान् राजगृहे विहरति स्म । गृध्रकूटपर्व्वते महता भिक्षुसंघेन सार्द्धं इत्यादि । अथ खल्वायुष्मानानन्द उत्थायासनादेकांशमुत्तरासङ्गं कृत्वा दक्षिणं जानुमण्डलं पृथिव्यां प्रतिष्ठाप्य येन भगवांस्तेनाञ्जलिं प्रणम्य भगवन्तमेतदवोचत् । एवमेव भगवता विप्रसन्नानि इन्द्रियाणि ।

End. इदमवोचद्भगवानात्तमना अजितो बोधिसत्त्वो महासत्त्व आयुष्मानानन्दः सा च सर्व्वावती पर्षत् सदेवमानुषासुरगरुडगन्धर्व्वलोका भगवतो भाषितमभ्यनन्दन्निति । भगवतोऽमिताभस्य तथागतस्य गुणपरिकीर्त्तनं बोधिसत्त्वानामवैवर्त्तभूमिप्रवेशः अमिताभस्य परिवर्त्तः सुखावतीव्यूहः सम्पूर्णः ।

No. B,

SUMA'GADHA' AVADA'NA.

सुमागधावदानम् ।

Substance, palm leaves, 12 × 1¾ inches. Folia, 22. Lines on a page, 6. Extent in ślokas, 350. Character, Newárí. Date, ? Appearance, old. Prose. Incorrect.

Story of Sumágadhá, daughter of Anáthapiṇḍada, a rich banker of S'rávastí. The young lady had been given in marriage to Vṛishabhadatta, son of Sus'íla, a banker and rich householder of Puṇḍravardhana. When dwelling with her husband, she was once asked if she knew of any very great teacher in existence. She said, "Yes, I know the Lord Buddha, bright as the champaka flower, and of profound learning; he is now dwelling in my father's garden, and is the greatest on earth." She then spoke in high praise of the saint. Vṛishabhadatta asked her, "Can you show him to me?" Sumágadhá replied, "Collect, sir, the materials for a good feast, and I shall show him to you."

She then repaired to the top of the house, drew a circle on the roof towards the side where the Lord was, and, respectfully offering a handful of flowers and a little water, said, "O thou most merciful, deign to favour me with thy presence!"

Through the miraculous influence of the Lord, the flowers and the water rose high in mid-air, and like a flight of geese passed on westwards for six hundred and forty miles and fell at the feet of the Lord at the Jetavana garden. The Lord received them very graciously. On the following morning, along with Ajṇátakauṇḍinya, S'áriputra, Maugha, Mahákás'yapa and others among his chief disciples, the Lord miraculously passed on through the sky, and appeared at midday before his devotee. Sumágadhá worshipped him with every mark of respect and veneration, and entertained his retinue with lavish hospitality. The people of Puṇḍra-vardhana crowded round the Lord, and received benedictions and advice. One of the congregation asked how it was that the Lord was so merciful to Sumágadhá ? and in reply the Lord said, this is not the only occasion when he had been so, he had been so before. In the 20th Kalpa, when men lived for a thousand years, Kás'yapa was the Buddha. He dwelt in the Deer Park at Benares. At that time Kṛiki was the reigning king, whose daughter was named Káṉchanamálá. The king dreamt some unpleasant dreams, and the expounders of dreams in his court recommended that the flesh of the most prized being on the earth should be given away in a feast to avert the consequences of the evil dreams. This implied Káṉchanamálá, who was the most beloved being in the kingdom, and the king could not listen to such a proposition. "Rather" said he, "that I should die immediately, or lose all my kingdom, than allow any evil to befal my dearest daughter." The king's grief brought the daughter to the place, and she advised that her father should abide by the advice of the Lord Kás'yapa. The king did so, taking Káṉchanamálá with him. Kás'yapa expounded the dreams, and assured him and his daughter that no evil would befal them.

Tho Bhikshus then enquired what was the cause of Káṉchanamálá's having been born with a chaplet of jewels on her head ? Thereupon the Lord said in a former life the lady, born as a poor woman, had respectfully offered an iron garland to the Chaitya of a Pratyeka Buddha, and through the merit thereof had been blessed to be born with a chaplet, and she who was the poor woman, was born as Káṉchanamálá, and was now born as Sumágadhá.

A different version of this story occurs in the Avadána-śataka, *ante*, p. 73.

Beginning. ॐ नमो बुद्धाय। बुद्धो भगवान् सत्कृतो मानितः पूजितो राजभी राजामात्यैर्धनिभिर्धनैः श्रेष्ठिभिः सार्थवाहैर्देवैर्नागैर्यक्षैरसुरैर्गरुड़ैर्गन्धर्वैः किन्नरैर्महोरगैरिति देव + + + + सुरगरुड़गन्धर्वकिन्नरमहोरगाभ्यर्चितो बुद्धो भगवान् ज्ञातो महापुण्यो लाभी चीवरपिण्डपातशयनासनग्लानप्रत्ययभैषज्यपरिष्काराणां संश्रावक-श्रावस्त्यां विहरति स्म।

End. इदमवोचद्भगवानात्तमनास्ते च भिक्षवो ,बोधिसत्त्वाः सा च सर्वावती पर्षत् सदेवमानुषासुरगरुड़गन्धर्वांश्च लोको भगवतो भाषितमभ्यनन्दन्निति।

No. B,

SUPRABHATA-STAVA.

सुप्रभातस्तवः ।

Substance, Nepalese paper, 10 × 4 inches. Folia, 88. Lines on a page, 7. Extent in ślokas, 700. Date, N. S. 932. Appearance, old. Verse. Incorrect.

A collection of 49 hymns by different authors in praise of S'ákya and other Buddhas and saints. The hymns are addressed to—1, Das'abala; 2, S'ákya as bhaṭṭáraka, by Yaśodhará; 3, the mercy of Avalokiteśvara; 4, Dharmadhátu; 5, Mahábuddha; 6, on the feet of Avalokiteśvara; 7, Dharmadhátu, in another measure; 8, Vágís'vara; 9 Buddha; 10, the ten guardians of quarters; 11 Buddha, in another measure; 12, Avalokites'vara, by Rájá Pratápamalla; 13, Chaitya of Dharmadhátu; 14, Sáradá; 15, For redemption from hell; 16, Vajramahákála; 17, Devás' 100 names; 18, Five Tathágatas; 19, Vajrayoginí; 20, Váṇí; 21, Avalokites'vara's rosary; 22, Prayer to Avalokites'vara; 23, Ananta, the Nága king; 24, Lokes'vara; 25, Avalokites'vara, by Chandradantá; 26, Ditto, by Chandriká Bhikshuṇí; 27, Mahábuddha, in another measure; 28, Dharmadhátu; 29, Mañgalá; 30, Vásukí, the Nága king; 31, Lokes'vara; 32, Ditto for redemption from hell; 33, Ditto; 34, Avalokiteśvara as the dweller of Pátála; 35, Buddha on the discomfiture of Mára; 36, Names of the Nakshatras; 37, Ditto of the signs of the Zodiac; 38, Ditto of the Yátrás; 39, Ditto of Yogas; 40, Ditto of the six Páramitás; 41, Sixteen stanzas on Adhyeśvara; 42, 14 stanzas on the diagram called Vajradhátu; 43, 25 ditto on Dharmadhátu; 44, 10 ditto on the knowledge of the original; 45, 44 ditto on perception; 49, 34 ditto on affection; 47, 25 ditto on gratitude; 48, 5 ditto on the 5 Tathágatas; 49, Verses addressed by S'ákya to Mañjus'rí.

Beginning. ॐ नमो बुद्धाय । ॐ नमो धर्म्माय । ॐ नमो संघाय ।

स्तुतमपि सुरसंघैः सिद्धगन्धर्व्वयक्षदिविभु

विबुधविधिज्ञैः स्तोत्रमाविकासिसै ।

अहमपि तवशक्ति नौमि संबुद्धमार्गे

नभसि गरुडयान्ति किं न यान्ति द्विरेफाः ॥ १ ॥

क्षयितदुरितपक्ष चीणनिः शेषदोष द्रवितकनकवर्णे

स्थूलपद्मायताक्ष सुरुचिर परिवेता सुप्रभामण्डलश्रीः

End. दृग्रवक्ष नवमित्यं सुप्रभातं प्रभातं ॥ २ ॥

No. B, .

SÚRYAPRAJNAPTÍ-ṬÍKÁ.

सूर्य्यप्रज्ञप्तिटीका ।

Substance, Nepalese paper, 10 × 4 inches. Folia, 223. Lines on a page, 15. Extent in ślokas, 5,000. Character, Nágara. Date, ? Appearance, old. Prose. Generally correct.

A commentary on a work on the motions of the sun and the moon, on the increase and decrease of the durations of days and nights, and on other astronomical phenomena. By Malayagiri.

Beginning. ॐ नमः सर्व्वज्ञाय ।

यथास्थितं जगतसर्व्वमीक्षतेऽदः प्रतिक्षणं ।
श्रीवीराय नमस्तस्मै भास्वते परमात्मने ॥ १ ॥
श्रुतकेवलिनः सर्व्वे विजयन्तां तमश्छिदः ।
येषां पुरो विभान्तिस्म खद्योता इवतीर्थिकाः ॥ २ ॥
जयति जिनवचनमनुपमसज्ञानतमः समूहविध्वंसि ।
शिवसुखफल कल्पतरुं प्रमाणनयभङ्ग सवङ्कलं ॥ ३ ॥
सूर्य्यप्रज्ञप्तिमहं गुरूपदेशानुसावतः किञ्चित् ।
विवृणोमि यथाशक्तिस्पष्टं स्वपरोपकाराय ४ ॥

End. इति श्रीमलयगिरिविरचितायां सूर्य्यप्रज्ञप्तिटीकायां विंशतितमं प्राभृतं समाप्तं ।

वन्दे यथास्थिताशेषपदार्थं प्रतिभासक ।
नित्योदितं तमोस्पृष्टं वेने सिद्धान्तभास्करं ॥ १ ॥
विजयन्तां गुणगुरपे जिनतीर्थनाशनैकपराः ।
यद्वचनगुनाद्ऽमपिलेशेन प + + ङ्किः ॥ २ ॥
सूर्य्यप्रज्ञप्ति मिमां अतिगम्भीरा विवृन्वता कुशल।
यदवाप मलयगिरिणा साधुजनस्तेन भवतु कृती ॥

No. B. 9.

SUVARṆA-PRABHA'SA.

सुवर्णप्रभासः ।

Substance, paper, 15½ × 3½ inches. Folia, 84. Lines in each page, 6. Date, ? Extent in ślokas, 1,845. Character, Newárí. Appearance, old. Incorrect. Prose and verse.

The philosophy of Nihilism developed in the course of describing the merits of a certain mystic formula named Suvarṇa-prabhásottama. The codex is incomplete, and comprises only the first twenty chapters, each of which is called a *parivarta.* The work was translated into the Chinese language by Dharmatatsin of the northern Liang dynasty (circa, 502—565 A. D.), and published under the name of Kin-kwong-ming-king. The Chinese have also an abstract of this work in two volumes under the name of Kin-kwong-ming-wan-ku. (Beal's *Tripiṭhaka*, pp. 15 et 99.)

Contents, I.—Once on a time the Lord was residing on the Gṛidhrakúṭa hill, when Lakshmí, Sarasvatí and other goddesses sat around him. Many Devas, Nágas, Yakshas, and Rákshasas were also present. The Lord was contemplating on the essence of religion (धर्मधातु), which is perceptible only to the profoundest of Buddhas. A'nanda asked him as to what were the religious duties of Bodhisattva congregations. The Lord said, "whoever hears, preaches, sympathises with, or honours the great sútra Suvarṇaprabhásottama, obtains the substance of all Samádhi residing in the breasts of the purest of Bodhisattvas, and is followed and protected by the gods with great attention." He then, by way of enumerating the benefits to be derived from the mantra, gave a summary of the work under notice.

II.—When the Lord was on the aforesaid hill, Ruchiraketu, a Bodhisattva, was at Rájgṛiha. He had worshipped millions over millions of Buddhas. The germ of everything good was ingrained in his soul, and he had a thorough knowledge of all the doings of ancient Buddhas. All of a sudden a strange thought crossed his mind—"How is it," thought he, "that S'ákya Muni should live for eighty years only?" Thus musing he was startled at the sudden transformation of his cell into a splendid drawing-room studded with gorgeous gems of different colours. Four jewelled thrones were seen on the four sides of the room, with four great Buddhas seated on them. High on the eastern throne sat Akshobhya; on the southern Ratnaketu; on the western Amitáyuh; and on the northern Dundubhis'vara. Other Tathágatas, too, were there.

The brilliancy of their persons illuminated the whole city of Rájagṛiha, and extended even to the loftiest of the three thousand great regions. Now the sight of the blind was restored; the deaf gained the power of hearing; memory was restored to those that had lost the balance of their mind. Astonished at this transformation, Ruchiraketu, saluated his celestial guests, but still remained musing on the short span of S'ákya Muni's life. The Buddhas, perceiving his anxiety, addressed him in the following manner, : "O thou of noble birth, do not think that there is any one under the sun, who can measure the length of S'ákya Muni's life. We know of no such person. It is easier to count the individual drops which fill the ocean, than to measure the long period of his existence. No one can form an idea of the period of a Jina's life."

Then Devaputras of all conceivable forms, Yakshas, Nágas, Gandharbas, and Bráhmaṇas, such as Kauṇḍilya and others, made their appearance in the assembly. They had heard the sound of S'ákya Muni's great Nirváṇa. Kauṇḍilya fell at the Lord's feet, and asked of him a boon. The Lord remained silent. Then a scion of the race of Litsa, Sarvasattvapriyadarshana by name, with a presence of mind miraculously obtained, answered for the Lord. He told Kauṇḍilya that he was authorised by the Lord to grant him any boon that may be asked. Kauṇḍilya asked for a very small fraction of the elements of which the Lord's body was composed, to the extent even of a mustard seed, in order that he might worship it when the Lord would be away, and, thereby obtain the lordship of heaven. He said he knew that the Suvarṇa-prabhása Sútra would ensure that; but it was extremely difficult even for the S'rávakas and Pratyeka Buddhas to learn it, and so there was no easy method of obtaining the sovereignty of heaven, except the worship of the lord's elements. The Litsakumára replied to him in the following terms: "The smallest fraction of the Lord's elements, even to the extent of a mustard seed, would be recreated at a time when flowers of their own accord would cross the stream of the Ganges, when crows would grow red and cuckoos white, when the blackberry would grow to the size of a palm fruit, and date trees would bear the blossoms of mangoes." Ruchiraketu and the congregation were glad to perceive from this that the duration of S'ákya Munis' life was immeasurable.

III.—Ruchiraketu dreamt a dream. He saw a kettle-drum made of gold, and bright as the sun, and assemblages of numberless Tathágatas and a Bráhmaṇa sounding it. He heard the gáthá they were chanting in harmony with the sound of the drum. Awakening from his sleep Ruchiraketu proceeded to the lord at the Vulture peak and prayed.

IV.—The prayer of Ruchiraketu was as follows:

"Let the drum of Suvarna-prabhása scare away the mundane pains of all sorts from the three thousand regions! May the people of this world be relieved from pains arising from vice, as well as those who dwell in the region of Yama! May they also be relieved from penury!"

V.—The Lord related an anecdote to the family divinity (Kuladevatá), of Bodhisattvas. He said, there lived in former days a king named Bhujendra, who prayed all the Tathágatas present, past and future, in the following manner: "I salute the Jinas; I shall worship the Jina-sañgha; I shall worship the tranquil, the pacified, the pure, the great Muni, radiant with the lustre of gold."

VI.—The Lord continued, "The principles of the absolute negation of existence have been explained at length in various Sútras. They are, as a matter of policy, now published in an abridged form, so that all creatures may learn how the body is nothing more than a deserted village. I now instruct you in the means of acquiring the knowledge of Nihility. The senses are like theives in a battle-field. They know not each other, though they are in the same village. The sense of vision is running after form alone, that of audition after sound, that of smell after smell, of taste after taste, and of touch after touch. The fickle mind busies itself only with enjoyable objects. The mind, dwelling on the senses which are like theives in a battle-field, is never after the deserted village. The human body to which the senses adhere is insentient—unsubstantial. It owes its origin to the residua of former perceptions. This material frame which creatures obtain in consequence of their doings in former existences is full of sputum, urine, fæces and worms. It is thrown away as a piece of wood at the end of life. Nonentity is the origin of everything. All animals and all the attributes of things have their origin in perception, through Avidyá or false notions. These attributes are sometimes existent, and sometimes non-existent. Therefore it is my opinion that these attributes are founded on deceptive perception. Rend asunder, O Bhikshus, with the sword of true knowledge, the feeling, the six senses, the form, the name, the knowledge and notion, and hold fast the attribute of Bodhi which is grand non-existence."

VII.—The Lord explained in the course of his conversation with Vais'ravaṇa, Dhṛitaráshṭra, Virúdhaka, and Virúpáksha, the four great

Mahárájas, the merits of hearing, reading, and bearing on the person the great Sútra Suvarṇa-prabhása.

VIII.—The goddess Sarasvatí, covering one of her shoulders with her outer garment, and placing her right knee on the ground, with folded hands asked the Lord's permission to wind up the net of illusions, spread round the chanter of the sutra (Dharmmabháṇaka), to grant him the Dháraṇí, and to show him the light of true knowledge. "I shall," said she, "restore the words or consonants that may have dropped from the great Sútra. I shall grant him the Dháraṇí that his memory may not fail. I shall teach him the mode of holy bathing which will enable the great Sútra to endure for a long time on earth, sowing the seeds of immense good, which will enable numberless creatures to cultivate their intellect, to learn various S'ástras, and to acquire immense merit." The ritual of the bathing is thus given. Orris root, yellow orpiment, *Trigonella corniculata*, Sirisha, and *Accacia suma* should be pounded when the Pushya asterism is on the ascendant, and a mystic formula is to be repeated a hundred times during the operation. Then a circle is to be drawn with cowdung, and the powder above described, with pearls, flowers and honey, is to be placed in it in a golden vessel. Four righteous men and girls with suitable decorations are to be employed on the spot. The fume of fragrant resins and the consort of five musical instruments are indispensable to the ceremony. The golden vessel is to be decorated with parasols, standards and flags. Its boundaries are to be set by the recitation of the mantra *Ake nayane hili hili gile khile sváhá*. Then the votary is to bathe, believing in the Lord, and chanting the following mantra: Sugate bigate Vigatávati, &c. "When a reciter, or hearer, or a writer of the Suvarṇa-prábhasa will have bathed in the aforesaid manner, I shall," said the goddess, "for his good remain with the Devas in the sky, and sweep away all sorts of diseases and distempers from his neighbourhood." So saying the goddess sat aside. The Lord praised her determination, and Kauṇḍilya extolled her good intentions.

IX.—Mahádeví saluted the lord, and said, "I shall also, my Lord, serve such a Bhikshu. He shall be supplied with beds, cushions, vestments and alms-bowls. Those who will listen to the great Sútra will remain in the enjoyment of terrestrial and celestial happiness for millions and millions of kalpas. Wherever Ratna-kusumaguṇaságara-vaidúryya-kaṇaka giri-suvarṇa-káṇchana-prabhása-s'rí, a Tathágata, went, and wherever he cast his eyes, there all creatures obtained affluence at my-hands. He shall be worshipped. I shall, by the power of the great mantra Suvarṇa-prabhása, increase the wealth of those that read it. Therefore those who desire wealth, should remember the following mantra—Pratipúrṇavare samantagate, &c.; and prosperity will certainly present herself at the instant when in a vihára, or a forest, cushions, aromatics, flowers, &c., are placed in the midst of a circle made of cow-dung to his honour.

X.—Mantras for the adoration of Tathágatas.

XI.—Dṛiḍhá, the presiding goddess of the earth, then offered to make the country prosperous in which the great mantra would be either known or preached. The Lord was very glad. He said "Any creature who would hear a line, nay a word, of the great mantra shall, after death, be born in the Trayastriñs'a and other celestial regions.

XII.—Sanjaya, the commander-in-chief of the Yakshas, who had twenty-eight great leaders under him, then offered to protect any one who would learn, or even hear one verse, nay one hemistich, of the great mantra Suvarṇa-prabhása. He offered not only to protect him, but also to make him prosperous.

XIII.—When the Lord was on the Gṛidhrakúṭa hill, Baladaketu asked his son Ruchiraketu, after he was anointed king, "do you know the science of government known as Devendrasamaya?" Then, without waiting for a reply, he proceeded, saying, "I learnt it from my father Varendra. Brahmendra first promulgated it on the mount Vajraprákára. Those kings are partial incarnations of the thirty-three Devarájas who protect the good and punish the vicious, and thereby establish virtue and destroy sin. No king should overlook crime, as such conduct is certain to increase vice, produce fraud and dissension, and court invasions from foreign powers. No king should displease the gods, for when the gods are angry, epidemics, bereavements, and invasions are sure to follow. Kings should be impartial, for if they have a predilection for sin, many will follow their example, cheating and fraud will increase, and the kings will be doomed to perdition. Therefore, my son, govern the kingdom according to the rules of the Devendra-samayarája Dharma." The principles of good government are detailed at considerable length.

XIV.—Susambhava was a king when Ratnas'ikha was the Lord of the earth. His capital was Jinendraghosha. Once he saw in a dream Ratnochchaya, a reciter of religion, reciting the great Sútra. He awoke, went in search of him, and found him repeating the great mantra in his house. The king heard it, and was purified.

XV.—Whenever a householder, or a woman of family, may be desirous of obtaining the knowledge of Buddhas, past, present and future, and of worshipping the Lord, he or she should hear and preach the great mantra Suvarṇa-prabhása.

XVI.—Bodhisattva-samuchchaya, a Kuladevatá, asked the Lord why the ten thousand Devaputras headed by Jvalanánanta were instructed by the Lord in the Bodhi knowledge immediately on their arrival at the monastery from the Trayastriñsa heaven? Three of these obtained the knowledge of perfect Bodhi. In one of the innumerable past kalpas, a good man named Ruchiraketu flourished in the region named Suvarṇaprabhásita, and there obtained perfect knowledge. Suvarṇaratnákarachhatrakúṭa and Suvarṇajambudhvaja-káṇchanábha flourished in succession in the region called Virajadhvaja. They preached and established the good religion in that region. After the demise of the last, a young man, named Rupyaketu, obtained the knowledge. But none of these Devaputras ever renounced the world, nor were they proficient in the six páramitás, how was it then that they were able to acquire the knowledge? The Lord said they were votaries of Suvarṇa-prabhása, and that was the secret of their success.

XVII.—In one of the innumerable past kalpas a Tathágata, named Ratnas'ikha, was born. After his demise, when the good religion was renounced by men, there was born a king, named Sures'varaprabha. He had a banker named Jaṭindhara, a man well versed in the knowledge of the pulse and of all the branches of the science of medicine. He had a son named Jalaváhana, who was very handsome and accomplished. During the reign of the irreligious king Sures'varaprabha his subjects were afflicted with various diseases. The only medical assistance procurable was from Jaṭindhara, who was extremely old, blind, and unable to move a step without support. Jalaváhana was deeply afflicted by the sufferings of these men. He learned the science of medicine from his father, and then cured his neighbours of their disorders.

XVIII.—Jalaváhana had two sons, Jalámbara and Jalagarbha, by his only wife Jalámbugarbhá. When he was passing in company with his sons by a tank inhabited by ten thousand fishes, it was on the point of being dried up. The presiding deity of the tank half discovering herself before the physician, implored his assistance to protect the lives of the fishes. Jalaváhana, finding no water in the vicinity, plucked leaves and branches, and threw them on the water, so that the small quantity of water in it may be protected from the scorching heat of the sun. He found at a great distance a river named Jalágamá; but he was sorely distressed for want of means to convey the water. At last he succeeded in procuring twenty elephants from the king Sures'varaprabha. By the help of these elephants he filled the tank with water, and supplied the fishes with plenty of food. When the fishes were made all comfortable, Jalaváhana, standing knee deep in the water, offered a prayer to the Lord, and begged that whoever hears the Lord's name at the time of death may be born in the Trayastriñsa heaven. With this prayer he repeated the mantra—Namastasmai bhagavate ratna-śikhiṇe, &c. He then taught the fishes some of the most abstruse doctrines of the Buddhist religion, and returned home. The fishes died that very night, and were born in the aforesaid heaven. Sures'varaprabha, in one of his subsequent existences was Daṇḍapáṇi, Jaṭindhara was S'uddhodana, Jalámbugarbhá was Gopá, Jalaváhana was the Lord himself, Jalámbara and Jalagarbha were Ráhula and Ánanda. The ten thousand Devaputras with Jvalanánanta for their chief, who were blessed with the Sambodhi knowledge, were the fishes that had heard the name of the Lord Ratnas'ikhi from the Lord, and the divinity of the waters was the goddess Bodhisattva Samuchchayá, at whose request the Lord gave the above explanations.

XIX.—A Bodhisattva should sacrifice his own body for the good of others. The Lord in the course of his perambulation through the country of the Páṉchálas, entered a forest. He sat upon a grass plot, and struck the earth with the palms of his hands and the soles of his feet. Thereupon a great stúpa made of gold, rubies, sapphires and precious stones rose like an aparition. The Lord ordered Ánanda to open the doors of the stúpa. Ánanda opened them, and found bones covered over with jems. The Bhikshus honoured them with salutation at the command of the Lord, and then the Lord, at the request of Ánanda, gave the following history of the holy bones. "There lived formerly a king named Mahâratha. He had three sons, Mahápráṇada, Mahádeva and Mahasattvaván. The king went to the forest. Rambling about his sons chanced to come to a secluded part of the forest. There they found a tigress who had by her side good looking cubs about seven or eight days old, but she looked sorely distressed for want of food, for she seemed to have had none since their birth. Mahádeva asked, "who is there that can sacrifice his ownself for this poor tigress, so famished, and in so much distress."

Mahásattvarán replied, "It is indeed difficult for us, self-seeking, narrow-minded mortals, to sacrifice ourselves for the good of others; but to great minds who are bent upon doing good to others at any risk, it is a task of no great difficulty." So saying he thought within himself that a better opportunity for offering his body, so full of impurities, in the cause of others, might not arrive in the course of his life. So musing he bade adieu to his brothers, and offered his body to the tigress. His mind was full of hope. He thought he would obtain Bodhi knowledge, have sympathy for all, and prove the means of saving millions from dangers of the mundane life. The tigress recognised a great Bodhisattva in him, and did not touch his body. The Bodhisatva thought the tigress was too weak to kill him, and so, cutting his own throat with a piece of bamboo, fell before her. She despatched his flesh and blood almost in no time. The princes were surprised at the spirit of self-sacrifice that actuated their brother, and went admiring home to tell the mournful news to their father. The whole royal family was in mourning, and came to the spot where lay the earthly remains of the magnanimous soul. After loud lamentations, the king caused the bones to be buried in golden boxes, and raised a stúpa upon them.

"I am, O Ánanda, the prince Mahásattvaván. I obtained by means of these bones the great Bodhi knowledge which nothing can equal."

XX.—Then a large number of Bodhisattvas, with folded hands, praised Suvarṇa-ratnákara-chhatraketu in the following words: "Thou hast, O Lord, sacrificed thy body which was more brilliant than gold. Thy limbs are shining gold. Thou art as it were a golden mountain." Then Ruchiraketu praised the Lord in the following terms: "Thou art the true one, O great Muni. Thou hast on thee the signs of a hundred merits. Thou hast a thousand beauties. Thou art adorned with various accomplishments, &c., &c.

XXI.—This chapter opens with an address by a Kuladevatá, but the concluding part of it is wanting.

Beginning. ॐ नमः सर्व्वबुद्धबोधिसत्त्वेभ्यः। नमः श्रीभगवत्यै आर्य्यप्रज्ञापारमितायै। तद्यथा, श्रुति स्मृति गति विजय स्वाहा। श्रुतं मयैकस्मिन् समये गृद्ध्रकूटे तथागतो विजहार धर्म्मधातौ गम्भीर बुद्धगोचरे। बोधिसत्त्वसमुच्चयया महाकुलदेवतया

सरस्वत्या महादेवतया श्रिया च महादेवतया इडया च महापृथिवीदेवतया हारीत्या च महादेवतया। एवम्प्रमुखाभिर्महादेवताभिरनेकदेवनागयक्षराक्षसगन्धर्व्वासुरगरुडकिन्नरमहोरगमनुष्यामनुष्यैः सार्द्धं। अथायुष्मानानन्दो भगवन्तमेतदवोचत्। किन्नामायं भगवन् धर्म्मविनय भविष्यति इति।

End. अथ भगवानासनादुत्थाय ब्रह्मस्वरेणावोचत। साधु साधु कुलदेवते आज्ञां ददामि साधु ते कुलदेवते कुलदेवते पुनश्च साध्विति। इदमवोचद् भगवानात्तमनास्ते च बोधिसत्त्वा बोधिसत्त्वसमुच्चया कुलदेवता सरस्वती महादेवी प्रमुखा। अतःपरं समाप्ति सूचकवाक्यानामभावः॥

No. B. 19.

SVAYAMBHÚ-PURAṆA.

स्वयम्भूपुराणः।

Substance, paper, 17 × 4½ inches. Folia, 163. Lines on each page, 8. Extent in ślokas, 5,055. Character, Newárí. Date, ? Apparently old. Verse. Incorrect.

A poetical account of the manifestation of Svayambhú or Ádi Buddha in Nepal, and of the origin of that country. The work belongs to the class called *Vyákaraṇa* or descriptive, and is written principally in the Anushṭup metre, as Puráṇas usually are. There seem to exist, or to have existed, two recensions of the work, one an abridgment (*laghu*), and the other the full or elaborated one (*vṛihat*). The codex under notice contains the latter. It is divided into eight chapters, and extends to five thousand s'lokas. Its author is Manjus'rí, who lived in the early part of the 10th century. In every detail the work is a counterpart of the Hindu Máhátmyas, of which so many are affiliated to the Hindu Puráṇas, and, like them, is strictly local in character, being unknown beyond the limits of Nepal. According to Hodgson the work has the alternative name of Sambhu Puráṇa. It appears not to have been translated into the Chinese language.

Contents: Chapter I.—The scene is laid in the Bodhimaṇḍapa at Buddha Gayá, and the principal interlocutors are the Bodhisattvas Jayas'rí and Jines'vari. The latter, desirous of attaining the *Bodhisamvara* (a religious observance leading to Bodhi knowledge), asks the former as to the best means for its attainment. The former advises him to have recourse to the Poshadha ceremony,* which should be performed in a place of pilgrimage, in a Vihára, in the temple of Sugata, in a chaitya, or in any place honoured with the image of a Buddha. "But the best place for its performance," says he, "is Svayambhú-kshetra, where its performance is invariably attended with the best results." Questioned about the origin of the place Jayas'rí relates what, he said, he had heard on the subject as related by Upagupta to As'oka. According to this account this sacred place is situated on the crest of a hill called Gosṛiñga. In the Satya Yuga it was called Padmagiri, on account of its have borne five lotuses made of jewels. In the Tretá age it was called Vajrakúṭa, because it was the abode of holiness. In the Dvápára epoch it was called Gos'ṛiñga, because it had the appearance of a bull's horn. In the present Kali age it is called Gopuchchha, because it is long like a cow's tail. Svayambhú is kept concealed under stones, in order that bad men in this sinful age may not destroy the pure element of religion. A chaitya has been raised over the place where he lies hidden.

Once on a time S'ákya Muni, after showing various miracles to all creatures at Jetavana, went to the mountain of Svayambhú. Devas, Gandharvas, Yakshas, etc. came to welcome him. They honoured him with profuse worship. He saw Svayambhú and the chaitya over it studded with gems, and having a golden wheel attached. Maitreya questioned him about the origin of Svayambhú. In reply, the Lord told him that he was, in the Bhadra Kalpa, when the life of men lasted for eighty thousand years, born as Satyadharma, the son of Bandhumān, the king of Bandhumatí, His mother obtained Buddhahood. He became a disciple of Vipas'yí, who used to live under a Páṭalá tree. There was at that time a large square lake measuring 7 croshas, and named Kálíhrada. The author then gives a long account of the merits of this lake.

Chapter II.—After the emancipation of Lord Vipas'yí there was a king named Aruṇa, in the city of the same name. His son S'ikhí obtained Buddhahood, and the Lord was his disciple under the name of Kshemarája. It was at that time that a lotus was found to spring up in the Kálíhrada. It was as large as the wheel of a chariot. It had ten thousand golden petals. It had diamonds above, pearls below, and rubies in the middle. Its pollen consisted of jewels. Its seed-lobes were gold, and stalks lapis-lazuli. In its centre sat a crystal figure, one cubit high. That figure was Svayambhú.

* Cf. ante, p. 111.

III.—In answer to the question of Maitreya as to the period when Kálíhrada dried up and became dry land, the Lord said, "After the Nirvána of Lord S'ikhí, when man's life extended to sixty thousand years, there was a celebrated king. His son Vis'vabhú performed a great Samádhi under a S'ála tree. He obtained Bodhi knowledge. He had a disciple in Parvata, a celebrated king. Lord Vis'vabhú, in company with Parvata and all his disciples, came to visit the shrine of Svayambhú. At this time there arrived Manjudeva, the king of the mount Manjus'rí in China, with two of his wives, Varadá and Mokshadá. The mount Manjus'rí was anciently known as Panchas'írsha, from its having had five peaks made of diamonds, sapphires, emeralds, rubies and lapis-lazuli respectively. Manjudeva, finding the tank full of monstrous aquatic animals, and the temple of Svayambhú almost inaccessible, opened with his sword many of the valleys on the southern side of the lake. He opened the valleys of Kapotala, Gandhavatí, Mṛigasthali, Gokarṇa, Varaya, and Indrávatí in succession. The waters of the lake rushed through these openings, leaving dry land at the bottom. Manjus'rí excavated a lake at the south of Gandhavatí, and the side of Kálíhrada was made into a mountain by throwing mud on it. He then excavated on the top of the mountain a lake named Padmagiri. Its site is called Upachhanda, which is one of the ten most sacred Píṭhas. It has a temple of the goddess Khagánaná.

IV.—In the next kalpa, when man's life extended to four thousand years, after the Nirváṇa of Lord Vis'vabhú, a Brahmáṇa, named Krakuchchhanda, was born in the city of Kshemávatí. He performed austerities on a grass plot under a s'irísha tree (*Acacia sirisa*), and obtained Bodhi knowledge. The Lord was one of his disciples under the name of Jyotihpála. Krakuchchhanda preached the good religion to all creatures. He remained for some time in Padmagiri, in Nepal, and then proceeded with all his disciples to the inaccessible peak of the S'aṅkhagiri. In one of the largest of its caves he preached the good religion. He found that a number of Bráhmaṇas, with Guṇadhvaja for their chief, a number of Kshatriyas with Abhayandada for their chief, and many Vais'yas and S'údras, eager to obtain the Bodhi knowledge. After their heads had been shaved and nails pared, he made them enter the Pravrayá. To them the Lord pointed out the rules of Poshadhavrata. The votary should every day implore the protection of the three jewels Buddhamaṇḍala, Dharmamaṇḍala, and Sanghamaṇḍala. He should salute his spiritual guide, and honour the Buddhas in all the ten quarters. The acceptance of anything not given, conduct contrary to the rules of Brahmácharya, drinking, dancing, singing, flower wreaths, perfume, unguents, ornaments of gold and silver, high bedsteads, and untimely meals are forbidden to a Bhikshu when engaged in this rite. Incontinence is specially reprehensible. A Bhikshu who fails in the observance of these rules is doomed to perdition. If he succeeds in their observance, he obtains the five experiences, *viz.*, divine vision, divine audition, the knowledge of other's thoughts, remembrance of previous existences, and the power of working miracles. Then he preached the thirty-seven virtues. These are, four causes of memory, four Samprahánkas, four points of miracle, five senses, five strengths, seven accessories to Bodhi, and eight secondary means.

The Lord then expounded the 27 virtues relating to Pukodhi. These are: 1st, The four causes of memory including the causes of the memory of matter, of feeling, of mind, and religion. 2nd, The four Samprahánakas, including the protection of merit already produced, production of new merits, destruction of prosperity, and the production of prosperity. 3rd, The four miraculous powers, including the superhuman power in meditation, in cogitation, in the settlement of points in dispute, and in strenuous exertion. 4th, The five senses including reverence, wisdom, concentration of mind, memory, and strenuous exertion. 5th, The five strengths including the power to emancipate, to protect, to meditate, to pardon, and to know. 6th, The seven accessories to Bodhi, including memory, accumulation of merit, love, exertion, purity, concentration, and resignation. 7th, The eight secondary means including perfect vision, perfect resolution, perfect speech, perfect work, perfect living, perfect exercise, perfect memory, and perfect concentration. A Bhikshu should abstain from the following ten vicious acts; viz., killing animals, accepting things not given, deception, wilful misrepresentation, wickedness, cruelty, prevarication, spiritual ignorance, mischievous intention, and false vision.

The Lord Krakuchchhanda spoke in high terms of the river Vágmatí which is as holy as the Gañgá, and which was produced from certain drops of waters which fell from the fingers of Tathágatas by the superhuman power of Vajrasattva. Then Vajrasattva, by the order of the Lord, threw half the quantity of the hair and parings of nails of the Bhikshus who had been ordained there, on the top of the mountain S'añkha, and lo, there came into existence a river named Kes'ávatí, emersion in the water of which washes away all sorts of sins arising out of anger, envy and folly. The other half of the hair and parings of nails were thrown on the top of the mount S'añkha, and it remained there, and looked like a large number of chaityas.

After the departure of the Lord Krakuchchhanda from Nepal, Svayambhú produced eight Vitarágas, or holy men who had mastered their passions. They exist there, and grant happiness and prosperity to all creatures. These are, (1) Maṇiliñges'vara, who grants increase of longevity to men. He lives in the vicinity of the valley on the river Maṇichúḍá. This river was anciently Rohiṇí. It derives its present name from Lord Maṇichúḍá's granting the jewel from his head to his suitors, on its banks. (2) Gokarṇes'vara, in Gokarṇa on the Vagmatí, where it falls from the mountain; he grants increase of fame. (3) Kítes'vara, on the crest of the mountain Cháru in the vicinity of Svelahrada; he grants increase of merit. (4) Kumbhes'vara, in Kumbhatírtha; he grants increase of knowledge. (5) Phaṇigarttes'vara, in Phaṇigartta on the Godavarí; he grants increase of happiness. (6) Phaṇilinges'vara, in Joytirlinga; he grants increase of fame in the valley of Phaṇis'itá. (7) Gauḍhes'vara, on the peak of Gandhavati; he grants increase of wealth. (8) Vikrames'vara, near the river Vikramasthalá; he grants increase of progeny. Thus, by the power of Svayambhú and Maṇjudeva, villages, cities and capitals were founded from the crest of the mount S'añkha down to the Chintámañitírtha. The country has a rectangular shape. It is bounded on the north, by the Vágmatí, on the east by the Kes'avatí, on the south by the mountain S'añkha, and on the west by Rágumañjarí. Dharmakara, a king of China, was anointed its king, and he governed it wisely as his own kingdom.

V.—The Lord gave the following enumeration of the holy places for ablution in, or near, the Vágmatí river, ḍetailing the meritorious consequences of bathing in them. (1) In the Vágmatí there is a serpent named Raktánga. (2) At the confluence of the Vágmatí with the Máradáraka is S'ánta-tírtha, which cures diseases. (3) At its confluence with the Maṇirohiṇí is S'añkara-tirtha, emersion in which brings health and peace. (4) At its confluence with the Rájamaṇjari is Rája-tírtha, emersion in which gives health and regal power. (5) At the confluence of the Kes'vatí with the Vimalávatí is Manorama-tirtha; and the serpent Karburakulis'a of that place grants clothes, &c. (6) At the confluence of the Kes'ávati with Bhadrá is Nirmala-tírtha, and the serpent Upanálaka of the place is the destroyer of sin. (7) At the confluence of the Kes'avatí with the Svarṇavatí is Nidhánaka; the serpents Nanda and Upananda of which place grants wealth and corn. (8) At the confluence of Kes'avatí with Pápanáśiní is Jṉána-tírtha; the serpent S'vetasubhranága of that place is the giver of happiness. (9) The confluence of the Kes'avatí and the Vágmatí is known as the Chintámaṇi-tírtha, and the serpent Váruṇa of that place fulfils all human desires. (10) The confluence of the Vágmatí with the Ratnavatí is known as the Ramodaka-tírtha. The serpent Padma of that place grants love and enjoyment. (11) The confluence of the Vágmatí with the Chárumatí is known as Sulakshaṇa-tírtha. The serpent Padma of this place is the granter of fortune. The confluence of the Vágmatí with the Prabhávatí is known as Jaya-tírtha, which grants wealth and beauty and destroys enemies.

Then the Lord proceeded to give the names of twelve other places of pilgrimage of a secondary character. They are resorted to on particular conjunctions (yogas.) These are, (1) Análiṅga; (2) Maṇis'ilá; (3) Gotrávalí; (4) Nadikrikaṇṭha; (5) Mátá; (6) Machchhamukha; (7) Hláti; (8) Navaliṅga; (9) Kákes'vara; (10) Techápa; (11) Vágís'vara; (12)—The merits of bathing in these tírthas are the same as those of the pools mentioned before. There are other holy bathing places. For instance the cataract of the Vágmatí named Darí. There is a she-serpent named Sundarí at Darí who fulfils all desires. On particular conjunctions the worship of Agastya, after bathing in the lake of the same name, conduces to the welfare of men. The worship of Ananta, on certain conjunctions like the Kumbha Saṅkránti, after the emersion in the lake Ananta, adds to wealth. The worship of Tárá, after bathing in the lake Tárá on the day of Vṛisha Saṅkránti, fulfils human desires. The worship of Avalokites'vara after emersion in the river Kapotará, which takes its rise from the opening of Kálíhrada, saves human souls from perdition. The ten lords of the ten quarters, Bráhma, Kṛishṇa with Rádhiká and other milkmaids went on pilgrimage to these tírthas.

VI.—Maitreya asked the Lord why was Svayambhú called Vágís'vara, and how the place became the abode of Devas and holy places? The Lord said, "In ancient times in the Bhadra Kalpa, when man's life extended to thirty thousand years, Kanaka, the son of the priest of the king of Sobhávatí, obtained Buddhahood under a Dumbílya tree, under the name of Sudharmarája. I was then a disciple of Kanaka. Lord Kanaka went with all his disciples to Nepal on pilgrimage to Svayambhú. Just at this time, a Bhikshu, named Dharmas'rímitra, came to Nepal with a view to proceed to China to learn from Manjudeva the explanation of the Námasañgíti and the meaning of the twelve letters. In his northward journey from the temple of Svayambhú he chanced to meet a cultivator driving his plough drawn by a tiger and a lion. The farmer welcomed him, requested him to halt with him for a night, and then to proceed to China which was, he said, a year's journey from the place. Then he caused the tiger and the lion to disappear in order to produce in the stranger's mind the impression that the land was ploughed by gods. This piece of ground so ploughed is called Jnánabhúmi. Dharmasrímitra had come to the mount Manjus'rí, the Nepalese residence of Manjudeva, where in the morning he discovered his host to be no less a person than Manjudeva himself. The wonder of the Bhikshu knew no bounds. Manjudeva, as a preliminary to his obtaining the explanations, made him perform the ceremony of Abhisheka in the following manner: The essence of Svayambhú was a circle. A circle was drawn with a radius of either one or ten or a thousand cubits measuring two spans each. It was decorated with eight squares of various colours. It had many openings. The Bhikhsu sat at the centre of the circle, and performed worship, contemplating in his mind the picture of Manjudeva with his wives. After the ceremony was over, Manjudeva instructed him in the explanation of the Námasañgíti, and initiated him in the mysteries of the twelve letters. The twelve letters are compounds of आ, á and ई í. By means of these letters all languages, all s'ástras, and even the Vedas are produced."

VII.—Why was Svayambhú concealed under stones, and who raised the chaitya for Svyambhú? In answer to these questions the Lord gave the following explanation: "In that very Bhadra Kalpa when man's life extended to twenty thousand years, Kas'yapa, the son of a learned Bráhmana of Váránasí, obtained Buddhahood under a pipal (Nyagrodha) tree. From Lord Kas'yapa the city of Váránasí is called Kas'í. I was then, under the name of Jyotirája, a disciple of Kas'yapa. Lord Kas'yapa went to Nepal to worship Svayambhú. Thence he went to Sumeru, where he was greatly honoured by Indra and other gods and goddesses. From Sumeru his journey was extended to Trayastriñs'a, where he preached the good religion to his mother, and he ultimately chose it for his residence. Manjudeva, in company with his wives, who may be compaired to Kes'iní and Upakes'iní, desirous of keeping constant company with the Lord, left his material frame behind, and in a celestial form proceeded to Trayastriñs'a. The place where his ashes fell is known as Patachchaitya or the Falling Temple. Devas and Asuras, who were on the mount Puchchhágra, called it Puchchhágra chaitya.

In the walled city of Gauḍa which had only one gate, Víravatí was the presiding diety. Prachaṇḍadeva, the king of Gauḍa, having abdicated his throne in favour of his son S'aktideva, devoted himself for a long time to the service of the goddess Víravatí. The fame of Svayambhú Kshretra as a holy place reached him there. He at once directed his steps towards the place. He renounced the world, and became a Bhikshu, under the name of S'ántikara. A short time before this, Vajrasattva, fearing that wicked men in the Kalíyuga, would steal away the jewels of Svayambhú and destroy his image, concealed him under a slab of stone. S'ántikara saw Svayambhú lying concealed. He placed a large piece of precious stone upon it, which Vajrasattva perforated in thirteen different places, so that any offerings in gold and silver may fall on Svayambhú's head, like so many flowers. Vis'vakarmá, at the request of the S'ántikara, built a chaitya upon it. A chaitya was also raised on the remains of Maṉjudeva on the mount Puchchhágra. The residence of Maṉjudeva was also honoured with a similar chaitya. S'ántikara consecrated all these chaityas. He also built five temples. (1) In the first of these he placed the image of Mahávíra, the giver of peace and final beatitude. This temple, facing the east, and extending from north to south, had only one entrance, and was divided into five apartments. (2) The second temple was situate to the south-east of the temple of Svayambhú. It was called Vasupurí, and was dedicated to Vasundhará, the giver of plenty. (3) To the south-west of Svayambhú was the temple of Váyupurí, dedicated to Váyu, animal sacrifice to whom frees one from transmigration into a bird's life. (4) The fourth was the temple of Agnipurí, sacred to Agni, by offering flesh and wine to whom one escapes from fire. The fifth temple was Nágapurí, consecrated to Varuṇa and other Nágas, by offering the five productions of a cow (Panchagavya) to whom a man attains peace and health, and gets copious rain. S'ántikara placed the images of the following gods all round the place. On the south of S'ántípura he placed Prithubhairava; to the east of Svayambhú Abhairavabali; a short way down the hill to the east, Tejobhairava; to the south-west of the mountain, Váyubhairava; to the west of the mountain, Khabhairava; to the east, S'únyabhairavạ; to the west of Svayambhú, Háritídeví facing the east; to the east of the mountain Ekanága, in the centre Kálínága. Two Ganes'as were placed in the forest region on the mountain, one facing the south, the other facing the west. Beyond these, at the foot of the mountain, were placed four circles (Maṇḍalas—Buddhist railings?)

VIII.—There was a continuous drought for seven years in Nepal. The drought brought on a famine. The people were dying of starvation. At the request of the king Guṇakáma, S ántikara undertook to allay the famine. He drew the figure of a lotus with eight petals, and invoked the Nágas. They came. In the centre of the lotus sat Varuṇa, of a white colour, with two hands and seven hoods. On the eastern petal came the blue coloured Ananta; on the southern petal, Padmaka of the colour of a lotus stalk, with five hoods; on the western petal, the saffron coloured Takshaka, with nine hoods; on the northern Vásukí, green, with seven hoods; on the south-west S'ankha, green; on the north-west Kullka, white, with thirty hoods; on the north-east the gold-coloured Mahápadma with as many hoods. But the blue coloured Karkaṭa, who was to have sat on the south-eastern petal, did not come. At the command of S'ántikara king Guṇakáma brought him, against his will, from his retreat in the Lake Ádhára to the south of the Gandhávati, by main force. S'ántikara worshipped these Nágas, and they sent a copious shower. S'ántikara, with the blood extracted from the bodies of serpents, painted the figures of these Nágas as seated on a lotus, and placed the picture in a city, named Nágapura, founded on the occasion, and consecrated it. The worship of the Nágas in this form was declared to be an antidote to famines and droughts. The Nágas were then dismissed, and Nepal was blessed with copious rain and plenty. Guṇakáma, in his old age, abdicated his throne in favour of his son Narendra, and renounced the world. By constantly worshipping Svayambhú and S'ántikara he obtained, after death, the blessed region named Sukhávati. S'ántikara performed a meritorious Samádhi named Ásphálana, and, excavating a large cave, a Yojana in extent, to the east of S'ántipura, remained there, like Gayas'írsha, having in his left hand the jewel named Chintámaṇi, the giver of food and clothing at the holder's desire, and in his right hand the waterpot named Chintámaṇi, having a tree of the same name behind him. The cave was known as Guṇagartta. It is a holy place; it grants wealth and prosperity; and one is sure to obtain success and attain final beatitude by repeating sacred mantras here. It is still the belief in the neighbourhood that S'ántikara rose again from his meditation as Vajrasattva, and preached the religion which alone can grant final beatitude.

The Lord gave the following account of the future condition of Nepal: "There will arise in the east, on the north-east of Káles'vara, on the trunk of a Champaka tree, a golden Lokes'vara, named Hariváhana, facing the west. Bráhmaṇas and others will worship him under the name of Náráyaṇa. Long after this, there will arise on the Vágmatí, in the valley of Mugasthata, a Lokes'vara, the subduer of the three regions, facing the south surrounded by Hari Hara, Hiraṇyagarbha and others. Him the people will worship under the name of Pas'upati. Long after that, during the reign of Yakshamalla, there will arise a Lokanátha in the place of Yamales'vara. For in the future there will arise on the Gandhavatí, to the south of Gandhes'vara, a red coloured Lokes'vara, named Khasarpa, facing the north. Later than that, during the reign of Narendradeva, there will be a continuous drought extending over a period of twelve years. Narendradeva will worship the Lokes'varas by the advice of Bandhudatta. He will bring Lokes'vara from the mount Kapota, and perform the ceremony of drawing the car. When the S aiva religion will be introduced in Nepal there will be a famine. The names here given clearly show that the Purána is not more than four or five hundred years old.

Mr. Hodgson has given a connected and interesting narrative taken from the Svayambhú Purána, of the origin of Nepal in his 'Essays,' pp. 115. But the standpoint from which he surveyed his subject was different from mine, and his version contains several short extracts which I have omitted.

Beginning. ॐ नमः स्वम्भवे ज्योतीरूपाय

ॐ नमो बुद्धाय धर्म्माय संघरूपाय वै नमः ।
स्वयम्भुवे विपद्धान्तभानवे धर्म्मधामवे ॥
भवार्णवसमुद्धारकारुण्यागारमूर्त्तये ।
जगदाह्लादरूपाय नमोऽस्तु स्वम्भवे सदा ॥
अस्ति नास्ति स्वरूपाय ज्ञानरूपस्वरूपिणे ।
शून्यरूपस्वरूपाय नानारूपाय ते नमः ॥
ब्रह्मेन्द्रादिगणैर्देवैर्दानवैः फणिभिस्तथा ।
विद्याधरै राक्षसैश्च यक्षैः किन्नरमानवैः ॥

मुनिभिर्भिक्षुभिक्षुणीराजन्यैर्वैश्यजैस्तथा ।
शूद्रादिभिर्जनैः सर्व्वैर्वन्दिताय च सर्व्वदा ॥
रागद्वेषसम्मोहादिनानादुःखविदारकं ।
सर्व्वलोकसमुत्तारं धर्म्मधातुं सदा भजे ॥
धर्म्मधातुर्जगन्नाथः सद्धर्म्मदेशको गुरुः ।
घोरसंसार उत्तारः पायाद्वः पावनं पदं ॥
श्रूयतां परया भक्त्या धर्म्मधातुसमुद्भवः ।
सर्व्वपापविनाशार्थं सर्व्वकामफलार्थिभिः ॥

End. ततःप्रभृतिकालेऽत्र अन्यजा अनजा अपि ।
पञ्चोपचारविधिभिः सदा तस्य प्रपूजितं ॥
प्रतिदिन प्रतिमास प्रतिपर्व्व मुदा सदा ।
तत् पुराणं प्रतिश्रुत्य श्रीस्वयम्भोश्च पूजितं ॥
तिथौ सुमङ्गलवरे शुभपूर्णयुक्ते स्वर्गेऽपि उष्णीषपदे सुरलोकश्रेष्ठः ।
शम्भोः पुराणमद्भिमां प्रतिश्रुत्य यत्नात् संतिष्ठते बुद्धगुणे सुगुणेन भुषः ॥

Colophon. इति श्रीस्वयम्भूचैत्यभाट्टरकोद्देशे महाप्रभाववर्णनो नामाष्टमोऽध्यायः परिसमाप्तः ।

No. B. 33.

TA'RA'SHṬOTTARAS'ATA-NA'MA-STOTRA.

ताराष्टोत्तरशतनामस्तोत्रम् ।

Substance, Nepalese paper, 7½ × 22 inches. Folia, 7. Lines on a page, 5. Extent in ślokas, 70. Date, ? Appearance, old. Verse. Incorrect.

One hundred and eight epithets strung together in the form of a hymn in praise of a goddess named Ekajaṭá A'rya Tárá or simply Tárá, who is the counterpart of the Hindu goddess of the same name. The hymn is alleged to have been imparted by Avalokita Bodhisattva to Vajrapáṇi Bodhisattva, and is intended to be worn as an amulet to avert evils proceeding from thieves, war, fire, lions, water, elephants, tigers, noxious animals generally, and other causes. Bhikshus were much exposed to these in their peregrinations, and Vajrapáṇi wanted a ready means of overcoming them. It is obviously an imitation of Hindu hymns of the kind, of which there are a great many extant. The Hindus usually prefer 108 to 100 epithets. The Muhammadans have also several hymns of the same kind. They call them in Arabic الاسماء الحسنى or "the most comely names of God." The number of epithets employed by them is 33, 99, or 990, according to the number of beads in their rosary. The usual number is 99.

Beginning. ॐ नमः श्रीएकजटा आर्य्यतारायै।

श्रीमत् पात + + + रम्ये नानाधातुविराजिते।
नानाद्रुमलताकीर्णे नानापक्षिनिकूजिते॥
नानानिर्झरसंस्कारे नानामृगसमाकुले।
नानाकुसुमजातिभिः समन्तादधिवासिते॥
नानाहृद्यफलोपेते षट्पदोद्गीतनिस्वने।
किन्नरैर्मधुरोद्गीर्णे मत्तवारणसङ्कुले॥
सिद्धविद्याधरगणैर्गन्धर्व्वैश्च निनादिते।
मुनिभिर्वीतरागाद्यैश्च सततं सुनिसेविते॥
बोधिसत्त्वगणैश्चान्यैर्दशभूमीश्वरैरपि।
आर्य्यतारादिभिर्दिव्यैर्विद्याराजसहस्रशः॥
क्रोधराजगणैश्चान्यैर्हयग्रीवादिभिर्वृतः।
सर्व्वसत्त्वहितो युक्तो भगवानवलोकितः॥
विजहार ततः श्रीमान् पद्मगर्भतले स्थितः।
महता तपसा युक्तो मैत्रीव कृपयान्वितः॥
धर्म्मं दिदेश तस्यान्तः महत्यां देवपर्षदि।
तत्रोपविष्टमागम्य वज्रपाणिर्महावरः॥
परमकृपयायुक्तं पप्रच्छ सोऽवलोकितः।
तस्करोरगसिंहाग्नि गजव्याघ्रादिसङ्कटे॥
खादन्त्यमी मुने सत्त्वा मग्नाः संसारसागरे।
बद्धाः संक्रूरकैः पाशैः रागद्वेषतमोमयैः॥
मुच्यन्ते येन संसारात् तन्मे ब्रूहि महामुने।
एवमुक्तो जगन्नाथः सर्व्वमानवलोकितः।
उवाच मधुरां वाणीं वज्रपाणि प्रबोधिनीः॥

End. प्रीतिमान् स महावाग्मी सर्व्वशास्त्रविशारदः।
कल्याणमित्रः संसेवी बोधिचित्तविभूषितः।
सदा विरहितो बुद्धैर्येन यत्रोपपद्यते॥

Colophon. इति आर्य्यताराभट्टारिकाया नामाष्टोत्तरशतकं बुद्धभाषितं परिसमाप्तं॥

No. B. 22.

TATHA'GATA-GUHYAKA *alias* GUHYA-SAMAGHA.

तथागतगुह्यकः ।

Substance, paper, 12 × 3 inches. Folia, 118. Lines on each page, 5. Extent in ślokas, 1,100. Character, Newárí. Date, N. S. 919. Appearance, old. Prose. Corrupt.

A ritualistic work belonging to the class Tantra, and treating of various esoteric rites and mantras, dwelling largely on the peculiar marks that are characteristic of the body of a Tathágata, and on various forms of meditation. It is written partly in Gáthá verse, and partly in Sanskrit prose, and is divided into eighteen chapters.

As a Tántric composition of the esoteric kind, it has all the characteristics of the worst specimens of S'ákta works of that type. The professed object, in either case, is devotion of the highest kind—absolute and unconditional—at the sacrifice of all worldly attachments, wishes and aspirations; but in working it out theories are indulged in and practices enjoined which are at once the most revolting and horrible that human depravity could think of, and compared to which the worst specimens of Holiwell Street literature of the last century would appear absolutely pure. A shroud of mystery alone serves to prevent their true characters being seen, but divested of it works of the description would deserve to be burnt by the common hangman. Looking at them philosophically the great wonder is that even a system of religion so pure and so lofty in its aspirations as Buddhism could be made to ally itself with such pestilent dogmas and practices. The chapters of the work are, as is usually the case with the Tantras, called *Paṭalas*, and the similitude is carried out in every respect. The first chapter opens with details about various kinds of Samádhi or meditation appropriate for the higher order of the Buddhist clergy. The second gives directions as to the mode in which Buddha is to be reflected upon. The third and the fourth describe various kinds of diagrams and mystical figures necessary to be drawn when engaged in the worship of Buddha. In the fifth are detailed the characteristics and qualifications necessary for a neophyte to undertake certain forms of secret worship, and among the practices enjoined which promote the attainment of perfection, debauchery of the most bestial character, not even excepting mothers, sisters and daughters, is reckoned as most essential.* These are followed by an account of how, during the height of meditation in the case of perfect devotees, the crown of their head bursts open, and rays of light issue therefrom. Certain prayers to be addressed by Bodhisattvas to Bhagaván are also given.

The sixth is devoted to secret mantras, like the Víja mantras of the Tantras, to meditation of mystic diagrams, and to training necessary for such meditation. The most appropriate food for devotees while engaged in this worship is said to be the flesh of elephants, horses and dogs,† to the exclusion of rice. The means of attaining perfection, described in the next chapter, are not to be austerity, privations and painful rigorous observances, but the enjoyment of all the pleasures of the world,‡ and the way in which some of the pleasures are described is simply revolting.§

The eighth opens with a hymn, by Ratnaketu, in praise of Bhagaván, and then gives the ritual of the worship aforesaid. The ninth is devoted to the ritual of the worship of Vajradhara, the diagrams, the forms of meditation, and the secret mantras required for the same. The tenth is a dialogue between Tathágata and Vajradhara, in course of which the latter explains the details of adoration with a secret mantra called *Mahá-siddhi-pradáyaka-mantra,* or that which grants the highest transcendental powers. In the next, Tathágata explains the mystery of the sacred syllables *om, áh, hum,* and the uses thereof. This is followed, in the next chapter, by instructions as to the rituals to be observed in performing particular kinds of meditations and the rewards derivable therefrom. All castes and classes are declared to be fit for the performance of such meditations, provided they follow the rules. The subject is continued in the next in which *japa* or silent recitations of mantras of various kinds are enjoined. These recitations may be accom-

* मातृभगिनीपुत्रीश्च कामयेद्यस्तु साधकः ।
स सिद्धिं विपुलां गच्छेन्महायानाग्रधर्म्मेषु ॥ fol. 15.

† हस्तिमांसं हयमांसं श्वानमांसं तथोत्तमं ।
भक्षयेदाहारकृत्यर्थन्न चान्नन्तु विभक्षयेत् ॥ fol. 20.

‡ दुष्करैर्नियमैस्तीव्रैः सेव्यमानो न सिध्यति ।
सर्वकामोपभोगैस्तु सेवयंश्चाशु सिध्यति ॥ fol. 21.

§ भगे लिङ्गं प्रतिष्ठाप्य बुद्धबिम्बं विभावयेत् । fol. 22.

plished by the body (*káyajápa*), by speech (*vágjápa*), by the mind (*chittajápa*), by the passions (*rágajápa*), and by other means.

The fifteenth section is particularly disgusting in its details, as it describes the adoration of Buddha through damsels of twelve years of age, daughters of Chaṇḍálas, dancing women, and other low castes, and by observances of rituals of the most revolting kind. Daily intercourse with daughters of the Chaṇḍála caste in out of the way places is deemed an essential of the highest importance,* and particular stress is laid on their personal charms.† A variety of mantras are given for the purpose of these adorations, and also incantations and charms for curing diseases, for causing hallucination or death, for acquiring superhuman powers, and for other purposes. The mantras are of the usual type, formed of the mystic syllables, *om, hum, hah, ah,* &c. One of these include twenty-three such syllables.

The sixteenth is exclusively ritualistic, giving directions for various kinds of secret worship, and the most appropriate diagrams, mantras, homas, and offerings of various kinds required for them. The oblations to be offered on the homa fire include, among other things, ordure, flesh, oil, &c.‡ The ceremonials described are throughout in the highest degree mystical.

The next two sections are quite as mystical and revolting as the last, but they are not so entirely ritualistic. They are made up of a great number of dialogues between Bhagaván, Vajradhara, Vajrapáṇi, and other Bodhisattvas, in which the esoteric doctrines of the faith are discussed at length, and various duties, discipline, forms, observances, rituals and practices are inculcated. All the ritualistic forms of *dhyána, dháraṇá, mudrá, nyása, sádhana,* &c., of reflection, meditation, gesticulation, regulation of breath, and other manifestations of mummery which characterize the Tántric cult of the Hindus are all faithfully reproduced, and interspersed with hymns, prayers, hallelujahs, &c. Some of these are in themselves of perfectly unexceptionable character. Others, absurd, unmeaning, or stupid as they are, are not in themselves such as to be particularly objectionable. But they are sometimes disfigured by in-

* द्वादशाब्दिकां कन्यां चण्डालस्य महात्मनः ।
सेवयेत् साधको नित्यं विजनेषु विशेषतः ॥ fol. 73.

† चारुवक्त्रां विशालाक्षीं नटीकन्यान्तु शोभनां । fol. 73.

‡ विण्मूत्रमांसतैलाद्यैराहुतिं प्रतिपादयेत् । fol. 78.

junctions which are highly repulsive. Not satisfied with the order given in the last chapter to make offerings of excrementitious matter on the homa fire, the author goes to the length of recommending such substance as human food,* denouncing all repugnance to such articles as sinful,† and enjoining that no food or drink should be taken by a worshipper, which has not been mixed with ordure, or urine, or flesh-meat of some kind.‡ Such injunctions would, doubtless, be best treated as the ravings of madmen. Seeing, however, that the work in which they occur is reckoned to be the sacred scripture of millions of intelligent human beings, and their counterparts exist in almost the same words in Tantras which are held equally sacred by men who are by no means wanting in intellectual faculties of a high order, we can only deplore the weakness of human understanding which yields to such delusion in the name of religion, and the villainy of the priesthood which so successfully inculcates them. No wonder the work was long kept away from Mr. Hodgson on the allegation that it was not available in Nepal, though he at last got it. (*Essays*, p. 49.)

Beginning. ॐ नमः श्रीवज्रसत्त्वाय । एवं मया श्रुतमेकस्मिन् समये भगवान् सर्व्वतथागतकायवाक्चित्तहृदयवज्रयोषिद्भगेषु विजहार । अनभिलाप्य अनभिलाप्यै बुद्धक्षेत्रसुमेरु परमाणुरजः सर्व्वैर्बोधिसत्त्वैर्महासत्त्वैः । तद्यथा, समवज्रेन च नाम बोधिसत्त्वेन महासत्त्वेन । कायवज्रेन च नाम बोधिसत्त्वेन इत्यादि ।

End. इदमुक्त्वा ते सर्व्वतथागतास्ते च बोधिसत्त्वा महासत्त्वाः स्वकाय वाक् चित्त वज्रेषु विचरन्तं कायवाक्चित्तवज्रस्य कायवाक्चित्तं स्वकायवाक्चित्तेनैवालभ्य तुष्णीमभूवम् इति ।

Colophon. इति श्रीसर्व्वतथागतकायवाक्चित्तरहस्याद् गुह्यसमये सर्व्वगुह्यनिर्देशे वज्रज्ञानाधिष्ठाने नामाष्टादशः समाप्तः ।

* समयचतुष्टयं रक्ष बुद्धज्ञानोदधिप्रभोः ।
विण्मूत्रं सदा भक्ष्यमिदं गुह्यं महाद्भुतं ॥ fol. 85.

† विण्मूत्रशुक्ररक्तानां जुगुप्सां नैव कारयेत् ।
भक्षयेद्विधिना नित्यमिदं गुह्यं त्रिवज्रजम् ॥ fol. 91.

‡ अन्नं वा अथ वा पानं यत्किञ्चिद्भक्षयेद् व्रती ।
विण्मूत्रमांसयोगेन विधिवत् परिकल्पयेत् ॥ fol. 92.

No. B. 37.

UPOSHADHA AVADA'NA.

उपोषधावदानम् ।

Substance, Nepalese paper, 12 × 3½ inches. Folia, 37. Lines on a page, 5. Extent in ślokas, 400. Character, Newárí. Date, ? Appearance, old. Prose and verse. Very incorrect.

An account of an optional fast called Uposhadha or Poshadha, (*ante*, p. 111). It is said to have been imparted by S'ákya himself. The work is divided into three chapters. The 1st treats of the history of the fast; the 2nd, its details; and the 3rd, its obligations.

When S'ákya was one day seated under a tree in the Nyagrodha Garden near the city of Kapilavastu, Vás'ishṭha, a Bráhmaṇ of the Vas'ishṭha gotra, came to see him. The Bráhmaṇhad long nails and unkempt beard, and was very much emaciated and weak. Being asked by the Lord why he was so, he replied by saying that he had adopted the mensial fast (*másavrata*) for the attainment of the fourfold blessing, fasting at a time for a month, and that having observed it for a hundred years he had been reduced to his present condition. The Lord said, "your nails and your beard and your abstinence from food for so long a time have not brought you at all near your object. Do you observe the fast of Uposhadha in honour of A'rya Avalokites'vara, and you will at once attain your end." In course of further discussion on the subject, the Lord said that he had acquired adamantine hardness of body by observing the fast. He also narrated a story about two Bráhmaṇs in connection with it. He said in the time of Kás'yapa, when Kṛikí was king of Benares, Paṭuvarmma and Hadivarmma, two Bráhmaṇ youths, saw a procession in the street. and on enquiry learnt that Kṛikí was going to the lord Kás'yapa to hear the merits of the Uposhadha fast. The youths followed, and, having heard the Lord's sermon about it, perfomed the ceremony. By virtue of this fast the elder youth was born under the name of Sujáta, a son of Kṛikí. The other, whose fast was vitiated by neglect in the observance of all the necessary details was born as a Nága. He remembered, however, the circumstances of his former life, and besought Sujáta for help. The king issued a proclamation offering a golden throne to whoever would furnish him with the ritual of the fast. An old woman came forward and said, "break that column before me and you will get the ritual." The column was broken, and at the foot of it was found the ritual, inscribed on a golden tablet. The Nága, having got the ritual performed the ceremony, and was translated to the heaven of Indra, where he was born a god, under the name of Uposhadha.

The proper time for the rite is the 8th of every waxing moon, whence the name *Ashṭamívrata.* A hut having been erected with five kinds of sacred wood, Lokes'vara should be worshipped in it with proper offerings and mantra, the performer observing the purification of the eight members of his body before and after it for a week. Especial merit is attained if particular kinds of articles be presented and particular musical instruments be sounded. The details about these extend to several pages.

The most important abstinence during the performance of the rite is from cruelty to animals, and this is illustrated by a story. A king of Vais'alí and his queen, having performed the rite and thereby obtained a precious jewel, was engaged in giving alms when Indra, having assumed the shape of a Bráhmaṇ, came forward and asked alms. The king said, "Let me know what you want, and it will be given." The Bráhmaṇ named the jewel. The king was greatly distressed at this; but not to break his promise to a Bráhmaṇ he was about to give it, when Indra, assuming the shape of a hawk, darted at the jewel and carried it away. Then in the shape of the Bráhmaṇ, he threw his sword at the bird and killed it The king finding that his jewel was about to be restored to him became glad, but Indra longing to have the jewel and frustrate the king's good word disappeared with it. The king and his country suffered long and grievously for the destruction of the hawk. and the evil was not removed until the king, under the advice of Krakuchchhanda, performed the rite once again.

Beginning. ॐ नमो रत्नत्रयाय । नमः श्रीआर्य्यावलोकितेश्वराय । एवं मया श्रुतमेकस्मिन् समये भगवान् कपिलवस्तुनि महानगर्य्यां स्वच्छनिर्म्मलसुगन्धिसुशीतलस्वादुलघुस्निग्धहृद्यवारिपरिपूर्णपद्मकुमुदोत्पलादिजलपुष्पप्रकाशमानद्युतिरञ्जितपुष्करिणीसम्पन्नन्यग्रोधारामे । तथावरूप (अपरूप) चम्पकवकुलपाटलजातिविटपनानापुष्पसुरभीकृते तस्मिन्नेव वने विहरति स्म । तस्मिन् खलु पुनः समये पञ्चभिर्भिक्षुशतैः षोड़शादिभिर्बोधिसत्त्वगणैस्तानेकैर्देवनागयक्षराक्षसासुरगरुड़गन्धर्व्वकिन्नरमहोरगसिद्धविद्याधरगणैरन्यैरनेकैर्मनुजराजादिभिः परिवृतः । तत्र न्यग्रोधारामे स्फटिकमणिशिलातले निषण्णः । तत्र भगवान् अर्हन् सम्यक्सम्बुद्धो धर्म्मव्याख्यानश्रवणश्रोतृजनपरिषदं दृष्ट्वा उपाख्यानं प्रारब्धवान् । ततस्तस्मिन

खलु पुनः समये तस्मिन्नेव कपिलवस्तुमहानगर्य्यां निवासितो वशिष्ठकुलसम्भवो-ब्राह्मणस्तथागतमर्हन्तं सम्यक्सम्बुद्धं न्यग्रोधारामविहारितं श्रुत्वा धर्म्मश्रवणाय समागच्छति स्म ।

End. प्रतिश्रुत्य स वशिष्ठो भगवतो वचनं मुदा ।
मुनेः पादौ नमस्कृत्य स्वगेहे च समागतः ॥
देवासुरमनुष्येश्च प्रणिपत्याजस्त्रं मुदा ।
देवनागासुरोयक्षाः किन्नराश्च महोरगाः ॥
गन्धर्व्वा गरुडाश्चैव स्वस्वगेहं प्रत्युद्गताः ।
प्रययौ भगवान्नाथ संविहारं मनोरथं ॥
सङ्घेन महता सार्द्धं दर्षैात्फुल्लितलोचनः ।

Colophon. इति श्रीमदार्य्यावलोकितेश्वरस्य सुगतवाशिष्ठसंवादे मानमत्तजदोषनिर्णयनामावदानं तृतीयोऽध्यायः ।

No. B. 51.

USHṆÍSHAVIJAYA DHÁRAṆÍ.

उष्णीषविजयनामकधारणी ।

Substance, Nepalese paper, 7 × 3 inches. Folia, 4. Lines on a page, 5. Extent in ślokas, 50. Character, Newárí. Date, ? Prose. Incorrect.

A mystic mantra bearing the name of Ushṇíshavijaya, a Bodhisattva. It begins with the words *Om krum krum krum sodhaya, &c.* It was imparted by Buddha Amitáyúh to Avalokites'vara. It is specially efficatious in curing diseases and prolonging life.

Beginning. ॐ नमो भगवते आर्य्यउष्णीषविजयाय । एवं मया श्रुतमेकस्मिन् समये भगवान् सुखावत्यां महानगर्य्यां यां धर्म्मसङ्गीतिमहागुह्यप्रासादे भवने विहरति स्म । सुखाप्रतिष्ठितो भगवान् अमिताyुस्तथागतो आर्य्यावलोकितेश्वरो बोधिसत्त्वमहासत्त्वानामन्त्रयते स्म । शान्तिकुलपुत्र दुःखितसत्त्वानामाजन्मव्याधिपरिपीड़ितानामल्पायुष्कानामर्थाय हिताय सुखाय । इमां सर्व्वे तथागता उष्णीषविजयो नाम धारयेत् देशयेत् पर्य्यवाप्नुयात् परेभ्यश्च विस्तरेण प्रकाशयेत् दीर्घायुष्कतायुमुपादायति अथ खलु आर्य्यावलोकितेश्वरोबोधिसत्त्वोमहासत्त्वो उत्थायासनादेव कृताञ्जलिपुटो भूत्वा भगवन्तमेतदवोचत देशयन्तु भगवान् सर्व्वतथागतोष्णीषविजयो नाम धारी देशयति स्म सुगतिः ।

End. इमां सर्व्वतथागतोष्णीषविजयो नाम धारणी वाचयित्वा अन्तेद्भूर्व्वा चलेन चैत्य-मुद्धिमर्चयेत । यस्यैव कृते अपरिमितायुः सप्तवर्षायुर्जीवति—। सप्तवर्षायुः सप्ततिवर्षायुर्जीवति—। परमायुश्शतं जीवति। स्मृतिमान् भवति। सर्व्वरोगविनिर्मुक्तो भवति॥ श्रीरायुरथसम्पन्नश्च भवति।

Colophon. आर्य्य उष्णीषविजयो नाम धारणी समाप्ता।

No. B. 34.

VAJRASÚCHÍ.

वज्रसूची।

Substance, Nepalese yellow paper, 10 × 3 inches, Folia, 9. Lines on a page, 6. Extent in ślokas, 140. Character, Newárí. Date, ? Appearance, old. Prose. Correct.

A disputation about caste. By As'vaghosha. The work has been translated, in a very spirited style, 'into English by Mr. B. H. Hodgson, and published in the' Transactions of the Royal Asiatic Society of Great Britain,' and also in his 'Essays,' (pp. 126f.). Mr. Hodgson writes the name of the author Ashughosha, but the MS. gives it as I have put it above. The meaning of the name is "he who has the voice" (*Ghosha*) "of a horse" (*as'va*). The first word (*As'va*) is put in contradistinction to the name of the tutor Manjughosha, "he of the sweet voice." Ashu is meaningless. The arguments used are very much of the same class with what is given on p. 225.

Beginning. ॐ नमो मञ्जुनाथाय।

जगद्गुरुं मञ्जुघोषं नत्वा वाक्कायचेतसा।
अश्वघोषो वज्रसूचीं सूत्रयामि यथामतं॥
वेदाः प्रमाणं स्मृतयः प्रमाणं धर्म्मार्थयुक्तं वचनं प्रमाणं।
यस्य प्रमाणं न भवेत् प्रमाणं कस्तस्य कुर्य्याद्वचनं प्रमाणं॥

इह भवतीयदिष्टं सर्व्ववर्णप्रधाणः ब्राह्मणवर्ण इति। वयमत्र ब्रूमः। कोऽयं ब्राह्मणो नाम। किं जीवः किं जातिः किं शरीरः किं ज्ञानं किमाचारः किं कर्म्म किं वेद इति।

End. अस्माभिरुक्तं यदिदं द्विजानां मोहं निहन्तुं हतबुद्धिकानां।
गृह्णन्तु सन्तोयदि युक्तमेतत् मुञ्चन्तथायुक्तमिदं यदि स्यात्॥

Colophon. कृतिरियं सिद्धाचार्य्याश्वघोषपादानामिति।

No. B. .

VAJRAVIDA'RAṆA NAMA-DHA'RAṆI'-HṚIDAYO-PA-HṚIDAYA.

वज्रविदारणनामधारणीहृदयोपहृदयं ।

Substance, Nepalese paper, 7½ × 3 inches. Folia, 3. Lines on a page, 5. Extent in ślokas, 25. Character, Newárí. Date, ? Appearance, old. Prose. Incorrect.

A charm which, on being worn in an amulet, or frequently recited, insures robust health. It was imparted by the Lord when he was dwelling in a thunderbolt. It begins with the words *Om taṭa taṭa toṭaya toṭaya sphaṭa sphaṭa sphoṭaya sphoṭaya ghuṇa ghuṇa ghuṇápaya ghuṇápaya svarvasattváni, &c.*

Beginning. ॐ नमो भगवत्यै आर्य्यमहावज्रविदारण्यै । नमो बुद्धाय । एवं मया श्रुतं एकस्मिन् समये भगवान् वज्रेषु विहरति स्म । सर्व्वशरीरं वज्रमयं अधिष्ठाय वज्रपाणिश्च बुद्धानुभावेन वज्रसमाधिसम्पन्नः । ततो वज्रपाणि बुद्धानुभावेन सर्व्वबुद्धाधिष्ठानाय महाक्रोधसम्भूतं वज्रधारपद भाषते स्म ।

End. हृदयमन्त्रः । ॐ नमो रत्नत्रयाय नमश्चन्द्रवज्रपाणये ज्ञन २ तिष्ठ २ बन्ध २ अमृते ह्रूँ फट् स्वाहा ।

Colophon. आर्य्यवज्रविदारणो नाम धारणीहृदयोपहृदयः समाप्तः ।

No. B. .

VASUNDHARA'-VRATOTPATTI AVADA'NA.

वसुन्धराव्रतोत्पत्त्यवदानं ।

Substance, Nepalese paper, 11 × 2¾ inches. Folia, 23. Lines on a page, 5. Extent in ślokas, 350. Character, Newárí. Date, N. S. 923. Appearance, old. Verse. Incorrect.

On the origin of a fast in honour of a goddess named Vasundhará. The account is said to have been imparted to A'nanda by S'ákya himself during his sojourn in the monastery of Ghoshírá, in the suburbs of Kauśámbí; but the work is palpably a modern one. The goddess claims the threefold form of Vasundhará or the earth, Mahá Lakshmí or great prosperity, and Kumárí or the virgin.

The story runs that in a remote period of antiquity, during the reign of a king named Súryodaya, the inhabitants of the earth were very viciously disposed, and suffered much from famine and disease. Once, when a famine was at its height, some maids of honour of the great goddess Vasundhará happened, in course of their rambles, to pass over the earth, and to behold the distress men were immersed in. Touched by sympathy they solicited their mistress at Tushita to afford them some relief. Thereupon the goddess sent for her stewards, Nándimukha and As'vaghosha, and thus expressed her behest:—"In the absence of a Tathágata mankind have run into vice, and it is my wish to reclaim them by giving currency to my worship. Do you, therefore, descend on the earth, and by some contrivance or other win over king Súryodaya, through whom my worship may be proclaimed?"

The stewards assumed the forms of bewitchingly beautiful damsels, and tried to win the king by sweet songs; but failed. Then assuming the forms of fierce boars they commenced to destroy the king's favourite garden. The king, hearing that two boars were destroying his garden, came forward with his men, who surrounded the place, and raised a dreadful uproar all round. The boars, thereupon, raised a hurricane, laid everything prostrate, enveloping the place in impenetrable darkness, and rushing past the king so as to strike against him, escaped. The contact knocked down the king, and made him insensible; but he soon regained his senses, and, mounting his horse, chased after them. The boars then gave up their swinish form, entered the body of the king's horse, and gallopped on across rivers and marshes till they reached a forest, when the horse stumbled and knocked down the king insensible on the ground. Of the king's retinue only one trooper was able to follow him in his wild run. He came to his help, and, when the king regained his senses and asked for a drink of water, ran to the nearest river for a supply.

When Senagupta, for that was the name of the soldier, had refreshed himself with a drink and was filling his can for his master, he beheld, on an island on the other side of the river, some Apsaras damsels engaged in frolic. The sight enchanted him, and he stood bewitched, When beckoned to approach near, he crossed the stream, and narrated to the damsels the history of his adventure. He then asked them what had brought them there. The Apsarases said they had come to perform the rite of Vasundharávrata. He then said, "if you will please instruct me in the details of the rite, I too would perform it." The damsels replied by saying that at early dawn on the second day of the moon in the month of Bhádra, or any other month, the performer should bathe himself, put on clean clothes, construct on a pure spot smeared with cowdung a diagram with metals, jewels, flowers, paddy or powdered stone, and place therein the emblems of the seven gods, and surround them with a line formed of paddy or any other of the articles aforenamed. The place should also be decorated with flags of yellow cloth, umbrellas and garlands of leaves and flowers, and the gods be there invited, and due offerings made to them. On the following morning the performer should bathe in a river, or a sacred pool, put on yellow cloth, and purify himself with the five products of the cow. Then facing the east contemplate and mentally worship the three jewels, and then worship the goddess Vasundhará with the usual mantras and offerings. After this worship he should tie round his wrist a protecting cord (*raksha*) formed of sixteen threads and having sixteen knots in it, and then pray for whatever he wishes. At night he should partake of barley-meal, and keep awake the whole night. Next morning he should again worship the goddess, and then bidding her adieu, worship a human virgin, and then give a feast to his spiritual guide and others.

After hearing this account of the fast, Senagupta brought water to the king, and explained to him the reason of his delay. On his return home the king appointed Senagupta his priest, and celebrated the fast with great pomp. It was, however, not accomplished in due order. The queen Chútadeví, who accepted the protecting cord at the time of celebrating the rite, afterwards thought it very offensive placed besides her jewelled bracelets, and tore and threw it out through a window. At this time a maid-servant of another queen who was residing in a Nimbá Park was passing by the window, and the cord fell on her head. She took it respectfully, accepted the hospitality of the king, and, returning to her mistress, told the story of the cord and the merits of the fast. Thereupon both of them mentally performed the fast.

A short time after the goddess Vasundhará assumed the form of an old woman, and, coming to the gate of the king, sent a message to the queen through one of her maids, saying, that the queen's grandmother had come, and wanted to see her. The maid duly carried the message to her royal mistress, but the queen felt annoyed at it, and exclaimed,

" my grandmother ! why she is long since dead; this is an imposter; go, and drive her away."

Thus repulsed, the old woman repaired to the Nimbá forest, and was there most respectully and hospitably entertained. This pleased her much, and she made herself manifest in her own real form. This is described as a handsome female of yellow complexion, having one head but six arms, holding in the right hands the emblems of blessing and of salutation to Buddha, and a handful of jewels, and in the left an auspicious jar (*bhadraghaṭa*), a volume of the Prajn̲á, and a sheaf of corn. Through her blessings everything prospered in the home of the Nimbá queen, and the king, forsaking his senior wife, lived with her.

Chútadeví was greatly incensed by the conduct of the king, and in a furious passion ran to the Nimbá Park. There, however, she heedlessly trod upon some flowers which had been offered to the goddess, and from the sin proceeding therefrom her head was immediately metamorphosed into that of a fierce sow. Looking at this the people of the neighbourhood raised an uproar, and out of shame she ran into a forest to hide herself. There she saw successively two birds quarrelling with each other, a large boar, a fox, a sow, and a big serpent. She repented of her sins, and, wishing to see the goddess herself, proceeded further, and, coming by a river, saw some damsels carrying golden pitchers on their hips. She asked them, " who are you? and where are you going to?" The damsels replied: " We are the maids of Vasundhará, come to fetch water from this river for her bath. This river flows only for her bath; wash your eyes with its waters and you will see what you desire."

She did so, and, immediately regaining her former shape, beheld the goddess before her. Saluting her most reverently she said, " Divine being, I have sinned most grievously. Do thou remit my sins; I shall now perform the fast most reverently."

The goddess was pleased with her repentance. She remitted her sins, and directed her to return home and perform the fast. In reply to further requests she explained the history of the sights Chútudeví had seen in the forest. " The two birds," said the goddess, " were formerly two sisters who quarrelled at meal, and therefore they have now become, two birds. The boar was formerly a housekeeper, and in that capacity he doled out half rations to the guests of his master, and purloined the other half, and this is his desert. The fox was formerly a learned Bráhmaṇ, and he dissuaded people by his sophistry from giving alms to Bauddhas, and therefore has he become a fox." Chútadeví explained to them their sins and ransomed them, and, returning home, performed the rite of Vas'undhará with her husband, and lived in peace and plenty.

Beginning. ॐ नमः श्रीसर्व्वबुद्धबोधिसत्त्वेभ्यः ।

जिनः श्रीभगवान् बुद्धः शाक्यमुनिस्तथागतः ।
सर्व्वज्ञोऽर्हञ्जगच्छास्ता धर्म्मराजो विनायकः ॥
स एकः समुपागत्य कौशाम्ब्या उपकण्ठके ।
विहारे घोषिरारामे विजहार ससांघिकैः ॥
अनेकैर्बोधिसत्त्वैश्च बहुप्रत्येकबुद्धकैः ।
श्रावकैर्जिनशिष्यैश्च भिक्षुभिक्षुण्युपासकैः ॥
देवपुत्रगणैः सार्द्धं ब्रह्मभिश्च महोत्तमैः ।
चतुर्भिश्च महाराजैरहिराजगणेश्वरैः ॥
किन्नरेन्द्रैश्च दैत्येन्द्रैर्गरुड़ैश्च महोत्तमैः ।
मनुष्यैर्मनुजेन्द्रैश्च राजामात्यगणैस्तथा ॥
धनिभिः सार्थवाहैश्च पौरैश्च जिनसेवकैः ।
ब्रह्मविष्णुशिवशक्रैरप्सरोभिर्मनोरमैः ॥
तत्र श्रीभगवान् तस्थौ खे रत्नमणिमण्डिते ।
सिंहासने समुत्थाय पूर्णेन्दुरिव भासयन् ॥
पर्षद्भिर्भगवांस्तेन समयेन चतसृभिः ।
गुरुपूजाकृतस्ताभिः सत्कृतो मानितोऽर्च्चितः ॥
शाक्यसिंहो दयाम्भोधिः स समालोक्य पार्षदं ।
प्रभाष्य धर्म्ममालोक्य तस्थौ लोकसमुज्ज्वलः ॥
अथ सर्व्वेऽद्भुतप्राप्तास्तमुनीनाथं व्यलोकयन् ।
वसुधाराव्रतोत्पत्तिं श्रोतुं सर्व्वे समीषिरे ॥

End. तदा भुवि तया देव्या स्वयं व्रतं प्रचारितं ।
इत्येतन्मुनिभिः सर्व्वैराख्यातं सत्त्वहेतवे ॥
इति श्रीमुनिनाख्यातं श्रुत्वा सर्व्वेऽपि सांघिकाः ।
एवमस्त्विति विज्ञप्य प्रत्यनन्दन् प्रसादिताः ॥

Colophon. श्रीवसुन्धराव्रतोत्पत्त्यवदानं समाप्तं ।

No. B. 49.

VASUNDHARÁSHṬOTTARA-S'ATANÁMA.

वसुन्धराष्टोत्तरशतनाम ।

Substance, Nepalese paper, 7½ × 3 inches. Folia, 3. Lines on a page, 5. Extent in ślokas, 30. Character, Newárí. Date, ? Appearance, fresh. Verse. Incorrect.

One hundred and eight epithets forming a hymn in praise of Vasundhará, apparently meant for the presiding divinity of the earth or Pṛithví Deví, but her abode is said to be in the Tushita heaven as described in the next preceding work.

Beginning. ॐ नमो भगवत्यै आर्य्यश्रीवसुन्धरायै ।
दिव्यरूपी सुरूपी च सौम्यरूपी वरप्रदा ॥
वसुधरी वसुधारी च वसुश्रीः श्रीकरी रवा ।
धारणी वरणी वाता शरण्या भक्तिवत्सरा ॥

End. अथवा सीरसम्पन्नसप्तजातिस्मरोदयं ।
प्रीयवाचयद्देवस्य रूपवान् प्रियदर्शनी ॥
विप्रचन्ति कुलेषु च आद्देयमुपजाते (?) ।
अन्त + भूमीश्वरं प्राप्ता पश्चात् प्राप्ता सुखावतिः ॥

Colophon. आर्य्यश्रीवसुन्धरानामाष्टोत्तरशतं बुद्धभाषितं समाप्तं ।

No. B. 16.

VI'RAKUS'A AVADÁNA.

वीरकुशावदानं ।

Substance, Nepalese paper, 12 × 4 inches. Folia, 96. Lines on a page, 8. Extent in ślokas, 640. Character, Newárí. Date, N. S. 947 = A. D. Appearance, old. Prose and verse.

This codex contains two works, both in the Newárí language, one a translation of the story of Kuśa of the Virakuśa Avadána and the other Ashṭamívrata-kathá, or story in praise of the Ashṭamí fast. Both are said to be extracts from the Divya Avadána, translated into the Nepalese language by Amṛitánanda. The Ashṭamívrata is the same with the *Uposhadha* or *Poshadha* rite described on page 265. The name here given refers to the age of the moon when it should be performed

The story given is in substance the same with what occurs in the Kus'a Jataka, (*ante*, p. 110), but some of the names and details are changed. The jewel referred to in the Kus'a Játaka is here said to have been obtained as a reward for performing the Ashṭamívrata. The name of Kus'a's mother here is Alindá, Kus'a has *aliases* in Virúpa and Upavása Kus'a, and he obtains in this story a handsome shape by observing the fast under notice.

Beginning. ॐ नमो रत्नत्रयाय । नमः श्रीमदार्य्यावलोकितेश्वराय । बोधिसत्वाय महासत्वाय महाकारुणिकाय । ॐ नमो लोकनाथाय । नत्वा गुरुं त्रिरत्नञ्च कथयामि समासतः । अष्टमीव्रतमाहात्म्यं नेपालीभाषयान्वितं । बुद्धगायसे बोधिमण्डपमहाविहारस श्रीजय श्रीभिक्षुन आज्ञादयकलं । कुक्कुटाराममहाविहारस श्रीशाक्यसिंह-भगवानन आनन्दप्रभृतिसभालोकपात आज्ञादयकलं । हे नोह्न आनन्दादि-अनेक अष्टमीव्रतयाकथाकने धुना । आडा विरूपराजा उद्धारजुड़ोगू अष्टमी-व्रतयामहिमाकने । वारानसीधाया महानगरीस सुवन्धुनाम राजाजुलो । उप-

End. वासकुश महाराजां अष्टमीउपासयाहं सकलप्रजालोकपालयाहं रजाथी पाहाड़ो आणन्दसुखभोगयाहं चोहाजुलो ।

इति श्रीदिव्यावदानोद्धृतमष्टमीमाहात्म्यं, अम्हतानन्दोद्धृतनैपालीयभाषाष्टमी-व्रतकथा समाप्ता ।

No. A. 18.
VRATA'VADA'NAMA'LÁ.
व्रतावदानमाला ।

Substance, Nepalese yellow paper, 16 × 8 inches. Folia, 70. Lines on a page, 6. Extent in ślokas, 2,109. Character, Newárí. Date, ? Appearance, old. Prose. Incorrect.

The work in its entirety comprises a number of stories in praise of various optional fasts or Vratas, but the codex under notice is a mere fragment, containing only the story of Suvarṇavarṇa, in three chapters, in praise of a rite called *Laksha-chaityavrata*. From the name of the hero of the story the fragment is named *Suvarṇavarṇávadána*.

The principal interlocutors in this work are Jayas'rí and Jinas'rí, who quote the authority of Upagupta, who is said to have recounted the merits of the work to As'oka. Upagupta says that on the Nirváṇa of the Lord when Mahákás'yapa was at the head of the Church at Rájagṛiha, one Divákara, son of Ratuákara, a merchant of Rájagṛiha had reduced himself to great distress by excessive dissipation. Impelled by want and hunger and stung with the reproaches of his wife, he one day presented himself before Mahákasyapa, and sought his advice.

Mahákáshyapa advised Divákara to perform the ceremony of *Lakshachaitya*. "Once on a time", said he, "Lord Buddha discoursed on the importance and the merits of the ceremony. He was then residing in the Champaka grove belonging to Vis'vabhadra, a citizen of Padmapuri. While seated on a stone under the shade of a palm tree he, at the request of his followers, exhibited in the sky the model of a crystal chaitya surrounded by a hundred thousand other chaityas.

He brought them on the earth. He told them how Lord Vipas'yí showed the same thing to prince Pushpaketu, of Bandhumatí, to Chandraketu, to Súryyaketu, and to prince Svarṇaketu, of Svarṇavatí. He advised them to erect chaityas and worship them. Those that bathe the model chaityas with the perfumed waters of the Mandákiní river go to the residence of Sugata. One who desires to perform the ceremony of the Lakshachaitya should decorate the Dharmasálá of a Vihára by raising the flags of Dharma, Ratna, Padma, and Vajra at the four corners. On the day previous to the ceremony, he should worship the image of the three jewels, and fast during the night. On the day of the ceremony, he should take an early bath, gather from the field different kinds of clay, temper them with milk, curd, ghí, cowdung and cow's urine. The clay then should be purified by the repetition, twenty-one times, over it of the mantra called Virochaṇadháraṇí. Then it should be shaped into a solid sphere with a tapering spire. The sphere should be opened in the middle and grass, rice, and five jewels placed into it. Such models should be worshipped to the extent of one hundred thousand, or any less number that may be convenient.

Vis'vabhadra, on hearing this, entered the ascetic state, and became an Arhat. In one of his previous existences he had worshipped model chaityas, in consequence of which he obtained great excellence in this existence. He had then been a proud Bráhmaṇa, but was so humbled by poverty that he worshipped the models and obtained blessings from Vipas'yí.

II. The second chapter gives the story of Suvarṇavarṇa. The story runs that on hearing the merits of this fast from Kás'yapa, Divákara repaired to his home, and by the performance of the above ceremony obtained large profits in his own trade. Devendra advised him to worship the "three jewels," by virtue of which Divákara was blessed with a son named Suvarṇavarṇa. In his previous existence Suvarṇavarṇa was Puṇyamahes'a, a Devaputra of the thirty-third heaven.

A short time after the birth of his son, Divákara undertook a distant maritime expedition. While he was away on his voyage, his son, Suvarṇavarṇa resorted one day to the Veṇuvana grove, and there happened to hear gáthás chanted by a Bhikshu in praise of high moral sentiments. He at once sought conversion to the true faith; but the Bhikshu objected. He said he could not convert a youth who had not obtained the permission of his parents. After many attempts to obtain the permission of his mother, the youth was obliged to wait till the return of his father. In the meanwhile he began to mix with Paṇḍitas, S'ramanas and Bráhmaṇas. Whatever good sayings he heard he noted down in a book, which he used to read in his father's garden outside the city. Close by this garden there was a villa belonging to one Prachaṇda, a minister of Ajátas'atru, and the minister there enjoyed the society of a courtesan named Kás'ísundarí. This woman was over head and ears in love with Suvarṇavarṇa, but Suvarṇavarṇa contemptuously rejected all her advances. Desperate in her amour, she broke an engagement with Prachaṇda, and entered Suvarṇavarṇa's garden with a view to charm him with all her blandishments. Prachaṇda, impatient to have her society, sent messenger after messenger after her, and at last traced her where she was. He went to her, beat her, tore her hair, and, furious with rage, ordered an orderly immediately to put her to death. But the man charged with this infernal commission was moved by her piteous entreaties, and fled away. He was pursued to a long distance by Prachaṇda who, when he found the chase hopeless, returned with a view to destroy Kás'ísundarí with his own hands. During this interval Kás'ísundarí ran to the nearest wall of the garden in order to scale over it and escape, but failed in the attempt on account of the great height of the wall. No sooner Prachaṇda found her near the wall than he gave her a violent kick. Stunned by the blow she fell insensible, and was bitten by a black snake on whose body she fell. Prachaṇda, finding her dead, returned home, and sent officers to search the garden of Suvarṇavarṇa for the dead body, and to charge the owner of the garden with the murder. The king made over the investigation of the case to Prachaṇda, who, with only the show of a trial, ordered Suvarṇavarṇa to the stake. Just at this moment Divákara returned from his distant voyage, and Lord Kás'yapa, obtained Nirváṇa, leaving A'nanda at the head of his congregation.

A'nanda lived at Vaisálí. Divákara prayed for his intervention. A'nanda, by virtue of his power of working miracles, presented himself before the king, persuaded him to reverse the order of punishment; but, at the instigation of Prachaṇda, the executioner hurried on his business. Suvarṇavarṇa was already placed on the stake when the royal messengers reached the place of execution. But the stake had been already deprived of its sting. A'nanda had miraculously produced a lotus on the top of the stake whereon Suvarṇavarṇa felt himself very comfortable. By the instructions received from A'nanda, Suvarṇavarṇa obtained true knowledge. Kás'isundarí was resuscitated by a charm. She felt a dislike for womanhood on account of the manifold dangers by which it is surrounded. She prayed A'nanda to turn her into a man. Her feminity disappeared, she renounced the world, and was soon enobled as an Arhat. There was no bound to Divákara's delight when he heard of the sudden change of his son's fortune. Suvarṇavarṇa, renounced the world, and became an Arhat. The king no longer countenanced Prachaṇda. He withdrew his protection from him, and proclaimed him an outlaw. He was kicked, insulted, and severely beaten by those whom in his prosperity he had injured. In his distress Prachaṇda, too, sought the protection of A'nanda. He entered the Pravrajyá, and become an Arhat.

The king then enquired from A'nanda the reasons why Suvarṇavarṇa, Kás'isundarí, and Prachaṇda, though so different in their dispositions, should come to the same end. The reply is grain in the next chapter.

III.—When Lord Vipaśyí was at Bandhumatí, there lived a merchant named Karṇa in that city. His wife was enciente when he went on a distant voyage. During his absence his house was destroyed by fire, his lands inundated, and his wealth stolen. The son that was born unto him was extremely ugly, full of a putrid smell in his body, and universally disliked. His wife lived in a wretched hovel, and maintained herself by menial service. All her servants left her, except one faithful maid, who was personally attached to her. The son was named Virúpa on account of his ugliness. His mother maintained him by serving as a maidservant. But in a short time she could not even find menial employment. Virúpa was obliged to beg from door to door; but the offensive smell issuing from his body disgusted every one. People hooted him, and pelted stones at him. He had to pass days together without even a morsel of food. Mortified at this, Virúpa went to his father's garden, determined to put a period to his existence.

Karṇa, the merchant, returned home at this time, having lost all his wealth by a shipwreck. But there he found no relief. He found his house, his wealth, his land, everything gone. His wife was in a most wretched state, lean, lank and cheerless. These sudden and rapid reverses of fortune, induced him to worship the Lord. He went to Vipas'yí, and surrendered himself at his feet. By this piece of good work he obtained a boon never after to become poor even for a day. Virúpa was at this time lying almost dead in his father's garden; Lord Vipas'pi revivified him; removed the offensive smell from his person; and turned his ugliness into beauty. His skin became of a golden colour. That maidservant of Karṇa, who had not deserted his wife in her distress, also obtained Arhatship from Vipas'yí.

Karṇa invited the Lord to his house, and entertained him with his whole congregation. He also performed the ceremony of Chaityavrata.

When the king Bandhumán expired he was succeeded by his son S'rímán. S'rímán, dying without an heir, was succeeded by Virúpa, now called Surúpa on account of the transformation. Surúpa lived long and made his kingdom prosperous and happy.

Surúpa was Suvárṇavarṇa; Karṇa, Divakara; Karṇa's wife, Divakara's wife; her faithful maid was Kás'ísundarí; and the maid servant of Karṇa was Prachaṇda.

Ajátas'atru then asked A'nanda the reason why should Suvarṇavarṇa be placed on the stake though he was guiltless?

A'nanda replied:—

Chandra was a great Buddha. At the time of his advent there was in a Vihára a Bhikshu, who preached to Bráhmaṇas and others. Once on a time another Bhikshu, named Ajita, came to that Vihára. He was very eloquent, and a perfect master of the art of oratory. He soon eclipsed the fame of the Bhikshu of the Vihára. He wanted to ruin Ajita. He caused a calumny to be spread by a Bráhmaṇ girl that Ajita had unlawful connection with her. When Ajita complained that such ugly things should be whispered against his stainless character, he was told that he deserved to be placed on the stake for his crime. Ajita, disgusted at the conduct of the Bhikshu of the Vihára, left the place. Now the eyes of the new Bhikshu was opened. He found that he had done wrong. He pursued Ajita to a great distance, fell at his feet, and obtained his pardon. Suvarṇavarṇa was that Bhikshu. Because he had uttered the harsh words "you deserve the stake for your crime" he was placed on the stake. He was rich, because he performed the Chaityavrata.

After the relation of these stories both Ajátas'atru and Divákara performed the Chaityavrata.

Beginning. ॐ नमो रत्नत्रयाय। लोकानां परमानन्दमानन्दमानतोऽस्म्यहं।
मारजिच्छासनरतं निर्वृते परमात्मनि ॥
महाकाश्यपं काश्यपं ज्ञातकौण्डिन्यभिक्षुं गयाकाश्यपं चोरविल्वाख्यभिक्षुं नमामि।
महामौद्गल्यं शारिपुत्रं सुभूतिं महान्तं महाराहुलं भद्रकान्तं मुनीन्द्रात्मजं।
जयश्रीभिक्षुवर्म्मोऽसौ जिनश्रियमुवाच तं।
शूयतां कथयिष्यामि स्तचैत्यव्रतं महत् ॥
कुक्कुटाराम आसीनं उपगुप्तं व्यजिज्ञपत्।
चैत्यव्रतकथां ब्रूहि शृङ्गभेरीकथान्तथा ॥
समज्ञपद्गुप्तपुत्रः शृणु हे विन्दुसारज।
यथादिष्टं शोणवासिगुरुणा हितकाङ्क्षिणा ॥
एवमनू श्रूयते भगवति श्रीमति निर्वृतिं गतवति महाकाश्यपो भिक्षुरायुष्मान् महात्मा प्रज्ञया समन्वागतः तथागत इव कारुण्यात्तेषु तेषु ग्रामनगरपत्तनादिषु तांस्तान् वैनेयांस्तैस्तैरुपायैर्विनयति स्म। यावदपरेण समयेन विनेयवशादनेकानि सत्त्वकोटिशतसहस्राणि सद्धर्म्मदेशनामृतवर्षाभिषेकेन सन्तर्पयन् वैशाल्यां विहरत्याम्रपालीवने।

End. दिवाकरो महासार्थः पुनः पुनराराधनव्रतानुभावात् पुत्रपौत्रदासदासी सकुरथपदातिसम्पत्तिसमृद्धिमांश्चक्रवर्त्तीव सुखमनुतथा निर्वृतिपदमाप्तवान्।

Colophon. इति व्रतावदानमालायां सुवर्णवर्णावदाने चैत्यव्रतानुशंसायां तृतीयावदानं।

No. B, 43.
CHAITYA-PUṄGAVA.
चैत्यपुङ्गवः।

Substance, Nepalese yellow paper, 13 × 3 inches. Folia, 38. Lines on each page, 5. Extent in ślokas, 1,700. Character, Newárí. Date, N. S. 905. Appearance, old. Prose. Incorrect.

On a rite called *Chaitya-puṅgava* or the adoration of Chaityas, and the rituals and merits thereof.

When the Lord was seated under a palm tree in a grove of Champaka trees in the hermitage of Vis'vachandraka, near the town of Padmapuri, he noticed that his followers were thinking of what he had said regarding the rite of Chaityas. Thereupon he caused the apparition of a jewelled Chaitya to appear in the sky, and then, at the request of a Bodhisattva, Suchetana by name, caused a tumulus (*chaitya*) of crystals to rise on the earth, and gave directions for the performance of the rite in question. The chaitya is to be made of pure clay mixed with the five products of the cow, the five nectars, the five jewels and the five aromatics. The mixture is then to be kneaded seven times while repeating the Samantabhadra mantra. The shape is to be a rounded one with a tapering top. The figure, being then anointed with oil, is to be placed in the centre of an altar, duly worshipped, and then cut across in a slanting direction. From the womb of the bisected figure the light of chaitya, (*chaitya vimba*—what this is I know not) is to be extracted, and placed on a jewelled throne, and there worshipped according to the ritual given in the text. The six Páramitás are to be duly observed during the time the worship is made. This leads to questions from Suchetana as to—how men descend from the region of the Devas? how they become Devas? and how they pass from one mortal shape to another? The Lord replies that those who follow the practice of the Yoga, are merciful, attached to truth, devoid of anger, malice, and delusion, engaged in beneficent works, and follow the right path, repair to the region of the Devas. Those who are virtuous, obedient to their tutors, and respectful to good people, pass from one human body to another. Those who are otherwise become after death devils, Asuras and inferior animals, according to their deserts. Thereupon Vis'vabhadra, a person of noted charity, who was present in the assembly, immediately obtained conversion, and attained Arhathood. Requested to explain the cause of this sudden translation, the Lord said Vis'vabhadra was, in a former existence, a Bráhmaṇ of great learning, master of the four Vedas and of all the S'astras. Finding them to be false, he betook to the constant worship of Chaityas and to the dissemination of the true religion whereby many persons obtained the highest reward, and through the merit of those works he now attained Arhatship.

The rite here described is obviously the same with the Chaitya-vrata noticed in the next preceding work.

Beginning. ॐ नमः श्रीबुद्धाय ।

श्रीबोधिनाथमभिनित्यमनित्यतारं संसारसागर-महार्णव-दुःखतारं ।
ज्ञानांशुकोमलकलोज्ज्वलमादिदेवं तं नौमि देवमतिदेवमतिशान्तस्वभावरूपं ॥
सत्कर्म्मताडनमयं वरबुद्धसङ्गं लोकोत्तमं बहुविधं सुगतस्य वाक्यं ।
वैशेषिकमतनुकिल्बिषनाशहेतोर्वक्ष्यामि सद्गकुशलपुन्यमहार्णवस्य ॥
लोकस्य यत्कर्म्मकृतैस्तु शीघ्रमनादिकालार्ज्जितकर्म्मजानि ।
निहन्ति तस्मादिह मानवानां वक्ष्याम्यहं सर्व्वकताडनाख्यं ॥
सन्मृन्मयैर्लेचकचैत्यविम्बं विधानयुक्तं विनयोपचारं ।
किञ्चितप्रदानं फु + मप्रमेयं स्वर्गादिकं वा शृणुतावदामं ॥
एवं मया श्रुतमेकस्मिन् समये भगवान पद्मपुरिमहानगर्य्यां विहरति स्म ।
चम्पकवने विश्वभद्रकस्यारामे तालवृक्षमूले नानाद्रुमोपशोभिते इत्यादि ॥

End. इत्याह भगवान् बुद्धः संविहारं ययौ ततः ।
इति भिक्षवो ज्ञात्वा पुन्यमार्गं समाचरेत् ॥
देवा नागासुरा यक्षा किन्नराश्च महोरगाः ।
गन्धर्व्वा गरुडाश्चैव स्वस्वचेचे प्रत्युद्गताः ॥
इति चैत्यपुङ्गवकथा समाप्ता ।

No. B, 56.

CHÁNAKYA-SÁRASAṄGRAHA.

चानक्यसारसङ्ग्रहः ।

Substance, yellow Nepalese paper, 10 × 4½ inches. Folia, 58. Lines on a page, 7. Extent in ślokas, 830. Character, Newárí. Date, ? Appearance, old. Prose and verse. Incorrect.

An amplified version of Chánakya's collection of moral maxims. The recension current in Bengal contains only 108 stanzas. The quotations are mostly from the Mahábhárata and other Hindu works, and the collection professes to be a Hindu work. It has got currency among the Buddhists from the circumstance of the maxims inculcated being good, and not very sectarial.

Beginning. श्रीगणेशाय नमः । श्रीनारायणाय नमः ।

प्रणम्य शिरसाविष्णुं त्रैलोक्याधिपतिं प्रभुं ।

नानाशास्त्रोद्धृतं वक्ष्ये राजनीतिसमुच्चयं ॥ १ ॥

अधीत्यैवामितं शास्त्रं नरोज्ञास्यति तत्त्वतः।

धर्म्मोपदेशविनयं कार्य्याकार्य्यशुभाशुभं ॥ २ ॥

तदहं संप्रवक्ष्यामि नराणां हितकाम्यया।

येन प्रज्ञा प्रवर्त्तेत सावैव हितकारिणी ॥ ३ ॥

End. गोभिर्विप्रैश्च वेदैश्च सतीभिः सत्यवादिभिः।

अलुब्धैर्दानशीलैश्च सप्तभिर्धार्य्यते मही ॥ ९९ ॥

असारेऽपि हि संसारे सारमेतच्चतुष्टयं।

काश्यां वासः सतां सङ्गो गङ्गाम्भः शम्भुसेवनं ॥ १०० ॥

इति श्रीचाणक्यसारसङ्ग्रहे तृतीयशतकः समाप्तः।

No. B, 51.

DHVAJÁGRAKEYÚRI' DHÁRAṆI'.

ध्वजाग्रकेयूरीधारणी।

Substance, yellow Nepalese paper, 7 × 2½ inches. Folia, 7. Lines on a page, 5. Extent in ślokas, 80. Character, Newárí. Date, ? Appearance, old. Prose. Incorrect.

A charm for ensuring success in warfare. Indra, having been overpowered by other gods, sought the protection of the Lord, and the Lord, out of his overflowing kindness, taught him this charm which, he said, he had obtained from a Tathágata of the name of Dhvajá. The charm begins with the words *jaya jaya vijaya vijaya jayaváhiní saṅkari prasaṅkari prataṅkari bhanjani prabhanjani*, &c.

Beginning. ॐ नमो भगवत्यै आर्य्यध्वजाग्रकेयूरायै। एवं मयाश्रुतमेकस्मिन् समये भगवान्
देवपुच एस्मिन्नेषु विजहार। पादकलम्बशिलायां शक्रो देवानामिन्द्रः सुरैर्जितः
पराजितः सत्वरं त्वमानरूपं येन भगवान् तेनोपसङ्क्रान्तः उपक्रम्य भगवन्तः पादौ
शिरसाभिवन्द्य भगवन्तमेतदवोचत्।

End. इदमवोचद्भगवानात्तमनास्ते च भिक्षवस्ते च बोधिसत्वाः सा च सर्व्वावती
पर्षत् सदेवमानुषासुरगरुडगन्धर्व्वाश्च लोको भगवतोभाषितमभ्यनन्दन्निति।
ध्वजाग्रकेयूरीनामधारणी समाप्ता।

No. B, .

GI TAPUSTAKA.

गीतपुस्तकम् ।

Substance, yellow Nepalese paper, 10 × 3½ inches. Folia, 50. Lines on a page, 5. Extent in ślokas, 600. Character, Newárí. Date, N. S. 230. Appearance, old. Verse. Generally correct.

A collection of Newárí hymns adapted for singing, the tune and the music being regularly noted against each hymn.

Beginning. राग, गम्भारी। ताल ज्यान्तालमाखं। विश्वसरोरुह विम्बविम्बा विम्बविम्बामोकार
विथापित सुसम्भवा ॥ १ ॥
नमामि नमामि नमामि वागीश्वर स्वपरमुनिहृदया वागीश्वर स्वपरमुनिहृदया
विलासथि कूटागार मनोहर स्वपरहृदया ॥ २ ॥

End. कायचक्राश्राये ॐ भव श्मशानवज्रवद्धपीठ प्रेतपुरि महावज्रानि २ चक्रव्येगाद्यलि-
ङ्गित श्मशांघ्र च वुभुज जटार्द्धेन्दु श्मशानदारालङ्कृता ॥ ४ ॥
चतुर्विंशतिरीवेश्वर प्रचण्डाद्यालिङ्गन त्रिभुवनकम्पित त्रियाणस्थिता २ कचीस-
वीर देवी एकस्वभावाङ्गनमे भनथि श्रीकुलिशनील प्रासात ॥ ५ ॥

No. B, 62.

KAṬHINA AVADA'NA.

कठिनावदानम् ।

Substance, yellow Nepalese paper, 13 × 4 inches. Folia, 7. Lines on a page, 7. Extent in ślokas, 200. Character, Newárí. Date, ? Appearance, old. Prose. Incorrect.

On the merits of charity, abstinence, &c., during the period of the Buddhist lent called Kaṭhina. This period extends to thirty days from the 1st of the new moon in the month of A's'vina. Gifts to Bhikshus and recital of stories in praise of charity are the principal observances. The rules were expounded by the Lord himself at the request of Kás'yapa. The Lord thereafter repaired to the Gandhamádana mountain along with a following of 500 ascetics. Arriving at the Anavatapta Lake, the Lord and his following sat each on a jewelled lotus as large as a cart wheel, and then Nágira, a Bhikshu, said that having cheerfully given alms during the period of lent he had never suffered from any misfortune for thirty great kalpas, and for eighteen kalpas had enjoyed the pleasures of heaven; on sixty-four occasions he had become Indra, eighty times a Chakravarti monarch, &c., &c. Kás'yapa, Sumaná, Mañgalyáyana and others made similar confessions. The object of the work seems to be to enjoin confession during the lent.

Beginning. ॐ नमो रत्नत्रयाय। यः श्रीमान् ससुरासुरैरविरतम्पादारविन्दार्च्चितः साचात् पन्थनिधानमङ्गलगुरुश्चिन्तामणिः सर्व्ववित्। निःशेषोद्भृत दोषजालजटिलः शौद्धोदनिः पारगः पायाद्वो भगवान् मुनीश्वरवरो देदीप्यमानद्युतिः। अनन्तरमस्यावदानस्य निदानमाह। अथायुष्मान् काश्यपोजानन्नेवपरमार्थं भगवन्तमेवमाह। भगवन् कदा कठिनमुतपद्यते। भगवानाह। अश्विनीकृष्णप्रतिपदमारभ्य त्रिंशद्दिवसेषु यदहोरात्रं तत्र सङ्घस्य कठिनमुतपद्यते।

End. विभातिकरकासुरो नभसि यावदुष्णप्रभः प्रजाजटिलमण्डलो हरिणलाञ्छनश्चोदितः। स्फुरन्ति मकरालयाः स्वभुवियावदव्याहतं सुरासुरनमस्कृतं सुगतशासनन्तिष्ठतु।

इति श्रीकठिनावदानं समाप्तं।

No. A, 16.

KARUṆA'-PUṆḌARIKA.

करुणापुण्डरिकम्।

Substance yellow Nepalese paper, 13 × 5½ inches. Folia, 126. Lines on each page, 11. Extent in ślokas, 4,500. Character, Newárí. Date, ? Appearance, old. Prose. Incorrect.

Account of a continent called Padmadhátu, of its king Araṇemi, of his priest and 500 sons, and of its Tathágata Ratnagarbha, interspersed with many anecdotes and stories, concluding with directions for the dissemination of the true religion on the Nirváṇa of the Lord. The work is divided into five chapters *(parivartas)*, and its leading expounder is S'ákya himself, speaking in response to queries of Maitreya and others. The work was translated into the Chinese under the name of Pei-hwa-king by Dharmaraksha, of the northern Liang dinasty (Circa 502—555.)

CONTENTS, I.—Description of the continent of Padma. The scene opens with an account of an assembly held on the Vulture Peak near Rájagṛiha. The Lord commenced a discourse on the great secret Sútra entitled *Charyávaisáradya*, when suddenly rays of light of various colours issued forth and illumined all the three thousand regions, even to the depth of the darkest hell, where the light of the sun and the moon had never reached before; Buddhist sacred places became specially resplendent thereby; the earth shook in six different rays; heavenly flowers fell in showers; and celestial music resounded everywhere. Beholding these prodigies Ratnavairochana uncovered one of his shoulders and, kneeling on his right knee, addressed the Lord in order to know whence these wonders came forth. The Lord thereupon gave an account of a region named Padma. It was situated to the south-east of Jambudvípa. It contained Buddhist sacred places, innumberable as the grains of sand on the banks of the river Ganges. The Bodhi tree there was named Indra, and under it, there was a lotus 500 yojanas in circumference, seated on a stalk made of lapis-lazuli; the leaves of this plant were of gold, each leaf being 15 yojanas in circumference. On this lotus sat the Tathágata Padmottara, and around him were Bodhisattvas innumerable, each seated on a lotus. At the last watch of the night Padmottara attained Buddhahood, and at early dawn set the *avaivartika* wheel in motion, and thereupon millions over millions of rays of light issued forth, and these were the causes of the prodigies.

II.—In reply to the questions of Ratnavairochana the Lord gave further descriptions of the continent of Padma and of Padmottara. The size of the continent of Padma was such that were one by a miracle to pound down the great Sumeru mountain to grains each not bigger than a mustard seed, multiply those grains four times, and spread them smoothly side by side, the area covered would represent the extent of that continent. Padmottara had 30 kalpas for the duration of his life. After his Nirváṇa the true religion lasted for ten kalpas, and then Bodhisattvas who had been born there lived for 40 kalpas. Formerly this continent was named Chandanalokadhátu, and it had been ministered by the Tathágata named Chandrottama for 20 kalpas. At the request of Gaganamudra, a Bodhisattva, that saint had prophesied that ten kalpas after his Nirváṇa Padmottara would be born. He also taught that Bodhisattva certain Dháraṇís of great potency.

III.—On the miraculous powers of Padmottara. Sántimati, a Bodhisattva, enquired of the Lord how it was that while other Tathágatas acquired perfection by overcoming the five attachments, Padmottara attained Buddhahood while retaining them. The five attachments are—the attachment for existence (*A'yuh kasháya*); that of fancy (*Kalpa kasháya*); that of beings (*Sattva kasháya*); that of sight (*Drishṭi kasháya)*; and that of pain. He then related the story of Araṇemi. This king lived in a very remote kalpa named Dharma. His household priest was Samudrareṇu, whose son Samudragarbha, relinquishing his home, attained the perfect Bodhi knowledge, and assumed the name of Ratnagarbha. Attended by a numerous retinue of Bhikshus, he travelled from country to country, and at last arrived at a Jambu grove near the metropolis of Araṇemi. The news of this arrival reaching Araṇemi, the king immediately came to him, and solicited his abidance at the place as his guest for three months. On the expiry of this period one thousand sons of Araṇemi, one after another, made a similar request, and the saint granted it in every instance. When thrice one thousand months had expired Samudrareṇu invited and entertained his son for seven years. Once this Bráhmaṇa speculated on what could be the object of Araṇemi in entertaining the saint. Does he aspire to the position of a Deva? or of an Indra? or of the possession of illimitable wealth and power? or of the perfect Bodhi knowledge? That night he dreamt a dream. He saw that Buddhas from innumerable sacred places had sent him presents of lotuses having leaves of gold, stalks of silver, and pericarps of lapislazuli. On each lotus was seen a sun, with a jewelled umbrella over it, and six billions of rays issued from each sun, and fell on his face. He, moreover, saw his own self clear as a mirror of the expanse of a thousand yojanas, and in it he beheld sixty billions of Bodhisattvas seated on lotuses, and celestial music resounding therein. He saw, too, the king Araṇemi seated, with the face of a hog and his body bespattered with blood, under a castor plant after devouring various animals there. Other animals feasted on the bones that were left after the meal of their king. The Bráhmaṇ then saw some of the princes, with faces of jackals, wolves, boars, lions and dogs and bespattered with blood, chasing other animals, and after feasting on their bodies seating themselves under castor trees. Other animals feasted on the remains of the animals destroyed. He saw other princes richly dressed and ornamented, mounted on chariots drawn by buffaloes, addressing him thus: "Divide these lotuses among the king and the princes." He did so, and then, waking up, went to the saint, and asked the meaning of the dream. The saint did so, and also expounded the meaning of the details of the dream; adding—"Since you have for the good of creation entertained us for seven years, you will acquire the perfect knowledge." The Bráhmaṇ then learnt the true knowledge, and advised the king and fhe princes to retire from worldly affairs, and to devote themselves to the contemplation of true knowledge for seven years. They confined themselves in their chambers, and did so. After a time Samudrareṇu requested his son to invite them to his presence. The saint performed a Samádhi from which issued forth various lights; he then called the parties to his presence, and blessed them.

IV.—Lord Padmaprabha, having performed the Samádhi named *Bodhisattvachittápromosha*, gently smiled, whereupon a brilliant light spread all over the universe, and made all Buddhist sacred places manifest to the king and the rest of the congregation. The king then prayed the Lord to be translated to a world where there was no hell, no avarice, no region of Yama; where all beings were brilliant as gold and endowed with the memory of their former existence, and with such transcendental sight that they could behold all Buddhist sacred places, and be ever devoted to the true religion. The Lord directed him towards the west, to a world which was named *Sudrasuvirájita*, and which tallied in every respect with the description. The Tathágata of this world was Indraghoshas'vararája. After many ages this Tathágata would be followed by Achintamatigururája who would be followed by Maraprabha. The true religion would last for 16 kalpas and then disappear. It would be revived by Rashmi a thousand kalpas afterwards. Then will come Ravores'vara who will be followed by Aparameya, after whom you will be a Tathágata under the name of Amitáyúh, when that world would be called Sukhavati. The king's sons then, one after another, came forward, and prayed for the perfect knowledge, and each of them was assured that he would become a Buddha at some time or other. The five sons of the Bráhmaṇ and a number of others obtained the blessing of salvation. The Bráhmaṇ appeared last, and he was told that in the Kali age, he would appear as S'ákya Siñha, and that a thousand years after his ministry the religion would disappear, (a prophecy which has not been verified, unless we take it to mean India only).

V.—At the request of the Bráhmaṇ, Padmaprabha then gave descriptions, among many others of the following Samádhis, *viz.*, Surañgamá, Ratnamudrá, Siñha-vikṛiḍitá, and Suchandrá. He gave in detail also the merits of these Samádhis. Thereupon the king with his one thousand sons and numerous followers and officers retired from the world, and accepted the initiatory rite of asceticism. On the Nirváṇa of Ratnagarbha seven jewelled Chaityas were erected on his remains, and the Bráhmaṇ Samudrareṇu became the teacher, and spread wide the knowledge of the great truth for many kalpas, after which he was born in the family of a Chaṇḍála in Sañkarakaṇa, a Buddhist region of great sanctity. His teachings there were highly appreciated, and they served to raise the duration of human life to five hundred years from eighty years, which was the duration before his birth. He was, moreover, on the death of the king, appointed king, under the name of Punyabala. By his might and valour he brought the whole of Jambudvípa under his sway. Once he proclaimed that he would give any gift that his people sought of him. Thousands over thousands came and got what they wanted, but at last came one Páñsughosha, a Jívaka, who said he wished to become a Vidyádhara in his present existence, and for that purpose required the skin and eyes of a living man to be given him by that person cheerfully and without any scruple. This was a hard prayer to grant, but the king was not unequal to it. He plucked out his eyes from their sockets, and gave them away, and told the beggar to skin the body as he listed. After death, he was again born in the family of a Chaṇḍála, raised to the rank of a king, and ultimately brought to his end by giving away his tongue and ears to beggars. He was then born as king Indradhvaja. He had a thousand sons, all of whom, except six, retired from the world, and became hermits. He divided Jambudvípa into six parts, gave the parts to his householding sons, and himself retired to a hermitage. In his next birth he was king Pradípapradyota. On one occasion, having seen a man tied to a post, he asked why was the man so treated? His minister reported that the person had failed to pay the king's dues. The king ordered him to let the man loose at once.

The minister hesitated, adding if the man were let loose he would set a bad example, and no one would pay any government revenue.

The king enquired, " Do all people require pressure to pay revenue?"

He answered, " Yes, Sire, no one pays any revenue of his own accord."

Disgusted with the world, the king made over his kingdom to his five hundred sons, and retired to a hermitage. While there, he perceived, by his miraculous power, that five hundred merchants had lost their way on the ocean in darkness, and were in imminent danger of being lost. He then tied some cloth on his forearm, steeped it in oil, set fire to it, and held it up as a beacon for the merchants to find their way. In his next birth he was king Ambara *alias* Sarvandada. A Vedic student, named Jyotírasa, begged of him the kingdom of the earth, and it was forthwith given. Next came Rocha, a Bráhmaṇ, who asked and obtained the two legs of the king. Next came Dishṭárava, another Bráhmaṇ, who wanted the king's eyes. The king immediately plucked them out, and gave them away. Then came yet another Bráhmaṇ, who wanted the king's ears. Others came forward, all Bráhmaṇs, and begged successively for the remaining members of the king's person, and they were all readily satisfied. In his next birth he became a Nága king, Nidhisandarsana by name, and in this state he gave away a profusion of rare jewels, and this is the person who after a few other births has become S'ákya Siñha. The chapter concludes with an eulogium on the merits of hearing, reading, knowing, bearing on the person this auspicious Maháyána sútra.

Beginning. ॐ नमः सर्व्वबुद्धबोधिसत्वेभ्योऽतीतानागतप्रत्युत्पन्नेभ्यः ।
ॐ नमः आर्य्यप्रज्ञापारमिताभ्योबुद्धजननीभ्योनमोनमः ॥
ॐ नमोगुरुभ्योनमोनमः ।
गुरुं प्रणम्य सर्व्वज्ञं धर्म्मसंघं गुणाकरं।
करुणापुण्डरीकाख्यं प्रवक्ष्ये बोधिसूत्रकं ॥
एवं मया श्रुतमेकस्मिन् समये भगवान् राजगृहे विहरति स्म । गृध्रकूटे पर्व्वते महता भिक्षुसंघेन सार्द्धं द्वादशभिर्भिक्षुशतैः । सर्व्वैरर्हद्भिः क्षीणास्रवैर्निःक्लेशै-र्वशीभूतैः सुविमुक्तप्रज्ञैराजानेयैर्महानागैः कृतकृत्यैः कृतकरणीयैरपहृतभारै-रनुप्राप्तस्वकार्थैः परिक्षीणभवसंयोजनैः सम्यगाज्ञासुविमुक्तचित्तैः सर्व्वचेतोवशि-तापरमपारमिताप्राप्तैरभिज्ञानाभिज्ञातैर्महाश्रावकैः इत्यादि । तेन खलु पुनः समयेन भगवांस्ताभिः पर्षद्भिः परिवृतः पुरस्कृतः संस्कृतोगुरुकृतः पूजितो-मानितः अर्चितोऽपरोपितः । तदा बोधिसत्वविषयसन्दर्शनप्रणिधानव्यूहसमा-धिविषयधारणीमुखव्यूहं समाधानमुखनिर्द्देशं चर्य्यावैशारद्यं नाम धर्म्मपर्य्याय-सूत्रान्तं महावैपुल्यं बोधिसत्वानुगतं सर्व्वबुद्धपरिग्रहं भाषितुमारब्धवान् ॥

End. उद्गृह्ण त्वं महर्षे इमं धर्म्मपर्य्यायं यावत् पश्चिमायां पञ्चाशत्यां द्वे शान्तरगता-नामवैवर्त्तिकानां बोधिसत्वानां कर्णपुटेषु प्रकाशस्व । अद्य चावैवर्त्तिकचित्तं संस्थन-स्वाद्देवं भदन्त भगवन् चतुरशीतिमहाः कल्पा अतिक्रामन्ता यन्मया भदन्त भगवन् पूर्व्वप्रणिधानेन यचरिपिस्वराङ्गानुर्थ्या (?) नुत्तरायां सम्यक्संबोधौ बोधधा-रिकां चरमानोऽतिक्रान्तः। सत्वा मया चतुर्षु ब्रह्मविहारेषु प्रतिष्ठापिता अवैवर्त्ति-कभूमौ च प्रतिष्ठापिता अहश्च सत्वानां स्वयमेव परिपाचयामि । यावत् पश्चिमायां पञ्चाशत्यां य इमं धर्म्मपर्य्यायमुद्गृहीष्यति यावद्य इतश्चतुष्पदिकामपि गाथां धारयिष्यति । इदमवोचद्भगवानात्तमनाः सर्व्वावती पर्षत् सदेवमानुषासुरश्च लोकोभगवतोभाषितमभ्यनन्दन्निति ।

Colophon. करुणापुण्डरीकं नाम महायानसूत्रं समाप्तं ॥

No. B, 50.

RATNA-PARÍKSHÁ.

रत्नपरीक्षा।

Substance, yellow Nepalese paper, 9 × 3 inches. Folia, 45. Lines on a page, 7. Extent in ślokas, 650. Character, Newárí. Date, N. S. 934. Prose and verse. Incorrect.

On the merits and defects of precious stones and jewels. By Buddha Bhaṭṭácharya. The articles noticed are diamond, pearl, emerald, carbuncle, ruby, sapphire, lapislazuli, bhishma (?), crystal, and coral. The work is in Sanskrit verse, and its meaning is explained in Newárí prose. As usual in Sanskrit works of this class, great importance is attached to good and ill luck, the jewels are calculated to bring on under particular astrological and other circumstances.

Beginning. ॐ नमोरत्नत्रयाय। नमः श्रीगुरुपादपङ्कजेभ्यः। रत्नत्रयाय भुवनत्रयवन्दिताय तथा नमः। समखोक्य च रत्नशास्त्रं रत्नप्रवेशमधिकृत्य विमुच्य फल्गु संक्षेपमात्र-मिह बुद्धभटेन दृष्टं॥

End. सुरागकोमलविद्रुमनधनधान्यवृद्धियालं विशेषणं स्त्रीजननधररकाले भाग्यदयकरं दुष्टव्याधिमोचकरं विषव्याद्निसमस्तभयमोचकरं। इति विद्रुमपरीक्षा

Colophon. इति श्रीबुद्धभट्टाचार्य्यकृता रत्नपरीक्षा समाप्ता।

Nos. B 5, and B 65.

DHÁRAṆÍS.

No. B 5 has already been noticed, (p. 80) but the description given does not convey a full idea of its contents. It comprises 39 Dháraṇís designed for averting various evils, or securing certain desiderated blessings. B 65 contains 12, some of which are included in B 5. From the illustrations given of Dháraṇís in the preceding pages, the nature of Dháraṇís and the unintelligible jargon in which they have been written have already been made clear, and nothing further need be said of them here. All of them have been attributed to S'ákya Siṅha himself, who declares that he had got them from previous Buddhas, or designed them himself by his miraculous power. Each Dháraṇí is preceded by a brief account of the circumstances which led to its being promulgated, and followed by an enumeration of the benefits to be derived by wearing them enclosed in amulets, or hearing them frequently repeated.

No. B 5 comprises the following Dháraṇís, *viz.* :—

1, Haráhara-hṛidayá; 2, Abhayaṅkarí; 3, Sahasrávartá; 4, Siṅhanádá; 5, Shaḍaksharíta-mahávidyá; 6, Avalokiteśvara-siddhiniká; 7, Do. S'ílakaṇṭhá; 8, Amoghapás'á; 9, Tárá; 10, Chaṇḍá; 11, Mokshapádá; 13, Chaṇḍabhaṭṭárikáraksha; 13, Sarvalokes'vará; 14, Manjus'rí-pratijṇá; 15, Do. sádhana; 16, Maitreya; 17, Saddharmapáṭhá; 18, Vajratárá; 19, Páramitáyur; 20, Sarvadurgati; 21, Vasundhará; 22, Vajravidáraṇa; 23, Gaṇapatihṛídaya; 24, Ushṇisavijaya; 25, Maríchí; 26, Parṇasavarí; 27, Gṛihamátriká; 28, Dhvajágrakeyurí; 29-30, Pratisará, 1st and 2nd; 31 and Mahásáhasrapramardiní; 32, Mahámáyúrí; 33, Sítavatímahávidyá; 34, Mahárakshamantráṇusáriṇí; 35, Paṇchaviṅsatiká-prajṇápáramitáhṛidaya; 36, Hemagáthá; 37, Mahámáyavijaya-váhiní-náráyaṇa-pṛichchhá; 38, Laṅkávatára; 39, Vasundharávrata-púrvamúrtya-maṇḍala.

No. B 65 contains—1, Pítavarṇa-prajṇápáramitá; 2, Vajracharchiká; 3, Ushṇishavijaya-sádhana; 4, Mahánáma-sádhana; 5, Parṇasavarí; 6, Vajragandhá; 7, Vajravárábí; 8, Vajragándhári; 2, Bhadracharí; 10, Prajṇápáramitá-hṛidaya; 11, Vasundhará; 13. Tárábhaṭṭárikáyánámáshṭottara-s'ata—the hundred and eight names of Tárá.

No. B 55.

KALPADRUMA-AVADÁNA.

कल्पद्रुमावदानम् ।

Substance, yellow Nepalese paper, 14 × 3½ inches. Folia, 305. Lines on a page, 8. Extent in ślokas, 9,760. Character, Newárí. Date, Sм. 884. Appearance, fresh. Verse. Generally correct.

A collection of stories alleged to have been related to As'oka by Upagupta in illustration of the merits of various acts of virtue.

CONTENTS, I. *Story of Sundara.* When As'oka held his court at Páṭaliputra, some merchants came to his presence, and offered him many valuable presents. The king was greatly pleased, and, proud of the personal beauty of his son Kuṇála, showed him to them, and asked them if they had, in course of their peregrinations on the face of the earth, ever seen a more handsome boy. They replied in the affirmative, and said that the name of the youth they had seen was Sundara, and that on his birth a beautiful tank and a fine garden were produced, which were greatly attached to him, and followed him wherever he went. He was immediately sent for, and the king was greatly surprised at the unrivalled beauty of the boy, and his wonderful attendants. To solve the mystery, he repaired to his religious tutor, Upagupta, at the monastery of Kukkuṭáráma. He was followed by the youth who, listening to the teachings of the saint, begged to be ordained, and was immediately assigned the rank of an Arhat. Even more surprised than before, the king begged for explanation. Upagupta replied—on the nirváṇa of the Lord S'ákya Buddha his principal disciple Kás'yapa roamed about in great distress of mind. A farmer of the Magadha country, seeing him and his five hundred followers in their distress, received them kindly, offered them fresh clear water for bathing, and entertained them with food with every mark of devotion. Kás'yapa was much pleased with this hospitality, and at the request of the farmer, said that he would in a future life become, as he desired, an Arhat. "That farmer is born as Sundara, and his former good deeds have now fructified in Arhatship."

II. *Story of Púrṇabhadra* alias *Sampúrṇa.* Given in the Avadána-s'ataka, *ante*, p. 17.

III. *Story of Sárṭhaváha.* Ditto ditto, *ante*, p. 21.

IV. *Story of Chandana.* When the lord was travelling in the Magadha country, his followers noticed an old, weather-worn, dilapidated chaitya, and enquired to whose honour it had been erected. The Lord said it had been erected by the disciples of a former Buddha, named Chandana, and, in reply to further enquiries gave an account of the Buddha in question. In former times Brahmadatta, king of Benares, worshipped many gods in the hope of getting a son; but to no avail. Once he noticed with surprise an infant in the cup of a lotus. The child was very beautiful, and had the aroma of sandal wood on his body, for which reason he was named Chandana. When the boy grew up and walked about, at every step he moved, a lotus was produced. This lotus sparkled for a short time and then withered away. The youth, studying this fact, thought that since the produce of his body was evanescent, his body must likewise be so. Thinking so he lost all attachment for worldly objects, and devoted himself to religion. Through the effect of his former good deeds and his devotion he became, under the direction of Lord Kás'yapa, a Pratyak Buddha, and on his nirváṇa his disciples erected the stúpa. He was very assiduous in offering sandal-paste and lotus flowers to the chaitya of Kás'yapa, and thence resulted the peculiar aroma of his body and the production of lotus flowers from his feet. This story occurs also in the Dváviñsa Avadána, *ante*, p. 88. Anecdotes regarding Chandana occur on pp. 22, 23 and 198.

V. *Story of Pṛityapreta.* Given in the Avadána-s'ataka, *ante*, p. 30.

VI. *Story of Kṛishṇasarpa.* A householder of great wealth but of an excessively miserly disposition, dying in the town of Rájagriha, became a black serpent in a garden of king Vimbisára, and killed by his very sight whoever came near him. The king, not knowing how to destroy this dreadful reptile, went to the Lord, who was then sojourning in the Bamboo Grove, and sought his assistance. Thereupon the Lord repaired to the garden, and cast a benign look on the serpent. The serpent was charmed by the sight, and mentally abjured all wicked thoughts. The Lord brought him to his monastery, and instructed him in the principles of religion. So instructed, the serpent killed himself by continuous fasting, and repaired to the Trayasiñha heaven. There, however, he did not feel satisfied. He longed to serve the Lord, and therefore came back to the earth, and became a disciple of the Lord, who taught him all the rules, principles, and precepts of religion, and made him an adept. Thoroughly enlightened by this teaching, the serpent, now a Deva, pointed out to the king Vimbisára the spot where he had kept his wealth concealed in the garden, and, requesting him to devote it to religious purposes, returned to heaven.

VII. *Story of Suvarṇábha.* Given in the Avadána-s ataka, *ante*, p. 34.

VIII. *Story of Prabhavá.* She was the maiden daughter of a rich merchant of S'rávastí. Courted by princes and other great people of the town, she rejected their addresses, and betook to the Lord, who ordained her an Arhat. The good deed which secured her this high honour was her devotion, in a former life, when she was the chief queen of king Bandhumat, to the Lord Vipas'yí, to whom she gave all her valuable ornaments. This story forms the 71st Avadána of the Avadána-s'átaka, but the name given her there is S'uklá, *cf.* p. 35.

IX. *Story of Samudra.* Samudra was the son of a rich merchant of S'rávastí. He was born on board of a ship when his father was returning from a voyage to the island of Ratnákara, and thereby got his name of Samudra or the ocean. When he attained his majority, his father sent him to Ratnákara on a commercial mission, in the company of a large body of experienced merchants. Out in the sea, his vessel was overtaken by a hurricane, and was in imminent risk of being lost. His companions, finding all other resources vain, began to pray, invoking S'íva, Rudra, Gaṇeśa, Náráyaṇa, Indra, Yama, &c., each according to his fancy, but the gods granted them no help. At last an old Buddhist advised them to pray to Buddha, who alone could help them. They did so, and the Lord, knowing of it, created a golden coloured blaze of light the sight of which frightened the storm, which at once subsided. The voyage subsequently proved prosperous, and the merchants returned home, laden with wealth. Nor were they unmindful of the divinity who had helped them. They repaired to the Jetavana grove where the Lord was then sojourning, and offered rich presents. Listening to his religious discourses, they were induced to pray for initiation, and were accordingly ordained Arhats. In explanation of the merits which ensured them this blessing the Lord said, in former times there lived on the sea-shore a kind-hearted Buddhist hermit, learned in the Vedas, cherishing the sacred fire, dressed in a blanket, having matted locks on his head, and supporting himself on roots and fruits. A body of five hundred traders came to him from Benares, worshipped him, attained his blessings, and then proceeded to the island of Ratnákara for commerce. In the way, on their return voyage, their ship was overtaken by a fearful storm, and was on the point of foundering. They called to mind the hermit on the shore, and prayed for his help. They were saved, and they made their acknowledgments to the saint for his miraculous interposition, and prayed for spiritual blessing. The hermit said, " When I shall become a Buddha, the leader of men, I shall place you in the asylum of Buddhism. I am that hermit, and these merchants headed by Samudra, are the traders of old."

X. *Story of Subhúti.* During the ministry of the Lord S'ákya

Sinha a large number of his disciples were deputed to different parts of of the earth to disseminate his doctrines. Some of the disciples had taken their way to the top of the Himálaya mountain. When they were engaged in their meditation there, a Garuḍa perched on a peak, holding a serpent in its beak. The serpent, seeing the pious men, resolved to become one like them in his next birth. He was born as the son of a Bráhmaṇ householder of S'rávastí, and was named Subhúti, after his mother Bhútí. When grown up, he became passionate in his disposition, and the least annoyance would put him into violent fits of anger. His father sent him to school, and had him instructed in all the learning of the Bráhmaṇs, including the Vedas, but the education did not suffice to improve his disposition. His tutor, failing in his other endeavours, at last directed him to betake to a hermit's life, and pass his time in meditation in a forest. He did so, and while he was so engaged, a sylvan goddess appeared before him and said, "Why are you, good man, passing your time in meditation in this solitary place, converting yourself into a log of wood, or a block of stone? If you long for religion, betake to the doctrine of Buddha." She then exhibited a miraculous temple in the air, and disappeared. The sight of the temple purified the mind of the youth, and he sought the asylum of the Lord, and was duly ordained a S'rávaka of the highest rank. In reply to a question of his audience the Lord said, "in a former existence, when the span of human life extended to twenty thousand years, this man had performed Brahmacharya for a thousand years at Benares under the tuition of the Lord Kás'yapa, and obtained a boon that during my ministry he would become a S'rávaka of the highest rank. In a subsequent existence he was rough of speech and quarrelsome in the monastery where he lived, and that led to his being born a poison-mouthed serpent for five hundred generations."

XI. *Story of Yaśovatí.* When Lord S'ákya Sinha was sojourning in a palace on the bank of the Markaṭa tank, in Vais álí, he thought of Yaśovatí, the daughter in-law of Sinha Senápati, as a person who had been destined to become a Buddhist, and went to pay her a visit. He and his followers were received with great respect by the lady, and most sumptuously treated. Afterwards when he was seated at ease and discoursing on religion, the lady offered him a profusion of gold jewels and rich dresses. Through the miraculous power of the Lord these flew up in the air and formed a canopy over the head of the Lord. The Lord then smiled, and out from his mouth issued a flame of light which irradiated and filled the universe with joy, and, releasing the dwellers of hell from their bondage, disappeared in the matted locks of the Lord. The Lord then said, "three Kalpas hence this lady will acquire the highest perfection in true knowledge, and become a Buddha under the name of Ratnamati."

XII. *Story of the Kauravyas.* In course of his travels the Lord once came to the suburbs of the city of Kaurava, and the people of that place, hearing of his advent, felt great delight, and prepared to go and welcome him. The Tírthikas of the place, however, did not like this excitement, and went from door to door to dissuade the people from seeing the Lord. They spread evil reports of him, and reviled him in every way. Those among the people who were wicked listened to their advice, and refrained from visiting him; but a few good persons among them came. The Tírthikas, having prevented the people, themselves came to see him. The Lord felt that it was necessary to show some miracles, and accordingly willed. Thereupon Indra came down from heaven with heavy loads of Gos'irsha sandal-wood, and employed Vis'vakarmá to erect a palace. The palace was forthwith completed, and, when the Lord had entered it, the Devas worshipped him, and revelled in music, song and rejoicings. The news of the festival spread wide, and the people of Kaurava, thereby excited, rejected the advice of the Tírthikas, and, taking their seats before the Lord, listened to his lecture. The Tírthikas remained outside, admiring the sculptured ornaments and the beauty of the palace. The Lord perceiving this, suddenly suppressed the palace, and appeared seated in an open field. The Tírthikas could no longer resist the influence of the Lord; they fell at his feet, listened to his discourse, and got themselves converted. Some became S'rávakas, some Pratyakbodhis, some Anuttarabodhis, and some Arhats. Thereupon the Lord made the palace manifest again, and dwelt therein for three months. "Formerly," said the Lord, "there lived a Buddha named Brahmá, and a Kshatriya king erected for him a palace of Gos'irsha sandal wood and worshipped him there for three months. I am that Kshatriya king."

XIII. *Story of Padmottara.* When the Lord was passing through the highway of S'rávasti a young lady with her little boy stood on the roadside to behold him. When he came near her, the little boy threw a lotus to him, and the lotus immediately assumed the size of a cartwheel, and, rising in the air, formed an umbrella over the head of the Lord. "This lad," said the Lord to Ánanda, "will enjoy all the pleasures of the world for a thousand kalpas, and then become a Pratyak Buddha under the name of Padmottara."

XIV. *Story of Chandra.* This story occurs in the Avadána-s'ataka (story LII), but the substance of it as given on p. 32, is incorrect in some important particulars. The youth went to the Lord with Anáthapiṇḍada only once, and, on return home, fell ill of fever, and died. On his death he repaired to heaven, but, longing to visit the Lord again, came down, and saw his father crying with his corpse on his lap. Appearing before his father in the garb of a ṛishi, he asked him why he held the corpse in his lap instead of cremating it? The Bráhmaṇ said, "this is the body of my only son, and I want it to be revived." Chandra replied, "Were you to cry continuously for a thousand years, it still cannot revive. Were the sun to rise towards the West, were fire to be as cold as ice, were fishes to dwell on the crests of mountains, still the corpse will not regain its life. If you wish for your son's welfare, go and burn his body, and throw his bones into the river Ganges." The Bráhmaṇ could not, however, be induced to do as he was told. Chandra, thereupon, assumed the shape of a Deva, and gave an account of what had happened to him, and advised his father to dispose of the corpse, and betake to the asylum of the Three Jewels whereby he would be translated to heaven, and there enjoy the society of his son. The Chandra of the story was afterwards born as S'ákya. Anecdotes of this person occur on pp. 14, 96 and 279.

XV. *Story of Sugandhi.* Sugandhi, son of a merchant of Kapilavastu, and noted for having the aroma of the lotus and sandal-wood on his body, came to the Lord in the Nyagrodha monastery, and was ordained an Arhat. On being asked the reason of this sudden exaltation, the Lord said, "this youth had, in a former life, worshipped the chaitya of Vipas'yí, and anointed it with aromatic oil, and through the merit thereof he has the aroma on his body, and has been so exalted."

XVI. *Story of Supríyá.* Anáthapiṇḍada had a daughter, named Supríyá. Immediately after her birth she looked up towards her mother, and recited a gáthá to the effect that gifts should be given in profusion to Buddhists and Champaka flowers should be strewed on sacred places. Her father did as she wished. Afterwards, the instructions of a saint who came for alms to her father's house, made a deep impression on her mind in her early girlhood. She had, moreover, the faculty of recalling to mind the events of her former existences. On her 7th year she obtained the permission of her parents to become a nun, and Gautamí, by order of the Lord, ordained her. Soon after, a famine breaking out, the Lord directed his followers to seek the charity of Supríyá. She herself begged alms from poor householders, and relieved the distress of all suffering people. Three months after, when the Lord was proceeding from S'rávastí to Rája-gṛiha, he arrived at the middle of a forest where no food of any kind could be had. Supríyá, seeing that the followers of the Lord would be put to great distress, held forth her alms-bowl, and prayed that if she had any stock of former good deeds it should help her by filling her bowl with food. A forest divinity heard her prayer, and filled her bowl with nectar, with which she entertained the Lord and his followers. Her good deeds now sufficed to raise her to the rank of an Arhat, the adorer of gods. In explaining why he raised her to the rank of an Arhat, the Lord said, "formerly in the time of the Lord Kás'yapa, a maid-servant, in the city of Benares, was carrying some cakes for her master, but, meeting Kás'yapa on the way on his begging excursion, gave him the cakes intended for her master. The Lord converted her, and for ten thousand years afterwards she had bestowed alms to Buddhists. That maid-servant has now been born as Supríyá."

XVII. *Story of Sumaná.* There lived at S'rávastí a merchant, who had successively lost three sons immediately after their birth. He once invited a S'ramaṇa of the name of Aniruddha, and, after entertaining him with every mark of respect, prayed that he may have a son who should not die so early, promising that if the boy lived up to the 7th year he would present him to his guest. The blessing of the saint fulfilled the prayer, and the new-born boy was named Sumaná, and on his 7th year he was given away to Aniruddha, who made him a Bhiks   and ultimately an Arhat. One day Aniruddha asked the youth to bring same water for his drink. Sumaná went to the river, filled his pitcher and, rising aloft, came by an aerial passage to serve the water, then, carrying the pitcher in his hand, he flew high in the air and, following his aerial course, came to the Jetavana grove where the Lord then sojourned. The Bhikshus were struck with wonder at the sight, and enquired about the history of this remarkable personage. The Lord said, "when the Lord Vipas'yí dwelt at Bandhumati, there lived a rich merchant who, in his old age, seeing death imminent, worshipped the Lord, and prayed that he may be blessed with the absolute knowledge. That merchant is now born as Sumaná."

XVIII. *Story of Sthaviraka.* There lived at Rájágriha a rich householder, whose wife did not, on the tenth month of her pregnancy, bring forth a child. She conceived ten times afterwards, and brought forth ten sons, but her first conception remained in her womb. On her death, long after, her relatives proposed to open her belly to see what had become of her first conception. The Lord, with his followers, came to see the wonder, and lo! when the womb was opened, there appeared an emaciated little dwarf, with his body covered with grey hairs, ensconced in the womb. The dwarf saluted the Lord and said, "None of you should use harsh words against your parents and teachers; I did so, and have suffered for sixty years, confined in a noisome place." The Lord named him Sthaviraka "the old one." His father took him home and nursed him, and in a short time he grew up to a handsome man. On his 70th year he got himself ordained by the Lord, and became an Arhat. In explanation of the question why Sthaviraka had remained so long in the womb, the Lord said, "in the time of Jinendra Kás'yapa, a disciple of one Sthavira asked his tutor to go with him to Benares to behold a festival; the tutor declined, whereupon the pupil said, 'well, then, I must go alone, and you may remain here like an embryo in the womb.' That reproachful speech brought this punishment, for that pupil of yore, is the Sthaviraka before us."

XIX. *Story of S'rimatí.* King Vimbisára had once given a handsome palace, named Jyotishka, to one of his sons, whereupon another, named Ajátas'atru, felt very much aggrieved, and, through the instigation of his friend Devadatta, killed his father, and himself became king. Subsequently, when out on a hunting expedition in a forest, he received salutary instruction from a S'ramaṇa, and touched thereby, repairing to the Lord S'ákya Siñha, repented of his sins, performed the purifying fast of Poshadha, and became a follower of Buddha. In explanation of the reason why Vimbisára fell under the hands of his own son, the Lord said, Vimbisára in a former life was a banker of Benares. Seeing a Pratyak Buddha in the way he had said, "these bald-pated vagabonds should have their feet decorticated with a razor," and that sin led to his feet being amputated by his son. He further stated that this Ajátas'atru was at first a great enemy of Buddhism. He did everything to thwart the true religion. Through the instigation of his friend Devadatta, he issued a proclamation that he would behead every person and escheat his property who evinced any regard for Buddhism or Buddhists. Once a lady, seeing a stupa covered with dust, had it swept, and the news of this act being brought to Ajátas'atru he ordered her immediate decapitation, and the order was carried out. The spirit of the lady was transferred to heaven and, in her divine form, she came and worshipped the Lord.

XX. *Story of Ajátas'atru's conversion.* The subjects of Ajátas'atru rose against him for his opposition to Buddhism, and, other means failing, he felt obliged to betake to the asylum of the Lord to save his kingdom. Avadána-sataka, story XVI.

XXI. *Story of Dhanapála.* Given in Avadána-s'ataka, story XXXIII, p. 27.

XXII. *Story of Shaḍadanta.* Brahmadatta, anxious to destroy the credit of the Lord, consulted some wicked people, and induced them to depute to the Lord a young handsome woman, who should tell him that the embryo in her womb was due to him, and he should provide for the maintenance of herself and for the child about to be born. They soon found a woman ready to undertake this mission, tied a wooden bowl on her belly, dressed her up, and sent her to the Lord. She appeared before the Lord when he was seated amidst his followers, and made her request. At this juncture Indra, perceiving the mischief in contemplation, sent two mice to get within her dress, and to cut the fastenings of the wooden bowl. When the woman stood up to give emphasis to her claims, down dropped the unfastened bowl, and she was put to great shame. She cried loud, and begged that she may be at once burnt on a pyre. The Lord said, "this woman was inimical to me in a former life. There lived on the southern scarp of the Himalayas a six-tusked king elephant who had two wives, Bhadrá and Subhadrá; Bhadrá once saw her rival decorated with golden lotuses by her lord, and resolved to avenge herself. She repaired to a forest, worshipped an old saint, and prayed that she may, in her next birth, have the faculty of recalling to her mind the events of her former lives, and, becoming a queen, may enjoy life seated on a throne made of ivory from the tusks of a six-tusked elephant. Her prayer was granted, and she cast herself headlong from the edge of a precipice, and killed herself. She was then born as the daughter of Khanalita, and married to Brahmadatta. When she had won the affection of her lord, she desired that a throne may be made for her of the ivory of a six-tusked elephant that lived on the Himálaya. The king deputed a hunter to bring the ivory, and the hunter, assuming the garb of a Bhikshu, appeared before the king elephant, which lived amidst 500 other elephants. The elephant, seeing that he was a Bhikshu, received him with respect, and enquired the object of his mission. The hunter confessed what he wanted, and pleaded his poverty for the repulsive work he had undertaken. The elephant, pitied his poverty, and, knocking his tusks against a rock, broke them, and gave them to him. Thus was the vow realized. I am that king elephant, and this woman, the daughter of a Tírthika, was that Bhadrá."

XXIII. *Story of Kavikumára.* See page 102.

XXIV. *Story of Kritajna.* When the Lord was once dwelling in the Jetavana grove at S'rávasti, Devadatta, intent on destroying the Lord, repaired to that place, and, standing before him, prepared to carry out his intention, when the fire of the Lord's benevolence enveloped him, and burnt him down to ashes. The Lord, beholding him in hell-fire, related the following story: "There lived in the town of Ratighosha two brothers, one grateful, the other ungrateful. The former gave away a deal of his self-acquired wealth in charity, and started on a commercial voyage. His brother followed him. Their speculations proved highly successful, but, on the return voyage, the vessel of the two brothers encountered a hurricane, and was lost. Kritajna, the grateful, seeing his brother drowning, dragged him out, and, taking him on his back, swam to the shore with the help of a plank. He was greatly exhausted. His brother now revived, and, seeing that he had some precious jewels tied in his cloth, blinded him, and carried away the jewels. A kind merchant helped the now blinded man to come to the suburbs of Ratighosha, where he left him in the hut of a cow-keeper, and departed. The poor blind man had no wish to go home, so he lived on the charity of the cowherd. One day, the king's daughter, Janakalyání by name, saw him, and fell in love with him. She married him, and nursed him, and brought him round. One day she was late in bringing him food, whereupon he accused her of inconstancy. She protested and said, "I know none but you, and should I be truthful and chaste, the merit thereof should restore one of your eyes." No sooner was this said, then one of his eyes opened, radiant like a lotus. The man was gratified, and said, "though my ungrateful brother deprived me of my eyesight, I bear no ill-will against him, and if this be true, that truth should restore me my second eye." The second eye immediately opened as the first, and the happy couple returned to the palace, and the youth was anointed vice-king. The ungrateful brother, hearing of this, came to conciliate his brother, but, no sooner he stood before the grateful one, than he felt a fire burning within him. He cried out 'I am burnt, I am burnt,' and fell into hell-fire. "That grateful one" said the Lord, "is myself, and the ungrateful one Devadatta."

XXV. *Story of Ajátas'atru's conversion.* (Another version.) In course of time Ajátas'atru was afflicted with leprosy. His body was full of rotting sores, covered with noisome matter, and horribly stinking; his friends forsook him, and even his wife and children could not approach him. He groaned much, and, repenting of his sins, sought the asylum of the Lord. The Lord pitied him, and deputed Lokes'vara Bodhisattva for his conversion. Lokes'vara recommenced the Uposhadha fast, and dilated on its merits. Ajátas'atru faithfully performed the fast, took the shelter of the Three Jewels, and, becoming a Buddhist, disseminated that religion of the Lord in his kingdom.

XXVI. *Praise of the Uposhadha fast.* See *ante*, p. 265.

Beginning. ॐ नमो रत्नत्रयाय ।

यः श्रीमान् भगवान् बुद्धो लोके धर्म्मामृतं ददौ ।
जयन्ति शासनान्यस्य पादौ वन्दे सदा नतः ॥
पुरा भागीरथीतीरे पाटलीपुत्रसंज्ञिता ।
आसीद्‌ या नगरी श्रेष्ठा विस्तीर्णेवामरावती ॥
ऋद्धा स्फीता सुभिक्षा च दर्शनीया मनोरमा ।
साधु-सज्जनसंवासा पूर्य्यमाणा सुरासुरैः ॥
क्षेमा च कमलारामा प्रशास्तकलितस्फुरा ।
ईतिभिरनभिक्रान्ता गोमहिष्यादिसङ्कुला ॥
बहुशस्यवती रम्या विद्वज्जननिषेविता ।
नानापुष्पफलोपेतैरुद्यानैः परिमण्डिता ॥
तस्यां पूर्य्यामभूद्राजा नाम्नाऽशोको नृपाधिपः ।
लोकत्राणाय यत्नाढ्यो दीनोद्धरणतत्परः ॥

End. अथ ते सन्त्रपा लोकाः श्रुत्वा तद्धर्म्मदेशनां ।
अनुमोद्य त्रिरत्नानि स्मृत्वा धर्म्मं प्रचेरिरे ॥

Colophon. इत्यशोकोपगुप्तसम्भाषणे कल्पद्रुमावदानमाला समाप्ता ।

No. A, 8.

DIVYA'VADA'NA-MA'LA'.

दिव्यावदानमाला ।

Substance, yellow Nepalese paper, 17 × 5½ inches. Folia, 235. Lines on a page, 9. Extent in ślokas, 9,400. Character, Newárí. Appearance, old. Date, ? Prose. Incorrect.

A collection of Avadána stories, related when the Lord sojourned at S'rávastí in the garden of Anáthapiṇḍada. There are in it many stories, but most of them occur, in some form or other, in other Avadána works. The name of the work does not occur in the Chinese Tripiṭhaka.

CONTENTS. I. *Story of S'roṇakoṭikarṇa.* There lived in the village of Vás'ava a rich householder who had born unto him a son with a jewelled ring in his ear. The boy was named S'roṇakoṭikarṇa. On the day in which this boy was born Bálaseṇa a neighbour, got two sons, Dásaka and Pálaka. When S'roṇakoṭikarṇa had grown up, he obtained the permission of his parents to proceed on a commercial tour in company with five hundred other commercial travellers. When returning home after a successful mission, he missed the company of his fellow travellers, and lost his way in the midst of an awful forest. Oppressed by thirst, he roamed about in quest of water, and at last came to a village inhabited by bobgoblins. These beings had enormous bellies, mouths not bigger than pin-holes, and bodies covered with hair. On being asked the cause of their misfortune, they said, " For twelve long years we have searched for water and have not yet got it. We were once men of Jambudvípa, but, never having given any alms from our birth to our last day, we are doomed to this condition." Leaving their place, S'roṇakoṭikarṇa proceeded further, and at vesper came to a spot where he saw a man seated in a pavilion, and surrounded by four Apsaras maidens. This man received him kindly, entertained him hospitably, and allowed him to remain there for the night. Rising from his bed early in the morning, S'roṇakoṭikarṇa found that the pavilion had vanished, and the man was being torn to pieces by the four Apsarases who had assumed the form of brindled dogs. At nightfall the scene changed again; the pavilion re-appeared, and the man was seen dallying with the celestial maidens.

On enquiring into the cause of these sudden transformations, the man said, "In my last existence I was a butcher, and would daily slaughter sheep and sell the meat, but at night I used to go to the saint Mahákátyáyana, and listen to his discourses and act according to his instruction; hence it is that I am mangled during the daytime, and allowed to enjoy at night. My son is now carrying on our family profession in the village of Vásava. Pray, tell him what you have seen, and try to restrain him from his profession; induce him to go to Mahákátyáyana and offer him an alms-bowl for my redemption." S'roṇakoṭikarṇa promised to do as desired, and then retired.

Next morning he came to a place where he saw a pavilion in which a man was enjoying the company of celestial damsels. At nightfall the pavilion disappeared, and the damsels assumed the shape of a monster centipede, which held the man in its embrace and stung him continuously. When the sun rose the scene changed as before, and the man explained the occurrence by saying that in his preceding life he was a dissolute Bráhmaṇ at Vásava; he used to spend his nights with prostitutes, and devote the daytime to the service of Mahákátyáyana, and hence his diurnal enjoyment, and nocturnal suffering. He added, "Pray, tell my son that you have seen his father in his suffering, and that his father's earnest request is, that he should abstain from prostitution. Should he listen to you, pray, tell him to dig out from under our Agnishṭoma altar a pitcher full of gold, and always offer alms to Mahákátyáyana."

Proceeding on, S'roṇakoṭikarṇa saw a lady seated on a bedstead in a pavilion, and four hobgoblins tied to the foot of the bedstead. When the hobgoblins were let loose to feed, one of them began to chew iron bullets, the second eat chaff, the third began to munch her own flesh, and the last appeared engaged on feasting on blood and pus. On enquiring of the cause, the lady said, "the one who is eating chaff is my daughter-in-law; the next who is eating iron bullets is my husband; the third who is eating her own flesh is my maid-servant, and the fourth who is eating blood and pus is my daughter. At a festival I prepared rich viands, and gave them first to Kátyáyana and S'ramaṇas and then to Devas and Bráhmaṇas. Coming to know this, my husband, in great wrath, said, 'Why don't these bald-pated wretches eat iron bullets?' and this is his punishment. Once, a relative of mine sent me some cakes; my daughter-in-law eat them, and showed me only the vessel in which they had been sent, therefore is she made to feed on chaff.

Again, once I prepared some cakes, and sent them through my daughter to a relative; she eat the cakes in the way, and gave the vessel to my relative, and when my relative sent me word, how it was that I had sent her only a pot? my daughter said, 'You then must have eaten the cakes and sent the pot.' Hence is she doomed to live on pus and blood. (The offence of the maid-servant is not related in the MS.) At the time when these offences were committed I expressed a wish that I may be permitted to see their retribution, and hence I see it now. You are going to Vásava, pray, tell my only wilful daughter living there that you have seen her parents, and the punishment, they were under; advise her in my name that she should abstain from sin. There are buried in my father's room four iron chests full of golden ornaments. Let her take them out, enjoy them, and offer proper presents to Kátyáyana on behalf of me." S'roṇakoṭikarṇa lived at her place for twelve years, and was at last sent to Vásava by the lady in her own vehicle.

Arriving at his native village, S'roṇakoṭikarṇa first repaired to the hermitage of Mahákátyáyana, and paid him his respects. Then he went to execute the commissions he had received in the wilderness, and at last returned home to the great joy of his sorrowing family. His narrative of what he had seen in his travels wrought a change in the mind of his son, who, no longer willing to remain at home, became a Bhikshu, and prevailed on his father to betake to the hermitage. The father was ordained an Arhat. In accounting for the conversions, the Lord said that in former times there lived at Benares the great saint Kás'yapa to whose memory king Kriki had erected a chaitya. This chaitya was neglected and allowed to go to ruin during the reign of that king's son, but repaired by a merchant named Vánijyakara, and that merchant was now born as S'roṇakoṭikarṇa.

II. *Story of Púrṇa.* There lived at the village of Surpáraka a merchant named Bhava who had three sons, Bhavila, Bhavatrátá, and Bhavanandi. When Bhava, was very ill, his wife and children neglected him on account of his habitual roughness of speech, but a slave-girl tended him, obtained medical aid, and restored him to his wonted health. Bhava was greatly overcome by her kindness, and got by her a child named Púrṇa. When Bhava died, Bhavatrátá and Bhavanandi proposed that all the family estate on land and at home should make one share, all that was on water or in foreign countries another, and Púrṇa the third.

Bhavila remonstrated against this scheme of partition, urging that Púrṇa was a son of their father, and should have a share. The other brothers, however, would not assent to this, as Púrṇa was slave-born and, being himself property, could not claim a share of the patrimony. The law being on their side, the original scheme had to be accepted, and Bhavila took Púrṇa for his share. The two younger brothers then expelled from the paternal homestead the eldest and his family, who had to seek shelter in the house of a relation.

Driven away from home, Bhavila and his family were in great distress, and one morning, the children crying for breakfast, Púrṇa took a másha of gold and went to the market to procure some. On the sea-shore he met a man trembling from a drowning he had had in the sea and watching a raft of logs. Knowing the logs to be of Gośirsha sandal-wood, he purchased the lot from the stranger for five hundred Kárshá-paṇas, and immediately after sold one of the logs for a thousand. With the money so obtained he placed his master's family in comfort. Soon after, physicians having recommended an emolient of Gosirsha sandal-wood to the king of the place to relieve him of the burning he was suffering from a high fever, Púrṇa sold another log for a like sum. Cured of his fever, the king, thinking that it was unbecoming that the royal stores should not possess so valuable a remedy and it should be obtainable in the house of a poor man, ordered the whole lot to be purchased. This was done at a cost of three hundred thousand gold pieces. Thus enriched, Púrṅa continued to trade, travelling from place to place, and amassed great wealth. At last he surrendered the whole of his property to his master, and, having repaired to the Lord, got himself ordained. Subsequently he retired to a place called S'roṇápurantaka, to abide there. The people of that place were very rude and vain, but Púrṇa, by his mildness, wisdom and assiduity, soon overcame them, made them resign Indra and the other Hindu gods to which they were attached, and betake to the fold of the Lord. About this time, Bhavila had gone in quest of Gos'irsha sandal-wood, and had employed five hundred labourers to fell the wood. A Yaksha who dwelt in that forest was offended at this, and created a hurricane to drown the ship in which Bhavila had come there. Bhavila cried in great distress for the succour of Púrṇa, and Púrṇa, coming to know of it through the medium of a god, flew to the place through the air, got the storm pacified, and obtained the permission of the Yaksha to carry away the wood. Returning with his brother to Surpáraka he caused a pavilion to be erected of that wood, and prayed that the Lord may come and occupy it. The message reached the Lord through the air, and the Lord at once came to the spot, and gratified the wish of his devotee. He tarried there for some time, and by his preachings and discourses converted many. In reply to the question why so pious a man as Púrṇa should have been born of a slave-girl, the Lord said that in the time of Káśyapa he had, in a former life, once said of a Bhikshu "what slave girl's son is this man?" and for that fault he was doomed to be born of a slave-girl for five hundred births.

III. *Story of Maitreya.* When proceeding to the kingdom of Maha the Lord related the following account. On the death of his father, Praṇáda, Maháprаṇáda ruled his country with great severity and injustice. Thereupon Indra, who was a friend of his father, came to him, and advised him to abstain from vice. Maháprаṇáda said, "put up some sign in my palace to remind me of virtue, and I shall follow it." Indra, thereupon, set up in the palace a golden staff, a thousand fathoms high and 16 fathoms in girth. In connexion with this, the king announced a grand festival, and his uncle As'oka became the administrator of charities. People from all parts of the earth assembled to enjoy the festival and behold the wonderful staff, neglecting their agricultural works. The result was a famine in the country. Disgusted at this, the king caused the staff to be cast into the river Ganges. "He who was As'oka before," said the Lord, "is now Bhañgáli, the Bhikshu."

The Bhikshus asked, "when will this staff be rescued?" The Lord said, "when the duration of human life will be eighty thousand years, a king will be born of the name of S'añkha, and his wife, Brahmavatí, will bear him a son of the name of Maitreya. This Maitreya will be a pupil of Brahmáyúh and will himself have eighty hundred pupils. Four great kings will recover this staff and present it to S'añkha, who will give it to Brahmáyúh. Brahmáyúh will give it to Maitreya, and Maitreya will present it to his pupils, who will divide it among themselves. When Maitreya will behold this partition, he will retire from the world and, attaining the perfect knowledge, become a Buddha. Him will follow S'añkha, his family and eighteen hundred chiefs, as also the family of Maitreya. Maitreya, followed by this retinue, will repair to the Gurupádaka hill, and there, taking up a bow of Káśyapa with his right hand and placing it in the left, impart instruction in the true religion."

In reply to the query, through what merit will Maitreya become a Buddha, the Lord said, that in the middle country there lived a king of the name of Vásava. He was strictly just and religious, and his country prospered. A king of the north country, Dhanasammata, envied this prosperity, and came down with a large army to plunder the wealth of the people. Vásava went forth to meet him, and the opposing armies were encamped on the opposites sides of the river Ganges. At this juncture the great Buddha Ratnas'ikhi came to the place, and took his station on the bank of the river, and Indra and other gods came to worship him. Seeing this, Dhanasammata made peace with Vásava and retired to his country. Vásava worshipped the Lord, and prayed that he may become an imperial sovereign. The blessing was granted, but it was to be effectual when human life would extend to eighty thousand years. Dhanasammata also worshipped the Lord, and prayed that he may become a moral ruler of mankind, and this too was granted on a similar condition. "This Vásava", said the Lord, "will be S'añkha, and Dhanasammata, Maitreya."

IV. *Story of Svágata.* There lived on the S'is'umára hill a rich householder, named Buddha. He gave his daughter Rúpiṇí to the son of Anáthapiṇḍada. His wife then bore him a son named Svágata. From the day the son was conceived, he suffered grievous misfortunes. When his son grew up he died; his house and his trading vessels and his corn stores were destroyed by fire. Svágata tried to obtain his sustenance by begging, but none would give him alms. So at last, he sought the protection of his sister's husband. He reached his destination on the very day on which Anáthapiṇḍada had invited the Lord and his retinue. Eating of the remnant of food on the Lord's plate his mind was purified, and he was soon after ordained an Arhat. He then retired to his native place, and converted thousands.

To satisfy the curiosity of his audience the Lord said that formerly there lived a rich householder named Karvaṭaka. He was once in his garden with his family, relatives, and friends when a lean, weak, emaciated Pratyak Buddha entered the place in quest of alms. Karvaṭaka ordered his men to expel the intruder, but none obeyed his orders. He then himself seized the saint by the neck, and shoved him out. The poor beggar, weak as he was, sat down, and began to pray for the welfare of Karvaṭaka. This surprised the householder, and he prayed for pardon. It was immediately granted, and a blessing was also added that in a future life he would become a saint. That man is now born Svágata.

V. *Story of Dharmaruchi.* Given in the Bodhisattvávadána-kalpalatá, p. 71.

VI. *Story of Sañgharakshita.* Ditto, p. 64.

VII. *Story of Kaṇakavarṇá.* The text is here defective and the story breaks off after a few lines. The opening lines refer to a famine.

VIII. *Story of Chandraprabha Bodhisattva.* When the Lord was on the Gṛidhrakúṭa hill, Maudgalyáyana, son of Sárí, vanished like a fire when the fuel had been burnt out. The Bhikshus asked the Lord if this was his final deliverance, or the lot which his forefathers had been destined to? The Lord said, Maudgalyáyana had obtained final deliverance and not the lot of his forefathers, and then recounted the former history of the departed hermit. At a remote period there lived in the city of Bhadras'ilá a king named Chandraprabha He had established an alms-house at each of the four principal gates, of the city, and proclaimed that he would give whatever was asked of him. Thousands over thousands flocked at the gates, and got what they wanted, when at last a wicked Bráhmaṇ, named Rudráksha, came and asked the king's head. Offers were made to him of untold wealth, but he would have nothing but the head. The king said, "take then the best member of my body," and removed his crown for the beggar. The sight was horrifying to the two principal ministers, Maháchandra and Mahidhara, who fell down in a fit and died immediately. The beggar, seeing the company before him, and the feeling of rage and despair they displayed at his request, discreetly said that the king should retire alone to a private garden where he could be decapitated, but no witness should be present. The king assented, retired to his garden, closed its doors, and then recited a mantra, saying, "it is not for a kingdom, or for an empire, or for heaven, or for enjoyment, or for Brahmáhood that I give away my head to a Bráhmaṇ; I do so for the absolute Bodhi knowledge, acquiring which I may control the uncontrollable, restrain the unrestrainable, redeem the condemned, and quench the unquenchable. May my remains be preserved in a chaitya!" He then tied himself to a champaka tree, and ordered the beggar to do as he listed. The Bráhmaṇ decapitated him, took the head, and ran away. The Lord said, "the town which formerly was Bhadras'ilá is now called Takshaśíla. He who was king Chandraprabha is now myself; the two ministers are now Sáriputra and Maúdgalyáyana;* and Rudráksha, the beggar Bráhmaṇ, is Devadatta."

* Sárí had seven sons of whom Upatishya *alias* Maudgalyáyana was a favourite disciple of Buddha. I cannot make out the proper name of the second. Sáríputra is obviously an epithet meaning, son of Sárí. *Cf.* pp. 45 and 148.

IX. *Story of Pan̲chhaka.* A Bráhmaṇ was one day seated in a very sorrowful mood, with one of his cheeks resting on his palm. An old woman asked him the cause. The Bráhmaṇ told her his wife was *enciente*, and expected to be delivered soon, and as all his former sons had died immediately after birth, he expected the same calamity soon. The woman said, "send for me when she is about to be confined, and I will help you." On the day of delivery the old woman came, helped the patient, took the male child in her arms, filled his mouth with butter, covered it with a white cloth, and, handing him to a maid-servant, said, "take this child to the market place, and, standing on the crossing, say to every Bráhmaṇ or S'ramaṇa you meet, 'this child salutes you.' When the sun sets bring him back." This was done, and the child lived. He was named Mahápan̲chhaka. A second son was born, and he was saved in the same way. His name was Pan̲chhaka. After the death of the Bráhmaṇ, Mahápan̲chhaka became a hermit, and was soon raised to the rank of an Arhat. Pan̲chhaka was a stupid youth and could learn nothing, so his brother expelled him from the monastery, and he sat crying on the roadside. The Lord met him in this condition, directed a hermit to instruct him, and soon after ordained him an Arhat.

To explain the reason for this sudden transformation, the Lord related the following stories. There lived in a market town a rich merchant who had an only infant son. Being required to proceed to a distant country on business, he deposited the bulk of his property in the custody of a friend, and, leaving only a small sum of money with his wife to meet household expenses during his absence, went away. He died out at sea, and his wife had great difficulty in bringing up her child. When the child had grown up to man's age, he went to his father's friend to beg assistance. The friend said, "he who has manly determination can help himself with that dead mouse; he begs no one's help." The young man, being high-spirited, felt deeply the force of the rebuke, and, taking up the dead mouse which was lying there and to which reference had been made, went away. While standing at the market-place with the dead mouse in his hand, a cat belonging to a shopkeeper pounced on the mouse, and carried it away. The shopkeeper gave him a quantity of kidney-beans (*másha*) as the price of the mouse. The youth parched the beans on a fire, took a pitcher of cool, clear water, and placed himself in the way by which some wood-cutters returned from their daily work in a forest. The wood-cutters were greatly pleased with the refreshment at hand. Each took a handful of the parched beans and a draught of cold water, and gave the youth a piece of wood in return. A part of the wood so acquired was sold, and with the proceeds fresh beans were purchased, and parched, and the refreshment was taken to the wood-cutters as on the preceding day. In a short time the youth acquired enough wood to set up a fuel shop, and that proving lucrative, he had soon the means of trading on more precious articles. Prospering daily, he at last became a rich merchant; but the humble means of his first venture was known to his neighbours, and they always called him *Mushika-hairaṇyaka*, or "mouse gold," and he wanted one day to pay off his debt regarding the mouse. He got four golden mice to be made, filled them with jewels, and, appearing before his father's friend, said "here is the equivalent of the dead mouse you had lent, together with interest for the use of your capital." The friend, not to be outdone in generosity by the youth, said, "here is the wealth that your father had deposited with me. Take it, and, as a reward for your manly determination and perseverance, I bestow on you my only daughter." The friend was the Lord in a former birth, and Paṇchhaka the youth.

In another birth Paṇchhaka was, under the name of Tripita, a pupil of Kás'yapa. He was proud and did not recite the Gáthás. In another existence he was a seller of hog's flesh. One day when ferrying across a river to a market, his boat was swamped, and he was carried away by the stream to a hermitage where five hundred Pratyak Buddhas resided. One of the saints rescued him from the river and revived him. He lived long with the saints and became a hermit.

On one occasion a Jívaka invited the Lord and his retinue to a sumptuous repast, but did not include Paṇchhaka in his list of guests. The Lord pointed out the omission, and it was rectified. When the guests arrived, the Jívaka did not offer welcome to Paṇchhaka, nor did he assign him a seat at the repast. The Lord noticed this and, instead of giving his plate to Ánanda, as usual, offered it to Paṇchhaka. Paṇchhaka prepared a miraculous seat on the air, and seated thereon, stretched out his hand like the trunk of an elephant to receive the plate. Surprised at this miracle the Jívaka fell at his feet, and begged to be pardoned. The Lord said, this is not the first time that this Jívaka has begged pardon of Paṇchhaka. In times of yore a horse-dealer was passing by a village when one of his mares delivered a foal, the sight of which made his horses neigh loudly. This he took to be an inauspicious omen, and gave away the foal to a potter. He then went to king Brahmadatta, and offered him his horses for sale. The king wanted a horse with particular marks on it, and this could not be found. The dealer then said, "the foal I have given to the potter has such marks." The potter sold the foal for a hundred thousand pieces of gold. One day the king rode this foal and went out of the city to his garden, where he was soon after surrounded by a band of rebels. The king mounted the foal and wanted to escape, but the road was besieged by enemies, and he could not go; the foal, thereupon, swam across a river and saved him. The dealer, coming to know of this, fell at the feet of the foal and begged his pardon. That foal was Paṉchhaka, and the dealer the Jívaka.

. X. *Story of Syámávatí.* When the Lord was at Kulmáshadamya, a hermit of the name of Mákandika offered him his daughter Anupamá to marry, but the Lord declined. An old man then advanced and offered to take the girl, but the father declined. The Lord said, "this is not the first time I have declined to take her," and related the following story. Formerly a blacksmith had resolved to give his daughter to the most proficient in his art, when a youth came to him and became his apprentice, and soon excelled him in art, but declined to receive the daughter when offered. The Lord was the youth and the blacksmith Mákandika.

To explain why the offer of the old man was declined, the Lord related with slight variations the story of Siñhala as given on pp. 96, 97. The story then runs that after the refusal, Mákandika went to Kaus'ámbi, and gave his daughter to king Udayana, and himself became the king's chief minister. When the king had once gone out on an expedition against an enemy, Anupamá set fire to the inner apartments, which destroyed her five hundred rivals including the chief queen Syámávatí. On Udayana asking the Lord the history of these five hundred wives, the lord said, formerly king Brahmadatta, of Benares, had five hundred wives. One day these ladies had gone to a garden for recreation. Bathing in an adjoining river they felt cold, and the chief queen, seeing a hut on the bank, ordered her maid to set fire to it, so that she may have a good blazing fire to warm herself. The maid reported that the hut belonged to a hermit. But the queen did not care for this, and insisted upon her order being carried out, and her companions supported her. The hut was accordingly burnt. The hermit escaped from the hut, and, rising high in the air blessed her, whereupon they all begged that they may be duly punished for their sins, but after that they may obtain the absolute knowledge. Syámávatí and her companions were those ladies of yore.

XI. *Story of Nanda* or *Kaus'idya-víryots'áha Avadána.* Nanda, the son of a rich merchant, became a cripple in his youth. His family priest, Púraṇa, tried his utmost to cure him, but failed. At last the Lord, hearing of his utter inability to rise from his bed, came to see him, when lo! the youth jumped out of his bed to offer him welcome. The visit cured him completely, and he started for Ceylon on a mercantile mission. On his return after a successful voyage, he invited the Lord, and offered him and his followers rich presents, praying at the same time that he may in a future life become a Buddha. The prayer was granted.

XII. *Dadhipa Avadána.* This is a new name for the story of Chandana given on pp. 198-9.

XIII. *Story of the merchant's wife* or *Chakra Avadána.* Given in the Avadána-s'ataka. Story XXIII, *ante*, p. 25.

XIV. *Story of Vítas'oka* or *Víśoka Avadána.* Given in the As'oka Avadána, *ante*, p. 6.

XV. *Story of As'oka* or *As'oka Avadána.* Given in the As'oka Avadána, *ante*, p. 6.

XVI. *Story of Maṇichúda* or *Maṇichúdávadána.* Given on p. 162.

XVII. *Story of Sudhanakumára.* Given in the Bodhisattvávadánakalpalatá, *cf.* p. 626.

XVIII. *Story of a poor Bráhmaṇ* or *Chhinna-bhakta-bráhmaṇa Avadána.* When the Lord was proceeding on foot to S'rávastí, he met a poor Bráhmaṇ returning from his field with a plough on his shoulders. Perceiving that the traveller bore on his person the thirty-two auspicious marks, but was oppressed with fatigue, the Bráhmaṇ brought out from his hut a cupful of pure cool water, and offered it to the Lord. The Lord ordered it to be cast into an adjoining dried-up, old, neglected well; and as soon as the Bráhmaṇ did so, the well filled up to the brim with the clearest, sweetest cold water. The Lord and his followers refreshed themselves with this water, and then, preaching the true religion to the Bráhmaṇ, retired. The next morning when the Bráhmaṇ went to his field, he found it covered with waving corn with ears loaded with grains of gold. Wonder-struck at the sight of the barley which he had sown the day before growing up so rapidly and bearing grains of gold, the poor man went to the king, and reported the occurrence. The king caused the crop to be harvested and divided into two equal shares, one for himself and the other for the cultivator. When the division was made and the shares duly made over to their respective owners, the grains which fell to the lot of the king changed to ordinary grains of barley. The division was repeated again and again for seven times, and every time the king's share underwent the wonderful change, and thereupon he ordered the whole crop to be given to the cultivator, who spent it in alms and other benevolent work.

XIX. *Story of five hundred cultivators* or *Panchhas'atakrishakávadána.* Proceeding from the hut of the poor Bráhmaṇ, the Lord met in the way five hundred cultivators, who prayed that they may be at once ordained and were made Arhats. These men in a former life had been ordained Bhikshus by Kás'yapa, but they had relapsed into evil ways, and therefore had been punished for a long series of generations by being made cultivators.

XX. *Story of an agricultural Bráhmaṇ* or *Krishaka-bráhmaṇávadána.* This is the story of Chandra as given on p. 298.

XXI. *Story of Rúpávatí* or *Rúpávatyavadána.* Once when the Lord was at the Jetavana monastery his disciples remarked, how wonderful it was that beggars should be the most favoured of all persons to the Lord. The Lord replied, it was even so in his former existences, and then recited the following story in illustration. At Utpalávatí in the northern country (*Uttarápatha*), there lived at one time a lady of great beauty and highly virtuous disposition, whose name was Rúpávatí. Once when in a monastery she saw a famished woman confined there and that person, under the pangs of hunger, was about to eat her own infant son. Having nothing at hand to give, she cut off her breasts and gave them to the famished woman. On return home she related the circumstance to her husband, who declared that such incomparable virtue deserved to be rewarded with the restoration of the busts, and the breasts immediately grew up to their natural size. Thereupon S'akra, assuming the form of a Bráhmaṇ, appeared before her and asked, "did you feel no hesitation in giving away your busts?"

"No," replied she.

"Why did you do so?" "To save the life of the child. I long not for kingdom, or wealth, or supremacy; I yearn for the absolute knowledge, which would enable me to rescue the fallen, redeem the lost, and restore mankind to eternal beatitude. I wish therefore to become a man."

The wish was immediately gratified by the blessing of S'akra, and the name of the metamorphosed lady became Rúpávata, and she was elected king of Utpalávatí. On her death after a reign of 60 years, she was born as the son of a merchant, and was named Chandraprabha, because his beauty outshone that of the moon. When he was eight years old, he went one day to a cremation ground and, cutting his flesh bit by bit, gave it to vultures to feed upon. When he lay helpless, the birds plucked out his eyes from their socket, and he died. He was next born in that town as the son of a Bráhmaṇ, named Brahmaprabha on account of the unrivalled effulgence of his body. When he attained the age of sixteen years, he retired to a forest and, making a hut there, passed his time in the exercise of the most rigorous asceticism. In the neighbourhood of his hut he one day saw a famished tigress which had lately brought forth two cubs and was about to eat them. He immediately gave his own body to the tigress, and saved the cubs. "The town," said the Lord, "which was Utpalávatí before is now Pushkalávata. She who was Rúpávatí before, is now myself. The woman who was confined in the monastery, next became the tigress. Those who were the parents of Brahmaprabha next became S'uddhodana and Máyá, and the two cubs are now A'nanda and Ráhula."

XXII. *Story of Kus'a* or *Kus'a Játaka*. See *ante*, p. 110. An English translation of the Páli version of this story has been lately published.

INDEX.